TURNCOATS AND RENEGADOES

'*Turncoats and Renegadoes* is an important and sensitive study of an issue that has been critically absent from the ongoing debate on allegiance and political culture in the English Civil War period'

Dr Elliot Vernon, Reviews in History

'A painstaking exploration of social, cultural, political, chronological, and regional patterns and attitudes in and to a phenomenon conditioned by the changing tides of war, opportunism, and the pressing weight of external pressures'

R. C. Richardson, Times Higher Education

'By combining high-level storytelling with a thoroughness and shrewdness of judgment, it is a work that is more than the sum of its parts'

John Morrill, BBC History Magazine

Andrew Hopper is a Senior Lecturer in the Centre for English Local History at the University of Leicester.

Turncoats and Renegadoes

Changing Sides during the English Civil Wars

ANDREW HOPPER

OXFORD

UNIVERSITY PRESS

OXFORD

UNIVERSITY PRESS

Great Clarendon Street, Oxford, OX2 6DP
United Kingdom

Oxford University Press is a department of the University of Oxford.
It furthers the University's objective of excellence in research, scholarship,
and education by publishing worldwide. Oxford is a registered trade mark of
Oxford University Press in the UK and in certain other countries

© Andrew Hopper 2012

The moral rights of the author have been asserted

First Edition published in 2012
First published in paperback 2014

All rights reserved. No part of this publication may be reproduced, stored in
a retrieval system, or transmitted, in any form or by any means, without the
prior permission in writing of Oxford University Press, or as expressly permitted
by law, by licence or under terms agreed with the appropriate reprographics
rights organization. Enquiries concerning reproduction outside the scope of the
above should be sent to the Rights Department, Oxford University Press, at the
address above

You must not circulate this work in any other form
and you must impose this same condition on any acquirer

Published in the United States of America by Oxford University Press
198 Madison Avenue, New York, NY 10016, United States of America

British Library Cataloguing in Publication Data
Data available

Library of Congress Cataloging in Publication Data
Data available

ISBN 978–0–19–957585–5 (Hbk)
ISBN 978–0–19–871671–6 (Pbk)

Links to third party websites are provided by Oxford in good faith and
for information only. Oxford disclaims any responsibility for the materials
contained in any third party website referenced in this work.

I would like to dedicate this book to my parents, Brian and Heather Hopper. Their lifelong passion for history has guided me well, and afforded me much inspiration and support.

Preface

I first became interested in writing a history of civil-war side-changing whilst researching the clash between the Fairfax and Hotham families, parliament's commanders in Yorkshire during the first civil war. Study for this volume began in 2006, and it has proved a challenging and enjoyable experience. Civil-war historiography has traditionally concentrated more upon the parliamentarians, but in recent years royalist studies have grown in number and sophistication. There has also been a recent tendency to reinterpret civil-war allegiances as less fixed and more fluid in response to changing circumstances. Therefore, the time is particularly ripe for a detailed study of the extent and nature of side-changing, despite the need for this having long been recognised. This book aims to address this gap in the literature, and hopes to inspire further research into the ways in which our seventeenth-century forbears confronted the difficult problem of loyalty and allegiance. Whilst it has been written primarily for academics and students, it is hoped that the prose style adopted will make it accessible to a wider readership of civil-war enthusiasts.

Andrew Hopper
Marc Fitch House, Leicester

Acknowledgements

The research for this book began in 2006 with my arrival at the University of Leicester, whose 'new blood' lectureship scheme has allowed me generous time for this research, as well as a much-needed semester of study leave so that the book could be finished on schedule. I am particularly thankful to Richard Cust, Jason Peacey, and Stephen Roberts for their encouragement to me in developing this topic, reading draft chapters, and responding with valuable criticism and advice. I would also like to thank the Early Modern Society at Birkbeck and the University of Oxford's Social, Cultural, and Economic History in the British Isles *c.*1450–1750 Seminar, and the University of Cambridge's Early Modern Economic and Social History Seminar for hosting occasions that allowed me to air my ideas. I am grateful to Tim Wales for valuable discussion and help with sources for parliamentarian officers, and I would also like to thank Adrian Ailes, David Appleby, Lloyd Bowen, Charles Carlton, Stuart Carroll, David Finnegan, Henry French, Ian Gentles, Peter Marshall, Mark Stoyle, Emma Watson, and Andy Wood for useful suggestions in discussion of this topic. I am most grateful to Glenn Burgess, Amanda Capern, Stuart Carroll, and Henry French for providing excellent hospitality during my research trips.

I have received much generous assistance from the archivists and librarians at the British Library, the Beinecke Rare Book and Manuscript Library, the Folger Shakespeare Library, the National Archives, the Bodleian Library, the West Yorkshire Archive Service, Leicestershire and Rutland Record Office, Devonshire Record Office, and Hull History Centre. I am also particularly grateful to Evelyn Cornell, history subject librarian at Leicester University Library. At Oxford University Press I would like to thank Seth Cayley for approaching me about this project, and Stephanie Ireland for helping me see it through to completion. Finally, I am also grateful to the anonymous referees whose stimulating criticism and helpful suggestions have no doubt made this a much better book. Any remaining errors are mine alone.

Contents

List of figures

Abbreviations

BL	British Library
Bodl.	Bodleian Library
CJ	*Journals of the House of Commons*
CCAM	*Calendar of the Committee for the Advance of Money (Domestic), 1642-1656*, ed. M. A. E. Green, 3 vols. (1888)
CCCD	*Calendar of the Proceedings of the Committee for Compounding, 1643–1660*, ed. M. A. E. Green, 5 vols. (1889)
CSPD	*Calendar of State Papers Domestic*
DRO	Devonshire Record Office, Exeter
EHR	*English Historical Review*
HJ	*Historical Journal*
HHC	Hull History Centre
HMC	Historical Manuscripts Commission
JBS	*Journal of British Studies*
JSAHR	*Journal of the Society for Army Historical Research*
Keeler	Mary Frear Keeler, *The Long Parliament, 1640–1641: A Biographical Study of its Members* (Philadelphia, 1954)
LJ	*Journals of the House of Lords*
ODNB	*Oxford Dictionary of National Biography*
Newman	P. R. Newman, *Royalist Officers in England and Wales, 1642–1660: A Biographical Dictionary* (New York, 1981)
P&P	*Past and Present*
Portland MS	*Portland MS*, HMC, 29, 13th Report, Appendix, Part 1 (1891), vol. 1
TNA	The National Archives
TRHS	*Transactions of the Royal Historical Society*
TT	Thomason Tract
WYAS	West Yorkshire Archive Service
YAJ	*Yorkshire Archaeological Journal*
YASRS	Yorkshire Archaeological Society, Record Series
YML, CWT	Civil War Tract, York Minster Library

Note to the reader

The place of publication of printed works is London unless otherwise noted. Dates are given according to the old-style calendar, but the year is taken to begin on 1 January instead of 25 March. The spelling, capitalization, and punctuation of quotes from manuscripts have been modernized. All other quotations are given as they appear in the printed source.

Introduction

On 2 February 1659 Major Lewis Audley was summoned before the House of Commons for abusing two Surrey MPs. He was charged with having called one a 'base rascal' and the other 'a base stinking Fellow and a Shit-breech.' In his defence, Audley maintained that he was provoked by one of them goading him: 'That he was no Gentleman; had no Arms; and that he was a Turncoat.' Denial of gentility had long been considered a grievous insult for a gentleman and provocative of violence, but Audley explained that being denounced as a turncoat was to him, even worse. He was judged guilty and committed to the Tower, but protested further: 'I have faithfully served you these eighteen years, and was never guilty of being a turncoat. That sticks with me.'[1]

The experience of civil war and revolution politicized the vocabulary of insult. From the social, sexual, and scatological slights of the 1630s, new overtly political smears emerged reflecting a 'widening sphere of political discussion' and 'the perceived widening of political participation'.[2] Alongside 'Roundhead rogue' and 'popish Cavalier' stood 'turncoat'—a term in use since the 1560s but increasingly employed during the civil wars. From usage at Oxford and Westminster, it penetrated into everyday conversations in provincial villages and towns. Henry Cholmley, constable of Tunstall in Yorkshire's North Riding, stood accused of berating his neighbours as 'turncoats, saying they were not worthy to come into honest men's company.'[3] At Weymouth, the corporation court heard in May 1646 that John Jourdain had said to the bailiff: 'Thou art a double-faced man and Fabian Hodder [condemned to death by the parliamentarians] is an honester man then thou; for hee hath stood to what hee hath undertaken, but thou has turned on every side'.[4]

This book is the first monograph devoted to examining the phenomenon of side-changing during the civil wars. It hopes to address not just why people changed sides, but also when, where, and how. Although a full quantification of side-changing can never be recovered, this book aims to provide a realistic picture of its importance and extent. It reveals that there were different degrees of side-changing and a variety of kinds of side-changer ranging from unprincipled opportunists to those

---

[1] *CJ*, vii, 596–7; Thomas Burton, *The Diary of Thomas Burton, esq., Member in the Parliaments of Oliver and Richard Cromwell, from 1656 to 1659*, ed. John Towill Rutt, 4 vols. (1828), iii, 38.

[2] Michael J. Braddick, 'The English Revolution and its Legacies', in Nicholas Tyacke (ed.), *The English Revolution c.1590–1720: Politics, Religion and Communities* (Manchester, 2007), 39.

[3] TNA, SP 23/172/450–9.

[4] I owe this reference to Lloyd Bowen: *Weymouth and Melcome Regis MS*, HMC, 5th Report, Part I, Report and Appendix (1876), 587b.

compelled by changing circumstances and a reconsideration of their duty to switch their allegiance. Contextualizing the experience of side-changers strongly suggests that notions of 'turncoating' and attitudes towards it were culturally constructed. Side-changing was a practice that rankled with contemporaries, and yet was engaged in by many. It attracted widespread condemnation, and yet was encouraged and connived at. On occasions and under specific circumstances, side-changing might be praised, honoured, and welcomed. It brought many to the scaffold, but crowned others with prosperity and success. It is a subject fraught with complication and contradiction, but given the weight of historiography examining allegiance, side-changing demands a detailed investigation. Ivan Roots emphasized the importance of side-changers as long ago as 1966, and declared the potential value of such an investigation, commenting: 'An analysis of their motives might shed a good deal of light on the issues at stake in the civil war.'[5] More recently, Jason McElligott has explicitly called for such a study, remarking: 'a history of the "turn-coat" in the Civil Wars is long overdue.'[6]

I

In order to properly contextualize civil-war side-changing, it is necessary to revisit the vexed question of allegiance and the process of taking sides. Historians have long been concerned to analyse the causes of the civil wars and respond to the subtly different question of how both sides mustered support. Whig and Marxist historians shared a conviction, albeit for different reasons, that parliament enjoyed stronger support than the king among the common people, in particular amongst the 'middling sort' of people. Whilst Whigs saw this as part of England's progress towards constitutional liberty, Marxists interpreted it as evidence of class conflict.[7] By the late 1960s, critics of Marxist historiography recognised that allegiance was not pre-determined by long-term undercurrents of socio-economic change, but rather that the choice of sides was shaped by a huge range of factors, including kinship ties, principle, a mixture of idealism and self-interest, and the geographical factor of where an individual's personal and landed estates were located.[8] Alan Everitt considered that allegiances were shaped by the 'whole network of local society', including the 'pressures of personal influence, family connection, ancient amity, local pride, religious sentiment, economic necessity, and a dozen other matters, now often very difficult to track down.' Yet in explaining the loyalty of the common people, he privileged one factor. In his perception, their allegiance in a subsistence society 'was unavoidably dictated chiefly by economic necessity.'[9]

    [5] Ivan Roots, *The Great Rebellion, 1642–1660* (1966), 76.
    [6] Jason McElligott, *Royalism, Print and Censorship in Revolutionary England* (Woodbridge, 2007), 226.
    [7] Brian Manning, *The English People and the English Revolution* (2nd edn., 1991).
    [8] J. T. Cliffe, *The Yorkshire Gentry from the Reformation to the Civil War* (1969), 360.
    [9] Alan Everitt, *The Local Community and the Great Rebellion* (Historical Association Pamphlet, 70, 1969), 23–5.

By the 1980s the focus had shifted to religious factors. This was most memorably articulated by John Morrill, that it 'was the force of religion that drove minorities to fight, and forced majorities to make reluctant choices.'[10] In 1986 Gerald Aylmer agreed, pronouncing that almost all current historians agreed that 'religion was the single touchstone, more than any other, which determined people's political, and eventually in most cases also their military allegiance.'[11] Ian Gentles isolated the 'key factor in pre-combat motivation' as religion—particularly religious fear—and that this was reflected in the cornets, colours, and banners borne on both sides.[12] Morrill's contention that the civil war 'was not the first European Revolution: it was the last of the Wars of Religion' continues to spark debate and qualification, not least whether religion is too unsophisticated as a descriptive category.[13] Barbara Donagan has also suggested that constitutional arguments featured heavily in the often overlooked stage between choosing sides and taking up arms. Yet despite the persuasive power of these arguments for the process of taking sides, individuals' inner motives often remain difficult for historians to reliably demonstrate with evidence. Donagan has cautioned that the criteria by which people took up arms 'cannot be forced into any simple pattern', whilst P. R. Newman's studies of royalism led him to caution that allegiance choices 'arose from inclination, temperament, and other humours that will forever defy precise analysis.'[14]

Since the 1980s, historians such as David Underdown, Ann Hughes, and Mark Stoyle strove to explore further the process of allegiance formation in specific localities.[15] By doing so they did much to discredit the revisionist contention that the civil wars lacked widespread ideological division. When the processes of recruitment were examined closely, the idea that both sides, but in particular the king, relied primarily on unquestioning deference to rally support tended to fall apart. Underdown contended that popular allegiance was significant, that it could be discerned, and that it was affected by the agriculture, settlement patterns, social structure, and political culture of a region. He considered that popular royalism was most prevalent in arable regions dominated by nucleated villages and single resident landlords, with a settled, festive, and traditional way of life. In contrast, parliamentarianism was more a feature of woodland and upland areas inclined to pasture, dairying, and rural industries, with scattered patterns of settlement, weak

---

[10] J. S. Morrill, 'The Religious Context of the English Civil War', *TRHS*, 5th series, 34 (1984), 157.

[11] G. E. Aylmer, 'Collective Mentalities in Mid Seventeenth-Century England: 1 The Puritan Outlook', *TRHS*, 5th series, 36 (1986), 3.

[12] Ian Gentles, 'Why Men Fought in the British Civil Wars', *The History Teacher*, 26 (1993), 409–11.

[13] Michael J. Braddick, 'Prayer Book and Protestation: Anti-Popery, Anti-Puritanism and the Outbreak of the English Civil War', in Charles W. A. Prior and Glenn Burgess (eds.), *England's Wars of Religion, Revisited* (Farnham, 2011), 144.

[14] Barbara Donagan, 'Casuistry and Allegiance in the English Civil War', in Derek Hirst and Richard Strier (eds.), *Writing and Political Engagement in Seventeenth-Century England* (Cambridge, 1999), 90–1; P. R. Newman, *The Old Service: Royalist Regimental Colonels and the Civil War, 1642–46* (Manchester, 1993), 313.

[15] David Underdown, *Revel, Riot and Rebellion: Popular Politics and Culture in England 1603–1660* (Oxford, 1985); Ann Hughes, *Politics, Society and Civil War in Warwickshire, 1620–1660* (Cambridge, 1987); Mark Stoyle, *Loyalty and Locality: Popular Allegiance in Devon during the English Civil War* (Exeter, 1994).

manorial control, and multiple or absentee landlords. These regions were held to have greater populations of unsettled and landless labourers, alongside a middling sort seeking to impose order and Godly discipline upon them. The problems with this hypothesis have been highlighted by, among others, John Morrill.[16] Yet Underdown did much to inspire an important focus of post-revisionist historiography; that is, the interaction between the gentry and the people, how each courted the other's support, and the explicit recognition that this was often a two-way process.[17] As Ann Hughes has recently reiterated: 'It was painfully obvious that political obligation was not natural or innate, but a matter to be negotiated and constructed.'[18] This is no longer surprising, as historians now recognize that the commons had long been educated by participation in local government, interpreting official policy for themselves and pressuring their governors into acting for them.[19] One civil-war example of this process was when the miners of Derbyshire's High Peak negotiated an exemption from lead tithe for those among them recruited into the royalist forces.[20] John Walter depicts an expanding 'dialogue between rulers and ruled' during the 1640s, suggesting a move from class to popular political culture as an explanatory tool for assessing popular allegiances, focusing particularly on the power of cheap print, mass petitioning, and oath-taking.[21] These developments have done much to advance our approaches to allegiance, yet a recent historiographical turn has made this question, and particularly that of side-changing, more relevant than ever.

During the last ten years, historians have increasingly emphasized civil-war allegiance as no fixed, unchanging matter, but rather as unstable, shifting, and fluctuating in response to changing political circumstances such as the failure of peace negotiations, the Solemn League and Covenant, the Cessation in Ireland, and the calling of the Oxford Parliament. Allegiance choices were not snap decisions of summer 1642. Once taken, they were not irreversible. Many taking sides, reluctantly or not, subjected themselves to years of soul-searching thereafter, and struggled to maintain their alignments in the face of changing political circumstances. Both sides extolled the virtue of constancy in order to discourage such wavering, and were brutal in their denunciations of defectors. Yet to side-changers themselves, defecting risked attracting human condemnation, whereas persisting in a cause they considered unconscionable and against God might lead some to fear divine retribution.

Alongside recognition of the fluidity of allegiance there has been a growing realization of the high frequency of side-changing, despite Mark Stoyle's assertion that because changing sides met with derision, 'turncoats were the exception rather

---

[16] John Morrill, 'The Ecology of Allegiance in the English Revolution', *JBS*, 26 (1987), 451–67.

[17] Ann Hughes, *Causes of the English Civil War* (2nd edn., Basingstoke, 1998), 140.

[18] Ann Hughes, *Gender and the English Revolution* (2011), 92.

[19] John Walter, 'The English People and the English Revolution Revisited', *History Workshop Journal*, 61 (2006), 174.

[20] Andy Wood, 'Beyond Post-Revisionism? The Civil War Allegiances of the Miners of the Derbyshire "Peak Country"', *HJ*, 40 (1997), 32–3, 39.

[21] Walter, 'The English People and the English Revolution Revisited', 178–9.

than the rule.'[22] Side-changers may have been exceptional, but they were also numerous and significant. David Smith and Jason McElligott's recent collections on royalism have suggested that side-changing was more common than hitherto realized, that it possessed 'discernable patterns', and that we 'might no longer be able to think of allegiance as a fixed, unchanging, and unchangeable entity.'[23] Geoffrey Smith has argued that the frequency of side-changing is unsurprising, suggesting that 'volatility' in civil-war allegiance stemmed from a sense of confusion and indecisiveness fostered by wartime events.[24] Ian Gentles has concurred that popular allegiance was not static, but often unstable, and 'everywhere in constant flux'.[25]

Part of this historiographical shift is an increased appreciation of how the warring parties were heterogeneous and riddled with internal strife. John Adamson has recently argued that 'factional ascendancies' on both sides were so interdependent and mutually affected by transformations in political power at Oxford and Westminster that the internal politics of each cause can no longer be treated as 'the activities of two almost self-contained worlds'.[26] The parliamentarian coalition was broad, diverse, and fractured, even from its inception in 1642, with Ann Hughes recently characterising parliamentarianism as 'an inherently fissiparous movement in which different interpretations of the "cause" emerged under the pressures of war and religious choice.'[27] Similarly, Barbara Donagan has argued that varieties of royalism were so wide-ranging that they presented a 'rainbow coalition'. She has endorsed Austin Woolrych's observation that there was much shared common ground between moderates on both sides.[28] One manifestation of this was that individuals on opposing sides maintained amicable correspondence, despite attempts to ban the practice. Together with the code of soldiery honour and professional conduct usually observed by officers on both sides, such contact, Donagan argues, 'ameliorated relations between enemies'.[29] Such intercourse and common ground also facilitated side-changing.

---

[22] Mark Stoyle, *Loyalty and Locality: Popular Allegiance in Devon during the English War* (Exeter, 1994), 112.

[23] Jason McElligott and David L. Smith, 'Introduction: Rethinking Royalists and Royalism', in Jason McElligott and David L. Smith (eds.), *Royalists and Royalism during the English Civil Wars* (Cambridge, 2007), 11, 15.

[24] Geoffrey Smith, *Royalist Agents, Conspirators and Spies: Their Role in the British Civil Wars, 1640–1660* (Farnham, 2010), 38–9.

[25] Ian Gentles, *The English Revolution and the Wars in the Three Kingdoms, 1638–1652* (Harlow, 2007), 140.

[26] John Adamson, 'Introduction: High Roads and Blind Alleys: The English Civil War and Its Historiography', in John Adamson (ed.), *The English Civil War: Conflict and Contexts, 1640–1649* (Basingstoke, 2009), 31.

[27] Ann Hughes, 'A "Lunatic Revolter from Loyalty": The Death of Rowland Wilson and the English Revolution', *History Workshop Journal*, 61 (2006), 195.

[28] McElligott and Smith, 'Introduction: Rethinking Royalists and Royalism', and Barbara Donagan, 'Varieties of Royalism', in McElligott and Smith (eds.), *Royalists and Royalism during the English Civil Wars*, 4, 68–71; Austin Woolrych, *Britain in Revolution, 1625–1660* (Oxford, 2002), 248.

[29] Barbara Donagan, 'The Web of Honour: Soldiers, Christians, and Gentlemen in the English Civil War', *HJ*, 44 (2001), 365.

In 2008 Michael Braddick's *God's Fury, England's Fire* advanced the debate conceptually to suggest that it 'might be better to think in terms of people's responses to particular mobilizations rather than a fixed allegiance to one of two sides.' Both sides instigated an ongoing process of attracting support and 'continuous coalition-building' against a backdrop of differing local conditions and changing political circumstances.[30] These 'rival mobilisations' were also directed at those beyond the pre-war ruling elites, playing on fears of popery and sectarianism, thereby impeding negotiation and stimulating further conflict.[31] The competing coalitions grew more difficult to maintain because of the lack of clarity over their objectives.[32] In parliament's case the breakdown of peace negotiations and the conflict's escalation during 1643 entailed a transformation of 'the cause' which strained the choices many had made in 1642. Parliament's amassing of executive powers, use of sequestration, and promulgation of both the Vow and Covenant and Solemn League and Covenant led many of its supporters into reconsidering their position or even changing sides. Those alienated by these political developments perceived that the defensive war in which they had enlisted was no longer recognizable, and that a decisive victory for either side would have undesirable consequences. Suspicion that their cause was betrayed gathered momentum among parliamentarians throughout the 1640s.[33] Disaffected parliamentarians invoked war aims of 1642 to trumpet how they had remained constant, while the New Model and its allies had changed the cause for the worse.[34] As Sir William Waller explained in 1648: 'This change was not in me, but in others: or, if in me, yet occasioned by the alteration and change of others...I am of opinion that all are not of the Godly party that wear that badge and cognizance.'[35] Others claimed that the cause had initially been misrepresented to them. Sir Hugh Cholmley reflected that he had persuaded his wife to become a royalist once he 'unmasked to her the Parlament's intents.'[36] In September 1649, one Shropshire minister spoke for many when he claimed: 'Mistake me not, had I known of their design I would have seen the parliament hanged before I would have been of their side.'[37] Such comments from contemporaries complicate the issue of what constituted side-changing, and indicate how it became such a highly contested phenomenon.

---

[30] Michael Braddick, *God's Fury, England's Fire: A New History of the English Civil Wars* (2008), 233, 236.
[31] Braddick, 'Prayer Book and Protestation', 135–6.
[32] Braddick, *God's Fury, England's Fire*, 300.
[33] Ibid., 261, 296–7, 592; Braddick, 'Prayer Book and Protestation', 141; Anthony Fletcher, 'The Coming of War', in John Morrill (ed.), *Reactions to the English Civil War* (Basingstoke, 1982), 48.
[34] Rachel Foxley, 'Royalists and the New Model Army in 1647: Circumstance, Principle and Compromise', in McElligott and Smith (eds.), *Royalists and Royalism during the English Civil Wars*, 164.
[35] Robert Ashton, *Counter-Revolution: The Second Civil War and its Origins, 1646–8* (New Haven, 1994), 396.
[36] Sir Hugh Cholmley, *The Memoirs and Memorials of Sir Hugh Cholmley of Whitby, 1600–1657*, ed. Jack Binns (YASRS, 153, 2000), 105.
[37] BL, Stowe 184, fo. 156r. I owe this reference to Lloyd Bowen: Lloyd Bowen, 'Seditious Speech and Popular Royalism, 1649–60', in Jason McElligott and David L. Smith (eds.), *Royalists and Royalism during the Interregnum* (Manchester, 2010), 50.

II

This book combines prosopographical and thematic approaches to this problem of side-changing, hoping to make connections between political, religious, social, cultural, and military history. Part I attempts to establish the scale of side-changing. It discusses the identity and motives of side-changers among peers, MPs, army officers, and common soldiers, as well as the chronological and regional context behind their defections. Although a work of this length cannot be completely comprehensive, by restricting Part I to England and Wales during the first civil war it is hoped that a broadly representative impression might be reached. This risks appearing Anglocentric, but as Barbara Donagan has conjectured, there is a danger that amalgamating the Scottish and Irish wars with England's might cloud deeper understanding of 1642–1646 with undue comparisons; if anything, allegiances in Scotland and Ireland were even more fluid and multi-layered.[38] Chronological constraint will also guard against an old pitfall of civil-war political history: the act of generalizing 'back from later standpoints'.[39] This is critical because from 1646 to 1649 the character of both royalist and parliamentarian causes changed irrevocably.[40] Side-changing during the Restoration and thereafter invites a study separate from this undertaking.[41]

Part II develops a cultural history of side-changing in thematic chapters that draw upon contemporary notions of honour, the nature of oath-taking, rituals of retribution, and the descriptive language of treachery in print and propaganda. It also analyses the justifications of the side-changers themselves as they sought to shape a self-image for their contemporaries or posterity. Here, the approach combines primary sources such as correspondence between gentry, journals, diaries, memoirs, commonplace books, muster rolls, trial records, and state papers, with evidence from art and literature such as poems, plays, ballads, engravings, iconography, newsbooks, and propaganda. Here useful thematic comparisons can be made with side-changing in Scotland and Ireland, and the chronology is extended to 1651. In this way, the considerable realignment that occurred during and after 1647 will not be neglected. In explaining these transformations, Rachel Foxley has recently warned us against overplaying the fluidity of allegiance. The Scots and the earl of Essex's old faction were unnatural allies, as were the New Model Independents and the anti-Scots royalists headed by the duke of Richmond and marquis of

---

[38] Barbara Donagan, 'Atrocity, War Crime, and Treason in the English Civil War', *American Historical Review*, 99 (1994), 1138–9; Micheál Ó Siochrú, *God's Executioner: Oliver Cromwell and the Conquest of Ireland* (2008), 32.

[39] Valerie Pearl, 'Oliver St. John and the "Middle Group" in the Long Parliament: August 1643–May 1644', *EHR*, 81 (1966), 511.

[40] Jason Peacey, *Politicians and Pamphleteers: Propaganda During the English Civil Wars and Interregnum* (Aldershot, 2004), 281.

[41] G. E. Aylmer, 'Collective Mentalities in Mid-Seventeenth-Century England: 4 Cross Currents: Neutrals, Trimmers and Others', *TRHS*, 5th series, 39 (1989), 7.

Hertford. While some rapprochement was possible, terms such as 'Cavalier, Independent, and Roundhead' still retained contemporary meaning and identity, circumscribing flexibility and freedom of action.[42]

This study encounters several historical problems, including defining what actually constituted a 'turncoat', especially when so many side-changers proclaimed political constancy for their actions. 'Turncoat' was employed as a contemporary term of abuse to describe a whole range of highly different individuals. Therefore, there are obvious problems with historians utilizing it as a category, especially with so many grey areas over its application. For instance, those who withdrew their support from one side negotiated with the other, or who surrendered prematurely were vulnerable to charges of turncoating even if they did not thereafter support the enemy. Professional military officers who changed sides to protect their pay and career prospects appear very different from MPs defecting due to changing political circumstances and fears for their safety, or common soldiers changing sides after being captured, in order to preserve their liberty.

Reaching a definition of side-changing is also hampered by ambiguity over what constituted sufficient activism to be fairly categorized as a parliamentarian or royalist in the first place. McElligott and Smith have recently defined as royalists 'somebody who, by thought or deed, identified himself or herself as a Royalist and was accepted as such by other individuals who defined themselves as royalists'.[43] A similar line, rooted in contemporary self and peer perceptions, is difficult to adopt for side-changers, especially if activism for either side was unclear. The problem of discerning allegiance was keenly felt by contemporaries themselves, with the proliferation of loyalty oaths bearing witness to the discomfort and uncertainty surrounding such endeavours. Contemporaries resorted to judging upon outward and perceptible criteria such as an individual's physical whereabouts; both sides prosecuted and sequestered those who fled to enemy-controlled territory. Yet this is far from a guarantee of voluntary activism, and historians should be wary of uncritically accepting the assessment of contemporaries about whether an individual had changed sides. Rachel Weil has argued that individuals presented themselves to those in authority in a world with no universally 'uniform or coherent understanding of allegiance.'[44] Here, contemporaries read much into the politics of gesture found in symbolic acts of loyalty. For instance, in September 1645 Rowland Laugharne complained to Speaker Lenthall that Roger Lort had once kissed the king's hand at Oxford, whilst suspicions that Sir John Hotham would change sides were heightened when rumours circulated that his son had kissed the queen's hand when she landed at Bridlington.[45]

---

[42] McElligott and Smith, 'Introduction: Rethinking Royalists and Royalism', 4; Foxley, 'Royalists and the New Model Army in 1647', 155–6.

[43] McElligott and Smith, 'Introduction: Rethinking Royalists and Royalism during the Interregnum', 8.

[44] Weil, 'Thinking about Allegiance in the English Civil War', 190.

[45] *Portland MS*, 270; John Tickell, *History of the Town and County of Kingston-upon-Hull* (Hull, 1798), 465.

Individuals appeared as different things to different people, with the matter of allegiance often remaining in the eye of the beholder; when Viscount Inchiquin abandoned the English parliament in 1648, the Committee of the Estates of Scotland considered him faithful to the Solemn League and Covenant. They were 'very sensible of the great extremities the Lord Inchiquin hath been reduced to by the malice of the Independent party in England', and vowed to include him in all their future negotiations and treaties.[46] The Pembroke gentleman Arthur Owen was considered 'among the rigid Presbyterians a Royalist; among the unlimited Royalists a Presbyterian'.[47] These are clear indications that identity and allegiance were culturally constructed, with individuals labelled as turncoats when they were perceived as such by hostile contemporaries. Those parliamentarians who tightened their grip on the legislative, judicial, and executive arms of government during the later 1640s used the term 'turncoat' in a political way to marginalize opposition. Such labelling strategies purposefully discredited former comrades among rival factions. The New Model Army's charge against the eleven 'incendiary' MPs in 1647 likened them to the executed defectors Sir Alexander Carew and the Hothams as betrayers of the cause and their own better consciences.[48] By establishing their opponents as an out-group of turncoats, the Army's supporters legitimized themselves as the true upholders of parliament's cause. Their enemies—the earl of Holland's insurgents of 1648—accused the parliament of 'breach of faith' for maintaining the New Model and its 'levelling undertaking'. They pledged themselves for 'KING and Parliament' as had the parliamentarians of 1642, declaring 'we do not vary from those principles and grounds, we have been engaged in'.[49]

Denouncing former comrades as 'turncoats', 'renegades', 'ambidexters', or 'changelings' was therefore an act of self-definition that testified to one's ownership of 'the cause' and legitimized one's position. A similar 'naming and shaming' strategy was employed in Restoration France after 1815, where the term 'girouette', meaning 'weathervane', was directed at politicians as 'a metaphor for turncoat'. The ease with which many former revolutionaries and supporters of Bonaparte achieved political office angered many returning émigrés and royalists. In 1815 the satirical prosopography of turncoats entitled the *Dictionnaire des Girouettes* employed weathervane symbols to indicate the moments and levels of their turncoating. It was

---

[46] *Portland MS*, 469–70.

[47] Arthur Leonard Leach, *The History of the Civil War (1642–1649) in Pembrokeshire and on its Borders* (1937), 220–1.

[48] BL, TT E404(6), *The Araignment [sic] and Impeachment of Major Generall Massie, Sir William Waller, Col. Poyntz, Sir Philip Stapleton, Sir Iohn Maynard, Ant. Nichols, and one Cheisly, the Scotch Secretary, (Lately Taken at Sea by the Vice-Admirall) with Dives [sic] other Surreptitious Members of the Commons in Parliament, the Court of Aldermen, and Common Councell of the City of London; as namely Col. Sutton, Major Banes, Cap. Cox, now in safe custody, and Other Citizens of Meaner Ranke and Quality of the Presbyterian Faction*, 23 August (1647), 5.

[49] BL, TT E451(33), *The Declaration of the Right Honourable the Duke of Buckingham, and the Earles of Holland, and Peterborough, and other Lords and Gentlemen now associated for the King and Parliament, the Religion, Lawes, and Peace of His Majesties*, 8 July (1648), 2–4.

tremendously popular, and its 'raking over of recent betrayals' was intended to ridicule and marginalize its subjects.[50]

There are further problems in interpreting the motives behind defections. Outward behaviour is not necessarily a reliable indicator of an individual's mindset and motives. David Underdown argued that as many in arms were reluctant or coerced, it is difficult for historians to deduce political allegiance merely from military service.[51] In tackling the problem of popular participation in the English Reformation, Ethan Shagan has suggested that contemporaries 'confronted issues of resistance and collaboration' on a daily basis, subjecting themselves to questions such as: 'Was it ethical to obey authority if obedience tended to further the growth of heresy? By what practices could an authority de-legitimize itself? At what point did passive obedience slip into active support for the regime's policies?'[52] Royalists and parliamentarians a century later grappled with these very same questions as they engaged themselves and then wavered as the war lengthened and their cause transformed itself in unexpected directions.

Historians have tended towards cynical explanations of side-changing, seeing side-changers as opportunistic and unprincipled, thereby accentuating their individual decision-making and changeable natures. This is not always warranted. More remains to be done to properly contextualize individuals' defections and fully explore the relationship between side-changing and allegiance. When side-changers justified themselves at the time or subsequently, they may have been honest as well as crafty about their motives. Self-interest and ideological motives might overlap. They may have sought to 'spin' their past actions to suit changed political circumstances, or blended trustworthy testimony with untruths. Interested parties appropriated or exploited their stories, fashioning the motives behind their side-changing for particular political ends and audiences. Whatever the case, Gerald Aylmer warned against the inclination among historians to morally condemn side-changers, humanely reminding us that the mid-seventeenth-century crisis could be a terrifying experience for those living through it. Recourse to derision was felt keenly by contemporaries, but 370 years on we might hope for a more judicious detachment.[53]

Another enigma is the relationship between neutrality and side-changing—a conundrum that strained Aylmer's attempt to categorize and tabulate the allegiance of royal servants.[54] Those who followed the path of least resistance in attempting to accommodate the demands of both sides were particularly vulnerable. Some were unfairly stigmatized as turncoats who had never voluntarily engaged themselves in

---

[50] Alan B. Spitzer, 'Malicious Memories: Restoration Politics and a Prosopography of Turncoats', *French Historical Studies*, 24 (2001), 40, 42.

[51] Underdown, *Revel, Riot and Rebellion*, 186.

[52] Ethan Shagan, *Popular Politics and the English Reformation* (Cambridge, 2003), 12.

[53] Aylmer, 'Collective Mentalities in Mid-Seventeenth-Century England: 4 Cross Currents: Neutrals, Trimmers and Others', 22.

[54] G. E. Aylmer, *The King's Servants: The Civil Service of Charles I, 1625–1642* (2nd edn., 1974), 343, 389–416.

the first place. This was because activists on both sides frequently considered that those who proclaimed themselves neutrals really had underlying sympathies with the enemy. They perceived neutral sentiment as a cloak for disaffection, with local commanders seeing self-proclaimed neutrals as merely awaiting a fitting opportunity to declare for the enemy.[55] For example, in October 1642 John Hotham and Sir Edward Rodes requested instructions from parliament on how to deal with those who 'shroud their disaffection in a pretended neutrality.'[56] Colonel Herbert Morley warned Speaker Lenthall that the royalist advance towards Southampton in September 1643 'may raise a storm in Sussex, which county is full of neuters and Malignants; and I have ever observed neuters to turn Malignants upon such occasions.'[57] Sir John Meldrum agreed in May 1644 that Lancashire's inhabitants in the neighbourhood of the royalist garrison of Lathom 'who formerly lurked as neuters do now show themselves in arms for the earl of Derby'.[58] Propagandists in particular were quick to conflate neutrality with treachery and conspiracy. John Vicars proclaimed that hell awaited those who protested neutrality: 'I pray thee that a *Newter*, or Key-cold fellow in *Gods cause*, is a most despicable creature, despised both of *God* and the *Devill*, being apt to be false and faithlesse to them both'.[59]

III

Before the civil wars, allegiance was largely seen as congruent with confessional identity, therefore notions of side-changing often encompassed apostasy or changing one's religion.[60] The unflattering treatment of Andrew Perne, dean of Ely, in the Marprelate tracts helped establish 'Pernere'—the Latin for 'to turn'—into a byword for religious turncoating. Perne's vacillations were far from untypical in the period and attest to his success in weathering the storm of successive Tudor Reformations, yet he was so condemned for apostasy and acting against his conscience that he was dismissed in Godly circles as 'Old Andrew Turncoat', and the 'noteablest turnecoate in all this land'.[61] Another famous example was Thomas Bell, curate of Thirsk, who converted to Catholicism in 1570, but after political conflict with the Jesuits, surrendered himself in 1592. He provided Archbishop Whitgift with intelligence on missionary Catholicism in northern England, including naming seminary priests and lay sympathizers. In a case that prefigured the conversion narratives required by civil war side-changers, he was required to preach to recusants imprisoned in York

[55] Braddick, *God's Fury, England's Fire*, 421.
[56] Bodl., MS Nalson 2, no. 82.
[57] *Portland MS*, 130.
[58] *CSPD 1644*, 174.
[59] BL, E33(18), *A Looking-Glasse for Malignants: or, Gods hand against God-haters... Together with a Caveat for Cowards and Unworthy (either Timorous or Treacherous) Newters. Collected for Gods Honour, and the Ungodlies Horrour, by John Vicars* (1643), 32–3.
[60] Weil, 'Thinking about Allegiance in the English Civil War', 184.
[61] Patrick Collinson, 'Perne the Turncoat: An Elizabethan Reputation', in Patrick Collinson, *Elizabethan Essays* (1994), 179, 184, 189–91, 216.

castle, and publish a treatise of recantation entitled *Thomas Bels Motives*. Authorship of other anti-Catholic tracts followed, and he secured a modest royal pension.[62] Bell's treatises were followed by a popular and influential genre of printed accounts that claimed to represent the confessions of former British Catholics who had converted to Protestantism.[63] Robin Clifton has argued that these tracts vulgarly pandered to Protestant prejudices about the superstitious nature of Catholicism and 'were presented as lively and truthful accounts of the enemy camp written by men familiar with its workings.'[64] Later propaganda narratives supposedly penned by civil-war side-changers built upon this tradition, fulfilling a similar function by maligning the side they had deserted.

Notions of side-changing were also informed by the realities of continental warfare—especially the English intervention in war between Spain and the Dutch. Here, the English learned a painful lesson of the military costs of treachery. Sir William Stanley was a Catholic Englishman who served in the duke of Alva's administration of the Netherlands before entering Elizabeth's service in Ireland, where he was active in suppressing Irish insurgency during the early 1580s. Thereafter he accompanied the earl of Leicester to the Netherlands, where he was appointed governor of Deventer in 1586. After quarrelling with the natives over the supply of his forces, he defected to the Spanish in January 1587, handing over Deventer the same day as his fellow Catholic, Rowland York, delivered up the fort at Zutphen. This coordinated defection completely undermined Leicester's campaign, and was thought to threaten Ireland's security should Stanley return.[65] Englishmen who fought in the French Wars of Religion witnessed Catholic aristocrats placing prices on the heads of their Protestant counterparts, encouraging Protestant soldiers to change sides and murder their own commanders. The sieur de Maurevert who shot Admiral Coligny in 1572 had changed sides three years earlier, shooting his Huguenot captain in the back as he did so.[66] England experienced a comparable act of treachery in 1628, when the disaffected officer John Felton murdered his former general, the duke of Buckingham. There was considerable public sympathy for Felton, whose name lived on in popular discourse not only as

---

[62] I am grateful to Emma Watson for discussion of Bell's case: Alexandra Walsham, 'Thomas Bell (*b. c.*1551, *d.* in or after 1610), Roman Catholic priest and protestant polemicist', *ODNB*.

[63] Peter Lake, 'Anti-Popery: The Structure of a Prejudice', in Richard Cust and Ann Hughes (eds.), *Conflict in Early Stuart England: Studies in Religion and Politics, 1603–1642* (Harlow, 1989), 98. Examples include Richard Sheldon, *The Motives of Richard Sheldon, Priest for his Just, Voluntary and Free Renunciation of Communion with the Bishop of Rome* (1612); John Gee, *The Foot Out of the Snare with a Detection of Sundry Late Practices and Impostures of the Priests and Jesuites in England* (1624); James Wadsworth, *The English Spanish Pilgrime. Or, a New Discoverie of Spanish Popery* (1630); Thomas Abernethie, *Abjuration of Poperie, by Thomas Abernethie: Sometime Jesuite, but now Penitent Sinner, and an Unworthie Member of the True Reformed Church of God in Scotland* (Edinburgh, 1638).

[64] Robin Clifton, 'Fear of Popery', in Conrad Russell (ed.), *The Origins of the English Civil War* (Basingstoke, 1973), 148–9.

[65] I am grateful to Peter Marshall for bringing Stanley's career to my attention: Rory Rapple, 'Sir William Stanley (1548–1630), soldier', *ODNB*; Sarah Clayton, 'Rowland Yorke (*d.* 1588), soldier and traitor', *ODNB*.

[66] Roger B. Manning, *Swordsmen: The Martial Ethos in the Three Kingdoms* (Oxford, 2003), 69, 70, 77, 109; Stuart Carroll, *Blood and Violence in Early Modern France* (Oxford, 2007), 272.

a traitor, but also as a patriot, hero, and martyr.[67] For instance, fenland rioters in May 1643 threatened to serve one JP and drainage projector 'as Felton served Buckingham'.[68]

Pre-war understandings of side-changing recognized that it might entail abandoning Christianity entirely. Approximately 8,000 British captives were seized by Barbary corsairs in the early 1600s, and many of them apostatized to Islam.[69] Anxieties were voiced from the Privy Council to the theatre that Christians so enslaved would turn 'renegado' and become Muslims. Robert Daborne and Philip Massinger wrote plays depicting such renegades as violent, quarrelsome, and treacherous apostates, while the poet Samuel Rowlands pronounced that God would punish renegades with damnation and death.[70] The words 'turncoat' and 'renegado', with the latter also implying apostasy, were in considerable use by the early seventeenth century, and both carried deeply negative connotations. The former was employed in John Foxe's *Acts and Monuments* by 1570, and on the stage in Thomas Middleton's *Game at Chess* by 1624.[71] By 1658 a ballad tune known as 'Turn-coat' had emerged, suggesting that the civil wars popularized these terms.[72] Side-changers seeking honourable employment did not wish to be associated with them.

In Ireland, social, cultural, and colonial factors blended with religious ones to complicate side-changing. One trooper defected from the Lord Deputy's forces prior to the battle at Kinsale in 1601. According to his commander this was in order to seek the favour of the Spaniards and aggrandize himself as the foremost of his sept.[73] The failure of the Irish insurgents to seize Dublin Castle in October 1641 was due largely to the renegade conspirator Owen O'Connolly, who alerted the authorities the day before, despite his kinship to the leading plotters.[74] During the rising's early stages, many English settlers converted to Catholicism to secure promises of safety from the insurgents—some even joining their ranks—while in

---

[67] Braddick, *God's Fury, England's Fire*, 43–4; Alastair Bellany, 'John Felton (*d.*1628), assassin', *ODNB*.

[68] Keith Lindley, *Fenland Riots and the English Revolution* (1982), 157.

[69] Linda Colley, *Captives: Britain, Empire and the World, 1600–1850* (2002), 49–50.

[70] Nabil Matar, 'The Barbary Corsairs, King Charles I and the Civil War', *The Seventeenth Century*, 16 (2001), 247, N. I. Matar, 'The Renegade in English Seventeenth-Century Imagination', *Studies in English Literature, 1500–1900*, 33 (1993), 489, 495; Philip Massinger, *The Renegado a Tragaecomedie. As it hath beene often acted by the Queenes Majesties Servants, at the Private Play-house in Drurye-Lane* (1630); Robert Daborne, *A Christian Turn'd Turke: or, The Tragicall Lives and Deaths of the Two Famous Pyrates, Ward and Dansiker as it hath beene publickly acted* (1612).

[71] J. A. Simpson and E. S. C. Weiner (eds.), *The Oxford English Dictionary*, 20 vols. (Oxford, 1989), xviii, 710.

[72] Wing (2nd ed.)/K697D, *The Knight and the Beggar-wench. Which doth a Wanton Prank Unfold, in as Merry a Story as ever was told. The Tune is, The Kings Delight, or Turn-coat* (1658). Ballads thrived on the distaste that memories of civil war turncoats conjured, decrying such individuals as hypocrites, survivalists, and unscrupulous profiteers: W. G. Day (ed.), *The Pepys Ballads*, 5 vols. (Cambridge, 1987), ii, 210. See below, fig. E.1. on p. 219.

[73] Brendan Kane, *The Politics and Culture of Honour in Britain and Ireland, 1541–1641* (Cambridge, 2010), 119.

[74] Ó Siochrú, *God's Executioner*, 23; Brian MacCuarta, 'Owen O'Connolly (*d.* 1649), plot discloser and parliamentarian army officer', *ODNB*.

Cavan, native Catholics who had converted to Protestantism during the 1630s quickly reverted to their old faith.[75]

During the Bishops' Wars there were fears that those English who opposed the war might prove treacherous. Sir Edmund Verney lamented to his son Ralph that 'the poorest scabb in Scotland will tell us to our faces that two parts of Ingland are on theyr sides, and trewly they behave as if all Ingland were soe.'[76] Several Yorkshire gentry subverted the royal war effort from within, and by August 1640 the king was concerned that Yorkshire's militia colonels and deputy lieutenants were in league with the enemy.[77] Pro-Scots propaganda circulated widely, declaring that Charles was subverted by his popish ministers into seeking to break the power of Protestantism in his kingdoms.[78] Individuals were prosecuted for singing pro-Scots ballads, while one Yorkshireman was charged with declaring that the king was 'worthy to be hanged' for having attended Mass with the queen, and that the Covenanter General, Alexander Leslie, would make a better king.[79] A few Englishmen such as the Newcastle merchant John Fenwick actually defected to Scotland, only to return accompanying the invading Covenanters in August 1640.[80]

IV

Post-revisionist historians have sought to demonstrate that individuals did develop political allegiances to attack the revisionist maxim that the war involved little ideological conflict.[81] This contention is both supported and undermined by this book's emphasis upon side-changing as significant and extensive. For individuals to change sides they had to have engaged themselves politically first, by taking sides, however reluctantly. Conversely, extensive side-changing might suggest that many had no deep or lasting attachment to either side in the first place. The experience of side-changers suggests that neither side's war effort ought now to be studied in isolation. Explaining the prevalence of side-changing also raises difficult questions for the frequent depictions of early modern England as a society which venerated ancient usage, continuity, obedience, loyalty, and constancy. In a period of revolutionary change, many contemporaries found these values difficult to maintain against the

[75] Joseph Cope, *England and the 1641 Irish Rebellion* (Woodbridge, 2009), 60–1; Brian Mac Cuarta, 'Religious Violence Against Settlers in South Ulster, 1641–2', in David Edwards, Pádraig Lenihan and Clodagh Tait (eds.), *Age of Atrocity: Violence and Political Conflict in Early Modern Ireland* (Dublin, 2007), 163–6.

[76] Mark Charles Fissel, *The Bishops' Wars: Charles I's Campaigns against Scotland, 1638–1640* (Cambridge, 1994), 33.

[77] David Scott, '"Hannibal at our Gates" Loyalists and Fifth-columnists during the Bishops' Wars: The Case of Yorkshire', *Historical Research*, 70 (1997), 271, 292; J. T. Cliffe, *The Yorkshire Gentry from the Reformation to the Civil War* (1969), 300, 309, 323.

[78] Caroline Hibbard, *Charles I and the Popish Plot* (Chapel Hill, 1983), 114.

[79] TNA, ASSI 45, 1/3/47; James Raine (ed.), *Depositions from the Castle of York Relating to Offences Committed in the Northern Counties in the Seventeenth Century* (Surtees Society, 40, 1861), 3.

[80] Andrew J. Hopper, 'John Fenwick (*b.* in or after 1593, *d. c.*1670), merchant and parliamentarian army officer', *ODNB*.

[81] Weil, 'Thinking about Allegiance in the English Civil War', 183.

forces of individual conscience, pragmatism, and novelty. Whilst concepts of honour, duty, and service were refined during the conflicts of the 1640s, so too were notions of betrayal, conspiracy, and treachery. Above all, this book seeks to reveal how the practice of side-changing, and the hopes and fears associated with it, played a large part not only in determining the course of the civil wars, but also in the downfall of the Stuart monarchies and the transformation of political culture thereafter.

PART I

A PROFILE OF SIDE-CHANGING
IN ENGLAND AND WALES,
1642–1646

1

A turncoat aristocracy

In September 1647 John Lilburne warned Sir Thomas Fairfax that he would not comply with the Grandees' negotiations with the king, scorning Cromwell and his son-in-law, 'Prince Ireton', for their compliance with a 'turncoat Lordly interest'.[1] Lilburne's depiction of England's aristocracy as untrustworthy waverers owed much to the prominence of several nobles who had changed sides since 1642. Historians have long considered that a majority of peers supported Charles I as the best guarantor of their elevated place within the social hierarchy. Yet in reality, much noble allegiance was murky and shifting, and Jason McElligott has recently suggested that the peerage was particularly susceptible to side-changing.[2] This was potentially significant because they remained a highly militarized group. In 1640, 69 per cent of England's peerage had experience of military action. By 1645 it was 71 per cent, with about a third exercising command in the field during the civil war.[3] Despite very few English peers holding military command on both sides during the first civil war,[4] many travelled the road between Oxford and Westminster, in both directions and on multiple occasions. As with the practice among MPs and army officers, peers moved towards the king until 1644, and towards parliament thereafter. This chapter will examine the troubles behind some peers' choosing of sides during 1642, before contextualizing the dramatic defections from parliament's cause in 1643. These are compared with those peers who abandoned their royalism from 1644 to 1646, before briefly discussing the consequences of aristocratic side-changing for factional politics at Westminster after the first civil war. As with all side-changers, there is a difficulty in translating evidence about their behaviour into an analysis of their motives, but the interplay of conscience, honour, self-interest, duty, and changing political circumstances in shaping the contexts for lordly side-changing may at least be highlighted.

The great Whig historians Gardiner and Firth depicted the nobility as a reactionary force either arrayed behind the king or as a self-interested rump at

---

[1] BL, E409(22), *The Juglers Discovered, in Two Letters writ by Lieut. Col. John Lilburne, Prerogative Prisoner in the Tower of London, the 28. September, 1647, to his Excellency Sir Thomas Fairfax*, 1 October (1647), 4.

[2] Jason McElligott, *Royalism, Print and Censorship in Revolutionary England* (Woodbridge, 2007), 97.

[3] Roger B. Manning, *Swordsmen: The Martial Ethos in the Three Kingdoms* (Oxford, 2003), 17–19; Keith Thomas, *The Ends of Life: Roads to Fulfilment in Early Modern England* (Oxford, 2009), 49.

[4] A rare example is Henry Mordaunt, 2nd earl of Peterborough: Newman, 262.

Westminster.[5] Firth overestimated the resilience of the royalist peers, arguing that few defected because parliament invalidated all titles conferred since 20 May 1642 and that royalist lords with older titles would not be readmitted into the House of Lords, unless agreed by both Houses.[6] He neglected those peers abandoning their royalism after January 1644, because their defections were more piecemeal and less dramatic than those of the six lords who left Westminster in August 1643.

The peerage was critical because it was expected that their decisions would be exemplary, with their presence at Westminster or Oxford bestowing legitimacy to their chosen parties. The press keenly reported their whereabouts, as contemporaries judged lordly allegiance by where peers resided; diarists such as Thomas Juxon, Richard Symonds, and John Syms keenly registered noble movement between Oxford and Westminster.[7] Analysing motives behind noble allegiance is difficult, as their religious and political attitudes, concepts of honour, and kinship networks warrant consideration, as well as their personal relationship to Charles I and concern for their landed estates. For those holding land in multiple counties, protecting their patrimony and honour was especially troublesome. Aristocratic estates endured the depredations inflicted by soldiery of both sides. Most peers feared personal losses from continued warfare, inclining many to support a negotiated peace and more moderate politics. In its extreme form, this process led some peers into self-important delusions, considering their prestige might prove decisive in brokering peace. This led to several changing sides, and fostered suspicion that many more would do likewise.

I

The king's establishment of his court at York in March 1642 gave royalist nobles a rallying point. Charles' person attracted numerous peers, augmented by a string of departures from Westminster during April and May. From a parliamentarian vantage point in 1647, Thomas May blamed the outbreak of civil war on this 'great defection of Parliament Members'. He considered these peers and MPs guilty of a breach of trust, and a particularly corrupting example by their enabling the king to term the Westminster parliament 'a faction, a pretended Parliament and such like names.'[8] Yet such partisan and retrospective contemporary analysis ought not to persuade us to label these individuals as side-changers for joining the king before

---

[5] John Adamson, 'Introduction: High Roads and Blind Alleys: The English Civil War and Its Historiography', in John Adamson (ed.), *The English Civil War: Conflict and Contexts, 1640–1649* (Basingstoke, 2009), 9, 17.

[6] Charles Harding Firth, *The House of Lords during the Civil War* (1910), 131.

[7] Thomas Juxon, *The Journal of Thomas Juxon, 1644–1647*, ed. Keith Lindley and David Scott (Camden Society, 5th series, 13, 1999), 42n, 55; Richard Symonds, *Richard Symonds's Diary of the Marches of the Royal Army*, ed. Charles Edward Long and Ian Roy (Cambridge, 1997), 50; BL, Add. MS 35297, fo. 64r.

[8] Wing/M1410, Thomas May, *The History of the Parliament of England, which began November the third, MDCXL* (1647), Book II, 58–9; BL, E1317(1), Thomas May, *A Breviary of the History of the Parliament of England* (1650), 59–60, 70.

armed hostilities had even broken out. Many probably still harboured hopes of avoiding war. By 15 June, thirty-two lords were at York. A list that day showed forty-two peers remaining in parliament, but of these, twelve joined the king later that summer. Firth maintained that there were soon over twice as many peers on the king's side, and on 22 June forty-one lords at York pledged to raise the king cavalry to defend his person.[9] However, parliament was initially more militarily effective in mobilizing its peers; its army in 1642 contained twenty-two regiments and troops raised by peers, to the royalist army's sixteen.[10]

Many nobles suffered profound uncertainty during 1642, with the royalists benefiting from eleventh-hour recruitment as 'late and reluctant' peers such as Henry, Lord Spencer, recoiled in horror from armed rebellion.[11] In June, William, Lord Paget, arrived at York in response to a royal declaration offering a pardon to all except the six members and a few others. The lords at York subscribed to 'defend the King in his just rights and prerogative', and to oppose parliament's Militia Ordinance.[12] Paget was married to Warwick's niece and had executed parliament's Militia Ordinance as Lord Lieutenant of Buckinghamshire.[13] Soon after this, his deputy lieutenant, Bulstrode Whitelocke, remarked that Paget 'began to boggle, and was unfixed in his resolutions'.[14] John Hampden feared that volunteering for parliament might diminish owing to the late withdrawal of nine lords from Westminster to York. He warned of 'the great noise the withdrawing of the Lords made in the country', complaining on 14 June: 'Yet what discouragements do those revolting lords endeavour to bring upon honest men. They vote as they do, execute the votes as favourably as any, then desert them, as if there were neither principle of conscience or honesty left among them'.[15] Denzil Holles orated that the falling away of these nine lords belittled parliament in the people's eyes and might lead to an anti-parliament at York.[16] Paget's choice of sides surprised his former colleagues. Sensitive to being perceived as inconstant, he felt compelled to explain his volte-face:

> It may seem strange that I who with all zeal and earnestness have prosecuted ever since the beginning of this parliament the Reformation of the disorders of Church and Common-wealth, should now in a time of so great distraction desert the Cause. Most

[9] Firth, *The House of Lords*, 115, 128; Ronald Hutton, 'The Structure of the Royalist Party', *HJ*, 24 (1981), 555; BL, TT 669 f.6[42], *A Catalogue of the Names of the Lords that subscribed to Levie Horse to Assist His Majestie in Defence of his Royall Person, the Two Houses of Parliament, and the Protestant Religion, Yorke the 22. of June* (1642).

[10] Ronald Hutton, 'Clarendon's History of the Rebellion', *EHR*, 97 (1982), 71.

[11] Hutton, 'The Structure of the Royalist Party', 556.

[12] *CSPD 1641–3*, 342.

[13] John Adamson, *The Noble Revolt: The Overthrow of Charles I* (2007), 292n; *LJ*, v, 76.

[14] Bulstrode Whitelock, *Memorials of English Affairs from the Beginning of the Reign of Charles I to the Happy Restoration of King Charles II*, 4 vols. (Oxford, 1853), i, 170.

[15] HHC, Hotham MS, U DDHO/1/3 and 5.

[16] BL, E200(48), *The Speech of Denzell Holles Esquire. Delivered at the Lords Barr, Wednesday the 15th. of Iune. Vpon the impeachment of the Earles of North-hampton, Devon-shire, Monmouth, and Dover, and of the Lords Rich, Andever, Grey of Ruthen, Coventry and Capell, for their contempt in departing from the Parliament, and not returning upon summons*, 22 June (1642), 3.

true it is that my ends were the common good, and that it was prosecuted I was ready to lay down my life and fortune. But when I found a reparation of arms against the king under shadow of loyalty I rather resolved to obey a good conscience than particular ends and now am in my way to his Majesty where I will throw myself down at his feet and will die a loving subject.[17]

Paget's words are judged exemplary of the gut loyalty felt by most peers, but not all who subscribed at York were fully committed, with an appetite for armed struggle. The earls of Clare and Salisbury signed the declaration of royalist peers on 15 June before slipping back to Westminster.[18] Despite being commissioned colonel, Paget himself surrendered to parliament in September 1644, long before royalist defeat was assured.[19] Lords Lovelace and Paulet pledged the king money at York, but both subsequently abandoned the cause.[20]

The parliamentarian peers formed around what John Adamson has termed 'the Junto cousinage': the earls of Warwick, Essex, and Northumberland.[21] Aristocratic parliamentarianism also drew from the twelve peers who had petitioned for a parliament in 1640. The earls of Denbigh, Northumberland, Pembroke, Salisbury, and Holland enjoyed close court connections, but Godly sympathies and family ties to the 'Junto' drew them into cautious parliamentarianism.[22] Adamson argued that the opposition lords were inspired by medieval precedents to reassert their baronial responsibility to curb the king's 'evil counsellors'. Their initial support for Essex's claim to be made Lord High Constable, and his appointment as Captain-General, conferred vice-regal status on Essex and suggested that the king was incapacitated.[23] Yet the rebellious peers feared Essex's insistence that he alone would negotiate with the king. If Charles won outright victory they might face trial and execution. Yet if parliament won, their influence might be curtailed by the House of Commons. Headed by Northumberland, Pembroke, and Holland, several parliamentarian peers therefore sought to dictate the terms of compromise, aligning themselves with the peace party in the Commons.

Other peers who remained at Westminster in 1642 tried to keep their options open. The earl of Pembroke and his son Philip, Lord Herbert, offered the king their active support in return for favours and an apology to Pembroke for past slights, including his dismissal as Lord Chamberlain in 1641. They sent clandestine letters to Hyde during summer 1642 in an attempt to sell their allegiance.[24] Lord Herbert excused himself by ill health, taking the waters at Tunbridge in August, and informing Hyde: 'I am the unfortunatest man in the world not to be capable of appearing in his Majesty's service'. He excused his father, writing

---

[17] Bodl., MS Clarendon 21, fo. 89.   [18] Firth, *The House of Lords*, 116.
[19] Newman, 284.   [20] *CSPD 1641–3*, 344.
[21] Adamson, *The Noble Revolt*, xii.
[22] Barbara Donagan, 'A Courtier's Progress: Greed and Consistency in the Life of the Earl of Holland', *HJ*, 19 (1976), 319.
[23] J. S. A. Adamson, 'The Baronial Context of the English Civil War', *TRHS*, 5th series, 40 (1990), 93–6, 100, 105–6.
[24] Samuel R. Gardiner, *History of the Great Civil War, 1642–1649*, 4 vols. (1987), i, 53; Barbara Donagan, 'Varieties of Royalism', in Jason McElligott and David L. Smith (eds.), *Royalists and Royalism during the English Civil Wars* (Cambridge, 2007), 79–80.

that 'scruple of honour is the sole impediment' that detained Pembroke from joining the king. He bargained that his father would turn royalist and procure other lords to do likewise if Charles offered parliament constitutional guarantees. Pembroke even wanted royal councillors Hyde, Falkland, and Culpeper to 'find out some way to give a public security of the king's intentions'. During 1643, Herbert plied Hyde with hopes of his father's defection, blaming his own absence upon poor health.[25] Pembroke remained a lukewarm parliamentarian, but his support fluctuated between different Westminster factions, and his shifting became notorious. A broadside of 1693 fictitiously depicted Pembroke being sent to the Tower, satirizing him as an arch-trimmer full of hypocritical complaints of his own sufferings: 'No, my Lords, keep the *Tower* for *Malignants*, they can *endure* it, some of them have been Prisoners 7 Years; they can feed upon bare *Allegiance*, please themselves with Discourse of *Conscience*, of *Honour*, of a *Righteous Cause*, and I know not what: But what's this to me? How will those Malignants look upon *me*?'[26]

Yet Pembroke and Herbert's prevaricating and grooming contacts on both sides was not unusual. The earl of Kingston sought to protect his vast Nottinghamshire estates by delay, while his eldest son, Lord Newark, sided with the king, and his younger sons William and Francis supported parliament. He declined to loan the king money by pleading poverty, and according to Lucy Hutchinson declared to the local parliamentarian committee that if he took up arms for either side 'let a cannon-ball divide me between them.' On 2 May 1643 he was commissioned a royalist lieutenant-general; but his royalism remained unmeasured, as soon after, on 30 July, he was killed by artillery fire.[27]

Sir William Ogle (later Viscount Ogle) abandoned parliament in November 1642 through fear of being captured while in rebellion. Having arrived at Westminster to raise money for Munster's Protestants, parliament appointed him London's governor when the king's army reached Brentford. According to 'a friend' he went to bed that night 'where he slept very little; meditating with his self: that he was in rebellion and what course he should take to get out of it'. Just before dawn he departed, ostensibly to visit London's outer defences.[28] When captured by royalists he convinced them that he had defected and sought to surprise Winchester castle for the king. Yet he maintained parliament's trust, informing them that he left London because his wife was dying.[29] Ogle procured a secret royalist commission to hold Winchester, and maintained that the king agreed he should take no public action, but wait upon events to make his defection decisive. His attempt to postpone declaring himself ended only when military events forced him into open royalism in October 1643.[30]

---

[25] Bodl., MS Clarendon, 21, fos. 114, 118, 152, 154.
[26] Beinecke Rare Book and Manuscript Library, Osborn Shelves, fb159, fo. 96.
[27] Alfred C. Wood, *Nottinghamshire in the Civil War* (Oxford, 1937), 50; Newman, 297.
[28] BL, Add. MS 27402, fos. 86v–87r.
[29] Ibid., fos. 88v–89r.
[30] Ibid., fos. 92v–93v, 98v–99r; Donagan, 'Varieties of Royalism', 79; Newman, 277–8.

Among the first to change sides after hostilities commenced was Henry, Lord Mordaunt. His father, the earl of Peterborough, was Essex's general of artillery.[31] Mordaunt captained the earl's cavalry troop, but defected to Oxford in April 1643, two months before his father's death.[32] Given command of a royalist cavalry regiment, Mordaunt was the sole English peer who commanded on both sides during the first civil war. He was a highly active soldier before abandoning the royalist cause in 1645.[33] He petitioned to compound in June 1646, pleading that 'his minority and younger age' had misled him, and that his father's parliamentarian service might be remembered. His mother downplayed the young earl's royalism, stressing that his departure from Oxford to travel overseas was '5 weeks before Naseby field'. However, he joined Holland's royalist uprising in 1648, enduring a second exile thereafter. He successfully petitioned to compound a second time in May 1649, again attributing his royalism to 'the inconsiderateness of his youth'.[34] Although recently dismissed by Geoffrey Smith as 'indecisive and muddled', 'changeable in his loyalties', and an 'easily discouraged' royalist, such condemnation belies the skill with which Peterborough refashioned his allegiance to escape retribution on two occasions.[35]

II

There were several attempts at personal negotiation with the king by parliamentarian peers in 1643, which ultimately produced a string of defections. In November 1642, as the royalist army approached London, Northumberland and Pembroke sent Charles a message to open negotiations, but he disregarded it as a device to win time.[36] In February 1643 Northumberland and Holland led a delegation to Oxford to offer terms, raising royalist hopes of Northumberland's conversion.[37] Northumberland offered Charles a second set of secret, more lenient terms. Fearful that Northumberland was engaged in conspiracy, the radical MP Henry Marten opened the earl's correspondence during his absence. Upon his return on 19 April, Northumberland demanded 'private satisfaction' for this affront and struck Marten when he refused to apologize.[38] Secret peace negotiations continued in May with the queen's arrival in Oxford; Sir Edward Nicholas informed Rupert that the lords at London had sent one Ralph Skipwith 'to be a messenger for peace'.[39]

---

[31] Peter Young, *Edgehill 1642: The Campaign and the Battle* (2nd edn., Moreton-in-Marsh, 1998), 65, 238; BL, E117(3), *The List of the Army Raised under the command of His Excellency, Robert Earle of Essex* (1642), sig. A3v.

[32] BL, E99(22), *Mercurius Aulicus*, 15th week, 9–16 April (Oxford, 1643), 187.

[33] Newman, 262; Victor Stater, 'Henry Mordaunt, 2nd earl of Peterborough (*bap.* 1623, *d.* 1697), nobleman', *ODNB*.

[34] TNA, SP 23/181/610, 622–4, 638.

[35] Geoffrey Smith, *The Cavaliers in Exile, 1640–1660* (Basingstoke, 2003), 24.

[36] Folger Shakespeare Library, V.a.216, Belasyse Memoirs, fo. 9r–v.

[37] I. G. Philip (ed.), *The Journal of Sir Samuel Luke* (The Oxfordshire Record Society, 29, 1947), i, 46; Firth, *The House of Lords*, 116, 132; Hutton, 'The Structure of the Royalist Party', 557.

[38] BL, Harleian MS 164, fo. 374r.

[39] BL, Add. MS 18980, fos. 59–60.

Further doubts arose over Northumberland's loyalty after the discovery in late May of a conspiracy for an armed rising in London. The MP Edmund Waller was the leading conspirator and had served on Northumberland's commission to Oxford. When questioned, Waller and his fellow plotters implicated Conway, Pembroke, Portland, and Northumberland. In response, these lords took the new Vow and Covenant to be loyal to parliament, which included a declaration of their ignorance of the plot. Yet on 29 June the House of Lords consented that Conway and Portland be examined concerning the conspiracy. Both were imprisoned, and the Commons debated whether to arrest Northumberland.[40]

Waller claimed to have personally acquainted Northumberland with the plot, on assurances from Conway and Falkland that the earl was engaged. Sir Simonds D'Ewes, who was also under suspicion, noted that on 29 June Waller and Northumberland confronted each other at Whitehall, but the former failed to substantiate his charges.[41] Yet suspicions lingered as a result of the military disasters at Adwalton Moor, Roundway Down, and Bristol. Essex, considering himself ill-treated by parliament, became friendlier with Northumberland and Holland, and new peace proposals were prepared in the Lords on 3 August.[42] By then, royal declarations of pardon for all who came peaceably into Oxford grew more attractive by the day.[43]

Austin Woolrych has considered that the Lords' peace terms amounted to 'virtual surrender'. The Commons debated them on 7 August, provoking angry tumults outside Westminster. The throng was mobilized by libels scattered about London, warning that if peace proposals were even debated, then Northumberland and Holland would be seized. D'Ewes lamented the 'seditious multitude', and their abuse of Holland, Bedford, and Clare in Old Palace Yard with accusations that they had 'endeavoured to betray the Commonwealth, were perjured, and such like.' D'Ewes feared that the crowd intended to murder these peers, concluding they could no longer attend in safety. The Commons rejected the proposals by seven votes, leaving those lords supporting peace dejected and humiliated.[44] Within days, six defected, amounting to a third of the House's regular attendance: William Russell, earl of Bedford, John Holles, earl of Clare, Henry Rich, earl of Holland (see Fig. 1.1), Jerome Weston, earl of Portland, Edward, Viscount Conway, and John, Lord Lovelace.[45]

Disenchanted by parliament's war effort and the failed peace negotiations, and shocked by the Westminster tumults, these peers probably considered that they had no choice but to change sides. Changing political circumstances now rendered them unwelcome in their chosen coalition. They had also endured slights as

---

[40] BL, Harleian MS 165, fos. 98r, 100r–v; Edward Hyde, earl of Clarendon, *The History of the Rebellion and Civil Wars in England*, ed. William Dunn Macray, 6 vols. (Oxford, 1888), iii, 44–5; Austin Woolrych, *Britain in Revolution, 1625–1660* (Oxford, 2002), 257–8.

[41] BL, Harleian MS 165, fos. 104v–105r.

[42] Ibid., fos. 100v, 134v; Hyde, *History of the Rebellion*, iii, 102–3.

[43] BL, Egerton MS 2646, fo. 293.

[44] Woolrych, *Britain in Revolution*, 265; BL, Harleian MS 165, fos. 145v, 146v–147r.

[45] Firth, *The House of Lords*, 135; Gardiner, *History of the Great Civil War*, i, 199.

HENRY RICH, EARL OF HOLLAND.

OB. 1649.

FROM THE ORIGINAL OF VANDYKE, IN THE COLLECTION OF

HIS GRACE THE DUKE OF BUCCLEUGH.

Fig. 1.1. Henry Rich, Earl of Holland. (Special Collections of the University of Leicester, University of Leicester Library, Fairclough Collection of Portrait Prints, E61.)

parliamentarians. Soldiers had defied Holland's authority as Keeper of Windsor Forest in slaughtering the king's deer in October 1642.[46] During May 1643 anti-enclosure rioters despoiled Bedford and Portland's Whittlesey manors in the Isle of Ely, deriding the magistrate sent to quell them as 'but a Parliament justice'.[47] Northumberland retired to his seat at Petworth in Sussex, from where it was easier to defect if required. Bedford and Holland surrendered directly to Wallingford's royalist garrison by mid-August (see Fig. 1.2).[48] Intimidated out of parliament's coalition, they departed London for similar reasons to those compelling the king in January 1642.

These defections stirred rumours that all remaining peers would forsake Westminster. On 22 August intelligence from Nicholas Luke reported: 'That the King came to Oxford on Wednesday last to meet the 6 lords that came from the howse, and they say there is noe Parliament now because all the Lords are come away'.[49] Yet for Charles, busy besieging Gloucester, these defections were a troublesome distraction. Uncertain how to treat them, he feared he would provoke disunity whatever his decision. He left it to his Privy Council, who furiously contested the matter. Historians have long relied on Clarendon's retrospective account of the affair, which maintained that he and Lord Savile advocated welcoming these peers to encourage further defections. He believed that depleting Westminster's House of Lords would leave the parliamentarians with 'no reputation in the kingdom to continue the war.' Those who opposed this felt that the peers lacked remorse, had freely taken the Vow and Covenant, and had defected only because of royalist victories. Some even advocated their imprisonment, concerned that Bedford sought to settle personal scores with the marquis of Hertford. Others proposed that Holland and Bedford should 'neither be courted nor neglected', simply admitted to kiss the king's hand, and then left alone. Despite his evident pleasure 'with any sharpness that was expressed' towards Holland, Charles finally admitted them into Oxford.[50]

Of the six, Bedford and Holland aroused most royalist antipathy, despite having failed to distinguish themselves in parliament's cause. From July 1642 to February 1643 Bedford was general of horse—a rank placing him second only to Essex himself.[51] Yet his military credentials were unimpressive, and he had been criticized for his deportment at Sherborne castle.[52] Holland was Groom of the Stole from 1636 and a favourite of Henrietta Maria, so his rebellion smacked of personal betrayal. Holland's offer to kiss the king's hand at Beverley in 1642 had met with the royal reproof of 'how durst he looke him in the face'. One royalist libel accused him of

---

[46] *CSPD 1641–3*, 401, 471, Daniel C. Beaver, *Hunting and the Politics of Violence before the English Civil War* (Cambridge, 2008), 122–4.

[47] *LJ*, vi, 86, 88, 107; Keith Lindley, *Fenland Riots and the English Revolution* (1982), 157–60.

[48] BL, Harleian MS 165, fo. 227v; Hyde, *History of the Rebellion*, iii, 143; I. G. Philip (ed.), *The Journal of Sir Samuel Luke* (The Oxfordshire Record Society, 31, 1950), ii, 136.

[49] Philip (ed.), *Journal of Sir Samuel Luke*, ii, 139.

[50] Hyde, *History of the Rebellion*, iii, 146–51.

[51] BL, Add. MS 28721, fo. 14.

[52] *Manchester MS*, HMC, 8th Report, Appendix, Part II (1881), 59.

Fig. 1.2. William Russell, Earl of Bedford. (Special Collections of the University of Leicester, University of Leicester Library, Fairclough Collection of Portrait Prints, EP101, Box 2.)

having 'played the Judas' because of lost positions at court.[53] Sir Philip Warwick later derided Holland as a coward 'fitter for a shew, than a Field'.[54] According to Clarendon, Holland and Bedford were scorned by the townspeople and privy councillors alike, so that when presented before the queen, she also received them coldly. This disheartened Holland, who had probably persuaded the others to defect, and had hoped that the queen's friendship would reinstate him into favour. Clarendon thought he 'began to think himself betrayed, and invited to Oxford only to be exposed to contempt.'[55] To salvage their reputations, Holland, Bedford, and Clare tendered their service to the king outside Gloucester. He received them civilly but they were afforded neither favour nor commands, so they volunteered for the king's regiment of horse at the battle of Newbury on 20 September. After this service, Clarendon recalled that they 'now expected to be well looked upon'.[56]

However, the greatest obstacle to Holland's rehabilitation was his refusal to admit any offence. Bedford was pardoned when he kissed the king's hand and begged forgiveness, but Holland could not contemplate this. According to Clarendon, he thought 'nothing of former miscarriages ought to be remembered; that all those were cancelled by the merit of coming to the King now, and bringing such considerable persons with him.' Holland even allegedly named Commons MPs ready to defect, and claimed that 'Northumberland only expected his advice'. Yet Charles perceived self-interest and double-dealing behind Holland's defection, and resented the earl's magnifying parliament's power in conversations with the queen. Clarendon also explained Holland's speedy disenchantment with royalism as due to the appointment of the marquis of Hertford to Holland's former office of Groom of the Stole.[57]

The lukewarm welcome afforded these peers revealed division within the royalist leadership. Rather than encouraging further defections, it disappointed those who had changed sides, and ultimately stiffened the resolve of those remaining at Westminster. Ronald Hutton has interpreted it as an important failure to broaden aristocratic royalism, arguing that retrospective royalist commentators recognized this, despite attempting to absolve themselves from blame.[58] Further defections might have followed. Northumberland was deliberating, with several Commons MPs awaiting his decision.[59] In late July 1643 it was suspected that Northumberland had connived in a plan to meet his royalist brother's cavalry near Maidenhead.[60] By August he was rumoured to be mustering gentry and servants on his Sussex estates.[61] Colonel Herbert Morley maintained surveillance over Northumberland's

[53] BL, E108(5), *Strange Newes from Yorke, Hull, Beverley, and Manchester* (1642), 2; BL, Harleian MS 164, fos. 281r, 400v–401r.

[54] Beinecke Rare Book and Manuscript Library, Osborn Shelves, fb87, fos. 37r, 92r.

[55] Hyde, *History of the Rebellion*, iii, 154–6.

[56] Ibid., iii, 193.

[57] Ibid., iii, 194–9.

[58] Hutton, 'The Structure of the Royalist Party', 558; Hyde, *History of the Rebellion*, iii, 246–8.

[59] Robert Ashton, *The English Civil War: Conservatism and Revolution, 1603–1649* (2nd edn., 1989), 213.

[60] Philip (ed.), *Journal of Sir Samuel Luke*, ii, 125.

[61] *CSP Venetian, 1643–1647*, ed. A. B. Hinds, vol. 27 (1926), 11.

movements at Petworth; and when he informed Pym of a suspect intercepted letter, the Commons 'generally conceived' he was about to defect.[62] Northumberland's eventual return to Westminster met with considerable relief, and he took the Solemn League and Covenant, understanding that the Scots would soon be occupying his northern estates.[63] Clarendon noted that Northumberland was 'received with great respect, all men concluding that he had never intended to do what he had not done. And the other members, who had entertained the same resolutions, changed their minds with him, and returned to their former stations.'[64]

Another peer suspected of plotting to defect in August 1643 was Basil Feilding, earl of Denbigh, whose father had been killed in the royalist cause. On 31 August Pym reported to the Commons that an intercepted letter from Denbigh's widowed mother revealed that she expected him to deliver his forces to the king. Denbigh was arrested at Wellingborough, and returned to London under armed guard.[65] Pym explained that the Countess had advised her son not to believe accounts that Bedford, Clare, and Holland had been ill-received at Oxford. Denbigh acknowledged that his mother had sent several such letters, but argued that he had satisfied the Committee of Safety in sending negative replies, penned with the aid of the barrister Colonel Samuel Roper.[66] D'Ewes rallied Denbigh's defence in the Commons, arguing that the earl had not done 'any thing clandestinely or treacherously', and instead had frustrated royalist attempts to capture him. These suspicions inflamed a rivalry over precedence in command between Denbigh and the Warwickshire county committee, but Denbigh overcame these doubts to remain a parliamentarian throughout the civil wars.[67] Although his post-Restoration memorials expressed repentance for rebellion, he proudly defended his constancy against the attempts to procure his defection. He argued that 'he could not with honour desert that cause and the persons of those with whom he stood engaged' without a breach of trust. He claimed that if he had done so it would not have been to the king's advantage, because it would have inspired others to change sides and thereby deepen divisions 'in making the Breach wider then it was'.[68]

Whether or not Holland had really led the six peers to Oxford, his example heralded the reversion of all except Portland.[69] Holland returned first, and was placed in Black Rod's custody. On 7 November he was examined before a committee of both Houses. Although D'Ewes attended, the room was so crowded he could

---

[62] BL, Harleian MS 165, fos. 156r–159r.

[63] Valerie Pearl, 'Oliver St. John and the "Middle Group" in the Long Parliament: August 1643–May 1644', *EHR*, 81 (1966), 497n; George A. Drake, 'Algernon Percy, tenth earl of Northumberland (1602–1668), politician', *ODNB*.

[64] Hyde, *History of the Rebellion*, iii, 199–200.

[65] BL, Add. MS 31116, fo. 75r.

[66] BL, Harleian MS 165, fo. 160v.

[67] Ibid., fo. 161r–v.

[68] *Denbigh MS*, HMC, 7th Report, Part I, Report and Appendix (1874), 223–4.

[69] Sean Kelsey, 'Jerome Weston, second earl of Portland (1605–1663), politician', *ODNB*. Lovelace had offered Sir Henry Vane intelligence in January 1644 and delivered himself to parliament after Rupert's surrender of Bristol: Juxon, *The Journal of Thomas Juxon*, 42; *CSPD 1645–7*, 190; Whitelock, *Memorials of English Affairs*, i, 235–6.

scarcely hear proceedings. Some of the Commons wanted Holland impeached for treason and imprisoned in the Tower; John Gurdon declared 'rather we should pardon all the lords at Oxford than pardon this lord, and that we should consider how many good ordinances had past the Lords' house since his going away.' In response, D'Ewes echoed the arguments of Clarendon and Savile at Oxford three months earlier: that extending mercy to Holland would 'invite others to follow his example', and provoke further defections in parliament's favour.[70]

On 11 November D'Ewes noted Holland's self-justification, which subtly shifted blame onto others, and claimed he was misled into believing that the king intended compromise.[71] Downplaying his own agency, he portrayed himself as the victim of events. Holland argued that he left Westminster only because the tumults on 7 August endangered his life.[72] He maintained that he had no invitation from royalists and that he had informed no member of his intention to leave until Bedford joined him at Kensington immediately before his planned departure. He maintained that he was forced into Wallingford because parliamentarian troopers were sent to arrest him. He remained there twenty days before admittance into Oxford, and first saw the king outside Gloucester on 5 September. He was at Newbury, but deflected attention from his armed service by claiming that he stood 'near His Majesty all the time'. He denied taking any oath at Oxford, and merely advised Charles to 'comply with his great Council in all their just desires'. His claims not to have discussed the war's management and not borne arms against parliament were untrue. He declared that he returned because the Cessation with the Irish rebels made it 'impossible for any honest man to continue there any longer'. His narrative attracted sympathy in the Lords, but met with silence in the Commons until Sir John Wray moved 'send him back to Oxford and let the King do what he would with him'. D'Ewes replied that Holland's crime was merely 'rashness and indiscretion'; having intended parliament good service at Oxford, Holland risked his life to return to Westminster 'to live and die with us'. D'Ewes protested that parliament had pardoned many soldiers for deserting when in fear for their lives, suggesting that Holland's circumstances were no different.[73] Despite this, the Commons voted by 59 to 56 to demand Holland's imprisonment.[74]

Yet Holland remained under the Lords' protection. In December he petitioned them for readmittance and for discharge from sequestration. Essex wrote in support, and Holland trumpeted 'his fidelity to the Parliament, and reluctancy for his former apostacie.'[75] The affair provoked hot debates about the procedure by which

---

[70] BL, Add. MS 31116, fos. 90r–91v; BL, Harleian MS 165, fos. 223v–224v.

[71] John Rushworth, *Historical Collections of Private Passages of State*, 8 vols. (1721), v, 368.

[72] D'Ewes maintained that Holland told him 'it was by the singular providence of God that he escaped with his life, for he was assaulted by three several persons who not only gave him base and vile language but thrust him up and down and one of them had laid his hand upon his sword to draw it upon him': BL, Harleian MS 165, fo. 228r.

[73] Ibid., fos. 227v–228r.

[74] Ibid., fo. 230v.

[75] BL, E252(12), *A Perfect Diurnall of Some Passages in Parliament*, no. 22, 18–25 December (1643), 173.

side-changing MPs could be readmitted, and on 22 December Samuel Browne argued 'for an ordinance of grace and mercy that so we might encourage others to return to us'.[76] On 13 January 1644 the Lords voted to readmit Holland. In response, a divided Commons debated his impeachment but shrank from voting.[77] Considerable effort was made to communicate Holland's explanations to a mass audience, and a pamphlet was published in February 1644, supported by the newsbook, *The Spie*, which portrayed Holland's return as having hastened a series of defections by royalist politicians.[78] On 11 March 1644 an ordinance was framed in the Commons which stipulated that any member that deserted for Oxford would not be received back without both Houses' consent. Although hostility to Holland lingered in the Commons, where there was a further motion to impeach him in May, this ordinance did not discourage the return of other turncoat peers from Oxford.[79]

Among them was the earl of Clare, a member of the Committee of Safety who had followed Holland to Oxford (see Fig. 1.3). The king received him outside Gloucester, after which he fought at Newbury and was admitted to the council of war. Yet by 1644 he grew dismayed at royalist antipathy towards negotiating peace, and withdrew to Nottinghamshire to safeguard his estate papers. From there, fearing arrest by royalist troops, he fled to Cambridge. Arriving in Drury Lane on 2 April, he wrote to Essex 'that the Cause only, and no other particular By-respects, hath brought me back.' He argued that he had ill understood the goodness of parliament's cause until he arrived at Oxford, where his 'Eyes were opened', 'Contraries better setting forth one another'. He magnified his professed sacrifice by stressing that nearly all his estates now lay at the enemy's mercy. He took the Covenant in 1645, and his sequestration was lifted.[80] He was not readmitted into the Lords but served parliament in local offices, leading his biographer to suggest that his subsequent 'affiliations showed a consistency which had previously been absent.'[81]

Viscount Conway also surrendered himself in April 1644. Like Bedford and Holland, Conway's military record was poor. Clarendon and Belasyse suggested that he had acted treacherously during the Second Bishops' War, and that his public reputation was consequently in tatters.[82] Conway had remained in London in 1642 but was imprisoned for implication in Waller's plot, changing sides upon release.[83] He attended the Oxford Parliament, but, like Clare, grew dismayed at its

[76] BL, Harleian MS 165, fo. 253r.

[77] BL, Add. MS 31116, fos. 109r.

[78] BL, E32(14), *A Declaration made to the Kingdome by Henry, Earle of Holland*, 10 February (1644); BL, E33(27), *The Spie, Communicating Intelligence from Oxford*, no. 4, 13–20 February (1644), 28.

[79] BL, Add. MS 31116, fos. 123r, 136v.

[80] *LJ*, vi, 495, 503; BL, Add. MS 31116, fos. 130v.

[81] P. R. Seddon, 'John Holles, second earl of Clare (1595–1666), aristocrat', *ODNB*; Ruth Spalding (ed.), *Contemporaries of Bulstrode Whitelocke, 1605–1675* (Records of Social and Economic History, new series, 14, Oxford, 1990), 42.

[82] Folger Shakespeare Library, V.a.216, Belasyse Memoirs, fo. 5v; Hyde, *History of the Rebellion*, i, 190n.

[83] James Knowles, 'Edward Conway, second Viscount Conway and second Viscount Killultagh (*bap.* 1594, *d.* 1655), politician and book collector', *ODNB*; BL, Egerton MS 2647, fo. 162.

JOHN HOLLES EARL OF CLARE.

Pub.ᵈ Feb.ʳ 1.1806. by J. Scott 442. Strand.

Fig. 1.3. John Holles, Earl of Clare. (Special Collections of the University of Leices-ter, University of Leicester Library, Fairclough Collection of Portrait Prints, EP42B, Box 1.)

failure to prosecute peace. Ronald Hutton has suggested that Conway and George Brydges, Lord Chandos, grew disgruntled at the peerage's eclipse in command by newly promoted professionals, such as Nicholas Mynne in south-east Wales.[84] Conway surrendered himself at Coventry in April 1644, having notified parliament's governor of Warwick castle of his intentions in February. He persuaded Denbigh to intercede with Essex, and claimed to Northumberland that he would have defected sooner had safe passage been possible.[85]

The first to follow Holland's return was Bedford. Essex received him at St Albans in December 1643, and wrote a sympathetic letter to Speaker Lenthall. This largely rehashed Holland's earlier explanations: Bedford went to Oxford to attempt peace negotiations, but 'finding how strongly the king was misled by the ill counsel about him, and that there was little hope of doing any good there, he turned back to the Lord General's quarter with a desire to proceed in doing the best service he could to the parliament.' His case was referred to the committee that dealt with Holland, and he was committed to Black Rod's custody, before confinement in his sister's house at Holborn.[86] According to one newsbook, the royalist conspirator Lady Aubigny wrote to Bedford on 22 January 1644, misguidedly thinking he was restored to the House of Lords, and urging him to repair his reputation at Oxford by pushing Westminster towards negotiating peace.[87]

Historians have been ungenerous in assessing the six peers and have tended to follow Clarendon, condemning them for self-interest and opportunism dictated by military events. Yet they were little different from other peers in prioritizing their own interests, offices, estates, and reputations. Barbara Donagan has pointed out that Holland was similar to Hamilton and Pembroke, with conflicting pressures pulling him in different directions. He was condemned by both sides because his anti-Catholicism, Devereux cousinage, and Godly preferences sat uneasily alongside his status as the queen's favourite. Civil war rendered such multiple roles impossible to sustain. Charles's dismissal of Holland from court office in 1642 precipitated a personal financial crisis, forcing upon Holland an enduring need for restoration to royal favour, but his estates in St Bartholomew's and Kensington lay at parliament's mercy. Holland was not alone in this dilemma. His hopes of regaining courtly office and prestige through negotiation were shared by Bedford, Clare, and Northumberland. It is no longer enough to dismiss these peers as 'merely disloyal, morally inadequate or self-interested.'[88] Rather, their side-changing was rooted in the specific context of alienation from parliament after the failure of the August peace negotiations. They shared unifying consistencies: none had distinguished military records, committing them more towards negotiating peace than pursuing outright victory. In this they shared ground with several royalist peers who defected to parliament in 1644–5.

[84] Hutton, 'The Structure of the Royalist Party', 561–2.
[85] *LJ*, vi, 518.
[86] BL, Add. MS 31116, fo. 104r–v; BL, E81(14), *The Weekly Account*, no. 19, 3–10 January (1644), 5–6.
[87] BL, E31(21), *The Kingdomes Weekly Intelligencer*, no. 42, 30 January–7 February (1644), 322.
[88] Donagan, 'A Courtier's Progress', 317–19, 352–3.

III

Aristocratic defections to parliament did not begin until early 1644, but within twelve months so many peers abandoned the king that even Prince Rupert and James Stuart, duke of Richmond, favoured peace. David Scott has revealed that by spring 1645 Richmond was even involved in secret negotiations to surrender Oxford.[89] Those peers most inclined to negotiating found their strongest voice in the Privy Council. Edward Sackville, earl of Dorset, and Lucius Cary, Viscount Falkland, shared ground with moderate peers at Westminster. Falkland negotiated with Northumberland's commissioners in March and April 1643, while in May Dorset corresponded with Essex over exchanging prisoners.[90] These peers were usually supported by Hyde and they hoped the king would accept Northumberland's secret terms to isolate Pym's junto at Westminster.[91] Those sharing their views were heartened by the opening of the Oxford Parliament on 22 January 1644. The king hoped this institution would lure MPs over from Westminster and legitimize his war administration's growing demands.[92] Although Oxford's peers outnumbered their Westminster counterparts by more than two to one, the king grew disappointed with the assembly, considering it more inclined to negotiate than support his war effort. Misplaced hopes that it would end hostilities through diplomacy were frustrated, so that its first sitting from January to April 1644 witnessed the retreat of several peers from the king's cause.

These shifts were also prompted by the Cessation in Ireland and parliament's Declaration of Both Kingdoms that promised pardon to all royalists not among the war's 'prime authors' in return for a fine to reclaim their estates. The first to compound was Mildmay Fane, earl of Westmoreland, who obligingly cited disgust at the Cessation as his motive. Imprisoned since 1642 and sensing that his continued suffering for royalism was needless, he applied to the House of Lords to take the Covenant and compound for his delinquency.[93] His adopted conversion narrative on 16 February 1644 declared: 'blesse[d] God who hath discovered unto him the danger church and state were in…whereby his judgement is now fully convinced that it had formerly been seduced and wandered out of the right way.'[94]

In Ireland, the Cessation provoked the spectacular defection of Murrough O'Brien, Viscount Inchiquin, in July 1644. Slighted by the king's passing over him for the Lord Presidency of Munster, Inchiquin took many of his Protestant forces with him into parliament's camp.[95] The earl of Leicester, whose sons clashed with

[89] David Scott, 'Counsel and Cabal in the King's Party, 1642–1646', in McElligott and Smith (eds.), *Royalists and Royalism*, 125.

[90] David L. Smith, 'Lucius Cary, second Viscount Falkland (1609/10–1643), politician and author', *ODNB*; David L. Smith 'Edward Sackville, fourth earl of Dorset (1590–1652), politician', *ODNB*.

[91] Scott, 'Counsel and Cabal', 123.

[92] Woolrych, *Britain in Revolution*, 274.

[93] Paul N. Hardacre, *The Royalists during the Puritan Revolution* (The Hague, 1956), 20–2.

[94] Rachel Weil, 'Thinking About Allegiance in the English Civil War', *History Workshop Journal*, 61 (2006), 186.

[95] Hardacre, *The Royalists during the Puritan Revolution*, 20–2; A. R. Bayley, *The Great Civil War in Dorset, 1642–1660* (Taunton, 1910), 107.

Inchiquin, impugned his motives, depicting him as a double turncoat who served parliament or king whenever 'theyr affaires agreed best with his interest'.[96] In March 1644, John Tufton, earl of Thanet, returned to parliament despite having been among the first lords at York,[97] while Charles, Lord Paulet, brother of the marquis of Winchester, was bribed by the parliamentarian council of war to yield Basing House.[98] When his treachery was unmasked, Paulet was court-martialled on 2 May. Although he was later pardoned, this did not spare him the grisly task of being forced to hang his accomplices.[99]

Henry Bourchier, earl of Bath, withdrew to his Devon estates after the Oxford Parliament's first sitting. Having been a commissioner of array in 1642, he was rumoured to be seeking Essex's protection in July 1644. He aided the New Model's siege of Barnstaple, and took the Negative Oath and Covenant in 1646.[100] James Hay, earl of Carlisle, was rumoured to have defected in December 1643. Whitelocke noted his conversion on 12 March 1644, and he took the Covenant on 6 May thereafter.[101] Later that month, Essex granted Lord Chandos a safe conduct to return to parliament, but was informed that Viscount Conway had endangered Chandos's life by writing to the earl of Dorset that Chandos intended to defect. Essex demanded Conway's examination for breach of trust in corresponding with Oxford, pointing out that the affair might have cost Chandos his life. Conway, who had changed sides himself only six weeks earlier, denied the charges on 5 June, maintaining that 'he loved not him [Chandos] so ill, nor them at Oxford so well as to give them advertisement of it.'[102]

Summer 1644 witnessed the return of Robert Sidney, earl of Leicester, and Lords Rich and Paget. On 24 June the House of Lords heard that Leicester had abandoned the king. He had spent 1643 in Oxford in a 'tortured state', stripped of his lord lieutenancy of Ireland for lacking resolution. Surrendering himself to parliament's forces at Warwick, he travelled to London, and his Welsh estates were sequestered by the king's orders.[103] On 27 July 1644 Warwick's errant son, Lord Rich, was examined by a Lords' committee at Westminster, having been recaptured approaching Marlow.

---

[96] G. Dyfnallt Owen (ed.), *Report on the Manuscripts of the Right Honourable Viscount De L'Isle, V.C.*, HMC 77, Volume VI, Sidney Papers, 1626–98 (1966), 566.

[97] Thanet briefly turned royalist again in May 1648, but served the Protectorate as sheriff of Kent in 1654. His descendants, 'with unconscious irony', assumed the words *Semper fidelis* as the family motto in his memory: BL, E35(23), *The Weekly Account*, no. 36, 29 February–6 March (London, 1644); Alan Everitt, *The Community of Kent and the Great Rebellion, 1640–60* (Leicester, 1966), 254–5, 294.

[98] Gardiner, *History of the Great Civil War*, i, 319; *CSP Venetian, 1643–1647*, 84.

[99] I. G. Philip (ed.), *The Journal of Sir Samuel Luke* (The Oxfordshire Record Society, 33, 1952–3), iii, 267; *CSPD 1644*, 143, 147, 151; Ronald Hutton, 'John Paulet, fifth marquis of Winchester (?1598–1675), royalist nobleman', *ODNB*.

[100] Amos C. Miller, *Sir Richard Grenville of the Civil War* (1979), 84–5; *CSPD 1648–9*, 344–5.

[101] Philip (ed.), *Journal of Sir Samuel Luke*, iii, 225; Whitelock, *Memorials of English Affairs*, i, 245; *LJ*, vi, 541.

[102] Beinecke Rare Book and Manuscript Library, Osborn Shelves, fb157, fo. 12, and Osborn Shelves, fb163; *LJ*, vi, 577–8.

[103] *LJ*, vi, 604; Ian Atherton, 'Robert Sidney, second earl of Leicester (1595–1677), diplomat and landowner', *ODNB*; Dyfnallt Owen (ed.), *Report on the Manuscripts of the Right Honourable Viscount De L'Isle*, 556.

He provided intelligence concerning Oxford's defences, and claimed to have awaited a safe-conduct to defect for three months. Richard Symonds sneered that Rich had 'renegaded to the rebels', but his loss to the cause was 'not considerable'.[104] On 18 September Essex requested favour for Lord Paget, who surrendered himself at Plymouth. Essex suggested that Paget's timing—after the disaster at Lostwithiel—suggested he had 'real and noble Intentions', and recommended that parliament 'will make him a Pattern for Encouragement to others'.[105] Paget prepared his defection from August in letters to Northumberland and Bedford, whilst according to White-locke he expressed humility, sorrow, and regret.[106] On 1 November Paget petitioned the Lords for favour, claiming to have been misled by a 'factious and ill-affected Party', and promising in future 'with all Zeal and Constancy, faithfully to serve you'. He complained that his Staffordshire lands were held by the enemy, but upon paying a £500 fine his estate was quickly discharged from sequestration.[107]

The king's lieutenant-general of horse, Henry, Lord Wilmot, was also investigated for treachery after his arrest on 8 August 1644.[108] Wilmot's clash with Lord Digby inclined him to write to Essex proposing negotiations, which the king considered treasonous.[109] Sir Philip Warwick considered that Wilmot had 'born too much kindness to Essex' and was 'much more affected to be an Umpire of Peace', than to have commanded in the field.[110] Wilmot's troopers petitioned the king to explain his arrest 'that they may not have reason to suspect themselves partakers of his crymes'. The king responded that 'in such cases, wherein a Crowne lyeth at the stake upon the decision of a battaile, a small suspition is grownd enough for Princes to remove any person but doubted from such a trust'.[111] Wilmot stood accused of having attempted to 'draw men to revolt from their allegiance' by claiming that the king was against peace and planning to give all power to his nephews. He was also charged with advocating that Charles submit to parliament.[112] The charges were eventually dropped, and Wilmot's joining the queen in France, rather than Essex at Westminster, strongly suggests that he never intended to change sides.[113]

Implicated in Wilmot's negotiations with Essex was Henry, Lord Percy, who was compelled to resign as general of the ordnance in August 1644. Charles ordered Percy's arrest on 14 January 1645, alongside Thomas Savile, earl of Sussex, and Lord Andover. The three were charged with giving intelligence to the enemy, speaking contemptuously of the king, and seeking to establish a faction in the Oxford Parliament aimed at forcing Charles to negotiate peace.[114] Savile was

[104] *LJ*, vi, 647; Symonds, *Richard Symonds's Diary*, 50.   [105] *LJ*, vi, 711.
[106] CSPD 1644, 454; Whitelock, *Memorials of English Affairs*, i, 324.
[107] *LJ*, vii, 42, 141.
[108] Symonds, *Richard Symonds's Diary*, 49.
[109] Hutton, 'The Structure of the Royalist Party', 562.
[110] Beinecke Rare Book and Manuscript Library, Osborn Shelves, fb87, fos. 68v, 80v.
[111] Symonds, *Richard Symonds's Diary*, 106–7.
[112] Ibid., 108–9.
[113] Ronald Hutton, 'Henry Wilmot, first earl of Rochester (*bap.* 1613–*d.* 1658), royalist army officer', *ODNB*.
[114] Bodl., MS Clarendon 24, fo. 6; Hutton, 'The Structure of the Royalist Party', 563; Stuart Reid, 'Henry Percy, Baron Percy of Alnwick (*c.*1604–1659), royalist army officer', *ODNB*.

previously imprisoned and indicted for treason in May 1643 for having negotiated with parliament through John Hotham.[115] He was also suspected of conspiring to seize Henrietta Maria upon her landing in February 1643.[116] Yet Savile's
skilful defence had satisfied the king, fashioning himself as a loyal sufferer who
had lost his estate to the rebels.[117] His experience of placating both sides informed
his recommendation of lenience for Holland and Bedford in autumn 1643. By
March 1644 he was beginning to be trusted, and was admitted to Oxford's council of war. By June he was ordering the deployment of Oxford's artillery.[118] However, he was suspected of secretly corresponding with the parliamentarian Temple
family, while the sparing of his Westminster house from plunder looked suspicious. Among the charges against him in January 1645 was that his daughter,
Lady Temple, had said 'there was one honest steadfast peer amongst the vermin at
Oxford'.[119] On 28 January he denied the charges, outraged that accusations from
which he was exonerated in June 1643 had once again resurfaced. He maintained
that since arriving in Oxford he had not received letters from 'any person living
of the enemy's party, which I believe few in this town can say besides myself.'[120]

In February 1645 Charles reassured his queen that he would stand fast against
backsliders: 'thou hast reason to bid me beware of going too soon to London, for
indeed some amongst us had a greater mind that way than was fit, of which persuasion Percy is one of the chief'.[121] On 13 March he added that he had freed himself
from the 'base mutinous motions' of 'our mongrel parliament here'.[122] When parliament published this in the *King's Cabinet Opened* after Naseby, Charles claimed
that he had been provoked into the term 'mongrel parliament' by 'Sussex's factious-
ness' undermining its proceedings.[123]

Savile was released from imprisonment before 13 March 1645 on condition that
he depart overseas. Instead, on 19 March he surrendered to parliament, where he
was examined by a Lords' committee and consigned to Black Rod's custody.[124] His
arrival was greeted with suspicion, especially after he accused Bulstrode Whitelocke
and Denzil Holles of conspiring with leading royalists during their engagement in
the Oxford negotiations of November 1644. To defend Holles, Sir William Lewis
scorned Savile as having already changed sides twice or even three times before, adding that as a newly created earl, perhaps he was sent 'as a service for his new honor
to cast a bone amongst them'.[125] Savile's servants were examined concerning the

[115] TNA, SP 23/115/603–4.
[116] Bodl., MS Clarendon 22, fos. 53–7; Bodl., MS Clarendon 23, fo. 230r.
[117] Bodl., MS Clarendon 22, fos. 58r–60v, 68r.
[118] BL, Harleian MS 6852, fo. 37r; Beinecke Rare Book and Manuscript Library, Osborn Files,
10843.
[119] Bodl., MS Clarendon 24, fo. 22r–v.
[120] Ibid., fos. 24r–26r.
[121] Beinecke Rare Book and Manuscript Library, Osborn Shelves, fb163, Charles I to Henrietta
Maria, Oxford, 15/25 February 1644/5.
[122] Ibid., Charles I to Henrietta Maria, 13 March 1644/5.
[123] Bodl., MS Clarendon 25, fo. 74.
[124] Andrew J. Hopper, 'Thomas Savile, first earl of Sussex (1590–1657), politician', *ODNB*; Bulstrode Whitelocke, *The Diary of Bulstrode Whitelocke, 1605–1675*, ed. Ruth Spalding (Records of
Social and Economic History, new series, 13, Oxford, 1990), 166.
[125] Spalding (ed.), *Contemporaries of Bulstrode Whitelocke*, 349.

manner of his journey from Oxford.[126] On 31 March Whitelocke noted that Savile had not answered satisfactorily, but due to 'grounds of suspicion that he came to do ill offices' he was ordered to depart London and parliament's quarters 'on payn to be proceeded against as one adhearing to the enemy.'[127] That he was invited back to London so quickly after this was a measure of Savile's success in exploiting factional infighting at Westminster. Ingratiating himself with Viscount Saye and the pro-New Model Independents, he proffered intelligence that held out the prospect of Oxford's surrender and the downfall of Denzil Holles.[128]

The defection of Richard Vaughan, earl of Carbery, by February 1646 was much more straightforward. Commissioned in 1643 as royalist lieutenant-general in south Wales, by late 1645 Carbery sought to safeguard his estates by complying with parliament. In February 1646 parliament discharged his fine of £4,500 for his former royalism. His erstwhile enemy, Rowland Laugharne, informed Speaker Lenthall that Carbery's compliance would 'induce many others to the Parliament's obedience'. He remained loyal to parliament thereafter, despite Laugharne's revolt in 1648.[129]

IV

Bulstrode Whitelocke joked that Bedford, Clare, and Holland had by their short-lived dalliance at Oxford performed great public service: 'It was said in drollery, that these three earls had much confirmed others to continue with the parliament; for they having tried both parties, found it by experience that this was the best to be in, and to adhere unto'.[130] His humour belied that their presence invited infighting and division. The ongoing vexed issue of their constitutional status influenced factional politics at Westminster until 1649. Unsuccessful attempts by Lincoln and Manchester to readmit Bedford, Clare, and Holland in 1647 generated further suspicion. Lord Willoughby recommended Holland's impeachment, arguing that 'he left us when we were at the lowest and after he had taken the oath, and then who can trust him afterwards'.[131] Leicester recalled that after the turncoat peers' failure to regain their seats in 1647, the earl of Bath informed him that he had granted royal pardons to several MPs who defected to attend the Oxford Parliament, many of whom were now readmitted into the Commons. Leicester reflected: 'it is a shame that so much scruple should be made to readmit some, when others sit there who have so offended.'[132] Holland considered himself harshly treated.

---

[126] BL, E260(8), *Perfect Passages of each dayes Proceedings in Parliament*, no. 23, 26 March–2 April (1645), 183.

[127] Whitelocke, *The Diary of Bulstrode Whitelocke*, 167.

[128] Patricia Crawford, 'The Savile Affair', *EHR*, 354 (1975), 76–93; Michael Mahony, 'The Savile Affair and the Politics of the Long Parliament', *Parliamentary History*, 7 (1988), 212–27.

[129] *Portland MS*, 353; P. R. Newman, *The Old Service: Royalist Regimental Colonels and the Civil War, 1642–46* (Manchester, 1993), 124; Ronald Hutton, 'Richard Vaughan, second earl of Carbery (1600?–1686), royalist army officer', *ODNB*.

[130] Bulstrode Whitelock, *Memorials of English Affairs from the Beginning of the Reign of Charles the First to the Happy Restoration of Charles the Second*, 4 vols. (Oxford, 1853), i, 208.

[131] Dyfnallt Owen (ed.), *Report on the Manuscripts of the Right Honourable Viscount De L'Isle*, 562–5.

[132] Ibid., 566–7.

Facing financial crisis and repeated impeachment attempts, his return to armed royalism in 1648 smacked of desperation.[133] He was joined by the earl of Thanet, and ironically, Willoughby, who had vehemently opposed his readmittance to the Lords. Impeached and imprisoned during January 1648,[134] Willoughby, shortly before fleeing overseas, penned a printed justification of his constancy, which maintained: 'I am still upon the same foundation I ever was.'[135] Yet Willoughby had articulated unease with the cause in 1644 when he lamented parliament's ill treatment of Essex and himself:

> Heare wee are all hasting to an erlei ruine, for I cannot see that any thing else can satisfy, selfe ends rules so much. For peace I cannot soe much as ever expect it nor see a though[t] by those that sitt at the healm tending that waise. Nobillity and gentry are going down apace ... I thought it a crime to be a nobleman.[136]

Holland, Thanet, and Willoughby's defections in 1648 renewed parliamentarian anxieties that the peerage were backsliders and turncoats. In 1649 these fears pre-cipitated the execution of the king and Holland, and helped drive the abolition of the House of Lords.

Despite depictions of the peerage as steadfast royalists, and more recently by John Adamson as rebellious conspirators, aristocratic allegiance was equally often fluid and responsive to changing circumstances. Side-changing peers were numerous, and were drawn from the more temperate ranks of their causes. Most shared com-mitment to negotiating peace, partly because they lacked the military credentials to win honour in the field. The speed of events transformed the causes for which they engaged in 1642, prompting those to defect whose coalition no longer accommo-dated them. Factional politics and personality clashes influenced defections on both sides, as did requirements of self-preservation and recovery of lost offices and endan-gered estates. James Daly once considered Savile and Holland 'utter time-servers', and of 'no fixed political principle'.[137] This now seems excessively condemnatory. Robert Ashton reminded us that parliamentarian nobles must have 'experienced some profoundly uneasy moments when reflecting on their rejection of the princi-ple of the indivisibility of obedience on which they had been reared.'[138] Likewise, Ruth Spalding cautioned critics of Holland for ignoring 'the dilemma of a man with little grasp of politics, fumbling in his search for peace in a revolution.' Side-chang-ing did not necessarily reflect lack of principles; Whitelocke considered that Hol-land's delight in Godly sermons was genuine enough, believing 'many of his notes were better then the sermons themselves.'[139] Rather, nobles such as Holland and

---

[133] Donagan, 'A Courtier's Progress', 348–9.

[134] Whitelock, *Memorials of English Affairs*, ii, 263.

[135] Beinecke Rare Book and Manuscript Library, Osborn Shelves, fb155, fos. 237–9; Robert Ashton, *Counter-Revolution: The Second Civil War and its Origins, 1646–8* (New Haven, 1994), 410; BL, TT 669, f.11 (124) *A Letter sent from the Lord Willoughby of Parham to the Speaker of the House of Peers* (1648).

[136] *Denbigh MS*, HMC, 4th Report, Part I, Report and Appendix, 268.

[137] James Daly, 'The Implications of Royalist Politics, 1642–6', *HJ*, 27 (1984), 749.

[138] Ashton, *The English Civil War*, 183.

[139] Spalding (ed.), *Contemporaries of Bulstrode Whitelocke*, 124.

Wilmot appear to have acted partly from an inflated conviction that their own importance as statesmen could broker a negotiated peace.

Overall, the tide of aristocratic defections reflected the fortunes of war, with parliamentarian peers turning royalist in 1643, but with a greater number abandoning royalism from 1644, if not becoming committed parliamentarian activists. This chapter has contended that much of the peerage adopted flexible views on loyalty to navigate the crises of the 1640s. Up to a third of those eligible to sit at Westminster were prepared to serve both sides, albeit to differing degrees.[140] Although few served both king and parliament in arms, more changed sides at some point than those who consistently remained at Westminster. With the passage of time, this pragmatism became less notorious. By 1656 it was even possible for former royalist stalwarts such as the marquis of Worcester to cultivate Cromwell's favour with the boast: 'I am able to do his highness more service than any one subject of his three nations.'[141]

---

[140] B. G. Blackwood, 'Parties and Issues in the Civil War in Lancashire and East Anglia', in R. C. Richardson (ed.), *The English Civil Wars: Local Aspects* (Stroud, 1997), 261.

[141] Jane Ohlmeyer, 'The Marquis of Antrim: A Stuart Turn-Kilt?', *History Today*, 43 (1993), 18.

2

'Ambi-dexter' MPs

This chapter charts side-changing among members of the House of Commons during the first civil war. It aims to reveal some of the motivations and consequences of these defections. Unlike with the peers, Commons' defections were strikingly towards the royalists, consisting of MPs deserting Westminster between August 1642 and the large-scale ejections of members with the onset of the Oxford Parliament in January 1644. Comparatively few MPs changed sides from king to parliament. Of those who did, most abandoned the king close to the end of hostilities, seeking an accommodation with parliament in order to mitigate their punishment.

Precisely defining what constitutes side-changer status for MPs is difficult, because so many sought to postpone or avoid taking sides. Many of those disabled from sitting at Westminster for defecting to the king had never been committed parliamentarian activists to begin with. Arduous and painful allegiance decisions often led to hesitation or advocacy of a negotiated compromise peace, and although such individuals were likely to be denigrated as turncoats by both sides, historians ought to be more careful.[1] Defining an MP as a royalist or parliamentarian in the first place raises questions concerning what constitutes activism. Nomination as a parliamentary committee man or commissioner of array is no sure guide, as often such appointments were designed to secure compliance from the uncommitted or wavering. The contribution of money, plate, horses, and arms might indicate choice, but may also have been performed under duress or political pressure. Some individuals defy easy labelling: Sir Ralph Verney stayed a firm parliamentarian until qualms at taking the Solemn League and Covenant compelled him to leave for France. He was ejected from the Commons and sequestered, but never renounced his parliamentarianism, so Aylmer's contention that he changed sides now seems unfair.[2] Firmer evidence of activism for both sides needs to be established to determine side-changer status because there is a mismatch between those contemporaries identified as turncoats and those who can be reliably identified as side-changers. Continued presence at Westminster or Oxford, and particularly the act of travelling from one to the other, was taken as a reliable indicator by

---

[1] G. E. Aylmer, 'Collective Mentalities in Mid-Seventeenth-Century England: 4 Cross Currents: Neutrals, Trimmers and Others', *TRHS*, 5th series, 39 (1989), 4.

[2] Michael Braddick, *God's Fury, England's Fire: A New History of the English Civil Wars* (2008), 227; G. E. Aylmer, 'Collective Mentalities in Mid-Seventeenth-Century England: 2 Royalist Attitudes', *TRHS*, 5th series, 37 (1987), 4.

contemporaries, but the firmest evidence for historians is in active military or civil service and the taking of political oaths.

These problems of classification have hampered attempts to quantify side-changing in the Commons. The Long Parliament returned about 550 MPs in November 1640. Brunton and Pennington's 'rough and ready' calculation of civil war allegiance claimed that 302 were parliamentarians and 236 royalists.[3] Christopher Hill warned against the labelling process behind such quantitative analysis, and that treating MPs as statistics lumped committed activists in with 'the marginal turncoat on either side'.[4] Brunton and Pennington admitted that the problem of side-changing complicated their figures, but they neglected to quantify the number of side-changers, preferring to allocate them to either camp. Robert Ashton has argued that thirty-five MPs defected from Westminster to the king during the war, but then revised the figure to forty-four, arguing that as many as thirty-two occurred in 1643, mostly during the summer months when parliament's military position deteriorated.[5] This is a significant number, but it remains conservative compared to Christopher Hill's claim that 'something approaching 100 MPs transferred their support to the King after 1642' in areas controlled by royalist armies.[6] Even a more elastic definition of side-changing cannot justify this inflated figure. However, if royalist defectors are added to Ashton's figures, then as much as 10 per cent of the lower house changed sides at some point between 1642 and 1646. It is surprising that such a significant contingent has evaded prosopographical investigation for so long.

A starting point for tracing defections from Westminster is to use the *Commons' Journals* to quantify those members disabled from sitting for 'adhering to the enemy' after the initial run of expulsions of the most notorious royalists in 1642. At least 112 MPs were excluded from Westminster between January 1643 and October 1645, yet not all can be classified as side-changers, as many had demonstrated themselves to be royalists from the outset. Firmer evidence of former parliamentarian activism is needed. Rather than providing a brief biographical account of each MP—a task better left to the forthcoming History of Parliament volumes—the purpose here is to trace the patterns behind defections and their political consequences.

I

Contemporaries were familiar with the notion of changing sides in parliamentary politics before 1642. For instance, Thomas Wentworth's public career in the 1620s was a balancing act of juggled identities, between affecting the role of

[3] Douglas Brunton and Donald H. Pennington, *Members of the Long Parliament* (2nd edn., 1968), 14.
[4] Christopher Hill, *Puritanism and Revolution: Studies in Interpretation of the English Revolution of the Seventeenth Century* (1958), 17.
[5] Ashton gave his authority for these figures as Keeler, Brunton, and Pennington, 'and a very wide variety of sources': Robert Ashton, *The English Civil War: Conservatism and Revolution, 1603–1649* (2nd edn., 1989), 134, 188, 403.
[6] Hill, *Puritanism and Revolution*, 18.

country patriot to some audiences, and appeasing the court to others.[7] Contemporaries among the opposition perceived him as a turncoat, anonymous pamphleteers and MPs charging him with apostasy for abandoning them. The earl of Bedford copied out Wentworth's speeches of 1628 in defence of the Petition of Right into his commonplace book. In 1641 these speeches were also published in print form by his enemies.[8] Even in death Wentworth proved a divisive figure, as his attainder provoked a royalist reaction at Westminster almost immediately afterwards. During May and June 1641 the earls of Bristol and Hertford, Viscounts Falkland and Savile, Lord Digby, and Edward Hyde distanced themselves from the opposition, fearing it had grown too militant and hoping for royal reward.[9] This reaction gathered pace after the late summer recess, strengthening misgivings over 'Root and Branch' abolition of episcopacy, and weakening the unity of opposition to Charles I, making civil war possible.[10] By 1642 it had led many future parliamentarians to consider their former colleagues among the opposition of early 1641 to be side-changers before armed hostilities in England had even broken out. As many as forty-four MPs who had been reformers in 1640 became royalists during the civil war, including the influential Henry Belasyse, Sir John Colepeper, Edward Hyde, and George, Lord Digby—the latter famously reversing his position during Strafford's trial.[11] Yet these individuals can hardly be considered side-changers, because they were responding to the changed political circumstances of 1641 that included the king's concessions and growing fears of tumult and religious anarchy.

Notorious among this group was Sir Edward Dering, because of his widely distributed speeches against Laudian prelacy.[12] Dering had moved the Root and Branch Bill in the Commons in April 1641. Yet on 21 June 1641 he spoke in favour of moderate episcopacy as a guarantor of order. Correspondence with his anxious constituents and experience of London's tumults had changed his thinking, despite his subsequent claims to constancy. His support for the Kent petition incurred his ejection from the Commons on 2 February 1642. Owing to his fame as an orator and his reforming activism, parliamentarians later considered him 'the most culpable turn-coat after Lord Digby'.[13] He joined the king at Nottingham and was granted royal pardon in September 1642, claiming in print that 'he had been bullied into moving the Root and Branch Bill, and that he had always supported "primitive episcopacy".'[14]

[7] Richard P. Cust, 'Wentworth's "Change of Sides" in the 1620s', in Julia F. Merritt (ed.), *The Political World of Thomas Wentworth, Earl of Strafford, 1621–1641* (Cambridge, 1996), 75, 77.

[8] Terence Kilburn and Anthony Milton, 'The Public Context of the Trial and Execution of Strafford', in ibid., 237–8.

[9] John Adamson, *The Noble Revolt: The Overthrow of Charles I* (2007), 312, 410.

[10] Austin Woolrych, *Britain in Revolution, 1625–1660* (Oxford, 2002), 170–2, 183.

[11] Keeler, 11–12, 103, 138, 157, 228; Aylmer, 'Collective Mentalities in Mid-Seventeenth-Century England: 2 Royalist Attitudes', 2.

[12] Beinecke Rare Book and Manuscript Library, Osborn Shelves, b297, nos. 19–21.

[13] Derek Hirst, 'The Defection of Sir Edward Dering', *HJ*, 15 (1972), 195–6, 203.

[14] BL, Stowe MS 184, fo. 73r; Aylmer, 'Collective Mentalities in Mid-Seventeenth-Century England: 2 Royalist Attitudes', 14.

Once armed hostilities commenced, both sides issued declarations aimed at procuring MPs ranged against them to defect. On 17 June 1642 a newsletter from
York reported that the king offered a 'full and absolute pardon' to all except 'those
six members formerly charged by his Majesty with treason', along with Alderman
Pennington, John Venn, Sir Henry Ludlow, Sir Peter Wentworth, Sir John
Hotham, and Henry Marten.[15] A parliamentarian sergeant, Nehemiah Wharton,
noted on 7 October 1642 that the earl of Essex had proclaimed that all royalists
returning to parliament would be favourably received, although returning MPs
would have to submit to the censure of the House.[16] Royalists were first to offer
attractive terms to prospective defectors. A royal proclamation at Oxford on 20
June 1643 was encouraged by the stream of early converts. Read at Westminster on
26 June, it offered royal pardon and protection to all members prepared to join the
king within the next ten days, except for thirteen MPs and five peers exempted
from pardon. It safeguarded royal authority by claiming that members had been
forced into 'unlawful and treasonable Protestations' to live and die with the earl of
Essex, while it played upon backbench dissatisfaction by denouncing parliament's
government as being conducted in secret by a close committee of arch-rebels. To
facilitate defections, it decreed that royalist forces were to permit MPs, their attend-
ants, and servants to come to Oxford unmolested.[17] This declaration was followed
by another on 22 December 1643, in which the king summoned Westminster's
MPs 'without exceptions' to join him against the Scots invasion and thereby gain
pardon through assembling at Oxford by 22 January 1644. This was intended to
marginalize those remaining at Westminster as traitors joined 'with a Foreign
Nation to ruine and extinguish their own.'[18]

Parliament countered with the Declaration of Both Kingdoms on 30 January
1644, offering free pardon to those not among the 'prime authors' of the war who
would return to Westminster by 1 March and take the Solemn League and Covenant. Prospective defectors were warned that they would be charged for the public
debts, but by such agents as would be 'as careful to prevent their ruin, as to punish
their delinquencies.' These declarations were not only intended to win converts,
but to spread doubt and anxiety among the enemy. According to Bulstrode Whitelocke the Declaration of Both Kingdoms was so widely circulated that the royal
council at Oxford made possession of it a felony, and martial law was threatened
against any that left Oxford without the governor's permission.[19] Both sides sought
to attract side-changers, and these declarations were a principal means, but so too
were the pre-war personal networks of the members themselves. Private correspondence with those on the enemy side was forbidden, but such rulings were

---

[15] *CSPD 1641–3*, 342.
[16] Ibid., 398–400.
[17] *LJ*, vi, 108–11; BL, Egerton MS 2646, fo. 293; BL, Harleian MS 164, fo. 278r–v.
[18] John Rushworth, *Historical Collections of Private Passages of State*, 8 vols. (1721), v, 559–60.
[19] Samuel R. Gardiner, *History of the Great Civil War, 1642–1649*, 4 vols. (1987), i, 300–1; Paul N.
Hardacre, *The Royalists during the Puritan Revolution* (The Hague, 1956), 20–1; *CJ*, iii, 380, Bulstrode
Whitelock, *Memorials of English Affairs from the Beginning of the Reign of Charles I to the Happy Restoration of King Charles II*, 4 vols. (Oxford, 1853), i, 240.

flagrantly breached. Defectors rarely acted impulsively, but rather formulated careful plans, so that few embarked upon a new allegiance when they lacked friends and protectors to intercede for them.

The first member to defect during hostilities was George Goring, MP for Portsmouth. His role in betraying the Army Plot in 1641 increased parliament's confidence in him, yet simultaneously he maintained his reputation with the king, who entrusted him to fortify Portsmouth. When summoned to answer charges of defaming parliament, Goring cleared his name convincingly, reminding the House that he too suffered under royal displeasure. He was granted money to complete Portsmouth's defences and was commissioned lieutenant-general of horse. He delayed leaving Portsmouth to take up this commission, prolonging his allegiance to parliament until it became evident that the king could raise forces. Yet his royalism was 'tempered by his instinct for self-preservation' and personal advancement.[20] When on 4 August 1642 news reached parliament that Goring had declared for the king, D'Ewes wrote that it 'staggered' many. Parliament ordered his arrest as a traitor for betraying his trust, and he was disabled from sitting on 16 August.[21] On 7 September he surrendered on favourable terms and was allowed to depart overseas.[22] Yet after his recapture at Wakefield in May 1643, the Commons voted that Goring's case, 'differing from those taken in open War', should be tried by martial law. He was considered guilty of breaking his engagement not to fight against parliament and for his betrayal of Portsmouth.[23] Goring's father was horrified at his son's predicament, and he was saved from execution only by a high-profile prisoner exchange.[24]

The incidence of defections from parliament increased during the war's first winter. Debates on the peace propositions were interrupted on 16 January 1643, by the claim that Edward Seymour was in the king's army, and he was disabled from sitting in the House. A similar move against another absentee, Sir James Thynne, was postponed at Pym's intervention, but only until 15 February.[25] Some changed sides through fear, such as John George, MP for Cirencester, who helped garrison the town and was taken at its capture by Rupert in February 1643. He was badly treated en route to Oxford, and was later threatened with execution.[26] After the Commons rejected a royalist proposal to exchange him, eventually he was induced to sit in the Oxford Parliament.[27] A more notorious defector was Sir Hugh Cholmley, not only disabled from sitting on 3 April 1643, but also impeached for

[20] Florene S. Memegalos, *George Goring (1608–1657): Caroline Courtier and Royalist General* (Aldershot, 2007), 112, 115; *CSPD 1641–3,* 15, 18, 23–5, 29, 179–80, 271; Edward Hyde, earl of Clarendon, *The History of the Rebellion and Civil Wars in England Begun in the Year 1641,* ed. William Dunn Macray (Oxford, 1888), ii, 270–82.

[21] BL, Harleian MS 164, fos. 259r–v; Keeler, 192; Memegalos, *George Goring,* 122.

[22] John Webb, 'The Siege of Portsmouth in the Civil War', in R. C. Richardson (ed.), *The English Civil Wars: Local Aspects* (Stroud, 1997), 85.

[23] BL, Add. MS 31116, fo. 53v; *CJ,* iii, 107.

[24] BL, Sloane MS 1519, fo. 12; *CJ,* iii, 191; *CSPD 1644,* 21.

[25] BL, Harleian MS 164, fo. 276r–v; *CJ,* ii, 966.

[26] Andrew R. Warmington, *Civil War, Interregnum and Restoration in Gloucestershire, 1640–1672* (Woodbridge, 1997), 27, 43; Hyde, *History of the Rebellion,* ii, 447.

[27] He was not disabled until 3 November 1646: BL, Harleian MS 165, fo. 114v; Keeler, 184–5; *CJ,* iv, 712.

high treason. This ominous development reflected Cholmley's breach of trust in delivering Scarborough castle to the enemy. Now parliament signalled to its governors elsewhere that such treachery merited death.[28]

Fear of treachery climaxed when on 31 May 1643 Edmund Waller was arrested for corresponding with royalists and plotting a rising in London itself. The king had permitted Waller to remain at Westminster, where he consistently advocated peace. While Waller surveyed the strength of London support for making peace, his fellow MP, Sir Nicholas Crisp, procured a secret royalist commission to raise forces. A servant of Waller's brother-in-law leaked the plot to Pym, who publicized it skilfully on the parliamentary fast day. Pym used the plot to demonstrate that those who pretended that they favoured peace, in reality were aiming to slaughter the well-affected. In response, a new loyalty test, the Vow and Covenant, was framed. MPs in favour of peace fell under increased suspicion. When questioned, Waller confessed much through fear, implicating the peers Conway, Portland, and Northumberland.[29] While two of his confederates were executed, judgement upon Waller was postponed. On 4 July he humbled himself in despair before the Commons, 'all clothed in mourning as if he had been going to execution itself'.[30] Yet he eloquently disowned knowledge of an armed rising, and his payment of a £10,000 fine moved the House to clemency. Lucy Hutchinson remarked that Waller, 'being more a knave than the rest and impeaching his accomplices', was permitted to buy his life. On 14 July 1643 he was disabled from ever sitting in parliament, and was imprisoned without trial until November 1644.[31] Unsurprisingly, Aylmer considered that Waller's most consistent principle was 'self-preservation',[32] while John Aubrey quipped that Waller's case was 'the first time a House of Commons was ever bribed.'[33]

These revelations engendered a feverish atmosphere at Westminster, and on 24 June 1643 three more members, including Sir William Ogle, former parliamentary governor of London,[34] were disabled from sitting for being at Oxford. Evidence from the conspirators' examinations also placed Denzil Holles, William Pierrepont, Sir John Maynard, and Sir John Holland under suspicion.[35] Alongside them were the two Sir John Evelyns, suspected for an intercepted letter written by the younger Sir John to the elder during the younger's stay with the earl of Northumberland at Petworth in August 1643. Lawrence Whitacre noted that the letter contained 'divers sentences darkly & suspiciously written',[36] while D'Ewes considered

[28] BL, Add. MS 31116, fo. 40r; CJ, iii, 28.
[29] Hyde, History of the Rebellion, iii, 38–53; Gardiner, History of the Great Civil War, i, 146–9; BL, E105(21), A Discovery of the Great Plot for the Utter Ruine of the City of London, and the Parliament. As it was at large made known by John Pym, Esq; on Thursday being the eighth of June, 1643. at a Common-hall: and afterwards corrected by his own hand for the presse, 9 June (1643), sig. B4r–v.
[30] BL, Harleian MS 165, fo. 144r.
[31] CJ, iii, 166; Warren Chernaik, 'Edmund Waller (1606–1687), poet and politician', ODNB; Lucy Hutchinson, Memoirs of the Life of Colonel Hutchinson, ed. N. H. Keeble (1995), 105.
[32] Aylmer, 'Collective Mentalities in Mid-Seventeenth-Century England: 4 Cross Currents', 4.
[33] John Aubrey, Brief Lives, ed. Richard Barber (Woodbridge, 2004), 311.
[34] BL, Harleian MS 164, fo. 247v; CJ, iii, 142–3.
[35] BL, Harleian MS 165, fo. 98r.   [36] BL, Add. MS 31116, fo. 74r.

that the evidence that the younger Evelyn intended to defect to Oxford was compelling, if not conclusive.[37]

Sir Henry Anderson, Sir Alexander Carew, William Constantine, and Sir John Harrison were disabled next, on 4 September 1643. Carew was disabled for attempting to betray St Nicholas Island at Plymouth, Anderson for joining the king's party, Harrison for leaving parliament for Oxford, and Constantine for joining the western royalists.[38] Anderson had raised men for parliament in Cleveland, but was in Oxford by September 1643.[39] On 25 September he wrote to Lenthall that his ejection was 'hard, if not unjust', because he was there to negotiate peace and procure pardons for his friends, having already suffered imprisonment in York castle for fourteen weeks. His son, a parliamentarian captain, had been imprisoned for twenty-four weeks, and he was eager to secure his release. He advised Denzil Holles that he and Sir Philip Stapleton were well-esteemed in Oxford, and devised peace articles, urging Holles to promote them in the belief that the king would acquiesce.[40] In November 1643 he was recaptured at Leicester, along with his incriminating petitions to the king and his letters criticizing parliament to Sir Edward Nicholas, Holles, and Lenthall.[41] Some of these were read in the House, showing he had chosen to abandon Westminster since 13 April 1643 and now solicited the king's pardon.[42] On 12 December 1643 the Commons voted Anderson into the Tower for assisting the enemy, denying him a defence before the House.[43] Anderson provides an example of those desperate for peace because they had been unable to protect their property, estates, families, and friends from wartime hazards. His efforts at negotiating peace were jeered at by some MPs 'as if he had been a fit instrument for such a work'.[44]

Carew's attempted defection was even more mishandled. D'Ewes and Clarendon agreed that he had supported parliament's opposition from 1640 with 'zeal and fury', but that after the royalist victory at Stratton, Carew doubted whether his governorship of St Nicholas Island would secure his Cornish estates. He contacted friends and neighbours who interceded with Sir John Berkeley for a pardon, but procrastinating over its terms, he was arrested before he could defect.[45] Constantine, the recorder of Poole, had initially supported parliament, writing to Lenthall in October 1642 that all Dorset demonstrated 'a unanimous consent and joy to be pliable to Parliament'.[46] Yet on 15 July 1643 he endeavoured to procure Poole's surrender to the royalists. Complimenting the royalists' kind usage of him, he wrote to advise Poole's municipal leaders to save themselves from pillage and

[37] BL, Harleian MS 165, fos. 156r–159r.
[38] BL, Add. MS 31116, fos. 75v–76r; BL, Harleian MS 165, fo. 165v; BL, E250(8), *A Perfect Diurnall of Some Passages in Parliament*, no. 8, 4–11 September (1643), 58.
[39] BL, Add. MS 15858, fo. 215; BL, Add. MS 18979, fo. 129r.
[40] *House of Lords MS*, HMC, 5th Report, Part I, Report and Appendix (1876), 107–8.
[41] BL, Add. MS 31116, fo. 90v; *CJ*, iii, 192, 305.
[42] BL, Harleian MS 165, fo. 225v.
[43] Ibid., fos. 241v–242r, *CJ*, iii, 338.
[44] BL, Harleian MS 165, fo. 225r.
[45] Ibid., fo. 165r; Hyde, *History of the Rebellion*, iii, 235–6.
[46] A. R. Bayley, *The Great Civil War in Dorset, 1642–1660* (Taunton, 1910), 60.

preserve their 'ancient government' by mayor and justices. He held that relief was impossible, and warned of the dangers of royal disfavour. If a siege were necessary, he threatened that Poole's poor inhabitants 'will endanger your persons as the cause of their sufferance'. Constantine later claimed that he was forced to write this letter and attend at Oxford, but his final flourish that his conversion had been 'with a free & clean hart' undermined his case. He was sequestered on 28 September and recaptured the following year, he was imprisoned in the King's Bench.[47] Finally, Sir John Harrison was named to several Hertfordshire committees and had taken the Vow and Covenant on 6 June 1643, but defected by August and subsequently sat in the Oxford Parliament.[48] A combination of royalist military successes, failed peace initiatives, and disorderly crowds at Westminster may have prompted these changes of allegiance.

The next to be disabled on 7 and 8 September were Sir John Hotham and his son, John Hotham, MPs for Beverley and Scarborough (cases discussed in Chapter 8). The following week, D'Ewes noted that some grew suspicious of Sir John Holland, as although he was absent under license to recover his health, some considered his sickness counterfeited, as others had used this ploy to facilitate their defections.[49] On 28 September the Commons ordered the sequestration of the estates of fourteen long-term absentees for 'deserting the Service of the Commonwealth', and threatened a further twenty-six with sequestration if they did not attend the Sequestration committee and account for their absence. The same day, Sir Guy Palmes was disabled. Palmes had been nominated a militia commissioner in Rutland by both sides, and, after Edgehill, remained at Westminster to support peace negotiations. Concerned by royalist domination of the north, in May 1643 he retired to protect his Yorkshire estates. As in many cases, the whereabouts of his person entailed judgements about his allegiance; his claims to neutrality after being captured at Newark in 1646 were not entertained.[50] His son-in-law, Robert Sutton, was disabled on 25 December 1643, while John Dutton was disabled on 1 January 1644 for having raised forces against Gloucester despite having promised ten horses for parliament's service.[51]

Large-scale ejections reflected parliamentarian anxieties about the opening of the Oxford Parliament: fifty-two were disabled on 22 January 1644 for being in arms against parliament, residing in royalist-held territory, or being a long-term absentee.[52] A further thirty-four who subscribed to the letter of 27 January to persuade the earl of Essex to negotiate peace, and who had sat in the Oxford Parliament, were disabled on 5 February 1644.[53] Many of these had been committed

---

[47] Ibid., 111; Bodl., MS Tanner 62, fo. 171; *CCCD*, ii, 940; Keeler, 140–1.

[48] Keeler, 205–6; *CJ*, iii, 117–18; BL, Stowe MS 184, fos. 136, 161.

[49] BL, Harleian MS 165, fo. 190r–v.

[50] *CJ*, iii, 256; Keeler, 294; Simon Healy, 'Sir Guy Palmes (1580–1653), politician', *ODNB*.

[51] *CJ*, iii, 353; Keeler, 356; Rushworth, *Historical Collections*, v, 559–60. Dutton's loyalties were divided as his election was sponsored by the royalist Berkeley family: *CJ*, iii, 355; Keeler, 162; Brunton and Pennington, *Members of the Long Parliament*, 133; Hill, *Puritanism and Revolution*, 18–19.

[52] *CJ*, iii, 374; BL, Add. MS 31116, fo. 110r.

[53] *CJ*, iii, 389; BL, Add. MS 31116, fo. 114r.

royalists since 1642, whilst others such as Sir Gerard Napper illustrate how tardy parliament could be in disabling well-connected members. Continually absent, Napper was ineffectually summoned to attend in July and October 1642. His arrest was ordered on 10 April 1643, but Sir Walter Earle and John Browne interceded for him on 17 May, attributing his absence to his wife's imminent childbirth. They declared that he had already lent arms, horses, and money in Dorset, and that he would return to Westminster if granted a few more weeks leave. On 26 May the Commons acceded, but by 3 August Napper was acting as a royal commissioner for the surrender of Dorchester.[54]

Parliamentarians who remained at Westminster considered the defections to Oxford in 1643 to be more blameworthy than those who had fled to York in spring 1642. Thomas May drew a distinction between these individuals 'because this latter revolt must needs carry the face of a crime; as being no matter of opinion or conscience, by which the first justified themselves [those of 1642]; but proceeding, in all probability, from weaknesse, and feare for their private fortunes'. In writing the official history of the Long Parliament, May could scarcely suggest otherwise, or that these MPs were responding to changed political circumstances. By denigrating their motives, he deliberately contrasted their feebleness with the constancy and strength of those that remained true.[55]

II

Another important consequence of these defections and ejections was a deepening of factional conflict at Westminster, fuelled by fears of further side-changing. Although only one in ten members actually changed sides, many more were suspected of the intention. On 19 August 1643 D'Ewes noted the order for all absentees to immediately return and attend. He considered that Pym promoted it 'in malice to Mr Holles, Sir William Lewes, and some others who had retired into the country', as well as Sir John Evelyn, who 'was at this time at Petworth with the earl of Northumberland, and intended as was guessed by many to go with him to Oxford to the king.'[56] This distrust surfaced in bitter arguments over how to deal with recaptured side-changers. On 11 November 1643 D'Ewes noted the sharp division over his motion that the returned earl of Holland's punishment be left to the House of Lords. His proposal sparked a counter-motion, defeated by just one vote, that the Commons should desire the Lords to send Holland to the Tower.[57] On 11 March 1644 an ordinance to prevent returning defectors from resuming their seats without consent from both Houses was long debated and left unresolved.[58]

---

[54] Keeler, 283; Bodl., MS Tanner 62, fos. 100, 217; Bayley, *Great Civil War in Dorset*, 31; Stephen Wright, 'Sir Gerard Napier, first baronet (*bap.* 1606, *d.* 1673), politician', *ODNB*.

[55] Wing/M1410, Thomas May, *The History of the Parliament of England, which began November the third, MDCXL* (1647), Book III, 91–2.

[56] BL, Harleian MS 165, fo. 152v.

[57] Ibid., fos. 229r–230v. [58] BL, Add. MS 31116, fo. 123r.

Suspicion and distrust over MPs' allegiance increased personal animosities in the Commons. In August 1643 D'Ewes noted that Holles's pass to go overseas was rescinded by a motion from Pym.[59] Doubts over Holles's loyalty kept him from being appointed to the Committee of Both Kingdoms. In December 1643 he was accused of corresponding with Oxford along with Sir John Clotworthy. In January 1644 Sir Walter Earle argued that Clotworthy was implicated in Sir Basil Brooke's supposed plot to deliver London to the king, adding that Clotworthy had aided an Irish Catholic officer to escape from the Tower.[60] William Pierrepont was also suspected of corresponding with royalists, and in November 1643 was forbidden by just one vote to withdraw overseas or into Nottinghamshire because he scrupled over taking the Covenant. Even Samuel Browne's defence of Pierrepont acknowledged the suspicions about him by observing Pierrepont 'had not wanted invitations from the other side.'[61]

The flight to Oxford of so many MPs inclined to a negotiated settlement left their 'peace party' colleagues at Westminster weakened and politically suspect. Yet the treachery associated with peace negotiations was exaggerated because although many on both sides professed desires for peace, they usually intended to impose it on highly partisan terms.[62] The continued suspicion of Holles was inflamed on 2 July 1645 when the side-changer Lord Savile accused him of betraying parliament's cause during the Oxford peace talks of November 1644. Savile accused Holles and Whitelocke of advancing their own peace terms and charged Holles with providing royalists with intelligence and corresponding with Digby. Lord Saye was eager to ruin Holles, but needed more evidence from Savile, as many argued that 'Oxford could ruin a man simply by naming him'. Historians have dismissed the affair because of Savile's devious reputation, and the two MPs considered it an Independent plot to oust them from the Commons. However, the charges placed them in a precarious position, because Savile's information was partly true and appeared to be vindicated by the publication of the *King's Cabinet Opened* after Naseby.[63] Holles was particularly vulnerable because his loyalty was questioned already by Sir Henry Anderson's letters in 1643. Robert Baillie considered Holles's supporters were 'in great feare for his undoeing'. Although parliament was unsatisfied with Holles's defence and some MPs demanded he stand trial by martial law, no firm evidence was proven, and Holles was cleared by ninety-five votes to fifty-five. Yet charges of treachery persisted in shaping Westminster politics after the king's surrender, as Savile's allegations against Holles were resurrected by the Army's charges against the eleven 'incendiary' members in July 1647.[64]

---

[59] BL, Harleian MS 165, fo. 151v.

[60] Valerie Pearl, 'Oliver St. John and the "Middle Group" in the Long Parliament: August 1643–May 1644', *EHR*, 81 (1966), 512.

[61] BL, Harleian MS 165, fo. 224v; BL, Add. MS 31116, fo. 90v.

[62] Aylmer, 'Collective Mentalities in Mid-Seventeenth-Century England: 2 Royalist Attitudes', 3.

[63] For a detailed discussion of these complicated intrigues see Patricia Crawford, 'The Savile Affair', *EHR*, 90 (1975), 76–7, 79, 83, 85; Michael Mahony, 'The Savile Affair and the Politics of the Long Parliament', *Parliamentary History*, 7 (1988), 220, 225.

[64] Crawford, 'The Savile Affair', 84–9; BL, Egerton MS 1048, fos. 51–80.

Holles and Whitelocke's attempt to impose a peace upon parliament raised royalist hopes that infighting at Westminster would weaken their adversaries. It also provided the royalists with intelligence to exploit factional divisions within parliament.[65] Mark Kishlansky considered these intrigues marked the birth of organized, adversarial party politics at Westminster, yet in contrast Michael Mahony used the affair to stress 'the evolutionary nature of factional politics, based firmly upon techniques already apparent in 1643.'[66] Yet the historiographical debate on the emergence of party politics overlooked the central role in these episodes played by side-changers, charges of treachery, and discord over what constituted betrayal of 'the cause'.

Notwithstanding the recriminatory atmosphere, some MPs skilfully negotiated a return to their seats, despite offences that would have disabled others. One such was Sir Edward Baynton who commanded Wiltshire's parliamentarian forces, but stood accused of disarming fellow parliamentarian gentry.[67] In May 1643 he was reprimanded for duelling and attempting to have Sir Edward Hungerford court-martialled, after Baynton and Hungerford had exchanged accusations of treachery and corresponding with the enemy.[68] Fleeing to the Isle of Wight, on 26 August 1643 he wrote to Sir Edward Hyde, desiring him to intercede to procure royal pardons for him and his son-in-law, Hugh Rogers, MP for Calne. He offered to return home to Wiltshire, and reassured Hyde 'that your greatest enemies shall never justly reproach you for procuring my pardon'.[69] He was recaptured by 5 September, and Colonel Thomas Carne, deputy governor of the island, informed Lenthall that Baynton had made seditious speeches, called the Committee of Safety 'a company of boys', and accused Saye and Pym of destroying the kingdom.[70] Imprisoned by parliament for eight months, he petitioned successfully for his release on 4 June 1644, and parliament appointed members to mediate his dispute with Hungerford. Despite having come very close to changing sides, Baynton quickly recovered his seat, while Rogers took the Covenant and was commissioned colonel.[71]

Another success was the courtier Sir William Uvedale, who was somehow able to maintain credit on both sides. He was with the king at Nottingham in August 1642 and was present among Hampshire's royalists in November 1643, yet was named to several parliamentary committees and allowed to regain his seat at Westminster in October 1644.[72] In February 1643 Sir Robert Pye retained his seat

---

[65] Crawford, 'The Savile Affair', 92.

[66] Mahony, 'The Savile Affair and the Politics of the Long Parliament', 214, 225.

[67] BL, Harleian MS 164, fos. 276r, 306v.

[68] BL, Add. MS 31116, fos. 53v–54r; BL, E85(37), *A Letter to the Earle of Pembroke from Sir Edward Baynton in Glocester*, 22 January (1643); Edmund Ludlow, *The Memoirs of Edmund Ludlow, Lieutenant General of the Horse in the Army of the Commonwealth of England, 1625–1672*, ed. C. H. Firth, 2 vols. (Oxford, 1894), i, 440–7.

[69] Bodl., MS Clarendon 22, fo. 119r.

[70] BL, Harleian MS 165, fos. 167v–168r; BL, E250(8), *Perfect Diurnall of Some Passages in Parliament*, 59.

[71] BL, Add. MS 31116, fos. 142r; Keeler, 101, 325.

[72] Keeler, 369–70; Hyde, *History of the Rebellion*, ii, 304; Whitelock, *Memorials of English Affairs*, i, 324; G. E. Aylmer, *The King's Servants: The Civil Service of Charles I, 1625–1642* (2nd edn., 1974), 391–2.

despite the discovery of his letter to Sir Edward Nicholas desiring the king's pardon, which also pointed out he had furnished Sir Nicholas Crisp with £3,700 for a 'secret service done for his majesty'. Pye protested his ignorance of the purpose of this money, and no attempt was made to eject him. D'Ewes remarked that Pye's son's marriage to Hampden's daughter protected him from the censure of 'the fierie spirits', despite other MPs having been disabled for less.[73] Crisp was interrogated, and slipped away to Oxford soon after.[74] Aylmer considered Pye's allegiance 'very lukewarm' and more due 'to his determination to retain his office than to any principled convictions.'[75] Another MP who rehabilitated himself after imprisonment for negotiating with the royalists was Sir John Evelyn the younger, who was released from custody by a Commons' vote of 71–66 on 2 March 1644. Such occasions could generate close divisions, contradictory pressures, and political embarrassment; in this case Oliver St John, Sir William Waller, and Sir William Brereton absented themselves and had to be recalled by the Speaker to vote. D'Ewes remarked bitterly that Evelyn was eventually reinstated in October 1644 because he had agreed with the Independents that henceforth he would oppose Presbyterian church government.[76]

III

The opening of the Oxford Parliament on 22 January 1644 represented a change in political circumstances and further complicated the positions of MPs. There were no fresh elections; Oxford MPs were the royalist element of the Long Parliament displaced from Westminster. The royalists were now more credible respecters of constitutional legality and had a king-in-parliament behind them who could pose as a defender of England against a Scots invasion. Those MPs who left Westminster and now sat at Oxford could argue that it was not they but the circumstances that had changed. The Oxford Parliament's two sessions lasted from 22 January to 16 April 1644, and from 8 October 1644 to 10 March 1645. The king promised his Oxford MPs their traditional parliamentary freedoms and privileges, but detailed analysis of their attendance and political positions is hampered because its records were burnt prior to Oxford's surrender in June 1646. David Smith maintained that forty peers and 100 commoners attended in January 1644, yet forty-four and 117 signed the letter to Essex of 27 January. The royalists also claimed the support of a further thirty-eight peers and fifty-five commoners who were absent.[77] These numbers compared favourably with the twenty peers and 200 active commoners remaining at Westminster, and represent the high

[73] BL, Harleian MS 264, fo. 277r.

[74] Robert Ashton, 'Sir Nicholas Crisp, first baronet (c.1599–1666), merchant and royalist', *ODNB*.

[75] BL, Harleian MS 164, fo. 277r–v; Keeler, 317; G. E. Aylmer, 'Sir Robert Pye (*bap.* 1585, *d.* 1662), exchequer official and politician', *ODNB*; Aylmer, *The King's Servants*, 381.

[76] Pearl, 'Oliver St. John and the "Middle Group" in the Long Parliament', 492n, 517; *CJ*, iii, 414; BL, Harleian MS 165, fos. 156r–159r.

[77] David L. Smith, *Stuart Parliaments, 1603–1689* (1999), 131; Rushworth, *Historical Collections*, v, 566.

tide of royalist support.[78] If Hyde and the king hoped the Oxford Parliament would win over more members from Westminster, then they were largely frustrated. Despite the difficulties of precisely dating defections, most occurred before it sat, with few abandoning Westminster thereafter.[79]

The prospect of a royalist parliament instilled considerable excitement in Oxford. One anonymous correspondent erroneously claimed that Sir Simonds D'Ewes was in town after an overnight ride from Westminster, and that another MP, 'a lawyer for some part of Northamptonshire, now much reformed' had joined him. It was alleged that these defections so pleased the king that 'he hath given order that such as repair to this assembly need not apply to him for pardon, but immediately enter their names in the office, and the pardon is consummated.'[80] The arrival of individual side-changers generated excited political speculation, but the initial parliamentarianism of many Oxford MPs had never been particularly active. For example, Thomas Coke had been a parliamentary assessment commissioner, Thomas Tomkins had pledged horses in June 1642, and Sir Henry Bellingham had been appointed commissioner for scandalous ministers and a committeeman for Westmorland.[81] It is unlikely that these men considered themselves committed parliamentarians in the first place. Most members at Oxford that were not ardent royalists in 1642 drifted into royalism in an inconspicuous manner.

Another MP whose side-changer status is questionable, but who was considered one by contemporaries, was the lawyer Edward Bagshaw, who had been an active supporter of Pym's group in 1642 and had lent the parliamentary cause £50 in plate. By February 1643 he was urging the House towards negotiating peace and complaining that City radicals were breaching parliament's privileges.[82] He was angered by attempts to separate the kingly office from Charles I's person, protesting that allegiance 'being a corporeall service, is to be done to a visible, corporeall, and local person; not to a thing invisible, [and] incorporeall.'[83] In June 1644 Bagshaw was recaptured and sent to London, where Whitelocke noted with satisfaction that he was imprisoned for high treason and desertion of parliament.[84] The parliamentarianism of Sir Thomas Eversfield was also questionable, despite having been vouched for by Sir Walter Earle in October 1642. He was appointed to the Sussex county committee, but was sequestered for absence on 28 September 1643 and later sat in the Oxford Parliament.[85] Michael Wharton's change of side is more demonstrable, as he was still a committeeman with Sir John Hotham

---

[78] Braddick, *God's Fury, England's Fire*, 315.

[79] Ashton, *English Civil War*, 213; Woolrych, *Britain in Revolution*, 274.

[80] Francis Bickley (ed.), *Report on the Manuscripts of the late Reginald Rawdon Hastings, esq.*, HMC, 78, 4 vols. (1930), ii, 118.

[81] Keeler, 105, 137–8, 362.

[82] Ibid., 94; BL, Harleian MS 164, fos. 295v, 304v–305r.

[83] Howard Nenner, 'Loyalty and the Law: The Meaning of Trust and the Right of Resistance in Seventeenth-Century England', *JBS*, 48 (2009), 861.

[84] *CJ*, iii, 546; Whitelock, *Memorials of English Affairs*, i, 272.

[85] *CJ*, ii, 802, iii, 45, 77, 256; Keeler, 170.

at Hull in October 1642 and was later killed defending Scarborough castle for the king in 1645.[86]

Others attending at Oxford had previously taken the Vow and Covenant of June 1643. Some of these may have complied under duress or with mental reservations, so again their status as side-changers is not straightforward, despite their condemnation at Westminster. These included William Bassett, Henry Brett, Sir Alexander Denton, John Fettiplace, William Glanvile, Sir Edward Littleton, and Sir George Stonehouse.[87] Stonehouse was named on the parliamentary committee for Berkshire, and appears not to have abandoned parliament until October 1643.[88] Bassett was a parliamentarian committeeman from August 1642, but continued to serve as a local magistrate when the royalists overran Somerset the following summer. David Underdown maintained that Bassett was politically constant, being, like many fellow gentry, determined to maintain local government, placing 'the unity of their county above partisan considerations.'[89]

D'Ewes noted further ejections from Westminster on 4 March 1644 when Sir John Borlase and Sir Edward Littleton were disabled without being summoned or heard.[90] Littleton of Pillaton, Staffordshire—not to be confused with his namesake the Lord Keeper—had supported parliament until 1643, but thereafter sought reconciliation with the king. Lord Paget vouched for Littleton's royalism on 17 October 1643, arguing that he would raise men and money for the king once royal forces 'shall come into the country to countenance him'. Littleton risked imprisonment by parliament's forces if he declared himself prematurely, but made good his pledges by joining the Oxford Parliament in January 1644.[91]

The Oxford Parliament was finally dissolved by the king in March 1645, after he had referred to it as a 'Mungrill Parliamt' in a letter to his wife that cast aspersions upon its allegiance after the defection of Viscount Savile and the exile of Lords Wilmot and Percy.[92] It may have enjoyed limited initial success in winning some converts, but failed to deliver the unified support for which the king had hoped. Most of the movement away from Westminster seems to have occurred before rather than after it sat. After the royalist capitulation in 1646, several members denied or downplayed their attendance. John Borlase refuted his involvement, despite having been in Oxford when it met.[93] William Morgan and Sir Walter Smith argued their attendance was forced, the latter claiming to be sick and infirm.[94] Others argued that they attended merely to negotiate peace, such as Roger

---

[86] Keeler, 379; Bodl., MS Nalson 2, no. 153; Jack Binns, *Yorkshire in the Civil Wars: Origins, Impact and Outcome* (Pickering, 2004), 118.

[87] *CJ*, iii, 117–18.

[88] Keeler, 352.

[89] Ibid., 100; David Underdown, *Somerset in the Civil War and Interregnum* (Newton Abbot, 1973), 39, 69.

[90] BL, Harleian MS 166, fos. 21v, 24r.

[91] Keeler, 254; Bickley (ed.), *Report on the Manuscripts of the late Reginald Rawdon Hastings*, ii, 107.

[92] H. G. Tibbut (ed.), *The Letter Books of Sir Samuel Luke, 1644–45* (Publications of the Bedfordshire Historical Record Society, 42, 1963), 218; Bodl., MS Clarendon 25, fo. 74.

[93] Keeler, 111.   [94] Ibid., 279, 344.

Matthew, who also claimed to have maintained his two sons in parliament's service.[95]

IV

Defections of royalist MPs to Westminster were fewer and arguably of less political consequence. Some were double side-changers, and very few recovered their seats. Their defections did not proceed until early 1644, in response to the Declaration of Both Kingdoms. Before then, prospective defectors lacked inducement to change sides, and until parliament acquired the Scots Army of the Covenant the king was perceived as holding the military ascendancy. The first defections included Sir Gerard Napper, Sir Anthony Ashley Cooper, and Sir Edward Dering—the latter two having held military commands. Robert Ashton considered that Dering's defection reflected the frustration of moderate voices at Oxford, yet James Daly considered that these defections had no unifying political characteristics beyond a reaction to the king's declining military fortunes.[96]

Dering was the first to defect, and his example provoked particular anxiety among royalists. On 22 February 1644 Sir Arthur Gorges wrote: 'I fear here be more of his mind undiscovered, but time will make them known to be knaves.'[97] One newsbook observed that Dering was in London by 2 February, only a day after parliament published the Declaration of Both Kingdoms. In response to his arrival, a committee was appointed to discuss how to receive others.[98] Dering obligingly took the Covenant on 7 February 1644, and wrote against his former comrades.[99] Yet his attempts to recover his rents were thwarted by parliament and the Kent county committee, scarcely enticing others to follow his example. *Mercurius Aulicus* eagerly pointed out that 'after all his Protestations, Declarations, and Overtures', Dering 'could only recover 200¹ *per annum* out of his whole estate, nor would his tenants pay him that; which with other discontents (whereof himselfe was Author) hath doubtlesse shortned his life.'[100] Dering lamented that his family were destitute, and bereft of their gentry status contrary to the declaration's promise that side-changers would be 'received into favour' and not ruined by their coming in (see Fig. 2.1).[101]

Napper had been an active royalist for only a few months when he submitted to parliament in March 1644. He took the Covenant on 20 September 1644, apologizing for his disloyalty. Not readmitted, his lands remained sequestered before he

[95] Ibid., 270.
[96] Ashton, *English Civil War*, 211; James Daly, 'The Implications of Royalist Politics, 1642–6', *HJ*, 27 (1984), 748–9.
[97] Bickley (ed.), *Report on the Manuscripts of the late Reginald Rawdon Hastings*, ii, 122.
[98] BL, E32(11), *The Parliament Scout Communicating his Intelligence to the Kingdome*, no. 33, 2–9 February (1644), 278–80.
[99] *CSPD 1644*, 13.
[100] BL, E2(6), *Mercurius Aulicus*, 26th week, 29 June (Oxford, 1644), 1050.
[101] BL, Stowe MS 184, fos. 61r–105r, esp. fo. 81r.

Fig. 2.1. Sir Edward Dering, MP. (Special Collections of the University of Leicester, University of Leicester Library, Fairclough Collection of Portrait Prints, EP41B, Box 1.)

eventually compounded for £3,514. Patrick Little considers Napper indecisive, and that his reversion to parliament was influenced by his close friend, Sir Anthony Ashley Cooper.[102]

Ashley Cooper was commissioned a royalist colonel in spring 1643, was president of the royalist council of war in Dorset, and governor of Weymouth from August 1643.[103] Yet on 29 December 1643 he requested Hyde for a licence to leave

---

[102] Bayley, *Great Civil War in Dorset*, 101, 107; *CCCD*, 1061–2; Patrick Little, 'Four Dorset Turncoats', unpublished paper delivered at a civil war conference at the Dorset Record Office, Dorchester, 2002.
[103] Hyde, *History of the Rebellion*, iii, 163–4; William Dougal Christie, *A Life of Anthony Ashley Cooper, First Earl of Shaftesbury, 1621–1683*, 2 vols. (1871), i, 40–6.

Dorset, complaining of insufficient pay and supplies, and that impressment was alienating the population.[104] In January 1644 he resigned his governorship and all his royalist commissions to defend himself from charges of breaking his trust, and subsequently presented himself to parliament's garrison at Hurst castle on 24 February. Hyde vindictively suggested that he defected out of bitterness at being replaced as Weymouth's governor, but according to Ashley Cooper the royalists had treated him well and he changed sides for political principles.[105] Like Dering, he insisted his conversion was before 1 March 1644 in response to the Declaration of Both Kingdoms. He defected when the royalists held the military ascendancy over his Dorset estates, and he soon became an uncompromising military commander for parliament.[106]

Another successful defector was Sir John Fenwick, deputy lieutenant for Northumberland, who raised forces against the Scots in early 1644, while his son was a royalist colonel killed at Marston Moor. Once captured in December 1644, he chose to serve parliament and was eventually reinstated into the Commons on 26 June 1646 after the sheriff and county committee of Northumberland had falsely stated to 'the best of their knowledge, Sir John Fenwick had always adhered to the Parliament and not to the King.'[107]

Unlike the 1644 defections, which occurred when the king's armies might still have emerged victorious, the four Cornish MPs who renegotiated their allegiance in 1646 did so whilst facing defeat. Mark Stoyle has argued for the particular and conditional nature of Cornish royalism, and once it became apparent that the New Model would not ruin their county, these MPs and their associates were quick to treat with Fairfax at Millbrook on 5 March to arrange the surrender of garrisons in east Cornwall.[108] Colonel William Coryton had his composition fine reduced for surrendering Mount Edgecumbe and assisting Fairfax thereafter in mobilizing forces. He did not take up arms for parliament, but was still regarded as a turncoat, while his wife was said to spy for Fairfax.[109] Lieutenant-Colonel William Scawen, controversially returned as recruiter MP for St Germans, also signed the treaty, thereby securing a satisfactory composition.[110] Colonel Piers Edgecumbe had offered to defect with his forces on 22 January 1646, eventually securing them favourable terms, and when Fairfax confirmed Edgecumbe's services his composition fine was also reduced. His epitaph later claimed that he had supported church

---

[104] Bodl., MS Clarendon 23, fo. 6r.

[105] Hyde, *History of the Rebellion*, iii, 362–3.

[106] Bayley, *Great Civil War in Dorset*, 107, 208–9, 227–8; Christie, *Life of Anthony Ashley Cooper*, i, 47–9, 59.

[107] Keeler, 174; *Portland MS*, 352, Mark Nicholls, 'Sir John Fenwick, first baronet (1579–c.1658), politician and landowner', *ODNB*.

[108] Mark Stoyle, *West Britons: Cornish Identities and the Early Modern British State* (Exeter, 2002), 142–3.

[109] Coryton was not disabled during the war, because he had already been deprived of his seat in August 1641: Keeler, 143; Newman, 87; P. R. Newman, *The Old Service: Royalist Regimental Colonels and the Civil War, 1642–46* (Manchester, 1993), 119; Joshua Sprigge, *Anglia Rediviva; Englands Recovery* (1647), 203–4.

[110] Newman, 333; Brunton and Pennington, *Members of the Long Parliament*, 22.

and king 'to the utmost of his power and fortune' in an attempt to wipe the memory of this betrayal.[111] His brother, Major Richard Edgecumbe, defected with him and took the Covenant in London in May 1646.[112] On 6 March 1646, all were recommended by Fairfax as 'Persons whose Interests and Endeavours have been very useful in reducing of the West'.[113] The precise nature of their parliamentarian service is unclear, but their example alone probably induced others to surrender more swiftly.

There were also several Welsh MPs that defected from the king, some of whom changed sides more than once. Sir John Price had sat in the Oxford Parliament but returned to Westminster in October 1644. He was not disabled until 20 October 1645, when his attendance at Oxford and his military commission from the royalist Lord Capel were belatedly discovered. Charles Carlton claimed that Price changed sides no less than four times and was well rewarded each time.[114] Sir Hugh Owen was another multiple side-changer, alongside most of Pembrokeshire's major landowners, who supported the king in 1643 and later aided or submitted to parliament.[115]

However, Westminster never attracted the number of convert MPs it might have done once it gained the military ascendancy. Defectors from the king are not numerically comparable to those who changed sides in 1643. Part of the explanation for this lies in the contrast between the king's free pardon and embracing of converts with Westminster's very public refusal to readmit royalist MPs into the Commons. Parliament's declaration of 29 June 1644 theoretically excluded all who had deserted the Commons from readmittance during that parliament.[116] Even by late 1645, as it became clear that parliament would win and there was increased incentive to defect to obtain a favourable composition, converts remained surprisingly limited.

Yet despite parliament's comparative harshness, it executed only three MPs during the first civil war. Carew and the Hothams were beheaded—not merely for changing sides, but for betraying their trusts. Owing to the privileges of parliament, they were not subject to the summary justice meted out to many army officers and soldiers. They were granted lengthy trials, albeit by martial courts, but were also heard in the House before their colleagues.[117] That they were treated harshly when others such as Baynton, Pye, Uvedale, and Price were allowed to return to

[111] Newman, 119; Keeler, 163–4; Barbara Donagan, *War in England 1642–1649* (Oxford, 2008), 231; *CCCD*, 1082–4; *CSPD 1645–7*, 317–18.

[112] Newman, 119–20; Keeler, 164; *CCCD*, 1082.

[113] *CJ*, iv, 495.

[114] Keeler, 314–15; *CSPD 1644*, 533–4; BL, Add. MS 31116, fo. 238v; BL, Harleian MS 166, fo. 270v; Charles Carlton, *Going to the Wars: The Experience of the British Civil Wars, 1638–1651* (1992), 255; *CCAM*, 664.

[115] Arthur Leonard Leach, *The History of the Civil War (1642–1649) in Pembrokeshire and on its Borders* (1937), 33; *CJ*, iii, 390, iv, 643.

[116] This had been discussed as early as 11 March 1644: *CJ*, iii, 547; BL, Add. MS 31116, fo. 123r.

[117] Although Nathaniel Fiennes was condemned to death for his surrendering Bristol prematurely, he was pardoned by the earl of Essex: BL, Harleian MS 165, fo. 179v; BL, Add. MS 31116, fos. 181v, 183r.

their seats indicates that there were degrees of culpability in turncoating. Much might be condoned by extenuating circumstances, claims of compulsion, skilful lobbying, and exploitation of political connections, but conspiring to betray vital port towns during the nadir of the parliamentary cause placed these men beyond rehabilitation.

V

Christopher Hill once assumed that while principled men on both sides were a minority, 'the marginal turncoat on either side...had no principles at all.'[118] Now this seems unduly harsh, yet until recently civil-war historians have been slow to acknowledge that politicians might reassess their allegiance in response to changing circumstances. Contemporaries recognized the fluidity of the political situation through repeated attempts to convert their enemies. The defections of 1643 may have reflected parliament's declining military fortunes, but they also demonstrated alienation from the radicalization of parliament's rhetoric and its increasingly punitive wartime administrative measures which made the defensive war envisaged in 1642 seem increasingly distant.[119] Faced with these defections, parliament grew increasingly reliant on those prepared to travel further in their rebellion. John Morrill argued that parliament's activists were split between 'those who had only joined the cause to preserve existing values and structures, to conserve their own power and influence, and those who saw the war as preparing for a transformed world.'[120] This analysis neatly describes the experience of side-changers in the Commons; puritan defectors from Westminster were conspicuously few. All four defectors among Yorkshire's MPs were religious moderates, whilst no defections occurred among their Godly colleagues.[121] The politics of side-changing also fuelled infighting and the emergence of adversarial party politics. Personal connections were utilized to persuade others to defect, or employed to urge lenience or severity upon prodigal returnees. Westminster was recognized by contemporaries as 'riven by factions, which could be analysed in terms of their internal structures and relationships.'[122] The prevalence of side-changing, along with broader perceptions of treachery, lay at the heart of this development in MPs' mentalities.

---

[118] Hill, *Puritanism and Revolution*, 17.

[119] Braddick, *God's Fury, England's Fire*, 303.

[120] John Morrill, *Revolt in the Provinces: The People of England and the Tragedies of War, 1630–1648* (1999), 164.

[121] J. T. Cliffe, *The Yorkshire Gentry from the Reformation to the Civil War* (1969), 346.

[122] Jason Peacey, 'Perceptions of Parliament: Factions and the "Public"', in John Adamson (ed.), *The English Civil War: Conflict and Contexts, 1640–1649* (Basingstoke, 2009), 104.

3

Military professionals: 'renegado' army officers

This chapter examines the incidence and significance of defections among army officers on both sides. While it highlights the contextual factors behind their defections, analysis of their motives remains problematic. This is because a combination of factors impacted upon their side-changing, ranging from opportunism and career prospects to slighted honour and changing military fortunes, whilst much of the surviving evidence for their defections comes from others impugning their motives. The chapter devotes a specific focus to 'professionals'—defined as career officers with military experience prior to 1642—because contemporaries viewed this group to be most susceptible to side-changing. English knowledge of side-changing practices in Europe is outlined first, before examining the experience of two particular and overlapping sub-groups of professionals who were notorious for defecting: officers under the earl of Essex, and continental foreigners in parliament's service. The chapter raises some of the important political consequences of this side-changing before turning to the defectors' possible motives and the circumstances behind their defections.

Professional officers were those English, Irish, Scots, and Welsh gentry who had served for pay overseas, largely owing to increased British and Irish interventions in continental warfare since 1585. Having been immersed in a violent culture of martial honour, they returned to offer their services in the Wars of the Three Kingdoms. Their numbers have been long underestimated by historians, and in 1642 both sides sought their services. In 1639 a list was compiled of nearly 200 officers and gentlemen who had served abroad and were available for Charles I's forces against Scotland.[1] Their numbers were augmented by foreign officers or 'outlanders' seeking employment with the outbreak of war in England.[2] This demand instilled in some military professionals the conviction that their indispensability endowed them with greater latitude to misbehave.[3] Professionals developed reputations for inflated self-regard, swearing, drinking, reveling, and importing frightful continental practices

---

[1] Barbara Donagan, 'Atrocity, War Crime, and Treason in the English Civil War', *American Historical Review*, 99 (1994), 1139; Barbara Donagan, 'Halcyon Days and the Literature of War: England's Military Education before 1642', *P&P*, 147 (1995), 71n.

[2] Mark Stoyle, *Soldiers and Strangers: An Ethnic History of the English Civil War* (New Haven, 2005), 91–109.

[3] Ian Roy, 'Royalist Reputations: The Cavalier Ideal and the Reality', in Jason McElligott and David Smith (eds.), *Royalists and Royalism during the English Civil War* (Cambridge, 2007), 104.

into English military life. Ian Roy has recently underlined how the practice of swearing among some professional officers became associated with royalism very early on.[4] Parliamentarians increasingly viewed professionals of questionable morality as politically suspect, despite the patronage afforded them by the earl of Essex. Their suspicions were vindicated when a large number, enticed into Essex's army by attractive pay, changed sides by 1643. The political consequences of this merit attention, including the resultant parliamentarian concerns to privilege ideological attachment to 'the cause' over self-interested or mercenary service. Also, the concept that military experience was a guarantor of victory, largely assumed in 1642, became increasingly questioned thereafter. Professional officers returning from abroad attracted satire in literature and verse in which their supposed martial glories were exposed as empty bluster.[5]

The notion that professionals considered themselves free agents in taking and changing sides was rooted in British perceptions of the Thirty Years' War. Contemporary publications such as Philip Vincent's *Lamentations of Germany* titillated and appalled readers with the horrors of a dehumanizing and corrosive war, whose Godless soldiers subjected civilians to barbaric depredations and torture.[6] The reputation of such soldiers has long suffered under the pejorative connotations of the term 'mercenary', while historians have assumed high desertion rates and that soldiers served whoever paid most.[7] Geoffrey Parker has observed that every European army employed at least some 'men who had fought on all sides'.[8] Side-changing was probably most prevalent among German-born soldiers, such as the Bavarian and Imperial prisoners, who, pressed into Swedish service, reverted to their former allegiance after the battle of Nördlingen in 1634. The following year they were joined by many of Sweden's other German allies, and the strategies of Axel Oxenstierna, John George of Saxony, and even Emperor Ferdinand II himself, were shaped by concerns to encourage defections among the enemy or prevent defections in their own ranks.[9] Despite the prevalence of side-changing, recaptured defectors risked execution. After the battle of Lützen, Albrecht von Wallenstein conflated treachery with cowardice in executing men from units that had fled the field, while in 1635 Count Johann Philipp Cratz von Scharffenstein, recaptured at Nördlingen, was executed for his defection to the Swedes and conspiracy to betray Ingolstadt.[10]

One Englishman, Sydenham Poyntz, provided a memoir of his service in Germany during the 1620s and 1630s, where he changed sides, first serving

---

[4] Ibid., 106.

[5] STC (2nd ed.)/5423, Richard Crimsal, *The Joviall Broome Man: Or, A Kent Street Souldiers Exact Relation, of all his travels in every nation* (1640); BL, E866(3), Robert Cox, *Acteon & Diana with a Pastoral Storie of the Nimph Oenone followed by the Several Conceited Humours of Bumpkin the Huntsman, Hobbinal the Shepherd, Singing Simpkin, and John Swabber the Seaman* (1656), 11–17.

[6] Philip Vincent, *The Lamentations of Germany. Wherein, as in a Glasse, We May Behold her Miserable Condition, and Reade the Woefull Effects of Sinne* (1638), 11, 18, 27.

[7] Peter H. Wilson, *Europe's Tragedy: A New History of the Thirty Years War* (2009), 827–8.

[8] Geoffrey Parker (ed.), *The Thirty Years' War*, 2nd edn. (1997), 204.

[9] Wilson, *Europe's Tragedy*, 549–50, 574–9, 829.

[10] Ibid., 511; Sydnam Poyntz, *The Relation of Sydnam Poyntz, 1624–1636*, ed. Rev. A. T. S. Goodrick (Camden Society, 3rd series, 14, 1908), 24–5.

under Ernst von Mansfeldt and the Elector of Saxony, before joining the Imperialists. This defection also entailed his conversion to Roman Catholicism—something he later explicitly denied once employed in parliament's service as Colonel-General of the Northern Association.[11] Poyntz's case indicates that even if side-changing was widespread, this does not mean that contemporaries felt there was no stigma attached. Poyntz carefully excused his defection as resulting from his ill-treatment by the Saxon Elector and the kindness showed him by Colonel Butler, his Imperialist captor. Poyntz turned the charge of breach of trust upon his employer, accusing the Elector of failing in his obligations to him and neglecting his ransom. Poyntz claimed that he intended to change sides sooner so that he might 'serve according to my owne conscience', but lacked the opportunity. Poyntz maintained he was within his rights because his only alternative to starving in prison was to defect—'which is the custome on both sides in those German warres'. He deflected attention from his own inconstancy by depicting the Elector's side-changing as far more reprehensible.[12] Allegations of side-changing among British officers on the continent may have been overstated or shaped by retrospective political concerns. The Scots officer, Sir James Turner, reflected of his own time in Swedish pay: 'I had swallowed without chewing, in Germanie, a very dangerous maxime, which militarie men there too muche follow, which was, that so we serve our master honestlie, it is no matter what master we serve'.[13] However, Turner penned this in changed circumstances to help account for his covenanting past. David Trim has recently argued that the ideology of a 'Calvinist International' did exist among English career soldiers serving overseas, rendering defections to Catholic powers problematic, while Barbara Donagan has pointed out that Poyntz was unusual, and that most Englishmen served in Protestant European armies, not risking what Robert Monro called 'shipwracke of [their] consciences'.[14]

I

The largest identifiable group of officer-defectors in England had learned about side-changing from their continental experiences. These were the professionals in Essex's army who defected to the king in 1642–3, despite having vowed to 'defend, maintain, and obey' parliament and Essex as captain general (see Appendix 3).[15] Most had continental or Irish experience, had served in the Bishops' Wars, or had

---

[11] BL, E320(8), *The Vindication of Colonel General Poyntz, Against the False and Malicious Slanders Secretly Cast Forth Against Him*, 3 February (1646), sig. A4r; D. N. Farr, 'Sydenham Poyntz (*bap.* 1607), parliamentarian army officer', *ODNB*.
[12] Poyntz, *The Relation of Sydnam Poyntz*, 18, 25, 54, 75–6, 79; BL, E320(8), *The Vindication of Colonel General Poyntz*, sig. A4v.
[13] David Stevenson, 'Sir James Turner (*b. c.*1615, *d.* in or after 1689), army officer and author', *ODNB*.
[14] David Trim, 'Calvinist Internationalism and the English Officer Corps, 1562–1642', *History Compass*, 4 (2006), 1024–48; Barbara Donagan, *War in England 1642–1649* (Oxford, 2008), 42.
[15] *CJ*, ii, 696, 699.

enlisted for Lord Wharton's army for Ireland of June 1642. Nearly all of Wharton's projected force was shoehorned into Essex's army by September 1642. Therefore, many of its officers later justifiably claimed that they enlisted under 'false pretences', never purposing to serve against the king's person in England.[16] Prominent examples include Sir Faithful Fortescue, John Urry, and James Chudleigh.[17] Their self-justifications and notions of military honour are examined in greater length in Chapter 8.

This group was so politically significant because many in it stood among parliament's best regarded and most successful commanders. For example, Urry was credited with directing the assault which captured Reading in December 1642, while Clarendon considered that Urry had done much to preserve Essex's army at Edgehill.[18] Despite the reverses Urry had inflicted upon the royalists, he managed his defection expertly, and Rupert quickly entrusted him with important independent operations. The royalist press was quick to praise Urry's sufficiency, gallantry, and loyalty.[19] Similarly, in December 1643 Sir William Waller eagerly anticipated Sir Richard Grenville's assistance and 'did much rejoice to have so gallant a man command his horse.'[20]

In 1642 Horatio Carey and Francis Dowett had also been highly praised—the former for negotiating Chichester's surrender, and the latter for capturing the earl of Bath.[21] Carey had served in Germany and Ireland, and, after his defection, quickly rose to brigade command among the royalist cavalry.[22] A penchant for bawdy poems inspired his cornet's motto that scorned his former general, Essex, with: 'Cuckold wee come'.[23] After his defection at Edgehill, the king entrusted Sir Faithfull Fortescue to raise a cavalry regiment, commissioning him colonel on 25 November 1642.[24] When Joseph Wagstaffe was captured by royalists, they excused

---

[16] Malcolm Wanklyn, *The Warrior Generals: Winning the British Civil Wars* (New Haven, 2010), 236.

[17] Chudleigh is excluded from Table 3 as he held his commission direct from the House of Commons to command dragoons raised for service in the west before projected transfer to Ireland in March 1643: *CJ*, ii, 878.

[18] BL, TT E129(12), *A True Relation of the Proceedings of His Excellence the Earle of Essex, with his Army, since his Departure from these Parts, in Pursuite of the Cavaliers. With the Taking of Redding by Colonell Hampden, and Colonell Hurry with their regiments*, 8 December (1642), 6; Edward Hyde, earl of Clarendon, *The History of the Rebellion and Civil Wars in England Begun in the Year 1641*, ed. William Dunn Macray, 6 vols. (Oxford, 1888), iii, 55–6.

[19] BL, Egerton MS 2646, fo. 295; BL, Add. MS 62084B, fo. 15r; Wing/H2076B, *His Highnesse Prince Rvperts late beating up the rebels qvarters at Post-Combe & Chinner in Oxfordshire* (Oxford, 1643), 13–15.

[20] BL, Harleian MS 165, fo. 249r.

[21] Charles Thomas-Stanford, *Sussex in the Great Civil War and the Interregnum, 1642–1660* (1910), 52; *Earl de la Warr MS*, HMC, 4th Report, Part I, Report and Appendix (1874), 304

[22] BL, Add. MS 18980, fo. 131; H. G. Tibbut (ed.), *The Letter Books of Sir Samuel Luke, 1644–1645* (Publications of the Bedfordshire Historical Records Society, 42, 1963), 653–5; Richard Symonds, *Richard Symonds's Diary of the Marches of the Royal Army*, ed. Charles Edward Long and Ian Roy (Cambridge, 1997), 181.

[23] Aaron Graham, 'Finance, Localism and Military Representation in the Army of the Earl of Essex (June–December 1642)', *HJ*, 52 (2009), 892; Ian Gentles, 'The Iconography of Revolution: England 1642–1649', in Ian Gentles, John Morrill and Blair Worden (eds.), *Soldiers, Writers and Statesmen of the English Revolution* (Cambridge, 1998), 99, 101.

[24] BL, Harleian MS 6852, fo. 1r; BL, Add. MS 18980, fo. 20.

his parliamentarianism, arguing that he had been misled, and that he was a 'gallant old soldier and an honest man'.[25] Parliamentarian newsbooks had also lavishly praised the exploits of Sergeant-Major-General James Chudleigh, and the sea captain Browne Bushell before their defections.[26] The royalist high command was pragmatic about employing side-changing professionals. P. R. Newman stressed that Grenville, Wagstaffe, and Urry subsequently became royalist generals despite being defectors because their skills were so appreciated.[27] In November 1645, Edward Hyde was advised that the former parliamentarianism of the Falmouth sea-captain, George Bowden, actually recommended him to royalist service, because of his knowledge of parliament's shipping along the southwest coast.[28]

The political damage wrought by these high-profile defections from Essex's army was intensified by doubts over the loyalty of four of the earl's most senior officers. Commissary-General Sir James Ramsey, commander of Essex's left-wing at Edgehill, was cleared of cowardice and disaffection in the Commons on 18 November 1642 for failing to intervene in the engagement at Brentford. Only the day before, the Commons had acquitted Essex's Sergeant-Major-General and President of the Council of War, Sir John Meyrick, from charges of having said the 'Parliament grew too high'.[29] Bulstrode Whitelocke recalled that when Meyrick arrived with orders to withdraw at Turnham Green, some felt a fifth-column had subverted their commanders.[30]

In 1643, suspicion of Essex's commanders spread to the provinces, where Major-General Thomas Ballard was accused of treachery. Ballard was a Nottinghamshire professional appointed to Swedish service in Hamilton's expedition of 1631.[31] He had returned to England by December 1638, and soon became a lieutenant-colonel under Lord Grandison.[32] The Newark memoirist John Twentyman recalled that Ballard 'had served in forreign warrs and such were so renowned that they were thought able to do wonders among us in the beginning of our unhappy Discords.'[33] Clarendon agreed that Ballard was 'a soldier of good reputation and great trust' with Essex.[34] His regiment was originally intended for Ireland, but Essex

[25] *Portland MS*, 85; BL, E244(30), *Mercurius Aulicus*, 6.

[26] *Portland MS*, 50; BL, E112(15), *Some Speciall and Considerable Passages from London, Westminster, Portsmouth, Warwicke, Coventry, and other places*, 9–16 August (1642), 8; BL, TT E100(6), *A Most Miraculous and Happy Victory Obtained by James Chudlegh Serjeant Major Generall of the forces under the E. of Stamford, against Sir Ralph Hopton and his forces*, 29 April (1643), 3.

[27] P. R. Newman, 'The Royalist Party in Arms: The Peerage and Army Command, 1642–1646', in Colin Jones, Malyn Newitt, and Stephen Roberts (eds.), *Politics and People in Revolutionary England: Essays in Honour of Ivan Roots* (Oxford, 1986), 92.

[28] Bodl., MS Clarendon 26, fo. 49.

[29] BL, Add. MS 31116, fos. 9v–10r.

[30] Bulstrode Whitelocke, *The Diary of Bulstrode Whitelocke, 1605–1675*, ed. Ruth Spalding (Records of Social and Economic History, new series, 13, Oxford, 1990), 140.

[31] George William Marshall (ed.), *The Visitations of the County of Nottingham in the Yeares 1569 and 1614* (Publications of the Harleian Society, 4, 1871), 104; John Rushworth, *Historical Collections of Private Passages of State*, 8 vols. (1721), ii, 83.

[32] *CSPD 1638–1639*, 176; BL, Add. MS 28082, fo. 12.

[33] Stuart B. Jennings, *'These Uncertaine Tymes': Newark and the Civilian Experience of the Civil Wars 1640–1660* (Nottingham, 2009), 22.

[34] Clarendon, *History of the Rebellion*, ii, 288n.

retained it for Edgehill where Ballard commanded the reserve infantry.[35] Under pressure from Essex, on 2 December 1642 the Commons ordered a declaration be prepared to clear Ballard, alongside Meyrick, of suspected infidelity to parliament.[36] In January Ballard was commissioned Major-General of Lincolnshire, Nottinghamshire, and Derbyshire.[37] On 28 February 1643 he commanded 6,000 men drawn from across the East Midlands who launched a failed assault against Newark.[38] On 5 April 1643 *Mercurius Aulicus* reported that the Committee for Nottingham had sent two gentlemen to London to procure Ballard's dismissal for his ill-conduct.[39] These were probably the Captain Lummocks and the clergyman whom D'Ewes recorded as having denounced Ballard in the Commons on 30 March.[40] The charges were that day referred to the Committee of Safety.[41] They accused Ballard of treachery in delaying the attack, refusing to commit his cavalry, withholding reinforcements and ammunition, ordering a premature retreat, and abandoning his artillery.[42] Lucy Hutchinson later corroborated these charges, recalling that as Ballard was 'decayed in his family' and 'bred up in the wars abroad', he was reluctant to attack Newark because of his friends there among the enemy.[43] A London serial reported for 7 April that Ballard was to be tried by Essex's council of war at Windsor for 'deceiving the trust reposed in him by the Parliament'.[44] He appears to have been exonerated or pardoned, as in August Speaker Lenthall authorized him to pass into Holland.[45] Alfred Wood claimed that Ballard subsequently changed sides, and he may have been the Lieutenant-Colonel Thomas Ballard listed in a royalist martyrology as killed near Taunton.[46]

Another provincial commander from Essex's army suspected of treachery in 1643 was Colonel Thomas Essex, governor of Bristol, but originally lieutenant-colonel to Lord St John's regiment. His correspondence with Rupert and friendliness to royalists fuelled fears that he intended to betray the city, and promoted infighting within the parliamentarian coalition.[47] Colonel Nathaniel Fiennes utilized these suspicions

---

[35] BL, 669.f.6[31], *A List of the Field Officers chosen and appointed for the Irish Expedition, by the Committee at Guild-hall, London, for the Regiments of 5000 foot and 500 horse*, 11 June (1642); Peter Young, *Edgehill, 1642: The Campaign and the Battle* (Moreton-in-Marsh, 1998), 95, 247.

[36] BL, Add. MS 31116, fos. 9v–10r; *CJ*, ii, 873.

[37] TNA, SP 28/5/39; Ron Slack, *Man at War: John Gell in his Troubled Time* (Nottingham, 1997), 78.

[38] Clive Holmes, *Seventeenth-Century Lincolnshire* (Lincoln, 1980), 161–2.

[39] BL, TT E97(10), *Mercurius Aulicus*, 14th week, 2–9 April (Oxford, 1643), 175.

[40] BL, Harleian MS 164, fo. 347r.

[41] *CJ*, iii, 23.

[42] BL, Sloane MS 1519, fos. 80r–81r.

[43] Lucy Hutchinson, *Memoirs of the Life of Colonel Hutchinson*, ed. N. H. Keeble (1995), 102–3.

[44] BL, E247(21), *A Perfect Diurnall of the Passages in Parliament*, no. 43, 3–10 April (1643), un-paginated.

[45] *CJ*, iii, 203.

[46] Alfred C. Wood, *Nottinghamshire in the Civil War* (Oxford, 1937), 39–42; Wing/R2135, *The Royal Martyrs, or, A List of the Lords, Knights, Officers, and Gentlemen, that were Slain (by the Rebels) in the Late Wars, in Defence of their King and Country as also of those Executed by their High Courts of (In)-Justice, or Law-Martial* (1663), 6.

[47] Patrick McGrath, 'Bristol and the Civil War', in R. C. Richardson (ed.), *The English Civil Wars: Local Aspects* (Stroud, 1997), 101; BL, E97(6), *A Full Declaration of all Particulers concerning the March of the Forces under Collonell Fiennes to Bristolo*, 18 April (1643), 3.

against Thomas Essex to arrest him on 27 February 1643 and impose himself as the city's next governor. Essex was subsequently imprisoned alongside some of his officers in Berkeley castle, although evidence of his treachery remained inconclusive.[48]

These officers undermined the earl of Essex's reputation in parliament because he had invested so much trust in them. As the war lengthened Essex's favouring of continental veterans and foreign professionals began to look suspect.[49] John Aubrey gossiped that Essex twice saved the Croatian Captain Fantom from execution for 'Ravishing' because Fantom 'taught the Cavalry of the army the way of fighting with Horse'.[50] Clarendon considered that Essex's reputation drew many professionals out of the Low Countries into his service, while Sir Samuel Luke continued to pander to Essex's good opinion of Urry even after he had changed sides twice.[51] Ian Roy has suggested that without Essex's favour even fewer professionals would have enlisted for parliament, calculating that around three quarters of those returning from abroad or holding commissions in 1640 enlisted for the king.[52] Yet those professionals who did enlist for parliament were probably just as attracted by the regular, generous pay initially distributed as by Essex's favour and reputation.[53] During 1643, as pay receipts and parliament's military fortunes dwindled, many may have defected owing to anxieties that parliament would prove unwilling or incapable of settling their arrears. Worries over arrears may have inclined some to realign themselves, and one newsbook voiced this concern explicitly in September 1644, observing that many commanders 'are ready to subject themselves to every new Master their Maxime being to side with the strongest.'[54] According to Ludlow, one such was Colonel George Barnes, who supposedly changed sides when the frequency of his pay packets declined.[55]

Civilians feared that army officers sought to prolong the war for their own enrichment. As early as November 1642, Bulstrode Whitelocke was suspicious that it was only the 'old soldiers of fortune' that advised against pursuing the king's army after Turnham Green.[56] On 26 June 1643 Sir Gilbert Gerard, treasurer for parliament's army, complained that Essex's officers would exhaust the commonwealth by desiring 'not an end of the war, but a continuance thereof receiving great & continual pay thereby'. At this D'Ewes reflected: 'Divers spake to this particular, & some spared not to say plainly that it was to be expected from the Lord General'.[57] Essex responded on 28 June, claiming that despite recent defections, 'that

[48] I. G. Philip (ed.), *The Journal of Sir Samuel Luke* (The Oxfordshire Record Society, 29, 1947), i, 8, 22; John Lynch, *For King & Parliament: Bristol in the Civil Wars* (Stroud, 1999), 26–30, 49.

[49] Stoyle, *Soldiers and Strangers*, 102.

[50] John Aubrey, *Aubrey's Brief Lives*, ed. Oliver Lawson Dick (Harmondsworth, 1949), 193–4.

[51] Clarendon, *History of the Rebellion*, ed. Macray, ii, 249; Tibbut (ed.), *The Letter Books of Sir Samuel Luke*, 225.

[52] Roy, 'Royalist Reputations', 90.

[53] Graham, 'Finance, Localism and Military Representation', 892.

[54] BL, E256(12), *A Perfect Diurnall of Some Passages in Parliament*, no. 61, 23–30 September (1644), 486.

[55] Edmund Ludlow, *The Memoirs of Edmund Ludlow, Lieutenant General of the Horse in the Army of the Commonwealth of England, 1625–1672*, ed. C. H. Firth, 2 vols. (Oxford, 1894), i, 62.

[56] Whitelocke, *Diary of Bulstrode Whitelocke*, ed. Spalding, 141.

[57] BL, Harleian MS 164, fos. 233r–v.

never army served with more fidelity than this'. Despite offering his resignation, Essex was persuaded to continue in command.[58] Fears over the motives of his officers deepened division within parliament's coalition. Thomas Juxon considered that Rupert's victory at Newark in March 1644 owed much to the rift between the 'soldatesta' faction and the local commander, the 'honest' Sir John Meldrum.[59] Suspicions of Essex's officers lingered and resurfaced after the disaster at Lostwithiel, of which times Richard Baxter later reflected:

> Though none could deny but the Earl was a Person of great Honour, Valour, and Sincerity; yet did some Accuse the Soldiers under him of being too like the King's Soldiers in Profaneness, lewd and vitious Practices, and rudeness in their Carriage towards the Country; and it was withal urg'd, that the Revolt of Sir *Faithful Fortescue*, Sir *Richard Greenvile*, Col. *Urrey*, and some others, was a satisfying Evidence, that the irreligious sort of Men were not to be much trusted, but might easily by Money be hired to betray them.[60]

Baxter's fears that many parliamentarian officers lacked ideological commitment were reflected in continued anxieties about soldiers of fortune. A later defence of the New Model alluded to this in lauding their swift prosecution of the war: 'They did not loyter... as though, like Souldiers of Fortune, they would make the best of their trade, by lengthening out the Warre.'[61]

The professional officers who remained loyal to parliament came under suspicion because of the defections of their fellows. One example, which required the intervention of the House of Commons to avoid violence, was the case involving Colonel William Carr, a Scots professional under Waller. He claimed that Sir Arthur Hesilrige had defamed him in the House of Commons and cast aspersions upon his loyalty. Called before the bar on 10 April 1644, Carr admitted to having sent Hesilrige a threatening letter, the language of which Lawrence Whitaker considered was 'in the nature of a challenge for words':[62]

> This is not to beg your friendship but that you will be pleased to forbear your inveterate spleen and temperate your tongue which is a virtue in a woman. You know no man in England that [can] justly tax me with any appearance of deserting this good cause within I should think myself happy to sacrifice my body... Sir you said I was never an officer till I came to England with many other unjust calumnies, I will prove by an hundred gentlemen and officers that I commanded a troop of horse sixteen years before you could span a pistol.[63]

---

[58] *Portland MS*, 715.

[59] Lindley and Scott argued that the 'soldatesta' faction were the senior officers connected to Essex, such as Lord Willoughby: Thomas Juxon, *The Journal of Thomas Juxon, 1644–1647*, ed. Keith Lindley and David Scott (Camden Society, 5th series, 13, 1999), 49.

[60] Wing/B1370, Richard Baxter, *Reliquiae Baxterianae, or, Mr Richard Baxters Narrative of the Most Memorable Passages of his Life and Times Faithfully Publish'd from his own Original Manuscript by Matthew Sylvester* (1696), 47.

[61] BL, E372(22), *A Just Apologie for an Abused Armie. Shewing, the unreasonablenesse of that bad opinion that many are of late falne into, concerning the Parliaments army, under the command of his Excellencie Sir Tho: Fairfax* (1647), 10.

[62] BL, Add. MS 31116, fo. 131r.

[63] Bodl., MS Tanner 61, fo. 11.

Judged guilty of breach of privilege and refusing to name his informants, Carr was ordered to be imprisoned in the Compter, although his discharge was procured soon after on 14 May following his penitent submission.[64]

Professionals were viewed as susceptible to side-changing because of their assumed mercenary motives. The term 'soldier of fortune' had connotations of greed and earthly advancement, while stereotypes of the hard-drinking, duelling, and swearing professional officer forged in Germany hardly inspired expectations of constancy.[65] Godly parliamentarians feared that licentious officers offended God and jeopardized military success. In September 1642 Sergeant Nehemiah Wharton complained that his Lieutenant-Colonel Biddeman and his former Sergeant-Major Ballard were 'profane wretches'.[66] Lord Brooke articulated such disapproval in February 1643, having his officers at Warwick elected: 'I had rather have a thousand or two thousand honest Citizens that can onely handle their Armes, whose hearts goe with their hands, than two thousand of mercinary Souldiers, that boast of their forraigne experience.'[67] In January 1644 Cromwell's political attacks on Lord Willoughby of Parham linked the peer's military failures to ungodly officers serving under him, one of whom had supposedly ordered a constable 'to bring him in some wenches for his turne'.[68] Alongside disapproval of professionals' supposed low morals, the realization emerged that continental military experience did not guarantee success, nor even endow competence.[69] Ludlow became dismissive of such men, questioning the ability of the lieutenant commanding Essex's lifeguard in 1642, who was 'an old souldier (a generation of men much cried up at that time)', who nevertheless led them to defeat at Powick Bridge.[70]

II

Mark Stoyle has pointed to a particular sub-group among side-changing professionals: that of foreigners or 'outlanders'. From his list of 105 foreign army officers, he detailed 59 royalists, 40 parliamentarians, and six side-changers, all of whom defected from parliament to the king. The latter included John Dalbier, Francis Dowett, Carlo Fantom, Cosmo Manuche,[71] and John van Gerish. Stoyle claimed that parliamentarians turned against their foreign officers because of these defections, which in themselves were influenced by an escalating xenophobia amongst

---

[64] *CJ*, iii, 455, 492.

[65] Wilson, *Europe's Tragedy*, 845; Roy, 'Royalist Reputations', 90, 104–5.

[66] TNA, SP 16/491/21.

[67] BL, E90(27), *A Worthy Speech made by the Right Honourable the Lord Brooke, at the Election of his Captaines and Commanders at Warwick Castle*, 26 February (London, 1643), 7.

[68] BL, Harleian MS 165, fo. 280r.

[69] Donagan, *War in England*, 53.

[70] Ludlow, *Memoirs*, i, 41.

[71] The Italian Colonel Cosmo Manuche was drawing pay from parliament in February 1643, but defected, and was recaptured at Arundel castle in January 1644. He had escaped and rejoined the royalists by March 1644, before he was again retaken at Tiverton castle in October 1645: Stoyle, *Soldiers and Strangers*, 103, 217; Newman, 261.

English parliamentarians.[72] Aubrey's account of Carlo Fantom, as a serial duellist and rapist, was an extreme example of such attitudes—Fantom supposedly having declared: 'I care not for your Cause: I come to fight for your halfe-crowne, and your handsome woemen: my father was a R. Catholiq; and so was my grandfather. I have fought for the Christians against the Turkes; and for the Turkes against the Christians.'[73] Stoyle has pointed out how the highest-ranking foreigners remaining loyal to parliament were increasingly distrusted, and that consequently few non-English officers were commissioned in the New Model Army. Rumours circulated about the double dealing of Essex's Quarter-Master-General, John Dalbier. Suspicion hung over him and Commissary-General Hans Behr for treacherous acts during the Lostwithiel campaign.[74] During 1646 parliament rebuked Dalbier for negligence at the siege of Donnington castle, while John Harrington noted on 3 April: 'Talk that Dalbier had done most shamefully in accepting a giving up of Donnington castle upon unfavourable conditions. Suspicions that he is false, remember that he was to have brought the German horse into England to make us slaves.'[75]

However, not all foreigners in parliament's service were so derided. Reputations for reliability and constancy were an important means by which even professional soldiers, whose prime motivation may well have been pay, could market themselves. The Frenchman Major Francis Dowett was particularly entrusted by parliament and was granted fulsome praise. His cornet pandered to parliamentarian sensibilities, featuring Magna Carta and the Bible.[76] He was praised for 'fidelity, valour and wisedome' in raids on enemy quarters and at the battle of Lansdown.[77] Such exaltation prompted *Mercurius Aulicus* to seek to undermine him as a coward who fled at Edgehill, and falsely claimed to have captured royalist colours at Newbury.[78] Furthermore, parliamentarian suspicions of their foreign officers are less apparent in northern England. The foreign officers in Scarborough remained conspicuously loyal to parliament when Sir Hugh Cholmley defected with over three quarters of the garrison. Among those who left Cholmley and departed for Beverley were Captains Matthias Froom, Cornelius Vanderhurst, and Hans Ursin.[79] Sir John Hotham praised the two Dutchmen as 'exceeding gallant men', informing Lenthall, 'I have in your name, assured them of your constant respect to all fidelity.' Captain John Legard recounted that Froom and Vanderhurst, backed by their best troopers, suggested they should attempt Cholmley's arrest, while Froom told

[72] Stoyle, *Soldiers and Strangers*, 103–9, 221.

[73] Aubrey, *Aubrey's Brief Lives*, ed. Dick, 193–4.

[74] Stoyle, *Soldiers and Strangers*, 107, 126.

[75] Bodl., MS Clarendon 26, fo. 113; BL, Add. MS 10114, fo. 11r.

[76] Gentles, 'The Iconography of Revolution', 107.

[77] Bodl., MS Tanner 62, fo. 164; BL, E60(12), *A True Relation of the Great and Glorious Victory through Gods Providence, obtained by Sir William Waller, Sir Arthur Haslerig and others of the Parliament forces*, 14 July (1643), 2; Ludlow, *Memoirs*, i, 116–7n.

[78] BL, E75(13), *Mercurius Aulicus*, 43rd week, 22–28 October (Oxford, 1643), 606. *Aulicus* grew complimentary towards Dowett after he joined the royalists in April 1645: Ludlow, *Memoirs*, i, 474–5.

[79] TNA, SP 28/138/3; Jennifer Jones, 'The War in the North: the Northern Parliamentary Army in the English Civil War, 1642–1645' (York University, Canada, PhD thesis, 1991), 252.

Cholmley 'he would be ready to serve him in an honest way, but never used to bee of the Traytours company'.[80] Froom was later mortally wounded in parliament's service at Gainsborough, while Vanderhurst became a captain under Colonel Alured and petitioned to accompany Sir Thomas Fairfax into the New Model in 1645.[81] Ferdinando, Lord Fairfax chose Hans Georg von Strobelln, to captain his lifeguard of horse after Marston Moor, a German whose parliamentarian service went back to October 1642.[82] Lieutenant-Colonel Reinking was another successful German officer, whose 'good and faithfull service' was commended to parliament in 1648 by the Elector Charles Louis.[83]

The German siege engineer, John Rosworm, faithfully defended Manchester for parliament despite attempts to persuade him to change sides. He fashioned himself as the 'faithful stranger', who 'abhors all faithlesse and indirect courses', when petitioning for relief from Fairfax and Cromwell in 1649.[84] Admittedly Rosworm's exaggerations struggled to conform to the customary humility and modesty of such addresses, but his stress on personal constancy, and resistance to treachery and temptation carried weight. He came to England from Ireland in 1642 and was employed in Manchester to oversee the fortifications, despite, he claimed, the earl of Derby having offered him five times more money to join him at Lathom. He spoke out against the treachery and cowardice of Colonel Holland, fortified the Pennine pass at Blackstone Edge, and reinforced Sir Thomas Fairfax prior to the battle of Nantwich in January 1644. Rosworm claimed that Rupert sent the side-changer Captain Peter Heywood to persuade him to deliver up Manchester in June 1644, equipped with arguments of how poorly the town had dealt with him. Rosworm played along in order to discover the royalist plans, but informed six 'chief men of the Town' to keep him from suspicion.[85] His petition to the House of Commons played upon how side-changing had become a high-visibility phenomenon: 'I pray you how many of your own Nation betrayed you, whilest I stood firm?'[86] Stoyle has considered that Rosworm was 'spitting in the wind' against a prevailing parliamentarian prejudice against foreigners, yet if relief by invoking constancy was hopeless, Rosworm would have spared himself much trouble and expense. His petition was considered in June 1649, and in July the Council of State ordered Manchester and Lancashire's deputy-lieutenant to pay his arrears. In October he was voted £30 and recommended to Fairfax for employment. Parliament considered Rosworm's naturalization in May 1651, and on 19 August 1651

[80] BL, TT E95(9), *A True and Exact Relation of all the Proceedings of Sir Hugh Cholmleys Revolt deserting the Parliament, and going to the Queen, with the Regaining of Scarborough Castle, by the Courage and Industry of Capt. Bushel. Sent in Two Letters, the one from Sir Iohn Hotham to M. Speaker, the other, from a worthy Captain to a Member of the Honourable House of Commons. Die Martis 4 Aprilis 1643*, 7 April (1643), 2, 6.

[81] TNA, SP 28/265/171–5; SP 28/267/part iv/66–70; Robert Bell (ed.), *The Fairfax Correspondence: Memoirs of the Civil War*, 2 vols. (1849), i, 214.

[82] TNA, SP 28/266/part iii/105–119; SP 28/252/33; SP 28/261/part iii/320.

[83] BL, Sloane 1519, fo. 185.

[84] John Rosworm, *Good Service Hitherto Ill-Rewarded, Or, An Historicall Relation of Eight Years Services for King and Parliament done in and about Manchester and those Parts* (1649), sig. A2r.

[85] Ibid., 2, 4, 12, 16, 17–19, 23; *CJ*, iii, 617.

[86] Rosworm, *Good Service Hitherto Ill-Rewarded*, 39.

he was appointed Engineer General of all garrisons and forts in England on a salary of 10s per day. He drew a state salary for much of the 1650s, and his appointments included the Isle of Man in 1651, and accompanying General Monck to Scotland in 1654.[87]

The experience of northern officers such Froom, Vanderhurst, von Strobelln, and Rosworm suggests that sustained loyalty to a cause was not as alien to parliament's foreign officers as the extreme example of Carlo Fantom suggests. Even Dalbier, who did not defect until the changed circumstances of 1648, was constant in his loyalty to Essex, and thereafter to his cousin, the earl of Holland, suggesting that Gardiner was inaccurate in calling him 'the Dutchman to whom all causes were alike'.[88] Despite the defections among parliament's foreign professionals, P. R. Newman has reminded us that the 'true mercenary, one who made a living by drifting into other people's wars, shifting allegiance as his pocket dictated, was a rarity in Civil War England.'[89] This would indicate that there were more factors constraining the side-changing of professional officers than has been imagined previously.

In contrast to the high-profile defections from parliament's service in 1643, Newman has stressed the enduring constancy of royalist officers, even in the face of defeat. He argued that side-changing amongst royalists during 1646—where we might expect to find it at its most pronounced—is too easily confused with the submission of vanquished royalists seeking the best terms for their surrender. His study of royalist colonels indicated that of 603 identified, only twenty-four had changed sides by 1646, with the direction reflecting the fortunes of war, first favouring the king in 1643, and thereafter the parliament. Newman's arguments may reflect his admiration of elite royalism, and more research is needed to uncover royalist defectors at lower levels. Donagan has suggested that Newman's small percentage masks greater fluidity amongst their subordinates because colonels 'were less likely candidates for side-changing' than lower-ranking officers and common soldiers.[90]

III

A wide variety of reasons might impact upon an officer's decision to change sides. Hopes of superior rank, employment, and pay might play a positive part, but frequently defections appear as prompted by frustrated ambition, slighted honour, or disenchantment with the cause itself. Such defections could be long planned, and

---

[87] *CJ*, vi, 573; *CJ*, vii, 754; *CSPD 1649–50*, 190, 225, 365; *CSPD 1651*, 342, 450; *CSPD 1651–2*, 38–9, 265; *CSPD 1654*, 12, 82, 88, 108, 134; *CSPD 1655*, 128, 603, 605, 608; *CSPD 1655–1656*, 302, 585, 587.

[88] Robert Ashton, *Counter-Revolution: The Second Civil War and its Origins, 1646–8* (New Haven, 1994), 409; Samuel R. Gardiner, *History of the Great Civil War, 1642–1649*, 4 vols. (1987), iv, 159.

[89] P. R. Newman, *The Old Service: Royalist Regimental Colonels and the Civil War, 1642–46* (Manchester, 1993), 9.

[90] Ibid., 119, 125; Barbara Donagan, 'Varieties of Royalism', in Jason McElligott and David L. Smith (eds.), *Royalists and Royalism during the English Civil Wars* (Cambridge, 2007), 77.

were often facilitated by pre-warned friends and contacts among the enemy. Honour was a common theme among the self-justifications of side-changing officers (as discussed in Chapter 8), and the nature of honour was constantly debated. Sir Keith Thomas has recently argued that contemporaries used it as 'justification for almost any kind of self-aggrandizement', while noble honour was a 'flexible code' that did not exclude duplicity. Essex himself may only have become parliament's general because he felt slighted by the king's failure to grant him due favour.[91] Such personal grievances were among Rowland Laugharne's motives in 1648. During the first civil war he assured royalist gentry surrendering in South Wales that they would not be proceeded against as delinquents. Unable to make good this promise against parliament's fund-raising needs, he deemed that parliament had slighted him, and his defection thereafter was not wholly unexpected.[92] Ludlow considered with evident bitterness that Francis Dowett's defection in April 1645 was motivated by frustrated ambition and resentment of his authority.[93]

Some officers defected in response to harsh treatment from their superiors. In August 1642 one Lieutenant-Colonel Broughton of the Trim garrison was courtmartialled for his 'hard usage'—a severity that had prompted one of his subaltern officers to defect to the Irish rebels.[94] Ian Atherton has shown how Sir Barnabas Scudamore's abrasive style as Governor of Hereford, combined with the bleak royalist prospects of late 1645, did much to alienate his subordinates. These included his deputy-governor, Lieutenant-Colonel Hyde, as well as Major Chaplaine, Captains Alderne, Ballard, and Howorth, and Lieutenant Cooper. Captains Alderne and Howorth resigned their commissions and defected, while Scudamore blamed Ballard, his own captain-lieutenant, for giving intelligence to the enemy. Anticipating parliament's imminent victory, these officers sought to protect their futures at the expense of the cause they had served: 'preferring peace through surrender or treachery to continued resistance'.[95]

Concerted efforts were sometimes made to persuade captured officers to change sides. Sometimes, as with James Chudleigh, they bore fruit. After his capture at Bristol's surrender in July 1643, William Pretty was persuaded to change sides. A royalist colonel by late 1644, he ended the war among Raglan's garrison.[96] Essex feared that after James Wemyss, Waller's artillery commander, was captured at Cropredy, 'no art will be left untried to win him over to the enemy'.[97] Friends and relatives might exert pressure upon captives to defect. After Lostwithiel, Richard

---

[91] Keith Thomas, *The Ends of Life: Roads to Fulfilment in Early Modern England* (Oxford, 2009), 157–60.

[92] Arthur Leonard Leach, *The History of the Civil War (1642–1649) in Pembrokeshire and on its Borders* (1937), 136; *Sutherland MS*, HMC, 5th Report, Appendix (1876), 151.

[93] *CSPD 1644–5*, 362, 394; Ludlow, *Memoirs*, i, 116.

[94] *Calendar of the Manuscripts of the Marquess of Ormonde preserved at Kilkenny Castle*, new series, HMC (1902), i, 50–1.

[95] Ian J. Atherton (ed.), *Sir Barnabas Scudamore's Defence Against the Imputations of Treachery and Negligence in the Loss of the City of Hereford in 1645* (Akron, Ohio, 1992), 10, 23–4, 39–40, 46, 56.

[96] Newman, 305; Eliot Warburton, *Memoirs of Prince Rupert and the Cavaliers*, 3 vols. (1849), iii, 178; *CCCD*, 1693.

[97] *CSPD 1644*, 352.

Bulstrode spent two days persuading his captured cousin Colonel Thomas Bulstrode to change sides, promising him a colonelcy if he did so. He failed, finding Thomas 'seduced by the Zealots of that Army', and 'wilful, stubborn and full of rebellious Principles.'[98] As a means of underlining his own political importance, Ludlow reminisced that during his captivity Lord Hopton and Sir Francis Doddington had done their utmost to convert him. Doddington politely argued for the justice and probable success of the king's cause, while downplaying parliament's military strength. Hopton even suggested Ludlow meet Archbishop Ussher, with the recommendation, 'if he cannot work on you, I know not who can.' Ludlow clearly wanted to show that the royalists thought he was worth 'saving'.[99] Sometimes relatives among the injured party would remonstrate with the defector; in November 1645, Lord Hopton wrote to his cousin, Humphrey Mathews, seeking to repair the disagreement which he suspected had caused his recent defection, blaming General Gerard for 'the impediment between you and the Prince of Wales'.[100]

Personal fear and desperation were no doubt also factors in some defections. Numerous officers changed sides once their conspiracies with the enemy came to light. On 28 February 1644 Sir Samuel Luke noted that Colonel Robert Keys had defected to parliament after his plan to change sides was discovered by the royalists. He may have been seeking to take advantage of parliament's Declaration of Both Kingdoms, but sacrificed his Oxfordshire property by doing so.[101] In April 1646 royalists in Pendennis noted that Major Chapman and Captain Reeves defected after their plot to betray the castle was discovered.[102] The royalist Major William Reeve was court-martialled and condemned to death for surrendering Taunton castle in July 1644, but upon his subsequent escape joined the parliamentarians.[103]

Occasionally, officers in Ireland incorporated side-changing into their military strategies—such as Colonel Richard Bourke, whose cunning pretended conversion to parliament allowed the resupply of his forces at parliament's expense before his reverting to his royalist allegiance. Others defected for pecuniary advantage or self-preservation, such as Major Charles Kavanagh, hired by the government to hunt down their former comrades.[104] In England there are cases of officers seeking to avoid recognition when captured by masquerading as troopers or common soldiers. By so doing they might take advantage of the practice of enlisting among their captors and then await their opportunity to desert and rejoin their former comrades. In

---

[98] Richard Bulstrode, *Memoirs and Reflections upon the Reign and Government of King Charles the I*[st] *and K. Charles the II*[d] (1721), 111.

[99] Ludlow, *Memoirs*, i, 81, 84.

[100] *Portland MS*, 323.

[101] Newman, 214–15; BL, Add. MS 18980, fo. 20; Tibbut (ed.), *The Letter Book of Sir Samuel Luke*, 626.

[102] Bodl., MS Clarendon 27, fo. 123.

[103] David Underdown, *Somerset in the Civil War and Interregnum* (Newton Abbot, 1973), 74; Sir Edward Walker, *Historical Discourses Upon Several Occasions* (1705), 41–2.

[104] Micheál Ó Siochrú, *God's Executioner: Oliver Cromwell and the Conquest of Ireland* (2008), 210, 232.

December 1643 those royalist prisoners taken after an engagement on Sproxton Heath, Leicestershire, were suspected of this by Lord Grey.[105] Likewise, Major John Sanderson considered that many of the royalist prisoners in Newcastle in July 1648 were officers that had masqueraded as common soldiers.[106]

Behind some defections lurked a measure of opportunism in response to changing military fortunes. After York's surrender, in July 1644 the royalist Colonel Robert Brandling of Leathley was accepted into parliament's service by Lord Fairfax and the earls of Leven and Manchester. Before the war he had resided just five miles from the Fairfax seat at Denton, and in 1647 he petitioned the House of Lords that he had been misguided into royalism and that to redeem himself he had raised a parliamentarian cavalry regiment at his own charge. He claimed that the three generals had pledged to him that 'his former Mistake should not be made Use of to his future Prejudice either in Person or Estate', and he was much commended by Sir Thomas Fairfax for his 'Fidelity and Resolution'. The Lords quickly ordered his discharge from sequestration.[107]

Others defected in response to changing political circumstances. After Lieutenant-Colonel Henry O'Brien surrendered Wareham to parliament in August 1644, his brother, Viscount Inchiquin, persuaded him to emulate his recent defection. Inchiquin cajoled his brother that 'our duty to God and our own safeties calls upon us to neglect the king's service in other things, and to preserve the interest against these who are his most dangerous enemies'. Alongside such political arguments, Inchiquin was sure to promise regular pay and settlement of his brother's soldiers' pay arrears.[108]

In some cases, where necessity dictated, parliamentarians received back double side-changers, although this was scarcely followed with favour, trust, and reward. Colonel Thomas Morgan remonstrated that parliament had not properly rewarded Robert Kirle for his role in the capture of royalist-held Monmouth.[109] Acceptance of Sir John Urry's defection to Parliament immediately prior to the second battle of Newbury was facilitated only because he brought with him intelligence of the depleted state of the king's army.[110] In this way, politically astute officers ensured that they possessed something to enhance the value of their defection that would immediately prove their value and sincerity. This might entail bringing other converts, or providing intelligence. The defections of Sir George Goring and Sir Richard Grenville were rendered more acceptable to the king and more odious to his enemies because parliament had paid both men large sums immediately beforehand.[111] Similarly, Major Drake defected to Devon's royalists with his cornet, James

[105] *Portland MS*, 165.
[106] P. R. Hill and J. M. Watkinson (eds.), *Major Sanderson's War: Diary of a Parliamentary Cavalry Officer* (Stroud, 2008), 141.
[107] *LJ*, ix, 497–8, 511.
[108] BL, Add. MS 46928, fo. 40r.
[109] Kirle had defected to the king in March 1643, returning to parliament's service the following year: *Portland MS*, 280; Newman, 219.
[110] Ian Gentles, *The English Revolution and the Wars in the Three Kingdoms, 1638–1652* (Harlow, 2007), 241.
[111] Florene S. Memegalos, *George Goring (1608–1657): Caroline Courtier and Royalist General* (Aldershot, 2007), 122; Amos C. Miller, *Sir Richard Grenville of the Civil War* (1979), 67.

Chudleigh's brother, in June 1644, carrying with him his arrears as well as a large pay advance.[112] Discovering the treachery of others was also an effective way for officers to ingratiate themselves with their paymasters; the House of Commons recommended speedy payment of Colonel Searle's arrears in December 1645 after his discovery of a plot against Plymouth.[113] Prospective side-changers with little to offer but unsavoury reputations risked being scornfully turned away. Joshua Sprigge noted that in October 1645 Fairfax snubbed Colonel John Connock, royalist governor of Tiverton, because of his reputation for cruelty to civilians, bidding him leave parliament's quarters or 'be proceeded against as a Spy.'[114] Officers notorious for side-changing might also obstruct peace propositions, such as in November 1644 when the House of Lords desired Sir Faithfull Fortescue's exclusion from the general pardon in forthcoming treaty negotiations.[115]

IV

The evidence reviewed here suggests that during 1642–6, military fortunes and professional considerations exerted a stronger influence upon side-changing officers than did changing political circumstances. In this sense, these 'turncoat' officers represent a different kind of defector to their counterparts among peers and MPs. Whilst Ian Roy's emphasis on the fickle nature of side-changing professionals is no doubt true in many cases, it remains far from universally applicable. He argued: 'Those who considered themselves soldiers of fortune lacked loyalty to any cause, were able to change sides when convenient during the war, and returned to foreign employment at the end.'[116] He cited Grenville and Urry as examples of this process, but it should be remembered that not all could change sides frequently, or with impunity, nor did they choose to do so. Newman highlighted the subsequent constancy and resolution shown in the royalist cause by the professional officers who defected from parliament in 1643.[117] Furthermore, associations of side-changing with soldiers of fortune remain suspect because they were often politically motivated and retrospective. One Restoration martyrology denounced the regicide Sir Hardress Waller as a turncoat soldier of fortune 'minding Profit more then Conscience' merely to render him and the republican cause all the more despicable.[118] An important facet of a professional officer's military honour—and therefore

---

[112] BL, Add. MS 35297, fos. 34r–v; *CJ*, iii, 562.

[113] *CJ*, iv, 376.

[114] Joshua Sprigge, *Anglia Rediviva: Englands Recovery* (1647), 134; Newman, 78. This may have been the Major Connaught responsible for the cold-blooded massacre of twelve civilians at Barthomley Church in December 1643: James Hall (ed.), *Memorials of the Civil War in Cheshire and the Adjacent Counties by Thomas Malbon of Nantwich Gent and Providence Improved by Edward Burghall, Vicar of Acton, near Nantwich* (Lancashire and Cheshire Record Society, 19, 1889), 94–5.

[115] BL, Add. MS 31116, fo. 171v.

[116] Ian Roy, 'England Turned Germany? The Aftermath of the Civil War in its European Context', *TRHS*, 5th series, 28 (1978), 132–3.

[117] Newman, *The Old Service*, 121, 125.

[118] Wing/W3066, William Winstanley, *The Loyall Martyrology* (1665), 104.

employability—was a reputation for constancy, honest dealing, and reliability. One such was the experienced professional Colonel Thomas Morgan, who, although he remained loyal to parliament throughout the civil wars, was not ashamed to describe himself and his men as soldiers of fortune when claiming pay arrears in 1648. He pointed out that as soldiering was their living they would be 'reduced to an exigency if not speedily taken into consideration.' His soldiers included Yorkshire men who had served under him for more than five years.[119]

---

[119] *House of Lords*, HMC, 7th Report, Part I, Report and Appendix (1879), 68–9.

4

Popular allegiance and side-changing among rank-and-file soldiers

This chapter examines the operation of the 'laws of war' in theory and practice to demonstrate the conditions under which common soldiers changed sides. Parliament and king alike declared that deserting to the enemy was a capital offence, yet both sides refrained from consistently enforcing this ruling, and both benefitted from the practice. Although full quantification is impossible, side-changing was probably even more common among the soldiery than among officers, peers, and MPs. Recent historiography emphasizes the fluctuating nature of popular allegiance.[1] This approach needs to be adopted to analyse popular side-changing because the topic has been neglected by most historians, with the notable exceptions of Charles Carlton and Barbara Donagan. Their valuable contributions have established that many soldiers on both sides were side-changers. High rates of desertion, particularly among those pressed, and the widespread practice of re-enlisting prisoners amongst their captors led to a large turnover of men.[2] Carlton argued that so many served on both sides that it suggests most 'had very little ideological commitment to either side in the first place.' His argument that apathy minimized atrocities has been taken up by Donagan, who has advanced that an 'ameliorating and reconciling element in side-changing' resulted from the prevalence of the practice.[3] Carlton considered that most soldiers were more motivated by plunder than by religion or politics, thinking of themselves 'not as saints in arms but labourers, worthy of whoever happened at the time to have hired them.'[4] His argument is supported by Ian Gentles's suspicion that even in the New Model 'few foot soldiers understood or cared about the reasons for fighting against the king.'[5] Practical issues of food, shelter, and survival have been held to outweigh political commitment, rendering popular allegiance flexible and pragmatic. This was recognized by contemporaries who consistently suspected that soldiers would change

---

[1] Ian Gentles, *The English Revolution and the Wars in the Three Kingdoms, 1638–1652* (Harlow, 2007), 140; Michael Braddick, *God's Fury, England's Fire: A New History of the English Civil Wars* (2008), 233, 261.

[2] Barbara Donagan, 'Did Ministers Matter? War and Religion in England, 1642–1649', *JBS*, 33 (1994), 155; Barbara Donagan, *War in England 1642–1649* (Oxford, 2008), 8.

[3] Charles Carlton, *Going to the Wars: The Experience of the British Civil Wars, 1638–1651* (1992), 255; Donagan, *War in England*, 277.

[4] Carlton, *Going to the Wars*, 255, 264.

[5] Ian Gentles, *The New Model Army in England, Ireland and Scotland, 1645–1653* (Oxford, 1992), 33.

sides for better pay, billets, or even fresh shirts and footwear.[6] Most rank-and-file defections were therefore unlikely to be heartfelt political conversions. Instead they were led into defecting by their officers, or were required to do so when captured by the enemy.

Yet despite these being frequent experiences, they were not universal. Demonstrating soldiers' inner motives remains problematic in the absence of explicit evidence. While pay was no doubt an incentive, historians should be careful about over-emphasizing mercenary motives, as common soldiers' wages offered only a 'modest and precarious maintenance'.[7] Likewise, it is dangerous to assume that all were involuntarily forced, pressed, or led into changing sides. A minority, especially among the cavalry, actively chose to defect. Some displayed conspicuous loyalty in the face of treacherous officers. Although the masses lacked aristocratic notions of honour, Sir Keith Thomas reminds us that no social group was 'utterly shameless or for whom considerations of reputation were totally irrelevant.'[8] Accepting that the rank and file lacked political motivation panders to stereotypes of common people espoused by contemporary elites.[9] It also adheres to an unfashionably narrow conception of politics which clashes with the recent historiography that stresses the emergence of a popular political culture before 1640 and the increased agency of sub-gentry groups.[10] Historians such as Andy Wood and Edward Vallance have pointed to a 'partially submerged world of popular politics' from Tudor to late seventeenth-century England. Both support James C. Scott's thesis that locates a 'hidden transcript' of defiance within the strategic deference and submission employed by plebeian speech and gesture towards their elite masters.[11] While some tenants followed their gentry to war, others made their own decisions, and in some cases, opposed them. John Plowman, the servant of Thomas Barker of Chiswick, was liberated when his master, a royalist trooper, was slain at Lansdown. Having buried his master, he later maintained that he returned home to take up arms for parliament.[12] By 1642, the Protestation and petitioning campaigns did much to mobilize popular opinion. Gentry expectations of deference

---

[6] I. G. Philip (ed.), *The Journal of Sir Samuel Luke* (The Oxfordshire Record Society, 29, 1947), i, 44, 48.

[7] Ann Hughes, *Politics, Society and Civil War in Warwickshire, 1620–1660* (Cambridge, 1987), 150–1.

[8] Sir Keith Thomas, *The Ends of Life: Roads to Fulfilment in Early Modern England* (Oxford, 2009), 173.

[9] For examples of such denunciations see David Underdown, 'The Problem of Popular Allegiance in the English Civil War', *TRHS*, 5th series, 31 (1981), 69. John Walter has reminded us that elites considered popular allegiance to be irrational, fickle and bestial: John Walter, 'Politicising the Popular? The "Tradition of Riot" and Popular Political Culture in the English Revolution', in Nicholas Tyacke (ed.), *The English Revolution c.1590–1720: Politics, Religion and Communities* (Manchester, 2007), 96.

[10] John Walter, 'The English People and the English Revolution Revisited', *History Workshop Journal*, 61 (2006), 171, 178.

[11] Andy Wood, ' "A Lyttull Word Ys Tresson": Loyalty, Denunciation, and Popular Politics in Tudor England', *JBS*, 48 (2009), 838–9; Edward Vallance, 'The Captivity of James II: Gestures of Loyalty and Disloyalty in Seventeenth-Century England', *JBS*, 48 (2009), 849; James C. Scott, *Domination and the Arts of Resistance: Hidden Transcripts* (1990).

[12] I am grateful to Adrian Ailes for this reference: TNA, SP 19/123/27.

no longer automatically commanded armed obedience. Several side-changing officers discovered this to their cost.

I

Historians should be wary of contemporary explanations of rank-and-file side-changing. This is because elite stereotypes of common soldiers in England during the 1640s were highly negative, as Donagan has summarized: 'They were characterized as drunkards and predators who ran away, changed sides, and disobeyed orders.'[13] One captain published precise rules for his troop to follow, which required his men to inform him of any 'that means to fall off from the service.'[14]

Essex's council of war were in 'feare of a generall defection' when parliament proved dilatory in honouring its promise to pay Essex's soldiers twelve shillings each for sparing Reading from plunder.[15] Colonel John Venn considered his recruits 'the Scum' of the counties where they were pressed: 'Men taken out of Prison, Tinkers, Pedlars, and Vagrants that have no Dwelling, and such of whom no Account can be given.'[16] Officers withheld praise from their soldiers for victories yet quickly blamed them for defeats. Major Hercules Langrishe remarked to Colonel Nathaniel Fiennes in April 1643 that the recent victory over Hopton's Cornish royalists owed little to the 'valour of our common soldiers, who run away for the most part as well as Sir Ralph and his'.[17] Sir Samuel Luke explained parliament's defeat at Pontefract in March 1645 as the work of renegade troopers giving intelligence to the enemy.[18] Likewise, Lord Byron attributed Liverpool's fall to 'the treachery of the common soldiers', many of whom defected to parliament. He added 'Some few of them are since fallen into my hands, upon whom I have done justice'.[19] The need for harsh discipline to curb unruly soldiers partly arose from gentry fears, heightened by wartime turmoil, that armed commoners were all social subversives. In September 1642 Thomas Gardiner wrote to Sir Ralph Verney, elucidating the difference between the allegiance of discerning gentlemen capable of reasoned political choices and seditious commoners with baser motivations:

> I am persuaded that conscience hath much to do on both sides which, tho' it may chance to be erroneous, yet ought to be respected. But these considerations enter not into vulgar hearts. The gentry (say they) have been our masters a long time, and now

[13] Barbara Donagan, 'Codes and Conduct in the English Civil War', *P&P*, 118 (1988), 71.
[14] BL, E113(8), *Votes Concerning the Post-master. Also Rules of Direction for the Government of Souldiers, made by Captain Dowet, and Delivered to his Troopers*, 22 August (1642), 6.
[15] Wing/M1410, Thomas May, *The History of the Parliament of England, which began November the third, MDCXL* (1647), Book III, 39.
[16] *LJ*, viii. 268.
[17] Bodl., MS Clarendon 22, fos. 35–6.
[18] H. G. Tibbut (ed.), *The Letter Books of Sir Samuel Luke, 1644–45* (Publications of the Bedfordshire Historical Record Society, 42, 1963), 205–6.
[19] Carlton, *Going to the Wars*, 171.

we chance to master them; and now they know their strength, it shall go hard but they will use it.[20]

The gentry feared that the commons, once enlisted as soldiers, might do anything to better their condition. In August1642 Sir John Potts warned Sir Simonds D'Ewes that 'whensoever necessity shall enforce us to make use of the multitude, I do not promise myself safety.'[21] By August 1649, wild stories circulated that the poor would even join 'an army of Turks or heathens come to ease them of their burdens', and the Rump grew anxious that hunger might reincline many towards a royalist or rebellious politics.[22]

For these reasons, both sides determined that once the commons were armed they would be harshly disciplined. The sentence for most offences committed by soldiers under martial law was death. The *Lawes and Ordinances of Warre* issued by the earl of Essex in September 1642 stipulated death for soldiers who straggled from or deserted their company. Those who gave intelligence to the enemy were to be 'punished as Traitors and Rebels'. Speaking with the enemy's drum, trumpet, or messenger was 'upon pain of punishment at discretion'.[23] One royalist soldiers' catechism declared that the normal protections due to surrendering soldiers could be laid aside if the captives required interrogation, of if they had committed a 'breach of faith', by which it meant they had previously changed sides.[24] The laws of war were enforced by courts martial appointed by commanding generals from among their own officers.

Despite these severe laws of war and their selective application between 1642 and 1646, executions of large numbers of side-changing soldiers were rare in England until 1648. The first instance was at Reading on 27 April 1643, when the earl of Essex captured numerous defectors in the royalist garrison. These men had taken advantage of a royal proclamation of 18 April which promised Essex's soldiers pardon and employment if they defected. The king was distraught that the third article for surrender stipulated that these men would be delivered to Essex. The court martial duly hanged them, and Clarendon recalled 'I have not known the King more afflicted than he was with that clause, which he called no less than giving up those poor men, who, out of their conscience of their rebellion, had betaken themselves to his protection, to be massacred and murdered by the rebels whom they had deserted.' The royalist governor, Colonel Richard Feilding, claimed he strove to get the third article changed but that the enemy was implacable. Once the royalist forces returned to Oxford, Feilding's soldiers demanded justice against him for conducting a treacherous liaison with Essex, but Feilding countered that the king had approved the articles. The conflicting claims made about these side-changers

[20] *Verney MS*, HMC, 7th Report, Part I, Report and Appendix (1879), 441.
[21] BL, Harleian MS 386, fo. 233.
[22] Steve Hindle, 'Dearth and the English Revolution: The Harvest Crisis of 1647–50', *Economic History Review*, 61 (2008), 67.
[23] BL, E116(34), *Lawes and Ordinances of Warre, established for the Better Conduct of the Army by His Excellency the Earle of Essex Lord Generall of the forces raised by the Authority of the Parliament, for the Defence of the King and Kingdom*, 12 September (1642), sig. A3v, C1r.
[24] Donagan, 'Codes and Conduct', 77.

reflected the royalists' need to apportion blame for their executions. The king court-martialled Feilding, declaring the terms were 'most prejudicial to his service and derogatory to his honour'.[25] Feilding was condemned to death, although not executed, while the king published a proclamation on 12 May distancing himself from the abandonment of the hanged defectors and promising a fresh amnesty for defectors during the next six days, 'that their former Errors shall never be remembred in the least degree to their disadvantage.'[26] The king himself demonstrates how sharply attitudes towards side-changers fluctuated and were shaped by particular contexts. Charles' public pronouncements and concern that his honour had been impugned by the executions at Reading were somewhat removed from his correcting of Sir Edward Walker's thoughts on Sir John Urry, with the remark that 'a Turncoat Souldier can hardly prove an honest Man.'[27]

Smaller numbers of defectors were hanged by both sides for various practical reasons throughout the first civil war. Fairfax was concerned to establish discipline in the fledgling New Model Army in May 1645 with the exemplary hanging of a 'renegado', 'upon a Tree, at *Wallop*, in the way of the Armies march, in *terrorem*.[28] Sir Francis Mackworth, royalist garrison commander in Halifax, hanged three defectors retaken at Mixenden on 4 January 1644 for having joined the anti-royalist insurgency at Heptonstall.[29] A hierarchy of execution was established at Nantwich, where four renegade soldiers were hanged on 26 September 1644, while an Irish lieutenant who defected to the royalists was later shot.[30] Rupert hanged twelve recaptured defectors from one tree in 1645 as an exemplary deterrent.[31] Newsbooks such as *Mercurius Aulicus* promoted loyalty by nurturing a loathing of defectors among the soldiery, claiming that recaptured turncoats were hanged to appease the fury of their former comrades.[32]

Executions of recaptured defectors might contravene articles of surrender. Edmund Ludlow was angered when the royalists executed two of his soldiers after Wardour castle's surrender in March 1644, despite his garrison being promised 'quarter without distinction':

> Capt. Leicester, to whom I principally applied my self because he pretended to most experience in things of this nature, told me, that I only conditioned for my souldiers, and that these who ran from them were not mine, but theirs: I replied, that they were

[25] Edward Hyde, earl of Clarendon (ed.), *History of the Rebellion and Civil Wars in England begun in the year 1641 by Edward, earl of Clarendon*, ed. William Dunn Macray, 6 vols. (Oxford, 1888), iii, 24–31.

[26] BL, TT 669 f.7[13], *His Majesties Proclamation and Declaration Concerning a Clause in One of the Late Articles at Reading*, 12 May (Oxford, 1643).

[27] Donagan, *War in England*, 276.

[28] Wing/S5070, Joshua Sprigge, *Anglia Rediviva; Englands Recovery* (1647), 15.

[29] T. W. Hanson, 'Three Civil War Notes', *Transactions of the Halifax Antiquarian Society* (1916), 257–8.

[30] James Hall (ed.), *Memorials of the Civil War in Cheshire and the Adjacent Counties by Thomas Malbon of Nantwich, Gent., and Providence Improved by Edward Burghall, Vicar of Acton, near Nantwich* (Lancashire and Cheshire Record Society, 19, 1889), 149, 158.

[31] Donagan, *War in England*, 276.

[32] BL, E40(6), *Mercurius Aulicus*, 11th week, 9–16 March (Oxford, 1644), 881.

never theirs, tho they had forced them to be with them, having pressed them into their service, which they had no power to do.[33]

This example again underlines how conflicting claims could be made about side-changers, and Ludlow saw their execution as a slight to his honour. He protested that 'if I had expected such usage, I would have died before I would have delivered the castle'. He noted with satisfaction that Captain Bishop withdrew from the council that authorized these executions, and subsequently laid down his arms.[34]

The hanging of recaptured defectors became contested when the identity of victims was questioned and atrocity stories developed. Sir Francis Doddington developed an unsavoury reputation after capturing parliament's garrison at Woodhouse, Wiltshire, on 19 July 1644. Determined upon exemplary justice, he ordered a dozen hanged. To excuse this, he later claimed they were renegades and deserters from the royalist army, and that he was retaliating for the execution of royalists at Wareham.[35] Yet Ludlow later claimed that these men were clothiers, and that Doddington intended more executions had not Hopton ordered 'a stop to their butcheries.'[36] Another royalist commander with a penchant for hangings was Sir Richard Grenville. When his forces stormed Saltash, Joseph Jane related that Grenville hanged 'many in cold blood against whom changing sides could not be objected'.[37] Jane's need to make this distinction suggests that hanging recaptured side-changers was normally considered an acceptable practice.

Despite these executions, as the war lengthened both sides wooed converts from their enemy's soldiery. A royal proclamation of 28 November 1642 declared that deserters would be put to death.[38] However, the prevalence of desertion soon rendered this unenforceable. To preserve royal authority, on 24 March 1644 the king offered mercy to all who deserted out of 'ignorance' and who were now penitent, provided they returned to their companies.[39] On 19 April 1645 the king again invited rebellious subjects to reconsider, arguing that the removal from Fairfax's commission of the clause protecting the king's person indicated that the rebels sought to destroy monarchy itself. This proclamation extended pardon to parliamentarian soldiers, providing they submitted by 31 May.[40] Carlton interpreted this

---

[33] Edmund Ludlow, *The Memoirs of Edmund Ludlow, Lieutenant-General of the Horse in the Army of the Commonwealth of England, 1625–1672*, ed. C. H. Firth, 2 vols. (Oxford, 1894), i, 79.

[34] Ibid., 80.

[35] John Wroughton, *An Unhappy Civil War: The Experiences of Ordinary People in Gloucestershire, Somerset and Wiltshire, 1642–1646* (Bath, 1999), 56; David Underdown, *Somerset in the Civil War and Interregnum* (Newton Abbot, 1973), 75.

[36] Ludlow, *The Memoirs of Edmund Ludlow*, i, 95; Sir Edward Walker, *Historical Discourses Upon Several Occasions* (1705), 40.

[37] Bodl., MS Clarendon 26, fo. 165. Symonds wrote that Grenville proposed to hang 300 while Luke recorded 100 executions: Richard Symonds, *Richard Symonds's Diary of the Marches of the Royal Army*, ed. Charles Edward Long and Ian Roy (Cambridge, 1997), 127; Tibbut (ed.), *Letter Books of Sir Samuel Luke*, 44–5; Amos C. Miller, 'Joseph Jane's Account of Cornwall during the Civil War', in Stanley D. M. Carpenter (ed.), *The English Civil War* (Aldershot, 2007), 468.

[38] J. F. Larkin (ed.), *Stuart Royal Proclamations. Volume II. Royal Proclamations of King Charles I, 1625–1646* (Oxford, 1983), 824.

[39] Ibid., 1018–19.

[40] Ibid., 1063–5.

as evidence of royalist recruitment problems, especially among the infantry. Yet it also suggests that the king and his advisers perceived that potential defectors were numerous, and that in response to changing military and political circumstances a fruitful appeal to them might be made.[41] It reflected the growing reality that allegiance was to be negotiated, not commanded. A way of winning back converts without compromising royal authority was to represent side-changers as deceived or compelled against their will into the rebel camp. One such declaration by the marquis of Montrose attempted to encourage conversions by offering free pardon and protection to those 'innocent and well meaning people' among the enemy 'who His Majesty from his wonted goodness and piety is rather willing to reclaim than punish.'[42]

Both sides used newsbooks to stimulate defections by promising better conditions in their service. In July 1642 one pamphlet claimed that the king offered pardon and a month's pay for any soldier or officer in Hull's garrison to join him.[43] On 17 April 1643 *Aulicus* boasted 'many of the Red coates (which is the name of the best Regiment of all the Rebels) tendered their service to His Majestie, and by His Majestie were not onely pardoned for their former fault, but listed and disposed of into severall Companies.'[44] The parliamentarian *Weekly Account* appealed to soldiers' instincts of self-preservation. In January 1644 it reported that hundreds of Hopton's pressed recruits had defected to parliament's garrisons at Poole and Lyme Regis, preferring to winter in towns, rather than enduring hardships in the field for the king. Threat of execution upon recapture was held up as an inspiration for future constancy: 'they are like to do good service, and run away no more, for they are sure (if ever they are taken) to suffer for it.'[45] In 1648 a declaration from the Prince of Wales circulated among Langdale's army pandered to material considerations, promising pardon, indemnity, and full pay arrears to parliamentarian soldiers that joined them.[46] The following year, whilst he was serving as a royalist admiral, Rupert offered indemnity and pardon to all parliamentarian soldiers and mariners who would change sides and join him.[47]

II

The most frequent situation in which large numbers of infantry changed sides was when they were captured after a battle or siege. Neither side had facilities to hold many prisoners long-term, so both frequently allowed captives to return home, having first sworn them not to take up arms again. Alternatively, they offered them

---

[41] Carlton, *Going to the Wars*, 197.
[42] Beinecke Rare Book and Manuscript Library, Osborn Files, 10,467.
[43] BL, E154(34), *Terrible and True Newes from Beverley and the City of Yorke*, 7 July (1642), 5.
[44] BL, E100(18), *Mercurius Aulicus*, 16th week, 16–22 April (Oxford, 1643), 197.
[45] BL, E81(14), *The Weekly Account*, no. 19, 3–10 January (1644), 3.
[46] BL, E454(8), *The Declaration of his Highnesse the Prince of Wales, to Sir Marmaduke Langdale, Lieutenant Gen. of His Majesties forces in the North of England, under His Highnesse* (1648), 4–5.
[47] Donagan, *War in England*, 276.

the chance to enlist with their captors. For many, this was safer and more practical. Partially enforced *en masse* defections of this nature became an important way to acquire soldiers, and such converts were usually considered less objectionable by those they had forsaken than voluntary, premeditated side-changers.[48] Based on reports of 645 engagements, Charles Carlton estimated that 32,823 parliamentarians and 83,467 royalists were taken prisoner in England and Wales during the three civil wars.'[49] Such numbers indicate that thousands potentially changed sides.

This type of side-changing began soon after Edgehill when the king's army captured Banbury on 26 October 1642, where most of the earl of Peterborough's regiment, 600-strong, re-enlisted as royalists.[50] Another large-scale defection occurred after Rupert's capture of Cirencester on 2 February 1643 where 1,000 garrison soldiers were captured. They were marched without sufficient food or clothing through appalling weather to Oxford. Once there, many agreed to defect to escape further depredations. Those who refused were sentenced to hard labour on Oxford's fortifications. This experience in itself, given time, persuaded many to enlist.[51] Early on there was some reluctance to trust such men, and some in Oxford feared the Cirencester recruits conspired to betray the city. Rupert ordered the dispersal of 140 Cirencestrians into the Reading garrison, splitting them into five per company, and in return drawing five of the best men from each to serve him in the field. The governor, Sir Arthur Aston, was unimpressed, and supposedly 'sent to the King that hee needed not to have sent him more enymies for hee had enowe already.'[52] Other more skilled captives might prove useful to garrison commanders. Experienced seamen were valuable commodities, and Sir John Digby offered captured parliamentarian mariners who were prepared to defect as currency in return for arms and supplies from his fellow royalist Edward Seymour, governor of Dartmouth.[53]

Another major instance was when 1,500 Welsh royalist prisoners taken at Highnam on 25 March 1643 were offered their freedom if they changed sides.[54] Several later served in parliament's Gloucester garrison.[55] In May 1643, after the royalists captured Rotherham, many of the garrison willingly defected, and according to the duchess of Newcastle thereafter proved 'loyal subjects and good soldiers'. Yet Lord Fairfax objected that the royalists broke the terms of surrender to force his

[48] Ibid., 275.

[49] Carlton, *Going to the Wars*, 203–4.

[50] Folger Shakespeare Library, V.a.216, 'A Brief Relation of the Life and Memoirs of John Lord Belasyse written and collected by his Secretary Joshua Moone', fo. 9r; Aaron Graham, 'The Earl of Essex and Parliament's Army at the Battle of Edgehill: A Reassessment', *War in History*, 17 (2010), 287.

[51] Wroughton, *An Unhappy Civil War*, 64–5; Philip (ed.), *The Journal of Sir Samuel Luke*, ii, 123.

[52] Philip (ed.), *The Journal of Sir Samuel Luke*, i, 9, 12, 42.

[53] DRO, 1392M/L 1644/22.

[54] J. R. S. Whiting, *Gloucester Besieged: the Story of a Roundhead City* (2nd edn, Gloucester, 1984), 7; Wroughton, *An Unhappy Civil War*, 54.

[55] Jeremy Knight, *Civil War and Restoration in Monmouthshire* (Logaston, 2005), 69.

common soldiers to change sides.[56] About 1,000 of Bristol's parliamentarian garrison changed sides, an informant of Sir Samuel Luke alleging that they were forced to do so because royalist soldiers 'wounded and beate them that would not.'[57] According to the royalists, their converts remained in the castle 'very willingly', but the vanquished governor, Nathaniel Fiennes objected that after the surrender the royalists had 'by threats and incitements' been 'drawing off our soldiers to serve them'. Yet Fiennes's own officers testified that defections were so numerous because Fiennes had badly mishandled the surrender, suggesting an element of voluntariness.[58] As such defections continued into 1644, both sides administered oaths and covenants to men recruited in this way. In parliament's case this involved tendering the Solemn League and Covenant to royalist soldiers at their surrender. Among the first were 500 royalist prisoners taken at Alton in December 1643, who took the Covenant and thereafter served under Sir William Waller.[59] The following month, these recruits were praised in a parliamentarian tract for their 'very good service' in the capture of Arundel, suggesting that by feats of valour turncoat soldiers could earn trust.[60]

After a negotiated surrender on an English battlefield, the combatants' shared language enabled fraternization between the soldiery. Donagan has highlighted how this facilitated side-changing and generated anxieties amongst defeated commanders that their soldiers might defect. Defeat often led to soldiers becoming disenchanted with their cause and leaders, leaving them ripe for changing sides if approached by a sensitive enemy.[61] Governors drafting surrender articles sought to prevent this occurring; article seven of the surrender of Chester insisted that 'no Souldie[r] in his marche shalbe Inveigled or entyced from his Colle[rs] [colours] or Comand wth any p'myse or inducem[t] whatsoeu'r.'[62] The same anxiety was reflected in Essex's revised articles of war of 1643, reissued to the New Model in 1645, which attempted to restrict communication with the enemy to senior officers. In September 1644 Philip Skippon attempted to have a proviso against fraternization included in the surrender articles at Lostwithiel.[63] Instead, the royalist terms imposed 'voluntary' re-enlistment: 'It is agreed that there be no inviting of any Souldiers, but such as will voluntarily come to His Majesty's Service shall not be

---

[56] Margaret Cavendish, duchess of Newcastle, *The Life of William Cavendish, Duke of Newcastle, To which is added the true relation of my birth, breeding and life by Margaret, Duchess of Newcastle*, ed. C. H. Firth (1906), 21; John Rushworth, *Historical Collections of Private Passages of State*, 8 vols. (1721), v, 268. Thomas Shircliffe of Whitby later claimed that he was captured at Rotherham and obtained his freedom by accepting a commission from Newcastle as captain of foot: *CCCD*, 1336.

[57] John Lynch, *For King & Parliament: Bristol in the Civil Wars* (Stroud, 1999), 105; Philip (ed.), *The Journal of Sir Samuel Luke*, ii, 30.

[58] S. Seyer, *Memoirs Historical and Topographical of Bristol and its Neighbourhood, from the earliest period down to the present time*, 2 vols. (Bristol, 1823), ii, 411–13.

[59] Bulstrode Whitelock, *Memorials of English Affairs from the Beginning of the Reign of Charles I to the Happy Restoration of King Charles II*, 4 vols. (Oxford, 1853), i, 230.

[60] Wing/B3751A, *A Wicked Plot against the Person of Sir William Waller*, 11 January (1644), sig. A2v.

[61] Carlton, *Going to the Wars*, 233.

[62] Hall (ed.), *Memorials of the Civil War in Cheshire*, 198.

[63] Donagan, *War in England*, 73, 148.

hindered.'[64] *Aulicus* claimed that several thousand did so, but Sir Edward Walker later agreed with parliamentarian newsbooks that only one hundred defected by the day following the treaty. Distinctions between voluntary and compelled defection were blurred, while royalist 'persuasion' could be a frightening affair. One tract lamented how Skippon's infantry were stripped as they passed through royalist ranks, and threatened with what would befall them if they did not 'desert the Parliament, and turn to the King'.[65] In Ireland, where racial, cultural, and religious hostilities hampered the absorption of defeated soldiers into the victors' ranks, massacres might ensue when prisoners proved too many to feed, guard, or ransom. Thousands of Thomas Preston's confederate army at Dungan's Hill were killed in cold blood—especially the English and the side-changers among them.[66]

The next most frequent situation in which soldiers defected was during sieges, when sanctuary among the enemy was close at hand. Garrison soldiers might wish to avoid the privations of a long siege or the danger of being slain during an assault. For these reasons, treachery within the walls was the perennial fear of town and castle governors. Royalist commanders at Pendennis castle noted in April 1646 that thirty of the garrison had defected, the 'soldiers preferring hardness abroad before the wants and closeness of a siege'.[67] Further large groups followed them, and were joined by garrison officers.[68] Dozens of Winchester castle's garrison defected to Cromwell's besiegers, nocturnally traversing the walls, fearing their commander, Viscount Ogle, had grown careless with their lives.[69] During an unsuccessful siege, besieging soldiers might defect to the garrison. A parliamentarian tract reporting their defence of Hull in October 1643 claimed that when 140 royalists were captured some of them 'were arrayed men, who have since taken up armes with us.'[70] At Colchester in 1648 many of the garrison defected out of hunger. On 20 August Fairfax deliberately enticed royalist soldiers to abandon their officers by offering more lenient terms to the rank and file—a practice which the royalist commanders predictably condemned as dishonourable.[71] His negotiation was designed to incite mutiny if the royalist commanders prolonged resistance, while the garrison's former parliamentarians were repeatedly exempted from the terms.[72]

[64] BL, Add. MS 78205, fo. 64; Walker, *Historical Discourses*, 79.

[65] Walker, *Historical Discourses*, 80; BL, E10(27), *A True Relation of the Sad Passages, Between the Two Armies in the West: Shewing the Perfidious Breach of Articles, by the Kings Partie: Their Horrid Crueltie, Offered to the Lord Generals Souldiers in their March from Foy*, 2 October (1644), 8; Gentles, *The English Revolution and the Wars in the Three Kingdoms*, 228.

[66] John Morrill, 'The Drogheda Massacre in Cromwellian Context', in David Edwards, Pádraig Lenihan and Clodagh Tait (eds.), *Age of Atrocity: Violence and Political Conflict in Early Modern Ireland* (Dublin, 2007), 264n; Micheàl Ó Siochrú, *God's Executioner: Oliver Cromwell and the Conquest of Ireland* (2008), 49.

[67] Bodl., MS Clarendon 27, fo. 123.

[68] BL, Add. MS 35297, fo. 119v.

[69] BL, Add. MS 27402, fo. 97v.

[70] BL, E51(11), *Hull's Managing of the Kingdom's Cause* (1644), 24.

[71] Barbara Donagan, 'The Web of Honour: Soldiers, Christians, and Gentlemen in the English Civil War', *HJ*, 44 (2001), 376.

[72] Donagan, *War in England*, 327, 336, 354, 356.

Changing sides during battlefield engagements was more risky, rare, and unpredictable. The most notorious example was the defection of Sir Faithful Fortescue's troop during Edgehill. Fortescue was so confident that his troopers shared his intentions that at the outset of the battle he sent his quartermaster, John van der Gerish, to parley with Rupert. Gerish removed his orange scarf which identified him as part of Essex's horse, and told Rupert that the whole troop would defect upon the signal of Fortescue discharging his pistol into the ground. Rupert accepted but lacked time to notify all his troops of the arrangement. During a lull in firing, Fortescue's troop advanced out of the parliamentarian line and, upon the prearranged signal, turned about and attacked their former comrades. Several did not remove their scarves, and about twenty were cut down by the royalists in the confusion of the mêlée. A battlefield defection of this scale was rare in England, and Clarendon deemed it instrumental in undermining the parliamentarian cavalry's morale, as they were quickly broken by Rupert's charge. Its psychological impact was keenly felt years later in Baxter's explanation of the rout of parliament's cavalry at Edgehill.[73]

Troopers were more capable than foot soldiers of defecting successfully, as they could move swiftly and over greater distances with less chance of recapture. Cavalry were frequently employed to surprise enemy quarters, often before daybreak. This afforded them plentiful opportunity to desert their units under cover of darkness. When half his troop defected, Ludlow explained that they did so 'under pretence of beating up a quarter of the enemy'.[74] Troopers were harder to billet than foot soldiers, because the required horse-feed necessitated their dispersal over a wide area. This made defining desertion more difficult, and led to much frustration and distrust amongst cavalry officers. Captain Thomas Evans wrote to Sir Samuel Luke from Salisbury on 15 October 1644:

> In the last letter I received from you I understand the soldiers that ran away from their colours are sick. They were well enough when they left their colours… In all service that I have served in, once mustered in a troop and received pay, [troopers] dare not go away without leave of their commanders though their horses were their own… Henry Garlington and Mr Jones are both gone. I mean the Jones you sent down, who was once a cornet in the King's army-he is a great plunderer and as great a coward. Command them all to come to their colours and then I shall take a course with them that shall please you.[75]

Parties of cavalry often voluntarily deserted, looking for preferential conditions in another force, which might not necessarily entail changing sides. John Cruso's popular military handbook actually recommended that commanders send 'defector' troopers into enemy ranks, 'feigning some discontent for want of pay or otherwise',

---

[73] BL, Add. MS 62084B, fo. 10r; Hyde, *History of the Rebellion*, ii, 360, 363; Christopher L. Scott, Alan Turton and Eric Gruber von Arni, *Edgehill: The Battle Reinterpreted* (Barnsley, 2004), 87, 91, 96; Richard Baxter, *Reliquiae Baxterianae, or, Mr. Richard Baxters Narrative of the Most Memorable Passages of his Life and Times Faithfully Publish'd from his Own Original Manuscript by Matthew Sylvester* (1696), 43.

[74] Ludlow, *Memoirs*, i, 116.

[75] Tibbut (ed.), *Letter Books of Sir Samuel Luke*, 355.

in order to procure them intelligence.[76] Some troopers sought reward for giving intelligence, such as Waller's men, who defected and were briefly entertained by the royalists before deserting them also on 11 October 1644.[77]

III

The widening of the war during 1644 to include a large presence of Scots and Irish soldiers in England further complicated the issue of side-changing, and lent the practice a 'three kingdoms' dimension. Most conspicuously, the English regiments brought back from Ireland after Charles I's cessation of hostilities with the Irish were a source of mass defections from royalist armies. Once withdrawn into England, they became more exposed to parliamentarian propaganda that undermined Charles I's commitment to the Protestant cause in Ireland. Those from settler families distrusted the king's relations with the confederates and grew unsettled at the number of Catholic officers in English royalist armies, especially in the north.[78] There was trouble soon after the first regiments landed at Bristol in October 1643. One royalist observed they became 'infected with the rebellious humour of England', and they soon mutinied, causing Hopton to execute 'two or three of the principale offendours'.[79] One of Sir Samuel Luke's scouts reported in December 1643 that the royalists were disciplining further companies from Ireland stationed at Newbury, imprisoning some and threatening hangings.[80] Parliamentarian agents and commanders soon proffered officers returning from Ireland their full arrears if they would bring their men over to parliament.[81]

Their first mass defection occurred after Lord Byron's defeat at Nantwich in January 1644, where 1,500 common soldiers were captured, most of whom had previously served in Ireland. Incarcerated in Nantwich parish church for three days, this experience must have concentrated their minds, because 'many of theim took up Armes for the pliam^t, And weire listed vnder Seu'all Captyns'.[82] Between 700 and 800 defected, taking the Covenant as they did so. This defection obliterated Byron's faith in English soldiers recalled from Ireland; he warned that none were to be trusted 'excepting such as are gentlemen'. His brother, Sir Robert Byron, suspected that many changed sides during the battle itself, and that afterwards many prisoners 'especially of Warren's, have taken conditions with them.'[83] On 30 January 1644 Lord Byron complained to Ormond that the returning English

---

[76] Wing/C7433, John Cruso, *Militarie Instructions for the Cavallrie* (Cambridge, 1644), 36–7.

[77] Symonds, *Richard Symonds's Diary*, 127.

[78] Gentles, *The English Revolution and the Wars in the Three Kingdoms*, 202.

[79] Charles E. H. Chadwyck Healey (ed.), *Bellum Civile: Hopton's Narrative of his Campaign in the West (1642–1644) and other papers* (Somerset Record Society, 18, 1902), 62–5.

[80] Philip (ed.), *The Journal of Sir Samuel Luke*, iii, 220.

[81] John Lowe, 'The Campaign of the Irish Royalist Army in Cheshire, November 1643–January 1644', *Transactions of the Historical Society of Lancashire and Cheshire*, 111 (1959), 53–5.

[82] Hall (ed.), *Memorials of the Civil War in Cheshire*, 115.

[83] BL, Add. MS 31116, fo. 112v; Samuel R. Gardiner, *History of the Great Civil War, 1642–1649*, 4 vols. (1987), i, 295–6; Lowe, 'The Campaign of the Irish Royalist Army in Cheshire', 70, 73.

troops were 'so poisoned by the ill-affected people here, that they grow very cold in this service'. He urged Ormond to send native Irish in future: 'since the rebels here call in the Scots, I know no reason why the King should make any scruple of calling in the Irish, or the Turks if they would serve him.'[84]

The allegiance of English regiments returned from Ireland was sorely tested during 1644 as native Irish arrived to fight alongside them. Further defections were stimulated by and celebrated in parliamentarian newsbooks. In May 1644 one reported that at parliament's garrison of Stafford:

> divers have come voluntarily unto us lately, and of some quality, especially such as were in *Ireland*, who assured us it went against the light of their conscience to march and Command those *Irish Rebells*, against whom they formerly fought, my Lord hath made one of them a Serjeant Major, Captaine *Pinkny*, who brought 100. men to us, from Prince *Rupert*, he is a very gallant Souldier and an honest man, and doth us good service.[85]

Historians have long pointed out that royalist recruits brought from Ireland—English and Irish alike—were 'more of a liability than an asset'.[86] They presented parliament with a golden propaganda opportunity, and undermined the allegiance of English royalists. Yet it now appears that they also deserted to parliament's forces in large numbers. Mark Stoyle has argued that of the approximately 9,000 troops returning from Ireland, about 2,000 were native Irish.[87] Many even of these, quite remarkably also defected to parliament.[88] In 1645 Ferdinando Fairfax's lifeguard of horse included, among its troopers, a Thurlough O'Donnell, who was later commissioned cornet to Colonel Thomas Morgan.[89] John Lambert's council of war at York in December 1647 felt itself unable to prosecute the suspected rebel, Patrick McCourt, one of their soldiers in Colonel Thornton's regiment, because of the protection afforded him by a treaty between the Irish Confederacy and the Lords Justices and Council of Ireland.[90] In November 1644 Sir William Brereton noted that the 'very Irish' in Liverpool mutinied against their officers to negotiate for themselves better terms of surrender from the parliamentarian besiegers that allowed them transport homeward.[91]

When royalist soldiers surrendered in England and Wales between 1644 and 1646 it was not uncommon for them to take the Covenant and volunteer to fight the Irish. After Wareham's surrender in August 1644, 500 did so, and many of them served under Lieutenant-Colonel Henry O'Brien, the brother of Viscount

---

[84] Thomas Carte, *A Collection of Original Letters and Papers Concerning the Affairs of England from the Year 1641 to 1660. Found among the Duke of Ormonde's Papers*, 2 vols. (1739), i, 39, 42.

[85] BL, E49(29), *Letters by Which it is Certified, that Sir Samuell Luke tooke at Islip. Fiftie horse, and fiftie pound in money, twentie seaven prisoners: Sir—Fortescue being one, three were taken prisoners at New-Castle underline: by Collonell Ridgley*, 28 May (1644), 3.

[86] Gentles, *The English Revolution and the Wars in the Three Kingdoms*, 202–3.

[87] Mark Stoyle, *Soldiers and Strangers: An Ethnic History of the English Civil War* (2005), 209–10

[88] Braddick, *God's Fury, England's Fire*, 317.

[89] TNA, SP 28/266/iii/118–9; TNA, E121/5/4, 29 June 1650, sale of Ticknell House and Bewdley Park.

[90] WYAS Wakefield C469/1.

[91] Tibbut (ed.), *Letter Books of Sir Samuel Luke*, 377.

Inchiquin who had recently defected to parliament. They agreed to reinforce Inchiquin against the Irish rebels, and were readied for transport to Munster.[92] A year later, of 700 royalist prisoners captured near Haverfordwest, 440 agreed to go to Youghal as reinforcements for Inchiquin. William Batten reported that all had taken the Covenant and shown 'great forwardness to serve against the Irish'. As all but two of their officers refused the Covenant and remained in prison, Batten sent the recruits off without their officers.[93] All this movement contributed to the accumulation of many former royalists among parliament's troops in Ireland by the late 1640s. In November 1649 Viscount Muskerry warned Ormond not to rely upon English royalists because so many had defected to the New Model since that August. They were even joined by natives who might convert to Protestantism to ease their defection. Micheàl Ó Siochrú has pointed out that surrendering Irish Catholics were increasingly recruited into Cromwell's invading army after 1649. The New Model could not sufficiently recoup their losses from England or from among Irish Protestants, while service to parliament offered native Irish the prospect of pay, self-preservation, and survival.[94] The tendency of the rank and file to change sides in such circumstances appears to have adopted a three-kingdoms dimension, and cut across national boundaries. From 1644 the presence in England of soldiers from Ireland appears to have stimulated rank-and-file side-changing in a parliamentarian direction.

IV

Sustained military success was another factor prompting rank-and-file side-changing, particularly after it became clear that parliament would win the first civil war. This is evidenced by the 1,000 or more royalist soldiers joining the New Model Army during the year after Naseby. They were attracted by the regular pay and relative safety of service, as by summer 1646 little fighting appeared necessary.[95] A week after Naseby, 3,000 prisoners were marched through London and Westminster, and were kept in the Artillery Ground near Tuttle Fields while a parliamentary committee considered their disposal. During July, 102 took the Covenant and were sent on barges to Reading to be admitted into the New Model.[96] All who refused to forsake armed royalism risked deportation overseas. About 800 volunteered for Ireland, but many spent the next year or more in prison. Glenn Foard has explained how this was designed to end the war quickly by denying the king the opportunity to re-recruit these men subsequently.[97]

---

[92] A. R. Bayley, *The Great Civil War in Dorset, 1642–1660* (Taunton, 1910), 208–9.

[93] J. R. Powell and E. K. Timings (eds.), *Documents Relating to the Civil War, 1642–1648* (Navy Records Society, 105, 1963), 210; Whitelock, *Memorials of English Affairs*, i, 501.

[94] Micheàl Ó Siochrú, *God's Executioner: Oliver Cromwell and the Conquest of Ireland* (2008), 206–9.

[95] Donagan, *War in England*, 217n.

[96] TNA, SP 28/34/464.

[97] Glenn Foard, *Naseby: The Decisive Campaign* (2nd edn., Barnsley, 2004), 307–8.

During the post-Naseby campaign, Fairfax enlisted many more royalists. According to Bulstrode Whitelocke, of 2,000 taken at Langport 800 took the Covenant and enlisted. At the taking of Bridgwater another 500 royalist prisoners took the Covenant and assisted in the town's capture.[98] Colonel Venn complained that many of the pressed recruits he collected at Northampton in April 1646 were formerly royalists.[99] Richard Baxter noted that many of the New Model infantry were 'such as had been taken Prisoners, or turned out of Garrisons under the King, and had been Soldiers in his Army.'[100] Although Baxter's hostility to the Army suggests exaggeration, his assertion demonstrates that the former royalist component of the New Model was well known. Similar complaints were made about the cavalry in Scottish service in Yorkshire during 1646. On 25 May the Godly minister Thomas Smallwood lamented that the regiment under Major-General Jonas Vandruske consisted of 'many Papists, French, Dutch, Irish, Scotch, and those that are Englishmen are (as their own chaplain confessed to me) four parts of them the king's reduced, or rather subdued officers, who, now our conquerors and tyrants, came from Newark, Oxford and other of his garrisons.'[101] A list of former royalists sheltering in Scottish service was compiled, and on 31 May the Scots commissioners ordered Vandruske's regiment disbanded.[102]

While such defections did little for the cohesiveness of parliament's forces, it undermined royalist efforts to revive their flagging cause. Fairfax's victory at Langport so destroyed royalist morale that Goring reported that now his army 'could not be brought to fight against half their number.' He perceived correctly that the clubmen associations would now 'take the strongest part' and associate with Fairfax more openly.[103] Joshua Sprigge recalled that on 13 October 1645 one of Goring's captains defected with his troop. The pattern continued over the winter as royalist officers defected, bringing small parties with them. On 1 February 1646 Sprigge noted 'a Lieutenant and ten Horse, well armed, came in to Sir Hardress Waller from the Enemy, and that night the Plymouth Regiment took a Major and twenty Horse neer Barnstable; and Tuesday following a Lieutenant Colonell and fifteen men more with their Armes, came in from the Enemy'.[104] Further large-scale defection followed after the royalist defeat at Torrington on 17 February 1646. Of 433 prisoners, 200 changed sides, claiming to have been pressed by the royalists. A similar number defected during the next week, emerging from woodland in small parties, expressing 'that they onely waited for an opportunity' to defect. 1,000 soon offered to serve parliament in Ireland. Sprigge considered that these defections

---

[98] BL, Add. MS 18979, fo. 204; Whitelock, *Memorials of English Affairs*, i, 477. John Syms suggested only 500 from 1200 taken at Langport did so, and that this was subject to approval by MPs: BL, Add. MS 35297, fos. 71r, 78r.

[99] *LJ*, viii, 268.

[100] Baxter, *Reliquiae Baxterianae*, 53.

[101] Henry Cary (ed.), *Memorials of the Great Civil War in England from 1646 to 1652*, 2 vols. (1842), i, 66.

[102] *LJ*, viii, 348–9, 366.

[103] Bodl., MS Clarendon 25, fo. 44.

[104] Sprigge, *Anglia Rediviva*, 134, 181.

amounted to 'the very ruining of all their Foot.'[105] As this became common knowledge, it prompted more defections—a process which parliamentarian newsbooks clearly sought to accelerate by reporting defections from Sir Richard Grenville's forces.[106]

Mark Stoyle has shown that defections continued as the New Model pursued Goring's cavalry into Cornwall. The contrast between an unpaid, broken royalist army prone to plunder, and a victorious, disciplined, and well-paid New Model, was not lost on the Cornish soldiery. Hugh Peter preached that the Cornish had been duped, providing many with a timely excuse to lay down arms. After the fall of Dartmouth and Torrington, Fairfax sent Cornish soldiers home with a generous two shillings each, while the arrest of their general, Sir Richard Grenville, by the Prince's council on 18 January 1646 speeded Cornish withdrawal from royalism.[107] East Cornwall's gentry negotiated a treaty at Millbrook with Fairfax on 5 March 1646 which surrendered all their men and garrisons.[108] Most Cornish soldiers deserted, surrendered prematurely, or went home—such as the garrison force Colonel Piers Edgecumbe, prevented from joining Hopton.[109] The royalist committeeman Joseph Jane later reflected that by 1646 the disgruntled Cornish felt that the burden of the royalist war effort had fallen too heavily and unfairly upon them.[110]

The service of former royalists in the New Model's ranks made a personal impression on Fairfax. After Oxford's surrender in June 1646, Sir Philip Warwick was granted an audience with him, during which he complimented Fairfax on the 'regularity & temperance of his army'. Warwick claimed that Fairfax replied that 'the best common soldiers he had . . . came out of our army, and from the garrisons he had taken in.'[111] The recruitment of former royalists became so notorious that the New Model's enemies in parliament used it to impugn the Army's reputation. In April 1647 Thomas Juxon noted how the earl of Pembroke claimed he had seen a petition from the New Model to the king:

> wherein they pray him to come to them, and they promise to r'establish him upon his throne and to strengthen it; told them 'twas no longer the New Model for there were 7,000 cavaliers in it, and that theirs and the king's hopes were upon the army. This was believed by some and divulged by others to serve their turn against the army.[112]

Although several hundred former royalists remained in the New Model, Pembroke's figure was a gross exaggeration intended to defame the Army. Ian Gentles has argued that ex-royalists were never more than a small percentage of the New Model's infantry.[113]

---

[105] Ibid., 196; Gentles, *The New Model Army*, 34.

[106] BL, Stowe MS 768, fo. 23.

[107] Mark Stoyle, *West Britons: Cornish Identities and the Early Modern British State* (Exeter, 2002), 84–5, 109–11.

[108] Ibid., 142–3.

[109] *CSPD 1645–7*, 317, 367.

[110] Miller, 'Joseph Jane's Account of Cornwall', 469.

[111] Beinecke Rare Book and Manuscript Library, Osborn Shelves, fb87, fo. 75r.

[112] Thomas Juxon, *The Journal of Thomas Juxon, 1644–1647*, ed. Keith Lindley and David Scott (Camden Society, 5th series, 13, 1999), 155–6.

[113] Gentles, *New Model Army*, 34, 153, 482.

Nevertheless, the extent of this royalist presence became a contentious issue on the political battlefield in 1647. In July, one royalist tract, entitled *The Riddles Unridled*, aimed at a New Model readership, pointed out that many of Goring's command had joined the New Model, but had not broken any oaths in doing so as both sides had been pledged to preserve the king's person and privileges of parliament.[114] Such arguments provoked an angry printed response from army radicals, unprepared to tolerate former royalists in their ranks.[115] Therefore the discussion to enfranchise parliamentarian soldiers at Putney was qualified to those who had joined before Naseby, in recognition that many recruited subsequently were former royalists.[116] Their presence compelled Fairfax in July 1647 to order that all former royalists who had joined the New Model during the last two months be removed from the muster rolls.[117]

There were persistent anxieties over the loyalty of parliamentarian recruits bound for Ireland. In December 1645 Colonel Jephson's soldiers stood accused of threatening to join the rebels, declaring that 'many of them that are there already are gone to the Irish, and if they should go some of them should do the like'.[118] In April 1649 the Council of State received reports that many of Colonel Tothill's men bound for Dublin 'openly profess to have served the enemy, and say they will do so again'. In response they forced an oath of loyalty upon them intended to weed out malignants prior to departure.[119] By 1652, those serving in English garrisons were forbidden to marry native Irish women, upon pain of forfeiting their lands and arrears.[120] Anxiety and speculation concerning the loyalties of the New Model could not be suppressed; in August 1650 one royalist exile complained 'doubtless there be but too many cavaliers in Cromwell's army to oppose the Scots.'[121] By the later stages of the civil wars, particularly in Scotland and Ireland, contemporaries were often uncertain about the loyalties of an increasingly heterogeneous rank and file.

V

The relationship between soldiers and their officers was not always the deferential one expected by the latter. Rare glimpses of the rank-and-file's concept of allegiance

[114] BL, E398(8), *The Riddles Unridled or, an Answer by way of Depositions of the free-commons of England, to Nine Proposalls, by way of Interogation to the Generall Officers and Souldiers in the Armie* (1647), 9.

[115] Rachel Foxley, 'Royalists and the New Model Army in 1647: Circumstance, Principle and Compromise', in Jason McElligott and David L. Smith (eds.), *Royalists and Royalism during the English Civil Wars* (Cambridge, 2007), 165, 169.

[116] I owe this reference to Jason McElligott: C. H. Firth (ed.), *The Clarke Papers*, 4 vols. (Camden Society, new series, 49, 1891), i, 366.

[117] Paul N. Hardacre, *The Royalists during the Puritan Revolution* (The Hague, 1956), 33. C. H. Firth, *Cromwell's Army* (Reprint of 3rd edn., 1962), 37; Rushworth, *Historical Collections*, vi, 639.

[118] *Portland MS*, 320.

[119] TNA, SP 25/94/65.

[120] *Portland MS*, 622–5.

[121] Letter by Lord Hatton, alias 'Charles Parker': BL, Egerton MS 2534, fo. 34.

are afforded by their attitudes towards officers who had changed sides. When one parliamentarian regiment was asked in 1650 whether they would have George Monck as their new colonel, they supposedly replied: 'What! to betray us? We took him, not long since, at Namptwick, prisoner: we'll have none of him.'[122] This memory from six years earlier caused Cromwell such trouble that he had to form a new regiment for Monck, as the strength of opinion could not be overturned.[123] This also suggests that soldiers developed their own opinions about side-changing officers that could diverge from those of their commanders, and that such views required a degree of respect.

When officers changed sides they frequently tried to bring their soldiers with them to enhance their defection's value, indicate their personal prestige, and demonstrate fidelity. In April 1643 Lord Mordaunt brought with him eight or nine troopers when he defected.[124] That June, John Urry rode into Oxford with four officers and eight troopers.[125] When Sir Richard Grenville defected in March 1644, troopers accompanied him—varying sources putting their number at eight, twelve, and seventeen.[126] According to Grenville's biographers, he lectured his troop at Bagshot concerning the evils of rebellion and invited them to accompany him to Oxford. Thirty-six agreed, and the eight who refused were allowed to return to Windsor.[127] In July 1644 the earl of Essex noted that twenty troopers accompanied Lieutenant Howard's defection to the royalists, and Ludlow remarked that his own major defected with thirty troopers in April 1645.[128]

Sometimes officers persuaded whole units to defect. In March 1643 the lieutenant of Sergeant-Major Griffiths's troop in Lincolnshire defected to the royalists, taking with him the entire troop along with elements of Lord Willoughby's.[129] In April 1643 Sir Thomas Fairfax complained that Captain Ratcliffe and his company had deserted to the royalists,[130] while in May 1648 Captain Thomas Wogan certified that four captains had defected from Colonel Laugharne's rebels, taking their entire troops to join Colonel Horton's parliamentarian force before their clash at St Fagans.[131] When the parliamentarian Captain Edward Wogan defected to the Scots

[122] Sir Walter Scott (ed.), *The Original Memoirs Written during the Great Civil War being the Life of Sir Henry Slingsby and Memoirs of Captain Hodgson, with notes* (Edinburgh, 1806), 139–40. I owe this reference to Derek Read. Hodgson was writing after the Restoration, and may have exaggerated the animosity against Monck. Nevertheless, his evidence appears to stand up.

[123] Ronald Hutton, 'George Monck, first duke of Albemarle (1608–1670), army officer and naval officer', *ODNB*.

[124] BL, E99(22), *Mercurius Aulicus*, 15th week, 9–16 April (Oxford, 1643), 187.

[125] Philip (ed.), *Journal of Sir Samuel Luke*, ii, 95.

[126] BL, Harleian MS 166, fo. 21v; BL, Stowe MS 768, fo. 3; Tibbut (ed.), *Letter Books of Sir Samuel Luke*, 629.

[127] Amos C. Miller, *Sir Richard Grenville of the Civil War* (1979), 67; Roger Granville, *The King's General in the West: The Life of Sir Richard Granville, Bart., 1600–1659* (1908), 52; William Hamper (ed.), *The Life, Diary and Correspondence of Sir William Dugdale* (1827), 62; BL, E35(23), *The Weekly Account*, no. 36, 29 February–6 March (1644).

[128] *CSPD 1644*, 351–2; Firth (ed.), *Memoirs of Edmund Ludlow*, i, 116.

[129] BL, E94(18), *A Continuation of Certaine Speciall and Remarkable Passages from both Houses of Parliament*, no. 38, 23–30 March (1643), 7.

[130] Robert Bell (ed.), *The Fairfax Correspondence: Memorials of the Civil War*, 2 vols. (1849), i, 44.

[131] Bodl., MS Tanner 57, fo. 67.

Engagers, he persuaded his troopers to accompany him on a remarkable ride from Worcestershire to Scotland, arriving in Edinburgh during March 1648.[132]

The average size of mass defections led by their officers increased dramatically in 1648 when Colonels Poyer, Powell, and Laugharne took thousands of troops into royalist service in South Wales. In England that year, Lieutenant-Colonel Henry Farr, a former deputy-lieutenant and commander of the earl of Warwick's regiment of Essex militia, led 1,000 trained bandsmen to join the royalist insurgents in what Robert Ashton has called 'the most spectacular, but certainly not the only, example of defections from the county militia'.[133] By 4 July Sir Thomas Honeywood conceded that half of Essex's trained bands had defected, including some from his own regiment.[134] After these soldiers surrendered at Colchester, Farr's success in procuring their defection was attributed to his calling them to muster without stating his intention of joining the insurgents.[135]

And yet soldiers were not always bullied or cozened into changing sides by their officers. Doubting their men's loyalty, some officers hesitated over changing sides, suggesting a less deferential soldiery not automatically inclined to follow orders. In August 1642 William St Leger assured Viscount Falkland that he regretted having 'entered deep into this rebellion' and now intended to bring his troop into the king's service. Yet he requested time to persuade all his troopers. Unsure how far his influence extended, he remarked: 'if the devil makes jealousies amongst ourselves so that I cannot bring my troop with me, I will be sure to come alone and doubt not but my example will be well followed'.[136] According to *Mercurius Verdicus*, when eight of Grenville's troopers realized he was taking them to Oxford, they declined, and returned to Windsor.[137] In September 1643 Captain Brooke, of parliament's warship *Providence*, was arrested by his crew when they discovered his intention to deliver the ship into Bristol harbour. His sailors sent word to the earl of Warwick and bound their captain below deck.[138]

Although Sir Hugh Cholmley carried most of Scarborough's garrison with him, his defection was opposed by junior officers and troopers. These were not Sir Hugh's trained band infantry but a mounted force, comprising twenty-eight troopers, sixty dragoons, four captains, a lieutenant, and three cornets.[139] Nevertheless, Sir Hugh inspired more loyalty than Sir John Hotham did during his failed defection

---

[132] Robert Ashton, *Counter-Revolution: The Second Civil War and its Origins, 1646–8* (New Haven, 1994), 415.

[133] Ibid., 465–6; Gentles, *The English Revolution and the Wars in the Three Kingdoms*, 338.

[134] *Portland MS*, 473. See also the articles against William and John Banson of Clavering, co. Essex, for persuading trained band soldiers to join the insurgents: TNA, SP 19/129/35–42.

[135] BL, E461(24), *A True and Exact Relation of the Taking of Colchester, Sent in a Letter from an Officer of the Army, (who was present during the siege in that service,) to a Member of the House of Commons*, 31 August (1648), 3.

[136] Bodl., MS Clarendon 21, fo. 120.

[137] BL, Stowe MS 768, fo. 3.

[138] Powell and Timings (eds.), *Documents Relating to the Civil War*, 91–2.

[139] BL, TT E95(9), *A True and Exact Relation of all the Proceedings of Sir Hugh Cholmleys Revolt*, 7 April (1643); TNA, SP28/138/3; SP 28/265/171–176; SP 28/267/part iv/66–70; E121/5/5, no. 1; E121/4/8, no. 12.

at Hull. Cholmley marvelled that Hotham 'found nott soe much as one man to lift a hand in his behalf.'[140] Rather than finding his soldiers rising in his defence, one musketeer battered Sir John, felling him from his horse and striking his face with a musket butt, inflicting a grievous wound from which Hotham suffered until his execution.[141]

Another victim of such violence was Sir Alexander Carew, parliamentarian governor of St Nicholas Island in Plymouth harbour. In August 1643 he ordered his gunners to fire on a parliamentarian warship. One gunner refused, and a brawl ensued. At this point Carew's own soldiers turned on him, 'whereupon the Governours owne man, tooke his Master by the choiler of his dublet, and strucke up his heeles, and then they bound him hand and foot and carried him aboard the great ship'.[142] Gentlemen were not accustomed to being abused by plebeian subordinates in this fashion. One tract praised the 'fidelity of his honest Souldiers' in so handling him, and D'Ewes agreed that Carew was ruined by his failure to persuade his soldiers.[143] Rather than acknowledge the loyalty of Carew's soldiers, Clarendon explained the arrest as 'the treachery of a servant'.[144] The executions of Carew and Hotham were made possible because their soldiers, aggravated by their parsimony with wages, were prepared to participate in arresting suspect commanders. Such action might even entail summary executions; in Ireland, Lord Kildare's captain-lieutenant was about to defect to the enemy in May 1649, but was arrested and hanged by his indignant soldiers.[145] Such conspicuous displays of loyalty challenge depictions of a largely apolitical soldiery changing sides with ease.

VI

As historians have found little evidence for the soldiery's political opinions, they have too readily generalized that soldiers remained apathetic, driven by baser motives, or easily carried along by their officers' commands. Yet when particular defections are examined in detail, this was not always the case. Rather, rank-and-file side-changing could be much more complicated, and might embrace a wider variety of motives. Robert Ashton considered that Viscount Inchiquin's 'spectacular' defection of 1648 led to the 'betrayal of a whole province', yet Michael Braddick has more recently highlighted Inchiquin's failure to persuade many of his Munster officers and men to follow his lead.[146] Parliament's sailors had so many

---

[140] Sir Hugh Cholmley, *The Memoirs and Memorials of Sir Hugh Cholmley of Whitby, 1600–1657*, ed. Jack Binns (YASRS, 153, 2000), 128.
[141] BL, E59(2), *A True Relation of the Discovery of a Most Desperate and Dangerous Plot, for the delivering up, and surprising of the Townes of Hull and Beverley*, 4 July (1643), 5–6.
[142] BL, E67(3), *Certaine Informations from Severall Parts of the Kingdome*, no. 34, 4–11 September (1643), 259–60.
[143] BL, E250(8), *A Perfect Diurnall of Some Passages in Parliament*, no. 8, 4–11 September (1643), 57; BL, Harleian MS 165, fo. 161r–v.
[144] Hyde, *History of the Rebellion*, iii, 235–6.
[145] Brian Howells, 'The Kidnapping of Griffith Jones of Castellmarch', *Trivium*, 15 (1980), 43.
[146] Ashton, *Counter-Revolution*, 402; Braddick, *God's Fury, England's Fire*, 530; *CSPD 1649–1650*, 225.

material grievances in 1648 that many went along with Admiral William Batten's conversion to royalism, but only until his denial of prize money to them soured their affections.[147] A pre-existing popular political culture lurked behind the defection of many rank-and-file soldiers that does not easily map onto the royalist versus parliamentarian divide.[148] Soldiers developed their own concerns that might only intersect with national politics at particular moments. They adopted their own sense of what constituted a trustworthy officer and fair conditions of service, whilst they might also develop loyalty to the well-being of their home district or neighbourhood, or the small group camaraderie of their company or file. Sir Arthur Hesilrige lamented that the troopers incarcerated at Newcastle in July 1648 had 'been in the same service formerly with the gentlemen that are prisoners', and would 'never change their partie so long as they live'.[149] Despite elite stereotypes of a base, ignorant soldiery, some protagonists recognized that they needed to appeal for popular allegiance in increasingly sophisticated ways, and that the outlook of soldiers among enemy ranks might be altered by exposure to rumour, exhortation, and print. In November 1645 *The Scottish Dove* admonished London's Godly ministers for not preaching to royalist prisoners, and noted a conference at Sion College to press the matter: 'many of them are men rationall but never came where preaching was, and might for ought any man knowes become new men.'[150] The royalist minister Edward Symmons made the same observation in connection with parliamentarian prisoners captured at Brampton Bryan in 1644.[151] Similarly, a royalist paper to be circulated among Cromwell's navy in 1656 endeavoured to incite mutiny.[152]

Many officers were daily consumed by fears and doubts over the fickle loyalty and two-faced temperament of their men. The radical Roger Crabbe observed a similar relationship in civilian life during the 1640s: 'labouring poor Men, which in Times of scarcity pine and murmur for want of Bread, cursing the Rich behind his back, and before his Face, Cap and Knee.'[153] While soldiers maintained a front of obedience and submission, some plotted to desert, defect, or even turn on their commanders. In 1640 the earl of Northumberland considered that those English who had not already deserted were 'readier to draw their swords upon their officers than against the Scots.'[154] He was proved correct that summer when two Catholic officers, William Mohun and Compton Evers, were murdered by common

---

[147] Richard Ollard, *This War Without An Enemy: A History of the English Civil Wars* (1976), 176; C. S. Knighton, 'Sir William Batten (1600/01–1667), naval officer', *ODNB*.

[148] John Walter, 'The English People and the English Revolution Revisited', *History Workshop Journal*, 61 (2006), 171.

[149] *Portland MS*, 476–7.

[150] BL, E309(24), *The Scottish Dove*, no. 109, 12–19 November (1645), 863.

[151] BL, E27(12), Edward Symmons, *Scripture Vindicated, from the Misapprehensions Misinterpretation and Misapplications of Mr. Stephen Marshall*, February (Oxford, 1645), preface, sig. A3r.

[152] Jason Peacey, *Politicians and Pamphleteers: Propaganda During the English Civil Wars and Interregnum* (Aldershot, 2004), 321.

[153] John Walter, *Crowds and Popular Politics in Early Modern England* (Manchester, 2006), 193.

[154] Ian Gentles, 'Why Men Fought in the British Civil Wars', *The History Teacher*, 26 (1993), 417.

soldiers.[155] John Dintch deserted royalist service for the Plymouth garrison, and later testified against his commanding officer.[156] In February 1644 Lord Byron lamented that two of his officers were forced to yield one garrison after their own soldiers threatened to kill them unless they surrendered, 'the greatest part of them runninge over to the Rebells' thereafter.[157] When Richard Browne disputed with his mutinous soldiers after Cropredy Bridge, they struck him in the face.[158] There were several attempts on John Hotham's life, while the prosecution witnesses at his trial included close family servants.[159] In Leinster it was claimed that Sir Charles Coote had been shot by one of his own men.[160] One parliamentarian musketeer, apprehended and hanged for trying to shoot Sir William Waller, merely replied 'that hee was sorry for nothing but that hee had not kild' him.[161]

[155] Braddick, *God's Fury, England's Fire*, 100.
[156] Mark Stoyle, *Loyalty and Locality: Popular Allegiance in Devon during the English War* (Exeter, 1994), 112.
[157] Bodl., MS Carte 9, fo. 123.
[158] Malcolm Wanklyn, *The Warrior Generals: Winning the British Civil Wars* (New Haven 2010), 113.
[159] BL, Harleian MS 165, fo. 117v.
[160] Kevin Forkan, 'Inventing a Protestant Icon: The Strange Death of Sir Charles Coote', in Edwards, Lenihan and Tait (eds.), *Age of Atrocity*, 213–15; Ó Siochrú, 'Atrocity, Codes of Conduct and the Irish', 62.
[161] Philip (ed.), *Journal of Sir Samuel Luke*, iii, 228; Wing/B3751A, *A Wicked Plot against the Person of Sir William Waller*, sig. A2v.

5

Chronological and regional patterns to side-changing

Changing sides during the first civil war was partly determined by chronological and regional factors. Military and political events influenced allegiance, as side-changing patterns reflected both the fortunes of war and the development of the coalitions. Charles Carlton and Barbara Donagan have both highlighted how the party perceived as winning attracted most defections.[1] Initially this was the king, but during 1644–5 the flow gradually reversed. As military control of particular regions shifted, so too did defections, reflecting that a key determinant of allegiance was the continued presence of armed forces, rather than popular sympathies or ideological conviction.[2] What mattered was not so much the presence of sympathizers as the ability to mobilize men, money, and munitions. Therefore it is unsurprising that provincial defections were so concentrated in the western, northern, and Welsh counties that changed hands most markedly. Alongside a desire to be among the victors existed natural concerns to protect one's home, family, and estates. Looking back from 1647, Thomas May concluded: 'scarce was there any City or Shire, but endured in process of time many Changes, and became altered from their first condition, either by unconstancy of affections, or else enforced to take a new side, as they were threatned by approaching Armies of either party, when the War grew to a greater height.'[3] Therefore this chapter will examine side-changing at a regional level, along with how military fortunes and changing political circumstances might transform provincial sympathies.

Gerald Aylmer pointed to the importance of region in allegiance formation, explaining that 'for someone to go against the prevailing trend of his region or district would seem to argue a greater measure of commitment to whichever side he took. Correspondingly, some very tepid loyalties or reluctant takings of sides can perhaps best be explained by a desire not so to stand out but to go with the trend.'[4] Protecting personal interests was not always considered dishonourable,

---

[1] Charles Carlton, *Going to the Wars: The Experience of the British Civil Wars, 1638–1651* (1992), 253; Barbara Donagan, 'Varieties of Royalism' in J. McElligott and D. L. Smith (eds.), *Royalists and Royalism during the English Civil Wars* (Cambridge, 2007), 80.

[2] David Underdown, 'The Problem of Popular Allegiance in the English Civil War', *TRHS*, 5th series, 31 (1981), 84; J. M. Gratton, *The Parliamentarian and Royalist War Effort in Lancashire 1642–1651* (Chetham Society, 3rd series, 48, 2010), 175.

[3] Wing/M1410, Thomas May, *The History of the Parliament of England, which began November the third, MDCXL* (1647), Book II, 100.

[4] G. E. Aylmer, 'Collective Mentalities in Mid-Seventeenth-Century England: 2 Royalist Attitudes', *TRHS*, 5th series, 37 (1987), 29.

and Lotte Mulligan has suggested that 'self advancement and the preservation of one's estate was a motive of which Clarendon and probably most others approved'.[5] Most propertied gentlemen, bred to preserve their estates for posterity, were reluctant to hazard all in a futile effort against those who dominated their locality. Instead, many waited upon events to declare themselves at a more opportune moment when military events permitted. Perceptions of who would win and the timing of defections were therefore critical.[6]

Many procrastinators awaited the result of the first battle before open commitment. After Edgehill proved inconclusive and the king withdrew from Turnham Green, it became increasingly difficult to delay such commitment. Thomas May later considered that one consequence of Edgehill was that it brought the king a wave of support from those gentlemen who had waited upon events and now considered the king likeliest to win.[7] The result of the next major confrontation in the Thames valley was eagerly anticipated by those deliberating their position. Sir Hugh Cholmley remarked that the Hothams delayed defecting because they awaited the issue of the siege of Reading. John Hotham was sensitive to such speculation, pledging to the earl of Newcastle on 4 May 1643: 'I am as much your servant as ever, and twenty such businesses as Reading shall make no alteration.'[8] Hotham was keen to stress his constancy, because after the town surrendered Sir Edward Nicholas confided to Rupert that the enemy would now make a 'great boast' that the king's support was falling away.[9] Side-changers were frequently portrayed as especially susceptible to military news when making political choices. For example, the Kent county committee was suspicious of Sir Edward Dering's delay in explaining his defection in print, admonishing him on 20 March 1644: 'it is verily believed you only look for the issue of the next battle between Sir William Waller and Hopton, before you will suffer any manifest under your pen to appear.'[10]

I

This chapter will first examine the link between the timing of MPs and peers' defections and the location of their estates. Lotte Mulligan examined 120 of the most active MPs at Westminster, arguing that their political alignment within parliament's coalition depended not just on their ideology but also on their wealth and their estates' location. She argued that MPs supporting a vigorous war against the

[5] Lotte Mulligan, 'Property and Parliamentary Politics in the English Civil War, 1642–6', *Historical Studies*, 16 (1975), 344.
[6] Conrad Russell, 'Why Did People Choose Sides in the English Civil War?', *The Historian*, 63 (1999), 8.
[7] May, *The History of the Parliament of England*, Book III, 29–30.
[8] Sir Hugh Cholmley, *Memoirs and Memorials of Sir Hugh Cholmley, 1600–1657*, ed. Jack Binns (YASRS, 153, 2000), 128; *Portland MS*, 707.
[9] BL, Add. MS 18980, fo. 61.
[10] BL, Stowe MS 184, fo. 73r.

king were likely to be poorer, with land in the most war-torn areas, or regions controlled by the royalists. Members inclined to peace negotiations were likely to be wealthier, with lands close to London or deep in parliamentarian-held territory that they might forfeit should they defect to the king. She adopted the rough and imperfect categories of war, middle and peace parties around which to base her analysis, and argued that peace-party MPs had 61 per cent of their estates in areas held by parliament, 24 per cent in areas that changed hands, and only 15 per cent in areas held by the king. In contrast, the estates of war-party MPs were located respectively 33, 45, and 22 per cent, with the statistics for 'middle group' MPs appropriately occupying the centre ground between these figures. Understandably, war-party members wanted their estates returned to their own control before the king was brought to terms. Their 'peace party' counterparts also faced a dilemma. They could defect and lose their estates to sequestration, or they could stay and thus lend legitimacy to an ever more radical war effort with which they were out of sympathy.[11] Clarendon considered Whitelocke cooperated with parliament not through sharing their principles but because 'all his estate was in their quarters'. Many MPs only began to think of a settlement 'which was much concerned with the rights of property, once their property was, in fact, safely back in their own hands.'[12]

Of the twenty-seven MPs identified in Chapter 2 who defected to the king between 1642 and 1644, the principal estates of fifteen of them at the time of their defection clearly lay in territory controlled by the king's armies, or precarious parliamentarian enclaves threatened by them.[13] The estates of six more were spread across several counties held by different sides, or located in strongly disputed areas.[14] Only six had most of their estates in undisputed parliamentarian territory.[15] These statistics support Mulligan's argument that an MP's estates' locations influenced their alignment considerably. Those 'peace party' parliamentarians alarmed by the radicalization of parliament's war effort in 1643 who did defect were the minority whose estates were in royalist hands or under direct threat of royalist occupation. This observation invites speculation that defections of MPs from Westminster would have been higher had more of those inclined to peace negotiations possessed estates in regions under royalist control in 1643. The correlation is even stronger among those MPs who defected from the king to parliament between 1644 and 1646. Of the ten identified in chapter two, all had their principal estates in areas that were either controlled by parliament or in imminent danger from resurgent parliamentarian forces.

---

[11] Mulligan, 'Property and Parliamentary Politics', 342, 348–50.

[12] Ibid., 345, 354.

[13] These were Sir Henry Anderson, William Bassett, Sir Henry Bellingham, Henry Brett, Sir Alexander Carew, Sir Hugh Cholmley, William Constantine, Sir Alexander Denton, John Dutton, William Glanvile, Sir John Hotham, John Hotham, Sir Gerard Napper, Sir Guy Palmes, and Michael Wharton.

[14] These were John Fettiplace, John George, Sir Edward Littleton, Sir William Ogle, Sir John Price, and Sir George Stonehouse. Ogle's prevarication and eventual defection was partly inspired by his bid to protect his estates in and near Winchester: Keeler, 289.

[15] These were Edward Bagshaw, Sir Thomas Eversfield, Sir John Harrison, Sir Thomas Peyton, and Edmund Waller.

The link between defections amongst the peerage and the location of their estates is more difficult to establish because most peers held property across several counties, with their estates therefore unlikely to lie in exclusively royalist or parliamentarian-held areas.[16] Of the six who defected to the king in August 1643, most of the estates of the earl of Bedford and Viscount Conway were in royalist-controlled areas, but those of the earls of Holland and Portland lay closer to London and remained under parliamentary control.[17] Lord Lovelace's Berkshire and Oxfordshire estates were in a disputed zone, while the earl of Clare's estates in north Nottinghamshire were under royalist control but his more lucrative Middlesex property was in parliamentarian territory.[18] As a group it would seem that their defection was more driven by royalist military success and their own increased political isolation within the parliamentary cause than out of any drive to protect their estates from royalist soldiery. The earl of Northumberland considered defecting soon afterwards, but his properties in Middlesex, Sussex, and London exercised a restraining influence upon him, despite the bulk of his northern lands being under royalist occupation. Others potentially wavering, such as the earls of Pembroke and Salisbury, were probably restrained by similar concerns; Clarendon predictably considered that they cooperated with parliament only because they feared confiscation of their seats at Wilton and Hatfield.[19]

However, those peers who abandoned royalism between 1644 and 1646 appear more influenced by estate concerns. This became more pronounced with the realisation that parliament would emerge victorious. The earls of Bath and Carbery were quick to negotiate in 1645 when their lands in Devon and Pembrokeshire were threatened by parliamentarian soldiers. The earls of Thanet and Westmorland made their peace with parliament in 1644, partly to protect their Kent estates from further ruin. After the death of the earl of Carnarvon at Newbury in September 1643, his 11-year-old son came to London so that his large Buckinghamshire estates could be safeguarded by his grandfather, the earl of Pembroke.[20] When the earl of Sussex defected to parliament in 1645 his Yorkshire estates were under parliamentarian and Scottish occupation. When the earl of Leicester returned to London the royalists sequestered his Welsh lands, but at least he could regain Penshurst and his Kent property. Likewise, the return of Holland and Clare from Oxford enabled them to safeguard their Middlesex estates. Aware of suspicions in parliament that such defections were motivated by seigneurial concerns, the earl of Essex stressed that Lord Paget's return from Oxford was timed immediately after parliament's

[16] G. E. Aylmer, *The King's Servants: The Civil Service of Charles I, 1625–1642* (2nd edn., 1974), 412–13.

[17] Bedford and Portland also held significant estates in the Isle of Ely, a district controlled by parliament.

[18] Peter Seddon, 'Landlords and Tenants: The Impact of the Civil Wars on the Clare Estates in Nottinghamshire, 1642–1649', *Transactions of the Thoroton Society of Nottinghamshire*, 113 (2009), 81–91.

[19] Mulligan, 'Property and Parliamentary Politics', 345.

[20] I. G. Philip (ed.), *The Journal of Sir Samuel Luke* (The Oxfordshire Record Society, 33, 1952–3), iii, 230; Bulstrode Whitelock, *Memorials of English Affairs from the Beginning of the Reign of Charles I to the Happy Restoration of King Charles II*, 4 vols. (Oxford, 1853), i, 226.

army was defeated in Cornwall, while Paget himself was quick to claim that his estates remained in royalist hands.[21] Although not all peers and MPs defected out of concerns to maintain their status and estates, such considerations were rarely entirely absent, particularly as the war lengthened and the administrative machinery of sequestration developed on both sides. An examination now follows of how military and political developments influenced side-changing in the regions where it was most pronounced: the West Country, Wales, and the north of England.

II

The six western counties of Cornwall, Devon, Dorset, Gloucestershire, Somerset, and Wiltshire were repeatedly fought over, and suffered many engagements. In his study of popular allegiance in Devon, Mark Stoyle uncovered a high incidence of defectors, and argued that 'as elsewhere, changing sides was commonplace, and at least 10 per cent of the county's knights and peers were turncoats.' Yet Devon was untypical. As military control of Devon fluctuated it became a regional hotspot for side-changing in a manner quite unparalleled in, say, Cambridgeshire or Suffolk. Stoyle identified Sir George Chudleigh, Sir John Davy, Sir Thomas Drewe, and Sir Peter Prideaux as parliamentarians in 1642 who later abandoned their allegiance as the royalist military ascendancy in the west escalated. To these might be added the earl of Bedford, Sir Alexander Carew, James Chudleigh, and numerous captains, lieutenants, and ensigns, as well as rank-and-file soldiers.[22] The momentum established by the victory at Stratton on 16 May 1643 was reflected in military recruitment and the pattern of side-changing. One embittered parliamentarian tract proclaimed that the Devon militia defeated at Stratton now besieged Exeter for the royalists.[23] In July 1643 Sir John Berkeley confided to Rupert that if they captured Exeter it would 'awake our friends and render our enemies less active.'[24] Devon parliamentarians grew despondent, and Stoyle has argued that 'local behaviour underwent something of a sea-change'.[25] This may have been partly inspired by skilful royalist propaganda, but the local perception of royalist support swelling at parliament's expense enabled Prince Maurice to secure Barnstaple's surrender in August 1643. Maurice persuaded the corporation that royalist victories had convinced so many at Westminster to change sides that only seven peers and less than a fifth of the Commons remained.[26] Provincial anxieties about the evaporation of support for parliament at Westminster itself appear to have accelerated royalist successes. Predictably, London newsbooks postulated the reverse, placing blame

[21] *LJ*, vi, 711, vii, 42, 141.

[22] Mark Stoyle, *Loyalty and Locality: Popular Allegiance in Devon during the English Civil War* (Exeter, 1994), 111–12, 138–40.

[23] BL, E67(27), *Articles of Agreement Betweene his Excellency Prince Maurice, and the Earle of Stamford, vpon the delivery of the City of Excester, the fifth of September, 1643. Together with a Letter Relating the Earle of Stamfords Proceedings in the West. Sept. 20* (1643), 5.

[24] BL, Add. MS 18980, fo. 89.

[25] Stoyle, *Loyalty and Locality*, 33.

[26] BL, Add. MS 18980, fo. 110.

elsewhere and arguing that Barnstaple and Bideford had been betrayed by the treachery of their mayors, who feared for their estates.[27] A common response to defeat was to blame local elites for falling away; Plymouth's mayor was vituperated for joining 'Sir Alexander Carye and that knot of Utrusques who look onely to their owne preferment and estates'.[28]

This momentum was maintained by Sir Ralph Hopton's eastward march into Somerset and his meeting with the marquess of Hertford at Chard on 4 June 1643. Here, the opposing parliamentarian forces were weakened by the defection of Waller's own trusted major, Horatio Carey, just prior to the engagement at Chewton Mendip on 9 June. Two weeks later Waller remained concerned to prevent the rest of Carey's troop from following his example.[29] Waller's subsequent defeat at Roundway Down on 13 July heralded the near collapse of parliamentarian strength in the west. It also had repercussions further afield, Clarendon remarking that it stifled the recruitment of Essex's army and inclined the earl to become friendlier with Holland and Northumberland, and those favouring peace negotiations.[30]

Roundway Down was followed by further royalist gains in Somerset and Dorset. Sir Edward Nicholas claimed to Ormond on 1 August 1643 that 'all the west is in a fair and probable way to be speedily reduced to obedience', and that the Dorset gentry 'desire to submit to the king upon any terms.'[31] Patrick Little has claimed that Dorset hosted more side-changers during the first civil war than any other county except Yorkshire. Dubbing it 'the southern capital of coat-turning', he argued that because Dorset gentry society was coherent, homogenous, and inclined towards neutrality, county leaders were able to restrain extremists, accommodate necessitous shifts in allegiance, and moderate the divisive effects of civil war. The county was first mobilized for parliament, but by autumn 1643 royalists under Prince Maurice recaptured all Dorset except Lyme and Poole. The MPs Sir Gerard Napper and William Constantine, along with William Churchill, a Dorchester militia captain, anticipated this, announcing their defections several weeks before the royalist conquest was complete.[32]

By autumn, all Somerset was under royalist control. Local office-holders who had earlier supported parliament were now more compliant. David Underdown noted how some even expressed enthusiasm in their change of heart. George Smith,

[27] Richard W. Cotton, *Barnstaple and the Northern Part of Devonshire during the Great Civil War, 1642–1646* (1889), 219–21; BL, E250(11), *The Weekly Account*, no. 2, 6–13 September (1643), 2–3; BL, E67(14), *The Parliament Scoute*, no. 12, 7–15 September (1643), 90; BL, E250(8) *A Perfect Diurnall of Some Passages in Parliament*, no. 8, 4–11 September (1643), 64.

[28] I owe this reference to Mark Stoyle: BL, E257(10), *Some of Mr. Phillip Francis Misdemeanours, and Sir Alexander Caryes Treacheries Discovered* (1644), 6.

[29] Newman, 64; Barry Denton, *Only in Heaven: The Life and Campaigns of Sir Arthur Hesilrige, 1601–1661* (Sheffield, 1997), 69; Charles E. H. Chadwyck Healey (ed.), *Bellum Civile: Hopton's Narrative of his Campaign in the West (1642–1644) and other papers* (Somerset Record Society, 18, 1902), 89.

[30] Clarendon, *History of the Rebellion*, iii, 102–3.

[31] Bodl., MS Carte 6, fo. 139.

[32] Patrick Little, 'Four Dorset Turncoats' unpublished paper delivered at a civil war conference at the Dorset Record Office, Dorchester, 2002; A. R. Bayley, *The Great Civil War in Dorset, 1642–1660* (Taunton, 1910), 29, 31, 101, 108–11.

an Ilchester constable, implemented royalist orders despite having previously supported parliament. He enlisted under the town's new governor, denouncing his
enemies as 'roundheaded rogues'. Several parliamentarian committeemen in Somerset had acquired royal pardons by early 1644, while those who had paid parliamentarian contributions acquiesced to royalist occupation, determined to maintain
their stake in local administration.[33] Even towns such as Taunton and Dorchester,
despite their deservedly puritan reputations, quickly surrendered, leaving David
Underdown to underline their 'drastic changes of attitude' that accompanied the
royalist high tide.[34]

In Gloucestershire defectors from parliament included several MPs, while the
soldiers Rupert captured at Cirencester in February 1643 lamented that treachery
from their gentry and ministers had undone them.[35] The royalist capture of Bristol
on 26 July led to further defections from Gloucester. John Corbet, rector of St
Mary de Crypt, wrote that the news that royalists had taken Bristol 'made most
men infidels, or at least question all things'. The countryfolk around Gloucester
grew hostile as they feared loss of their crops and livestock to a besieging royalist
army.[36] Gloucester's governor, Edward Massey, claimed that the citizens were disaffected and uncooperative.[37] After Bristol's capture, Clarendon noted the arrival in
Oxford of peers and MPs from Westminster, happily reflecting how 'above all, the
prosperity of the King's affairs made every body wish to come into his quarters.'[38]

Despite the royalist ascendancy in August 1643, the king never quite consoli-
dated his hold on the west. The royalist governor of Weymouth, Anthony Ashley
Cooper, resigned in December 1643. His defection thereafter may have partly
been in response to the king's Cessation with the Irish confederates and the increasing presence in the west of soldiers brought back from Ireland. By February 1644
he had surrendered himself to parliament, alongside Sir Gerard Napper, in order
to take advantage of the Declaration of Both Kingdoms. Both defected when the
royalists still held the military ascendancy in Dorset, but the earl of Essex's summer
campaign in 1644 won back most of the county for parliament.[39] After Wareham's
surrender on 10 August, much of the garrison agreed to change sides and fight for
parliament in Ireland.[40] Even the king's triumph at Lostwithiel did not clear the
west for long, as the governor of Exeter was complaining of incursions from parliament's garrisons at Taunton and Lyme by December 1644.[41] Waller campaigned in

[33] David Underdown, *Somerset in the Civil War and Interregnum* (Newton Abbot, 1973), 69.

[34] Underdown, 'The Problem of Popular Allegiance in the English Civil War', 76.

[35] Andrew R. Warmington, *Civil War, Interregnum and Restoration in Gloucestershire, 1640–1672*
(Woodbridge, 1997), 38, 43.

[36] BL, E306(8), John Corbet, *A Historicall Relation of the Military Government of Gloucester: From
the Beginning of the Civill Warre betweene King and Parliament, to the Removall of Colonell Massie*
(1645), 39–40.

[37] Bodl., MS Tanner 62, fos. 197–9.

[38] Clarendon, *History of the Rebellion*, iii, 149, 152.

[39] Bayley, *Great Civil War in Dorset*, 107, 227–8; William Dougal Christie, *A Life of Anthony Ashley
Cooper, First Earl of Shaftesbury, 1621–1683*, 2 vols. (1871), i, 47–9, 59.

[40] Bayley, *Great Civil War in Dorset*, 208–9; BL, Add. MS 46928, fo. 40r.

[41] DRO, 1392 M/L 1644/56.

Dorset in March 1645, and noted how his lack of infantry left the local population uncertain about committing themselves, 'the people being universally disposed to receive us, but unwilling to engage till they see me with such a body as may give them assurance I mean to stay with them, and not to be gone tomorrow'.[42]

Thereafter, much of the west remained disputed territory until the New Model's arrival after Naseby. Although the Dorset clubmen movement in summer 1645 was more royalist-inclined, many clubmen from north-east Somerset rediscovered parliamentarian sympathies in rallying to Fairfax during the siege of Bristol in September 1645.[43] Another clubmen uprising in areas of north Devon previously noted for parliamentarian strength demonstrated their allegiance by crying out 'a Fairfax, a Fairfax' and disarming royalist troops that fell within their power.[44] Both David Scott and Ian Gentles have pointed to Fairfax's ability to channel clubmen loyalty to parliament's benefit in the west during 1645.[45]

This realignment accelerated the New Model's victory, particularly after Goring's defeat at Langport on 10 July 1645. Defections were especially pronounced in Cornwall—which appears surprising, as it had hitherto proved a fertile royalist recruiting ground, and thousands of Cornish remained in arms under Sir Richard Grenville. Cornwall's royalists gained a reputation for fierceness and rapacity after Essex's army surrendered at Lostwithiel in September 1644. Calls for vengeance, fostered in London's press, led the Cornish to fear a backlash from the resurgent New Model Army. To counter this threat, Grenville had recruited a substantial New Cornish Tertia by the summer of 1645, but by September he complained that the towns of St Ives and Helston were growing mutinous.[46] Fairfax wrote to Cornwall's high sheriff on 8 September 1645, promising fair terms if the Cornish withdrew from the war, but the utmost severity if they did not. This political ploy was designed to isolate royalist diehards and win over those wavering. That Fairfax was willing to treat with them separately from other royalists inclined an important clique of Cornish gentry to begin negotiations from January 1646. The depredations of Goring's royalist cavalry upon the civilian population and clashes with Grenville's infantry, followed by Grenville's arrest on 20 January, alienated the Cornish further. With Hugh Peter acting as an intermediary, the discontented Cornish gentry signed a treaty at Millbrook on 5 March 1646 which agreed to surrender royalist garrisons and forces in east Cornwall.[47] Fairfax later acknowledged that their 'seasonable coming in to me at my marching into Cornwall...did much further the accomplishment of my designs in those parts'.[48] Without these infantry

---

[42] BL, Sloane 1519, fo. 66.

[43] Underdown, *Somerset in the Civil War*, 106, 113.

[44] BL, E262(29), *Perfect Occurrences of Parliament*, no. 30, 18–25 July (1645), sig. Ggv.

[45] David Scott, *Politics and War in the Three Stuart Kingdoms, 1637–1649* (Basingstoke, 2004), 97; Ian Gentles, *The New Model Army in England, Ireland and Scotland, 1645–1653* (Oxford, 1992), 66.

[46] Mark Stoyle, 'Sir Richard Grenville's Creatures: the New Cornish Tertia 1644–46', *Cornish Studies*, 2nd series, 4 (1996), 26–44; Bodl., MS Clarendon 25, fo. 149.

[47] Mark Stoyle, *West Britons: Cornish Identities and the Early Modern British State* (Exeter, 2002), 142–3, 154, 187–9; Bodl., MS Clarendon 27, fos. 3, 7, 12, 15; Wing/S5070, Joshua Sprigge, *Anglia Rediviva: England's Recovery* (1647), 203.

[48] Bodl., MS Tanner, 59, fo. 745.

Lord Hopton was forced to surrender the royalist western army within two weeks.

After Langport, many western royalists laid down arms, embraced exile, or negotiated their own terms with parliament. This even encompassed the hitherto conspicuously royalist Cornish and Welsh, as they recognized that the New Model could end the war quickly and that the king was plotting to land Irish and French Catholic troops to restore his fortunes in the west.[49] Yet despite these changed political circumstances, other royalists took pride in their resistance and vied to hold out the longest. Ronald Hutton has argued that the wave of defections and premature surrendering among royalists in 1645–6 generated a reaction among hardcore royalists 'to testify to the intrinsic worth of their cause.'[50]

III

The next region in which side-changing was particularly prevalent was Wales. From autumn 1642 the king recruited successfully in Wales, partly owing to the hostility of London's press towards the principality. Godly parliamentarians considered Wales full of idolatry and superstition. A series of pamphlets scorned the Welsh as being motivated by a dangerous politics of subsistence. Welshness, religious backwardness, and royalism were linked in parliamentarian mentalities.[51]

Those few Welsh gentry harbouring parliamentarian sympathies wisely collaborated with royalist domination from 1642 to 1643, when attempted defiance would have been foolhardy. Such men may have included Sir William Williams of Vaynol, Thomas Glynne of Glynllifon, William Lloyd, and Thomas Madryn, who became commissioners of array but subsequently changed sides.[52] Those Pembrokeshire towns which had declared for parliament were soon persuaded by the earl of Carbery to lay down arms. However, Carbery's pacification of Pembrokeshire collapsed after parliament's military fortunes were revived under Rowland Laugharne's direction in spring 1644.[53] A string of Pembrokeshire gentry who had co-operated with Carbery went over to parliament, many establishing themselves on its county committee. Among them was Roger Lort, who had captured Tenby for the king in August 1643, but travelled to London to arrange his defection soon after his house at Stackpole was captured by Laugharne.[54] By October 1644 the

---

[49] Ivan Roots, *The Great Rebellion, 1642–1660* (1966), 99; Ian Gentles, *The English Revolution and the Wars in the Three Kingdoms, 1638–1652* (Harlow, 2007), 143; Woolrych, *Britain in Revolution*, 329.

[50] Ronald Hutton, *The Royalist War Effort, 1642–6* (2nd edn., 1999), 199.

[51] Lloyd Bowen, 'Representations of Wales and the Welsh during the Civil Wars and Interregnum', *Historical Research*, 77 (2004), 362–4, 366; Mark Stoyle, 'Caricaturing Cymru: Images of the Welsh in the London Press 1642–46', in Diana Dunn (ed.), *War and Society in Medieval and Early Modern Britain* (Liverpool, 2000), 162–3, 165.

[52] Norman Tucker, *North Wales in the Civil War* (Denbigh, 1958), 21–2; Newman, 159, 414.

[53] Malcolm Wanklyn, *The Warrior Generals: Winning the British Civil Wars* (New Haven, 2010), 48, 88.

[54] Arthur Leonard Leach, *The History of the Civil War (1642–1649) in Pembrokeshire and on its Borders* (1937), 39, 56, 67, 89.

parliamentarian Sir John Meyrick reported that the inhabitants around Monmouth and west of Chester, would, 'if the wheel of fortune should turn again', leave home and volunteer for parliament.[55]

Welsh allegiance was complicated with the king's arrival after Naseby. At Usk on 25 July 1645, Charles requested the recruitment of 8,000 men from the Association in South Wales.[56] These demands, along with the exactions of royalist troops under Charles Gerard, provoked a clubmen movement in South Wales from August that was soon dubbed the 'Peaceable Army' in Glamorgan.[57] Richard Symonds noted that Lord Astley subdued them in September, but that upon hearing of Bristol's surrender, they aligned with Pembrokeshire parliamentarians.[58] Thereafter, on 19 September royalist-held Cardiff fell and a committee of ten gentlemen assumed control of the town—five of them having previously served as commissioners of array. Adopting a parliamentarian language of anti-Catholicism, they proposed alignment with Rowland Laugharne and the Brecon gentry for their own security.[59] Soon afterwards, the Glamorgan gentry pledged themselves to parliament on 25 October, passing off their former royalism as forced upon them unwillingly:

> And we do all hereby declare, that albeit being formerly overmastered by forces so far, that wee were not able to appear so ready as the duty wee owed to his Majesty and the great council required of us, yet our affections ever sided and adhered to them. And our firm resolution is, from henceforward to hazard our lives for their preservation.[60]

This hasty refashioning was emulated by the neighbouring Monmouthshire gentry. There, on 11 September 1645, Sir Trevor Williams of Llangibby was arrested by the king at Abergavenny, alongside four others, accused of hindering the relief of Hereford. Williams had raised a royalist regiment in 1643, but declared for parliament soon after Rupert surrendered Bristol. Often seen as an 'ambitious weathercock', and dubbed 'an arch-trimmer' by Ronald Hutton, Williams headed an anti-Raglan faction within royalism that could mobilize considerable military force in the county by 1645.[61] His defection, alongside that of Colonel Humphrey Mathews, emboldened Colonel Thomas Morgan to take Chepstow castle for parliament in October 1645.[62] In January 1646 parliament granted Williams overall

[55] H. G. Tibbut (ed.), *The Letter Books of Sir Samuel Luke, 1644–45* (Publications of the Bedfordshire Historical Record Society, 42, 1963), 38.

[56] BL, Harleian MS 6852, fo. 302.

[57] John Morrill, *Revolt in the Provinces: The People of England and the Tragedies of War, 1630–1648* (2nd edn., 1999), 133–4, 140.

[58] Richard Symonds, *Richard Symonds's Diary of the Marches of the Royal Army*, ed. Charles Edward Long and Ian Roy (Cambridge, 1997), 239.

[59] Stephen K. Roberts, 'Office-holding and Allegiance in Glamorgan in the Civil War and After: The Case of John Byrd', *Morgannwg: The Journal of Glamorgan History*, 44 (2000), 18. Many Breconshire gentry declared for parliament after the fall of Hereford in December 1645: Jeremy Knight, *Civil War & Restoration in Monmouthshire* (Logaston, 2005), 101.

[60] Beinecke Rare Book and Manuscript Library, Yale, Osborn Shelves, fb156, fo. 141.

[61] Symonds, *Richard Symonds's Diary*, 205, 238; Knight, *Civil War & Restoration in Monmouthshire*, 56, 71, 97; Ronald Hutton, 'The Worcestershire Clubmen in the English Civil War', *Midland History*, 5 (1979), 46–7; Sprigge, *Anglia Rediviva*, 291; BL, Harleian MS 6852, fo. 79r.

[62] *Portland MS*, 286–7.

command of Monmouthshire's forces, many of whom had defected with him. His neighbour and fellow side-changer, Anthony Morgan of Marshfield, was discharged from sequestration and sought a parliamentarian colonelcy in a possible attempt to advance his claim to sequestered property in Sussex.[63] Williams engaged his forces in the siege of Raglan, alongside another local side-changer, Colonel Robert Kirle.[64] Many other Monmouthshire gentry followed suit, such as Thomas Morgan of Machen, a commissioner of array who occupied Newport for parliament in January 1646. Other Monmouthshire defectors included Edmund Jones and John Parry, parliamentarian committeemen from 1646, while another commissioner of array, William Herbert of Coldbrook, became parliament's high sheriff in 1646.[65]

On 17 November 1645 the House of Commons appointed another side-changer, Bussy Mansell, as its regional commander in south-east Wales, while also approving double side-changers such as Humphrey Mathews and Edward Carne as county committee men.[66] Just three months earlier Mansell had been appointed royalist Colonel-General of Glamorgan in the Association of South Wales against the Scots.[67] Subsequently Charles stripped Mansell of command for supporting the Peaceable Army, thereby inclining Mansell into secret negotiations with the enemy.[68] On 26 January 1646 Mansell and Edward Carne, another former royalist colonel, requested aid from Rowland Laugharne against the incursions of the Raglan cavaliers.[69] However, Carne soon reverted to his royalism, leading a short-lived insurrection in Glamorgan in February 1646. His force, denounced in London newsbooks as a 'Runnagado crew', briefly retook Cardiff before being quelled by Laugharne.[70]

In North Wales, the royalist grip was stronger, leading loyalties to waver at a slightly later stage. The king wrote to the sheriffs and justices of Anglesey, Caernarvon, and Merioneth on 20 July 1645 requesting them to join with the Association in South Wales to assist him in defeating the invading Scots. He declared: 'All Wales as we are informed being destined by the Rebells at Westminster as a more particular prey & reward to those Invaders'.[71] The king promised that these forces would be used for local defence, but the region did not hold up well to invasion by Thomas Mytton's parliamentarians in 1646. Lord Byron discovered

[63] *CJ*, iv, 402, 713; *LJ*, viii, 552; Newman, 262, 414; Knight, *Civil War & Restoration in Monmouthshire*, 89, 100, 106.
[64] BL, E339(9), *The Gallant Siege of the Parliament's Forces before Ragland Castle*, 30 May (1646).
[65] Jeremy K. Knight, 'Taking Sides: Royalist Commissioners of Array for Monmouthshire in the Civil War', *Proceedings of the Monmouthshire Antiquarian Association*, 22 (2006), 6–9, 11, 14, 16.
[66] *CJ*, iv, 346.
[67] BL, Harleian MS 6851, fo. 188; Stephen K. Roberts, '"Specially Trusted by the Parliament": Thomas Carne of Brocastle, a Lost Civil War Commander', *Morgannwg: The Journal of Glamorgan History*, 50 (2006), 70.
[68] A. M. Johnson, 'Bussy Mansell (1623–1699): political survivalist', *Morgannwg*, 20 (1976), 11–12.
[69] *Portland MS*, 345.
[70] Newman, 61–2; J. R. Powell and E. K. Timings (eds): *Documents Relating to the Civil War, 1642–1648* (Navy Records Society, 105, 1963), 233–4; Knight, *Civil War & Restoration in Monmouthshire*, 104.
[71] BL, Harleian MS 6852, fo. 141r.

a conspiracy to betray Caernarvon, while the local gentry were perturbed by the royalist plan to land an Irish army in North Wales.[72] Sir Thomas Hanmer may have had an eye on his Middlesex property when he made peace with parliament in November 1645, claiming to have been forced into arms.[73] By April 1646 the Caernarvonshire and Anglesey gentry had their first real opportunity to defect, and they did so enthusiastically, joining Mytton's forces. Large numbers of captured infantry changed sides too, attracted by the promise of regular pay.[74] John Williams, archbishop of York, despite posing as Byron's local ally, had done much to encourage this process by writing to the remaining royalist governors, urging them to defect.[75]

Stephen Roberts has commented that there 'was nothing simple about the nature of allegiance in South Wales in the autumn of 1645'.[76] Allegiances there after Naseby were extraordinarily fluid. John Morrill considered the region's 'ambidexters' were prepared to take any political stance which would limit the dangers to their livelihoods and estates. This showed a pragmatic loyalty to themselves and their communities.[77] They acted to save their estates and preserve their localities from a ruinous resistance.[78] The result was that by late 1646, so many Welsh royalists had changed sides that local parliamentarians were hardened with cynicism; the royalist Colonel Howell Gwinne, who held firm to the king for longer than most, was accused of declaring upon the king's surrender, 'Heigh God, heigh Devil, I will be for the stronger side.'[79] The mobilization of Welsh forces for parliament from autumn 1645 reflected a desire to terminate wartime depredations rather than a heartfelt political conversion. It was probably accelerated by the loss of key Marcher garrisons to treachery in 1645, as described in Chapter 6. Yet the superficial and pragmatic nature of these defections was confirmed by further royalist insurrection in South Wales during 1648.

IV

The largest regional heartland for side-changing was England's six northern counties, where allegiances proved particularly fluid and dynamic. East of the Pennines, the pattern of side-changing initially favoured the royalists owing to the mobilization of the earl of Newcastle's large field army. Under its weight, limited parliamentarian support in the north-east quickly collapsed. North Riding parliamentarian activists were imprisoned in York and threatened with sequestration until they

[72] Hutton, *The Royalist War Effort*, 197.
[73] P. R. Newman, *The Old Service: Royalist Regimental Colonels and the Civil War, 1642–46* (Manchester, 1993), 123.
[74] Tucker, *North Wales in the Civil War*, 22, 98; Bodl., MS Carte 130, fo. 67.
[75] Hutton, *The Royalist War Effort*, 197.
[76] Roberts, 'Office-holding and Allegiance in Glamorgan', 20.
[77] Morrill, *Revolt in the Provinces*, 124.
[78] Hutton, *The Royalist War Effort*, 189.
[79] *CCAM*, ii, 730.

subscribed to the Yorkshire Engagement to raise money for Newcastle's army.[80] The threat wrought by the sheer size of Newcastle's army worked alongside the political doubts felt by Sir High Cholmley and the Hothams to undermine parliamentarian allegiance in Yorkshire.

Sir John Hotham headed a large kinship network in the East Riding that administered garrisons at Hull, Beverley, Cawood castle, Wressle castle, and the family seat at Scorborough House. Having helped prevent a royalist victory during 1642 by securing Hull's large arms magazine for parliament, Sir John and his eldest son, John Hotham, both entertained second thoughts during 1643. Jealous that the Fairfaxes had eclipsed them as parliament's leading generals in the north, as well as worried by and disdainful of the Fairfaxes' 'clubmen' forces recruited from the West Riding cloth towns, the Hothams felt themselves slighted when their pay and supplies from London became less regular. John Hotham wrote to the earl of Newcastle from December 1642, offering the prospect of their changing sides and delivering Hull, Beverley, and Lincoln to the king. These remarkable letters reveal much of how the Hothams sought to change sides once favourable conditions presented themselves.[81] They feared that parliament's war effort might spin beyond the gentry's control, thereby threatening their estates and pre-eminent local standing, predicting 'the wounds of dissension made wider, and strangers brought in by degrees amongst us, to possess our Inheritances.'[82] The Hothams procrastinated too long, and were arrested by their own forces on 29 June 1643. This ignited a political battle over their subsequent trial and execution. How many of their officers and men they hoped to carry with them remains uncertain, but a large number were imprisoned and remained under suspicion after their arrests—in particular, Lieutenant-Colonel Christopher Legard and Sir Edward Rodes.[83] In a conspiracy to betray Lincoln that was most probably closely related, Sergeant-Major Purefoy, the governor, and his brother Captain Purefoy, who had served both in Hull and under John Hotham's command, were also arrested and sent for trial to the earl of

[80] TNA, SP 19/120/120–8.

[81] Andrew Hopper (ed.), *The Papers of the Hothams, Governors of Hull during the Civil War* (Camden Society, 5th series, 39, 2011), *passim*.

[82] HHC, Hotham MS, U DDHO/1/57.

[83] Sir William Dugdale, *The Visitation of the County of Yorke* (Surtees Society, 36, 1859), 386; James Digby Legard, *The Legards of Anlaby and Ganton* (1926), 27, 45, 83–5; HHC, C BRS/7/11; TNA, SP 28/7/168, SP 28/7/228, SP 28/7/478, SP 28/138/3; BL, E256(45), *A Perfect Diurnal of Some Passages in Parliament*, no. 71, 2–9 December (1644), 561; BL, E119(24), *Speciall Passages*, no. 8, 27 September–4 October (1642), 61–2; BL, E123(5), *Speciall Passages*, no.10, 11–18 October (1642), 88; BL, E124(14), *Speciall Passages*, no. 11, 18–25 October (1642), 96; BL, E121(2), *The Declaration and Votes of the Lords and Commons Assembled in Parliament: Concerning the late Treaty of Peace in York-shire . . . Together with the fourth article of the Lord Generals instructions, sent to Mr. Hotham and Sir Ed. Rodes*, 4 October (1642); BL, E97(9), *The Kingdomes Weekly Intelligencer*, no. 16, 11–18 April (1643), 125; John Tickell, *History of the Town and County of Kingston-upon-Hull* (Hull, 1798), 466; John Vicars, *Jehovah-Jireh. God in the Mount or England's Parliamentarie-Chronicle* (1644), 370–1; BL, E59(2), *A True Relation of the Discovery of a Most Desperate and Dangerous Plot for the delivering up, and surprising of the Townes of Hull and Beverley*, 4 July (1643), 6; BL, E61(16) *Certain Informations from Severall Parts of the Kingdome*, no. 27, 17–24 July (1643), 210; *CJ*, iii, 295–6; *CJ*, iv, 61, 417; J. T. Cliffe, *The Yorkshire Gentry from the Reformation to the Civil War* (1969), 328, 343.

Essex's council of war.[84] This sparked the abandonment of Lincoln and Gainsborough owing to mass desertions, and by 1644 one lieutenant-colonel openly questioned the allegiance of parliament's leader in the county, Lord Willoughby of Parham.[85]

The Hothams' eventual trials at London's Guildhall deepened factional infighting within parliament's coalition at a critical moment, shaping political divisions for years to come. Simultaneous to their court martial, on 11 December 1644 the Self-Denying Ordinance was brought before the Commons. Successful prosecution of the Hothams became a test of strength for those who favoured new-modelling parliament's armies. In this way the Fairfax interest became allies of Viscount Saye, Oliver St John, Oliver Cromwell, and the anti-Essex interest. This helped bring the many northern MPs connected with Lord Fairfax into sympathy with the war party and the Independents.[86] Conversely, those urging clemency for the Hothams opposed the new army and Sir Thomas Fairfax as its commander—in particular, Essex's supporters and the Presbyterian interest, often headed in the Commons by Sir Philip Stapleton, the commander of Essex's lifeguard and Sir John Hotham's son-in-law. When the Commons voted to reject clemency for Sir John, Cromwell was teller for the anti-Hotham vote, with Stapleton opposing him.[87]

The Hothams were the most important failed side-changers of the war. With almost 3,000 men under their command, their successful defection might have proved a decisive blow to parliament's cause.[88] With the Fairfaxes defeated at Adwalton Moor in the West Riding on 30 June 1643, and Hull thereafter in danger of siege, even the local Godly reconsidered their position. Thomas White, minister of Rowley, just nine miles from Hull, lamented to Sir Thomas Barrington on 14 July 1643 that many East Riding sympathizers:

> dare not come in (those that are willing) so freely as they would: many waver... So unexpressible is the disadvantage of playing an after game in war that we are in a very perplexed condition... The malignants here daily disperse rumours of ill successes on the Parliaments side in the south which daunts men exceedingly, the adversary trumpets and rails exceedingly... the clouds are so exceeding dark and thick.[89]

---

[84] BL, E126(1), *Speciall Passages*, no. 12, 25 October–1 November (1642), 103–4; BL, E97(9), *The Kingdomes Weekly Intelligencer*, 125; BL, E249(2), *A Perfect Diurnall of the Passages in Parliament*, no. 47, 1–8 May (1643), sig.Aaa2r; TNA, SP 28/138/3–4; SP 28/6/48; BL, E249(24), *A Perfect Diurnal of Some Passages in Parliament*, no. 55, 3–10 July (1643), 12; BL, E59(12), *The Parliament Scout*, no. 2, 29 June–6 July (1643), 14; BL, Harleian MS 165, fo. 107r; Vicars, *Jehovah-Jireh*, 372–3; Tickell, *History of the Town and County of Kingston-upon-Hull*, 464; *CJ*, iii, 86, 202, 303, 309.
[85] BL, Egerton MS 2647, fo. 120; BL, Harleian MS 165, fo. 148v; Clive Holmes, 'Colonel King and Lincolnshire Politics, 1642–1646', *HJ*, 16 (1973), 452–3, 459.
[86] David Scott, 'The "Northern Gentlemen", the Parliamentary Independents and Anglo-Scottish Relations in the Long Parliament', *HJ*, 42 (1999), 347–75.
[87] Andrew Hopper, *'Black Tom': Sir Thomas Fairfax and the English Revolution* (Manchester, 2007), 60–1.
[88] HHC, Hotham MS, U DDHO/1/35.
[89] BL, Egerton MS 2647, fo. 29.

White buckled under this pressure and obtained a written protection from New-castle. An acquaintance later remarked that it was fortunate that White died before Hull's siege was lifted, otherwise White would have 'taken some grief of heart, that he should so far doubt God's providence, as to shelter himself under the protection of the wicked, for the saving of his temporal estate.'[90]

With the Scots' arrival in Yorkshire from April 1644 the military ascendancy shifted towards parliament, and the flow of defections reversed. When Cawood castle surrendered in May 1644, most of the 140 prisoners took the Covenant and enlisted for parliament.[91] The royalist Colonel Sir Edward Duncombe had changed sides and assisted the besiegers, and later aided the allies' siege of York. When that city fell, Colonel Robert Brandling was captured and enlisted under Lord Fairfax. Punitive proceedings against Duncombe and Brandling were dropped.[92] After the disaster of Marston Moor, most committed royalists travelled south to serve the king or stayed to maintain royalist garrisons, encouraged to hold out by news of the king's western successes.[93]

In Lancashire, defections initially favoured the parliamentarians, who extended their control in early 1643. According to John Rosworm, parliament's initial local successes 'both animated, and increased' sympathizers.[94] Royalist attempts to mobilize Lonsdale's trained bands provoked them to revolt that January, and some may have defected to Colonel George Dodding's parliamentarian regi-ment.[95] Yet in May 1644 the pendulum swung back with the arrival of Rupert's army and the fearful sacking of Stockport, Bolton, and Liverpool, prompting parliamentarians to fear defections. By spring 1644 the loyalties of Colonels Dodding and Holland were in doubt. Sir John Meldrum lamented 'partialities and factions', while Sir Thomas Fairfax considered some of Lancashire's colonels so disaffected that they 'went as their peculiar safety or Interest swayed them.' Captain Peter Heywood was arrested for plotting to betray Manchester.[96] Adam Martindale, serving in Colonel Moore's troop, recalled that their captain had defected to the royalists in June 1644, before Rupert took Liverpool.[97] After Marston Moor, royalist military and civilian administrators in the county clashed, and William Legge, left behind by Rupert, lamented in August: 'I despaire of any good in Lancashire, who, to divert the war from themselves, have exposed their own quarter to be lost.'[98] In October 1644 Lord Byron urged Rupert to send reinforcements, as the parliamentarian conquest of the Wirral had led many

---

[90] Ibid., fo. 372.

[91] *CSPD 1644*, 176.

[92] Newman, 40–1, 116; Newman, *The Old Service*, 55–6.

[93] BL, E256(12), *A Perfect Diurnall of Some Passages in Parliament*, 486; Tibbut (ed.), *The Letter Books of Sir Samuel Luke*, 339.

[94] John Rosworm, *Good Service Hitherto Ill-Rewarded, Or, An Historicall Relation of Eight Years Services for King and Parliament done in and about Manchester and those Parts* (1649), 36.

[95] J. M. Gratton, *The Parliamentarian and Royalist War Effort in Lancashire 1642–1651* (Chetham Society, 3rd series, 48, 2010), 186.

[96] Ibid., 89–91, 109.

[97] Richard Parkinson (ed.), *The Life of Adam Martindale* (Chetham Society, 4, 1845), 40.

[98] Gratton, *Parliamentarian and Royalist War Effort in Lancashire*, 150.

countryfolk to reconsider their allegiance: 'for many who heretofore were thought loyal, upon this success of the rebels are either turned neuters or wholly revolted to them, no contribution comes in, for want of which the soldiers daily runaway'.[99]

A key factor in transforming northern allegiances during the 1640s was the repeated military interventions from north of the border. Oliver St John's speech to the Common Hall of London on 6 October 1643 claimed that with the Scots' military aid, parliament could win over neutrals.[100] However, anti-Scots prejudice was so strong in the north that the reverse was more likely; the earl of Newcastle probably benefitted from a surge in support when the Scots invaded. However, St John's speech served its purpose in spurring City aldermen and clergymen into a subscription to fund the Scots army.[101] London's press supported Scottish intervention by linking the Covenanters' arrival with a surge in defections to parliament. One newsbook applauded: 'Doe not the Earl of *Bedford*, Earle of *Westmerland*, Sir *Edward Deering*, Colonel *Gray* in the North give a very fair example? And I question not, but they will be followed by all that have any sence of honour, or loyalty.'[102]

After Marston Moor, the presence of large Scottish forces besieging Newcastle and Carlisle appear to have brought about a major realignment of politics in the region. The parliamentarian Richard Barwis, MP for Carlisle, enlisted the support of local royalists in opposing the Scottish presence. Barwis won further support at Westminster among war-party radicals, despite the north-west having previously shown little attachment to Godly politics or parliament's cause.[103] In September 1644 his brother-in-law, Sir Wilfrid Lawson, was appointed president of Lord Fairfax's council of war for Cumberland and Westmorland, despite having served as a royalist lieutenant-colonel and commissioner of array as recently as that spring.[104] Lawson was joined in local government by the former royalist Colonel Sir John Lowther, who surrendered quickly after Marston Moor, compounded, and took the Covenant, serving thereafter as a Westmorland JP.[105] Sir Patricius Curwen and other former royalists took the Covenant by October 1644.[106] By 1645 Sir George Dalston and Sir Henry Bellingham led the parliamentarian county committees in Cumberland and Westmorland, despite their former

---

[99] BL, Add. MS 18981, fos. 287–8.

[100] Valerie Pearl, 'Oliver St. John and the "Middle Group" in the Long Parliament: August 1643–May 1644', *EHR*, 81 (1966), 501.

[101] BL, E70(23), *The Parliament Scout Communicating His Intelligence to the Kingdome*, no. 16, 6–13 October (1643), 141.

[102] BL, E33(27), *The Spie, Communicating Intelligence from Oxford*, no. 4, 13–20 February (1644), 28.

[103] David Scott, 'The Barwis Affair: Political Allegiance and the Scots during the British Civil Wars', *EHR*, 115 (2000), 843–5, 858.

[104] Scott, 'Barwis Affair', 845–6; Newman, 225.

[105] In his defence, Lowther claimed that despite his royalist colonelcy, he had never raised forces against parliament: Newman, 239. Clark S. Colman, 'The Paralysis of the Cumberland and Westmorland Army in the First Civil War, c.1642–45', *Transactions of the Cumberland and Westmorland Antiquarian and Archaeological Society*, 3rd series, 1 (2001), 131–2.

[106] *Portland MS*, 185.

royalism.[107] David Scott has shown that of the seventeen men Barwis recommended as local justices, four had compounded for royalism, while a further nine
were politically suspect. C. B. Philips has argued that this shift was not so much
inspired by reconciliation as by the region's lack of genuine parliamentarian gentry
of sufficient status; Barwis and Lawson resorted to promoting and placing trust in
their kinsmen, despite doubts concerning their loyalty to parliament.[108]

When the Scots seized Carlisle in June 1645 they installed their own governor,
claiming that Lawson's forces could not be trusted. The Scots commissioners at
Westminster presented the Cumberland lawyer John Musgrave's charges concerning the former royalism of Barwis's supporters, but Barwis was repeatedly shielded
by the war party and Independents because he supplied them with political capital
in the shape of incriminating details of Scottish depredations.[109] A leading parliamentarian chaplain, Edward Bowles, excused and mitigated Lawson's former royalism as the product of his locality: 'consider the condition of this Gentleman, it's
true he cannot be justified throughout; he lived in an ill aire, and was infected with
it, but never stirred out of the County, to doe any prejudice to the Parliament: but
suffered imprisonment for his not ready complyance with the Commissioners of
Aray.' Bowles made the usual point that had Lawson defected to parliament earlier
it would have served little purpose, with the region dominated by the enemy. He
added that the Scots were hypocritical in distrusting Lawson when they employed
many who had previously opposed the parliament, including the notorious defector Sir John Urry.[110] John Lilburne was not so irenic, discrediting northern enemies
of the New Model in 1647 as having sought to betray parliament's cause from the
outset, and naming Sir Wilfrid Lawson in particular.[111] This was an effective ploy,
because Lilburne well appreciated that the depth of Lawson's loyalty and the effec-
tiveness of his militia remained highly questionable. There were accusations of
treachery and cowardice against the Cumberland forces in the wake of Sir Marmaduke Langdale's raid in late 1645. Once the royalists had seized Carlisle in April
1648, parliament's militia collapsed, Lawson was suspected of reverting to royalism, and Westmorland committee-men defected once again.[112]

David Scott has also pointed out that after 1646 the royalists were unable to
mobilize significant northern support because royalist credibility was compromised
by its attempts to enlist Scottish aid, forcing Sir Marmaduke Langdale into impress-
ments and threats to recruit during 1648.[113] During the second and third civil

---

[107] C. B. Philips, 'County Committees and Local Government in Cumberland and Westmorland,
1642–1660', *Northern History*, 5 (1970), 39.

[108] Scott, 'Barwis Affair', 847; Philips, 'County Committees and Local Government', 44.

[109] *Portland MS*, 257; Scott, 'Barwis Affair', 850, 852–6.

[110] Scott, 'Barwis Affair', 854; BL, E343(1), Edward Bowles, *Manifest Truths or An Inversion of
Truths Manifest. Containing a Narration of the Proceedings of the Scottish Army, and a Vindication of the
Parliament and Kingdome of England from the False and Injurious Aspersions cast on them by the Author
of the said Manifest* (1646), 59–60.

[111] John Lilburne, *Plaine Truth without Feare or Flattery, or, A Discovery of the Unlawfulnesse of the
Presbyterian Government* (1647), 12.

[112] Philips, 'County committees and local government', 52, 54; Leicestershire and Rutland Record
Office, DG21/275/c, Hazlerigg of Noseley MS.

[113] Scott, 'Barwis Affair', 859–61.

wars, many commoners in Northumberland supported parliament from hatred of the Scots and the military depredations they represented. After the battle of Worcester, many Cumberland and Westmorland civilians armed themselves to pick off Scots fugitives. Scott concludes that this shift was seismic enough to 'turn one of England's most malignant counties into a potential parliamentarian stronghold.'[114]

V

Side-changing was most pronounced in the regions that changed hands from 1642 to 1646. These were usually areas initially held for the king, but thereafter gradually brought under parliament's control. In contrast, those areas that parliament controlled throughout were comparatively unaffected by side-changing. Rather than attempting to build local support, East Anglian royalist gentry either left to serve the king outside their native region, fled overseas, or bided their time and remained at home.[115] The one occasion on which the Eastern Association's counties were seriously endangered was by Newcastle's army in August 1643. This threatened invasion of East Anglia sparked fears of treachery on its northern frontier at Wisbech and doubts over the loyalty of Sir John Palgrave's Norfolk regiment.[116] But on this occasion, eastern parliamentarians were rescued by other regional concerns; Yorkshire's royalists refused to expose their estates while Hull remained unreduced. They allegedly threatened Newcastle that if he persisted in marching southward 'they should say he had betrayed them.'[117] Militarily significant defections from parliament's heartlands in the southeast awaited 1648, when changed political circumstances turned many former parliamentarians against the New Model Army. Royalist rioting in Kent and East Anglia preceded the outbreak of the second civil war, while London itself became a 'hotbed of royalism', its crowds deriding the New Model as 'King Fairfax bastards', and its leaders recruiting disbanded parliamentarian soldiers for royalist insurgency.[118]

Political considerations as well as perceptions of military strength influenced the timing of defections. Chapter 2 noted that defections to the king were encouraged by the royal declarations of 20 June and 22 December 1643, while parliament procured its first flurry of elite side-changers from January 1644 in response to its Declaration of Both Kingdoms. Viscount Conway, Sir Anthony Ashley Cooper, Sir Gerard Napper, and Sir Edward Dering all attempted to time their defections

---

[114] Ibid., 862–3.
[115] Ann Hughes, 'The King, the Parliament and the Localities during the English Civil War', *JBS*, 24 (1985), 243; B. G. Blackwood, 'Parties and Issues in the Civil War in Lancashire and East Anglia', in R. C. Richardson (ed.), *The English Civil Wars: Local Aspects* (Stroud, 1997), 275; Clive Holmes, *The Eastern Association in the English Civil War* (Cambridge, 1974), 67.
[116] Bodl., MS Tanner 62, fo. 181.
[117] Bodl., MS Clarendon 23, fo. 229.
[118] Ian Gentles, 'The Struggle for London in the Second Civil War', *HJ*, 26 (1983), 286–90, 298; Robert Ashton, *Counter-Revolution: The Second Civil War and its Origins, 1646–8* (New Haven, 1994), 369–78.

to receive the benefits of this declaration; Dering complained on 11 March 1644 that he had been promised that a special 'consideration shall be had of the time of my coming in which is now almost 6 weeks past.'[119] Most side-changers with property and posterity to protect timed their prearranged defections to their own advantage. With jaded cynicism, committed activists came to expect a degree of side-changing in response to local conditions, political developments, and the fortunes of war; Richard Symonds commented that one Herefordshire gentleman was 'first for the Parliament, then for the King, then theirs, the taken prisoner by us, and [with] much adoe got his pardon, and now pro Rege, God wott.'[120]

[119] BL, Stowe MS 184, fo. 64r.
[120] I owe this reference to Mark Stoyle: Symonds, *Richard Symonds's Diary*, 196.

PART II

A CULTURAL HISTORY OF SIDE-CHANGING

.

6

Political oath-taking and the fear of treachery

Probing recent studies have investigated the factional infighting behind strategic decisions of the high command on both sides, but no concerted effort has yet been made to examine the influence of treachery in determining these counsels.[1] Instead, a traditional debate continues that tries to balance whether parliament's victory was due to superior generalship and decisive battles, or its superior material resources. For instance, Malcolm Wanklyn has recently argued that the decisive battle occurred at Naseby, before the king ran out of resources; therefore generalship was important in deciding the war's outcome.[2] Yet successful treachery in one's favour, or the act of unmasking traitors, could be perceived by contemporaries as equally decisive. For example, Sir Edward Nicholas congratulated the earl of Newcastle in January 1643 that his discovery of Lord Savile's supposed plot against the queen 'was no less acceptable to him than if he had won a battle'.[3]

This chapter analyses how side-changing and fear of treachery influenced strategy and the mobilization of support. The oaths, covenants, and protestations that both sides devised to bind supporters became established strategies because of fears of backsliding. Such anxieties were heightened because both sides knew the other was employing treachery and subversion to undermine them. In particular, commanders were well aware that enemy spies could masquerade as defectors. Victors ascribed successes to providence in order to demonstrate that God was on their side, but this practice raised problems for the vanquished in making sense of their defeats. They might argue that God was punishing them temporarily for their sins, and that if only they repented He would prevent the final triumph of their adversaries.[4] Yet more persistently, defeats were ascribed to human failures—in particular, treachery and turncoats. When such opinions circulated in print they intensified fears of traitors from within, undermining the war effort. These concerns might then be employed for factional purposes, to discredit individuals or interests. Insufficient activism and cowardice came to be conflated with treachery. So too was

---

[1] David Scott, 'Counsel and Cabal in the King's Party, 1642–1646', in Jason McElligott and David L. Smith (eds.), *Royalists and Royalism during the English Civil Wars* (Cambridge, 2007), 121–6; David Scott, 'Rethinking Royalist Politics 1642–9', in John Adamson (ed.), *The English Civil War: Conflict and Contexts, 1640–1649* (Basingstoke, 2009), 43–4, 50–1; Malcolm Wanklyn, *The Warrior Generals: Winning the British Civil Wars* (New Haven, 2010).

[2] Wanklyn, *Warrior Generals*, ix–x.

[3] BL, Harleian MS 164, fo. 281r.

[4] Margaret Griffin, *Regulating Religion and Morality in the King's Armies, 1639–1646* (Leiden, 2004), 132–4, 139.

correspondence with the enemy—a frequent practice, despite being forbidden by articles of war on both sides.[5] Fear of betrayal constantly exercised garrison commanders, leading towns to become dominated by surveillance. Accidents and setbacks were read as conspiratorial, and governors were quick to suspect subordinates of perfidy. With commanders mindful of planting spies among the enemy, how could incoming converts or returning prisoners be trusted?[6] Fear of treachery on occasions hampered strategy on both sides, and occasioned an atmosphere of near panic among parliamentarians in August 1643. However, the king's opponents were able to overcome this crisis, and by 1644, owing to superior military intelligence networks, they were clearly more effective in defending their cause from subversion, as well as procuring decisive defections from the enemy.

I

Oaths, vows, protestations, and covenants were employed on both sides to mobilize support, prevent backsliding, and minimize turncoating. They carried force because it was widely believed that God would punish those who failed to observe them once taken, and they became established political strategies because of fears of conspiracy and treachery. The Protestation of 1641 was a reaction to the Army Plot and attempts to free the earl of Strafford. Unspecific phrasing pledged its takers to protect the king's person, the privilege of parliament, and the Protestant religion 'from Counsels, Plots, Conspiracies, or otherwise'.[7] From 1642, both sides interpreted its ambiguity to their advantage, using it to mobilize supporters.[8] In particular, some parliamentarians appear to have associated it with a pledge of loyalty. Parliamentarians used copies of the Protestation as badges of allegiance, fixing them to pikes, hats, coats, and muskets. Some sought to use it as a test of political and religious reliability; in Yorkshire, Thomas Stockdale considered it a fit tool 'to distinguish the subjects' affections', and that by listing refusers, 'the strength of the adverse faction might appear'.[9] Above all, it invited greater popular political participation, reflecting what David Cressy has called 'the most ambitious political mobilization heretofore attempted.'[10]

After the outbreak of war the Protestation was adapted to address the military situation at Exeter in December 1642, pledging citizens 'never to desert' parliament's cause.[11] As John Walter has suggested, it provoked arguments at

   [5] Wing (2nd edn.)/C2497A, *Military Orders and Articles Established by His Majesty, for the Better Ordering and Government of His Majesties Army* (Oxford, 1644), 18; BL, E116(34), *Lawes and Ordinances of Warre*, 12 September (1642), sig. A3v. In 1645 the earl of Sussex insinuated that most of Oxford corresponded with someone among the enemy: Bodl. MS Clarendon 24, fo. 25r.
   [6] Barbara Donagan, *War in England 1642–1649* (Oxford, 2008), 104–6, 111, 122.
   [7] *CJ*, ii, 132.
   [8] Edward Vallance, 'Protestation, Vow, Covenant and Engagement: Swearing Allegiance in the English Civil War', *Historical Research*, 75 (2002), 411.
   [9] David Cressy, 'The Protestation Protested, 1641 and 1642', *HJ*, 45 (2002), 259, 266–7.
   [10] Ibid., 252.
   [11] Mark Stoyle, *From Deliverance to Destruction: Rebellion and Civil War in an English City* (Exeter, 1996), 180.

parish level.[12] Immediately before Hull was besieged by royalists in September 1643, Christopher Bacon of North Ferriby was charged with having said 'had I known so much as I do know now, I would not have taken the Protestation for within a little while you will see a great change.'[13] In districts where Catholic royalists were prominent, some parliamentarians turned on backsliders for breach of faith. For example, in April 1643 Sir John Hotham accused his kinsman Sir Hugh Cholmley of 'falsifying his Protestation' by his defection to the king and 'revolting to the Popish army.' Soon afterwards, Sir George Chudleigh defended himself against similar charges. Despite laying down arms, Chudleigh's printed defence maintained that he had 'done my utmost faithfully according to my Protestation.'[14]

Although royalists held that the traditional oaths of supremacy and allegiance remained adequate, occasionally they imposed protestations upon people to oppose parliament.[15] Sir Francis Otley did so at Shrewsbury in January 1643, binding the inhabitants to 'withstand & suppress' the rebels.[16] In January 1644 an association was imposed on all adult males in Devon, Exeter, and Cornwall that bore similarities to the Protestation, but pledged they would protect the Protestant religion from the 'Innovations of Sectaries and Schismatiques'. It was to be taken before the minister, constable, and churchwardens in every parish.[17] On 22 June 1644 Sir John Berkeley, governor of Exeter, advised Dartmouth's governor, Colonel Edward Seymour, to 'secure all' that refused it.[18] An oath was imposed on Exeter's inhabitants in 1645 to resist the New Model Army and to oppose all plots and treacheries intended against the city.[19] From April 1645 Rupert imposed a new protestation on adult males in Herefordshire and Worcestershire that abjured clubmen associations and repudiated the Solemn League and Covenant.[20] Oxford's city regiment undertook to defend the king, city, and university from all 'treacheries, plots and conspiracies whatsoever'.[21] Parliament's propagandists vilified royalists

[12] John Walter, 'Politicising the Popular? The "Tradition of Riot" and Popular Political Culture in the English Revolution', in Nicholas Tyacke (ed.), *The English Revolution, c.1590–1720: Politics, Religion and Communities* (Manchester, 2007), 104.

[13] HHC, C BRS/7/52.

[14] BL, E247(21), *A Perfect Diurnall of the Passages in Parliament*, no. 43, 3–10 April (1643); BL, E37(20), *A Declaration Published in the County of Devon by that Grand Ambo-dexter, Sir George Chudleigh baronet* (1644), 3.

[15] David Martin Jones, *Conscience and Allegiance in Seventeenth-Century England: The Political Significance of Oaths and Engagements* (New York, 1999), 112–13.

[16] TNA, SP 16/497/3.

[17] BL, E30(1), *Mercurius Aulicus*, 2nd week, 7–13 January (1644), 776; Stoyle, *From Deliverance to Destruction*, 208.

[18] DRO, 1392 M/L 1644/38.

[19] BL, E297(3), *Sir Thomas Fairfax's Letter to the Honorable William Lenthall Esq: Speaker of the House of Commons; Concerning the taking of Sherborn Castle… Also, the oath taken by the inhabitants of Exeter*, 19 August (1645), 7.

[20] Ronald Hutton, 'The Worcestershire Clubmen in the English Civil War', *Midland History*, 5 (1979), 46; BL, E260(25), *Perfect Passages of each dayes Proceedings in Parliament*, no. 27, 23–29 April (1645), 210–12.

[21] BL, Harleian MS 6852, fo. 22r.

for forcing prisoners taken at Leicester to swear to serve the king, while John Vicars blasted the 'Oxonian Protestation or Covenant against the Parliament.'[22]

From August 1642, Essex's officers were bound by an oath to 'defend, maintain, and obey' parliament and Essex as captain-general.[23] However, the wartime covenants parliament imposed were more far-reaching. Edward Vallance has argued that they met with equivocation in many quarters—not through political hostility, but because people feared forswearing themselves in an uncertain future or contradicting previous oaths.[24] The first was the Vow and Covenant administered from June 1643 as a reaction against Waller's plot. Capitalizing upon the climate of fear unleashed by the plot's discovery, Pym devised it to isolate royalists, cow those in favour of peace, and commit the people to war against the king in the name of the Protestant religion.[25] Unlike royalist oaths of allegiance to the king's person, this was a covenant, binding people together to participate in thwarting royalist treachery and winning God's favour.[26] It was unevenly enforced, leading some garrison commanders to take the initiative themselves. On 4 November 1643, Plymouth's council of war required all the 'officers, soldiers, inhabitants and strangers' to take a 'vow & protestation' to defend the town, and discover plots against it, to the mayor and governor. Refusers were duly noted.[27] The following month, Colonel Richard Norton drew up a 'vow and protestation' himself and imposed it on Southampton's inhabitants. The vow was to 'hold no secret correspondence with nor give intelligence unto the enemy and that they should discover all secret plots and attempts against the said town.'[28]

From October 1643 parliament's next covenant, the Solemn League and Covenant, pledged its supporters to a Scottish alliance and a Presbyterian church settlement. Returning side-changers such as the earl of Holland and Sir Edward Dering were offered it as a means of reconciling themselves with parliament. Some royalists wanted a loyalty oath imposed on Holland after his arrival at Oxford, and when he returned to parliament Holland denied having taken one. Sir Edward Dering complained that despite his having taken the Covenant three times, his loyalty was still doubted.[29] On 5 February 1644 an ordinance directed that the Covenant should be taken by every adult male in England and Wales.[30] Although local enforcement was patchy, parish ministers were ordered to send parliament

---

[22] BL, E33(18), John Vicars, *A Looking-Glasse for Malignants: or, Gods Hand Against God-haters* (1643), 23–4; Wing/S5070, Joshua Sprigge, *Anglia Rediviva; Englands Recovery* (1647), 51.

[23] *CJ*, ii, 696, 699.

[24] Vallance, 'Protestation, Vow, Covenant and Engagement', 408.

[25] *CJ*, iii, 117–18; Hyde, *History of the Rebellion*, iii, 38–53; Samuel R. Gardiner, *History of the Great Civil War*, 4 vols. (1987), i, 146–9.

[26] Ann Hughes, 'The King, the Parliament and the Localities in the English Civil War', *JBS*, 24 (1985), 259n.

[27] BL, Add. MS 35297, fos. 12r–13r.

[28] BL, Harleian MS 165, fo. 251v. According to the royalists, Thomas Essex imposed a similar protestation on Bristol in February 1643: BL, E246(41), *Mercurius Aulicus*, 8th week, 19–25 February (Oxford, 1643), sig. P3v.

[29] Edward Hyde, earl of Clarendon, *History of the Rebellion and Civil Wars in England begun in the year 1641*, ed. William Dunn Macray, 6 vols. (Oxford, 1888), iii, 146–7; BL, Harleian MS 165, fos. 227v–228r; BL, E32(14), *A Declaration made to the Kingdome by Henry, Earle of Holland*, 10 February (1644), 3; BL, Stowe MS 184, fo. 64r.

[30] *LJ*, vi, 411.

lists of refusers.[31] It was pressed on royalist prisoners of war and those compounding for their estates. It was intended to constrain the consciences of royalist captives to future good behaviour; one London newsbook claimed that Sir Thomas Gower and Viscount Dunbar had surrendered themselves to parliament before perfidiously returning to the royalists in Scarborough, and called for 'a searching Oth and Covenant, which would touch them to the quick' to be administered upon their apprehension.[32] However, most royalists considered the Solemn League and Covenant unlawful, not least because it contravened previous oaths and was therefore not binding.[33] During the first civil war, most gentry defections to the king took place before the Solemn League and Covenant was in place, but those side-changers who became royalists having previously taken it might face execution as covenant-breakers.[34]

This situation was inflamed by the mass defections in 1648. The parliamentarian newsbook *The Moderate* declared that August that any royalist who had previously taken the Negative Oath or Covenant could be executed without mercy.[35] Yet in practice, executions of side-changing officers in 1648 were for betraying trusts rather than breaking the Covenant. Parliamentarians were uncomfortably aware that the Covenant required its takers to preserve the king's person, a pledge which defectors in 1648 could forcefully argue that parliament had now broken. So despite their contested nature, claims to political constancy would be arbitrated by the victors of the second civil war as factional politics at Westminster came to define and determine who would be stigmatized as turncoats and oath-breakers.

II

While both sides employed oaths, protestations, and covenants to bind supporters to them, they also sought to subvert individuals among the enemy into defections that could prove militarily decisive. Royalist military strategy in 1643 was consistently diverted into failed conspiracies to capture parliament's garrisons by treachery. Gloucester, Hull, and Plymouth were particularly critical because they pinned down large royalist armies and prevented the king from completely dominating the north and west. All were difficult to take by assault, so the royalists combined siege and subversion against them.

The fateful decision to besiege Gloucester in August 1643 was frequently argued, even in Gardiner's day, as the point where Charles lost the strategic initiative.[36] The

---

[31] Jones, *Conscience and Allegiance*, 130.

[32] BL, E10(22), *The Kingdomes Weekly Intelligencer*, no. 74, 24 September–1 October (1644), 594.

[33] Jones, *Conscience and Allegiance*, 138.

[34] Charles Carlton, *Going to the Wars: The Experience of the British Civil Wars, 1638–1651* (1992), 198.

[35] The Negative Oath was required of compounding royalists from April 1645, and involved a pledge not to assist the king in the war and to submit to parliament: Jones, *Conscience and Allegiance*, 115; BL, E461(16), *The Moderate Impartially Communicating Martial Affaires to the Kingdome of England*, no. 7, 22–29 August (1648), sig. G2r–v; Robert Ashton, *Counter-Revolution: The Second Civil War and its Origins, 1646–8* (1994), 400.

[36] Gardiner, *History of the Great Civil War*, i, 194, 197.

argument goes that the king should have marched on London when parliamentarian morale and resources were at their lowest ebb.[37] Yet the decision to besiege Gloucester was informed by hopes that Governor Edward Massey and the citizens would defect and surrender. Initially, in 1642, Massey had offered his service to the king, but was refused. On 8 August 1643 the royalist Captain Prestland Mollineux advised that Massey would change sides, particularly if his father was allowed into Massey's presence to persuade him.[38] Since December 1642 there had been attempts to convert Massey's Sergeant-Major, Constance Ferrer.[39] On 4 August 1643 the royalist Colonel William Morton reported that Ferrer was inquiring what service from him was requisite to gain royal pardon. Morton claimed that many acquaintances in Gloucester had approached him to intercede for royal mercy; he advised that were it not for Massey and a few others, Gloucester 'should be delivered up without a stroke.'[40] Clarendon recalled that William Legge wrote to Massey, urging him to surrender, and although Massey replied with a spirited written refusal, he sent verbal assurance that he wished the king well and would not defy his person.[41] Here Massey was probably conducting a double game designed to ensure his safety should the city prove untenable (see Fig. 6.1).[42]

These considerations brought the king's army before Gloucester's walls on 10 August 1643. Despite refusal of the summons, royalist hopes remained high that surrender was imminent. The royalist council of war's papers include a list of loyal inhabitants that probably reflects another scheme to subvert the city from inside.[43] Massey warned parliament that he feared treachery from the disobedient citizens, claiming that '10 for one incline the other way'.[44] A gunner and fifteen musketeers defected to the besiegers, claiming that the defenders lacked bread, that more were ready to defect, and detailing where the defences contained weaknesses.[45] The *Perfect Diurnal* reported for 29 August that a conspiracy among the corporation to shoot Massey and his officers had been foiled; several conspirators were quickly executed.[46] Even after the siege was raised, Massey's loyalty was questioned by his own subordinates, some of whom were themselves approached by royalists to defect.[47]

[37] Wanklyn, *Warrior Generals*, 63.

[38] BL, Add. MS 18980, fo. 104.

[39] TNA, SP 16/493/1; *CSPD 1641–3*, 458.

[40] BL, Add. MS 18980, fo. 100; Newman, 265.

[41] Hyde, *History of the Rebellion*, iii, 130–1.

[42] Andrew Warmington, 'Sir Edward Massey (1604x9–1674), parliamentarian and royalist army officer', *ODNB*.

[43] BL, Harleian MS 6804, fo. 118.

[44] Bodl., MS Tanner 62, fo. 197.

[45] I. G. Philip (ed.), *The Journal of Sir Samuel Luke* (The Oxfordshire Record Society, 31, 1950), ii, 139; J. R. S. Whiting, *Gloucester Besieged: the Story of a Roundhead City* (2nd edn., Gloucester, 1984), 13.

[46] BL, E250(5), *Perfect Diurnal of the Passages in Parliament*, no. 7, 28 August–4 September (1643), 51–2; Bulstrode Whitelock, *Memorials of English Affairs from the Beginning of the Reign of Charles I to the Happy Restoration of King Charles II*, 4 vols. (Oxford, 1853), i, 210.

[47] *CSPD 1644*, 343–4; Whiting, *Gloucester Besieged*, 17; BL, E45(12), *A True Relation of a Wicked Plot intended and still on foot against the City of Glocester, to betray the same into the hands of the Cavaliers*, 7 May (1644); BL, E306(8), John Corbet, *A Historicall Relation of the Military Government of Gloucester: From the Beginning of the Civill Warre betweene King and Parliament, to the Removall of Colonell Massie* (1645), 71.

Fig. 6.1. Major-General Edward Massey. (Special Collections of the University of Leicester, University of Leicester Library, Fairclough Collection of Portrait Prints, EP36, Box 3.)

At Hull in the summer of 1642, despite an attempted siege, the royalists lacked the military capacity to wrestle this impressively fortified town from Sir John Hotham.[48] Consequently, they devoted their efforts to suborning the governor and his officers. Thomas Beckwith of Beverley attempted to bribe two garrison officers into betraying the town without success.[49] Lord Digby, disguised as a Frenchman, also met Sir John Hotham in early July, where, according to Clarendon, Digby persuaded him to deliver Hull if the king appeared in force before it.[50] Whether it was due to Sir John's second thoughts or his deliberate sabotaging of their efforts, the royalists' failure to secure Hull's arms magazine led to the king's army being poorly equipped at Edgehill—itself a decisive factor in their failure to inflict a crushing defeat on the earl of Essex.[51]

By the time of the second siege of Hull from September 1643 the town's government had passed to Lord Fairfax, who quickly regarrisoned Beverley owing to fears that the aldermen were conspiring to betray the town.[52] On 27 August 1643 Lord Fairfax declared that there were 'dangerous and malevolent' people in Hull giving intelligence to the enemy. He established a committee to guard against spies and treachery, which soon arrested one of its own members, Captain Bladen, for conspiring to deliver up the blockhouses.[53] On 4 September Fairfax informed parliament that he feared the enemy 'had some hope to carry the town by treachery', while Ralph Josselin confided to his diary how Hull was 'like to be betrayed'.[54] During the siege, when a careless gunner ignited a powder magazine, it was conspiracy, not negligence, that was immediately suspected.[55] The process of taking depositions concerning seditious words, traitors, and fifth-columnists increased fears further,[56] climaxing with the arrest of Sergeant-Major-General John Gifford on 3 October for having received letters from a royalist captain urging him to change sides.[57] Yet the royalists' failure to take Hull by force or treachery, owing to

---

[48] Audrey Howes and Martin Foreman, *Town and Gun: The 17th-Century Defences of Hull* (Hull, 1999).

[49] Basil N. Reckitt, *Charles the First and Hull, 1639–1645* (2nd edn., Howden, 1988), 45; *CJ*, ii, 587–8; Philip Saltmarshe, *History and Chartulary of the Hothams of Scorborough in the East Riding of Yorkshire, 1100–1700* (York, 1914), 124; BL, E107(31), *Terrible News from Hull: Concerning a Great Conspiracy which was intended against Sir John Hotham*, 20 July (1642).

[50] BL, E256(45), *A Perfect Diurnall of Some Passages in Parliament*, no. 71, 2–9 December (1644), 560; BL, E67(22), *Certaine Informations from Severall Parts of the Kingdome*, no. 35, 11–18 September (1643), 268; Reckitt, *Charles the First and Hull*, 49–52; HHC, Hotham MS U DDHO/1/35; Hyde, *History of the Rebellion*, ii, 257–67.

[51] Aaron Graham, 'The Earl of Essex and Parliament's Army at the Battle of Edgehill: A Reassessment', *War in History*, 17 (2010), 290.

[52] BL, Add. MS 31116, fo. 63r–v; *CJ*, iii, 704; BL, E249(29), *A Perfect Diurnall of Some Passages in Parliament*, no. 4, 17–24 July (1643), 32.

[53] The Bladens had been servants of the first baron Fairfax, and Captain Bladen joined Sir Thomas at a critical moment in January 1643: HHC, C BRS/7/19, 53; Bodl., MS Fairfax 30, fo. 129; Robert Bell (ed.), *The Fairfax Correspondence: Memorials of the Civil War*, 2 vols. (1849), i, 35.

[54] BL, Harleian MS 165, fo. 177r; Ralph Josselin, *The Diary of Ralph Josselin, 1616–1683*, ed. Alan Macfarlane (Records of Social and Economic History, new series, 3, Oxford, 1976), 13–14.

[55] BL, E69(13), *A True Relation from Hull of the Present State and Condition it is in* (1643), 5.

[56] HHC, C BRS/7/48, 52.

[57] Gifford had previously served the Hothams in Hull during 1642: TNA, SP 28/138/4; BL, E107(12), *An Extract of all the Passages from Hull, York, and Lincolnshire*, 19 July (1642), 8; Bodl., MS Tanner 62A, fos. 103–4.

parliamentarian vigilance and the strength of the town's defences neutralized the offensive capacity of the king's largest field army for the rest of 1643.

As at Hull, Plymouth's defences were so heavily fortified that they rendered direct assault problematic, so for three years the garrison was bombarded with conspiracies. There were five sieges and an intermittent blockade, and no less than six successive governors and colonels were approached to betray Plymouth, or its outlying forts and defences. In August 1643 Sir Alexander Carew, governor of St Nicholas Island in Plymouth Sound, was arrested by his own men before he could deliver his charge to the royalists.[58] In November 1643 an attempt to explode part of the defences was foiled.[59] Plymouth was reinforced by forces under Colonel James Wardlaw, who himself uncovered a plot against the town.[60] In February 1644 Richard Strode accused Wardlaw of conspiring to betray Plymouth and attempting to remove Colonel William Gould from his command of the fort and island.[61] Yet despite such discord among the garrison, the royalists failed to infiltrate Plymouth successfully.

In March 1644 Sir Richard Grenville's attempt to persuade Colonel Gould to surrender failed, as did Lord Digby's September efforts to convert Lord Robartes.[62] The royalist deserter Captain Joseph Grenville failed to suborn Colonel Michael Searle into betraying the outworks.[63] Another foiled conspiracy was noted by Thomas Juxon in December 1644.[64] A year later, Sir John Digby attempted to capitalize on parliament's ill-treatment of the governor, Colonel James Kerr, but Kerr scorned his approach, remarking that he had 'no reason to wonder much at your perswasion to Treachery', adding 'surely those principles came from Spain.'[65] The unfortunate Scotsman who attempted to pervert Kerr into betraying the town was hanged, drawn, and quartered there in December 1645.[66]

It might be argued just from these three sieges that the king lost his best chance of victory through misplaced hopes among the royalist high command of treachery in his favour. Royalists invested heavily in this strategy either because they lacked

[58] BL, E67(3), *Certaine Informations from Severall Parts of the Kingdome*, no. 34, 4–11 September (1643), 259–60; BL, E250(8), *A Perfect Diurnall of Some Passages in Parliament*, no. 8, 4–11 September (1643), 57; BL, Harleian MS 165, fo. 161r–v.

[59] DRO, 1392M/L 1645/35, *A True Narration of the Most Observable Passages in and at the Late Siege of Plymouth, from the fifteenth day of September 1643 untill the twenty fift of December following* (1644), 8.

[60] Wanklyn, *Warrior Generals*, 90.

[61] Bodl., MS Tanner 62, fo. 557.

[62] Miller, *Sir Richard Grenville*, 75; BL, E47(1), *A Continuation of the True Narration of the Most Observable Passages in and about Plymouth, from Ianuary 26. 1643. till this present*, 10 May (1644), 9–12; Roger Granville, *The King's General in the West: The Life of Sir Richard Granville, Bart., 1600–1659* (1908), 97.

[63] Amos C. Miller, *Sir Richard Grenville of the Civil War* (1979), 94; BL, Add. MS 35297, fo. 47r; *CJ*, iii, 667.

[64] Thomas Juxon, *The Journal of Thomas Juxon, 1644–1647*, ed. Keith Lindley and David Scott (Camden Society, 5th series, 13, 1999), 70.

[65] BL, E314(10), *Sir John Digby's Letter to Colonel Kerr Governour of Plymouth, perswading him to betray his trust, and deliver up the town and forts of Plymouth, to the Kings party. Together with Col. Kerrs answer.* 2 January (1646), 4.

[66] BL, Add. MS 35297, fo. 95v.

the resources for a successful siege or, as at Dover castle, because conventional attack was out of the question.[67] After the costly storming of Bristol, they also sought to avoid the casualties of an assault. Subverting enemy commanders was a more cost-effective strategy. Royalist perceptions of parliamentarians as hypocritical upstarts who used religion merely as a cloak for private interests and rebellion may have led them to consider parliamentarians as particularly susceptible to offers of money and social advancement.[68]

Although less critical than Gloucester, Hull, and Plymouth, the royalists repeatedly failed to capture parliament's garrisons at Aylesbury and Nottingham during 1643. Four attempts to subvert garrison officers were made at Aylesbury, and five at Nottingham; but they failed, despite polite letters from royalist commanders known personally to the recipients offering money, favour, and employment. Aylesbury was important as a frontier garrison, guarding the Chiltern route between London and Oxford.[69] During the third plot against the town, in October 1643, Sir John Byron informed the governor whom he thought he had subverted, Colonel Edward Aldrich, that the king grew impatient with such stratagems: 'His Majesty hath reason to be cautious in regard of the late failure of Poole[70] upon a treaty of the same nature; and therefore what you propound in this business let it be done with that clearness and ingenuity, that it may not undergo any such suspicion.' Having convinced Byron of his sincerity, Aldrich discovered the conspiracy to the earl of Essex, leaving Byron to indignantly declare him 'a fool and a knave'.[71] The failure of the fourth attempt on Aylesbury particularly embarrassed Rupert and Digby who had both been involved, while Essex was probably warned of it from the outset.[72] As at Hull, failed plots prompted a strengthening of defences. In January 1644 the House of Lords, recognizing that this was the fourth treacherous attempt on Aylesbury, prioritized its supply.[73] Charles grew personally frustrated by the consistent failure of such conspiracies, while his strategy of capturing Aylesbury the day before the Oxford Parliament first met was particularly damaging. It incurred a costly six-week delay to Rupert's implementing of his commission in the Welsh marches. Consequently, Rupert did not arrive in Shrewsbury until 19 February 1644, by which time Sir Thomas Fairfax had been victorious at Nantwich in his absence.[74]

[67] Alan Everitt, *The Community of Kent and the Great Rebellion, 1640–1660* (Leicester, 1966), 203.
[68] This social snobbery was so pronounced in the parliamentarian Edmund Ludlow that he claimed that 'Col. Brown the woodmonger' changed sides because he failed to control his 'ambitious temper' after the king gave him a pair of silk stockings: Edmund Ludlow, *The Memoirs of Edmund Ludlow, Lieutenant General of the Horse in the Army of the Commonwealth of England, 1625–1672*, ed. C. H. Firth, 2 vols. (Oxford, 1894), i, 139.
[69] Wanklyn, *Warrior Generals*, 37.
[70] One serial claimed that this failure resulted in the massacre of 300 royalists, admitted through Poole's gate only to be riddled with musket and artillery fire: BL, TT E250(16), *A Perfect Diurnall of Some Passages in Parliament*, no. 11, 25 September–2 October (1643), 87.
[71] *Portland MS*, 139–40, 144–5; BL, Add. MS 18980, fo. 144.
[72] I. G. Philip (ed.), *The Journal of Sir Samuel Luke* (The Oxfordshire Record Society, 29, 33, 1947, 1952–3), i, 39, iii, 238; BL, Harleian MS 165, fo. 152r, 283r–v; BL, Add. MS 18980, fo. 144; BL, Add. MS 31116, fo. 111r; see also papers referring to the plot to betray Aylesbury: Bodl., MS Tanner 62, fos. 434–8; Juxon, *Journal of Thomas Juxon*, 4.
[73] *LJ*, vi, 394.
[74] Wanklyn, *Warrior Generals*, 253n.

At Nottingham from August to December 1643 the governor, Colonel John Hutchinson, his brother, Lieutenant-Colonel George Hutchinson, and his cousin, Captain Thomas Poulton, were all offered, in letters from the earl of Newcastle and Sir Richard Byron, large sums to betray the castle. The letters warned that the king held keeping a castle against him as more treasonous than service in Essex's army.[75] Mindful of the arrests of Carew and the Hothams, Hutchinson dared not conceal these letters from parliament 'least some suspicion might be had of his fidelity'.[76] Hutchinson and his officers penned disdainful refusals, sending copies to the county committee and parliament, and took the important step of printing them in a pamphlet.[77] Through print, sieges became media stories, where rumours of side-changing and conspiracy might impact upon the course of events. Allegations of treachery could undermine trust in garrison commanders, so the Hutchinsons sought to fashion themselves as beyond temptation. Resorting to print also raised their stock within parliament's coalition by showing that the royalists thought them sufficiently important to try to subvert. It also enabled them to advance themselves as heroic, incorruptible, and constant, whilst traducing the royalists as devious, conniving, and treacherous. They would 'starve and rot' before betraying their trusts, declaring that the royalists might better employ their 'despised Coyne to tempt some fraile waiting-woman' instead.[78] Print helped allay their fears that the royalists had spread falsehoods about them in order to undermine their reputations with their comrades. Strengthening their position within their coalition's shifting factions was vital, because Colonel Pierrepont was attempting to secure the castle's governorship for himself, and suspicion of disloyalty would play into his hands. Lucy Hutchinson used the same means to discredit Pierrepont, claiming that the Fairfaxes had intelligence that he intended to change sides.[79]

Royalist military planning was also badly compromised by the king's inclination to secrets, duplicity, and the simultaneous pursuit of multiple strategies. For instance, Charles approved Sir William Ogle's secret plans to surprise Winchester castle without Sir Ralph Hopton's knowledge. This undermined the latter's strategy, diverting him from his projects against parliament's important garrisons at Lyme and Poole.[80]

III

In contrast to the king's repeated failures, from 1644 parliamentarians became successful in suborning royalist garrisons while further frustrating royalist attempts against

---

[75] Lucy Hutchinson, *Memoirs of the Life of Colonel Hutchinson*, ed. N. H. Keeble (1995), 121–6.

[76] Newcastle had offered Hutchinson a barony and £10,000: BL, Harleian MS 165, fo. 258r; Bodl., MS Tanner 62, fo. 467.

[77] Hutchinson, *Memoirs*, 142.

[78] BL, E79(30), *A Discovery of the Trecherous Attempts of the Cavaliers, to have Procured the Betraying of Nottingham Castle into their Hands* (1643), sig. A2v, A3v.

[79] Hutchinson, *Memoirs*, 110, 122, 135, 358n.

[80] Charles E. H. Chadwyck Healey (ed.), *Bellum Civile: Hopton's Narrative of his Campaign in the West (1642–1644) and other papers* (Somerset Record Society, 18, 1902), 63.

their own. In November 1643 Sir William Brereton captured Hawarden castle when the governor Colonel Ravenscroft, assisted by another side-changer, Colonel Aldersey, opened the gates and changed sides. Yet Brereton insisted that it was surrendered not through treachery, but because it was poorly supplied.[81] *Mercurius Aulicus* mocked Waller's capture of Arundel castle soon after, claiming that, failing to take it by force, he had learnt from Brereton how to bribe his way in.[82] Royalist and parliamentarian sources alike confirm that Monmouth fell to parliament by treachery in September 1644, the double side-changer Lieutenant-Colonel Robert Kirle betraying the town.[83]

Lord Digby failed to subvert Major-General Richard Browne, the parliamentarian governor of Abingdon in late 1644. By allowing Digby to think he would surrender the town for a baronetcy, Browne gained time to reprovision and refortify.[84] This strategy was risky, as Sir John Hotham was tried and executed for secretly conducting such a strategy at Hull during the previous year. Yet Browne was more circumspect in securing parliament's trust. Even Edmund Ludlow, who loathed Browne as a mean woodmonger, considered his service at Abingdon worthy of praise, while the royalist Sir Philip Warwick remarked: 'Brown was a man of clear courage, & of a good understanding, and very crafty, as his treaty with the Lord Digby... whilst he lay at Abingdon, will hereafter show'.[85]

In February 1645 parliament's Colonels Mytton and Reinking captured Shrewsbury in suspicious circumstances. In the previous October the governor, Sir Michael Earnley, had complained to Rupert that Shrewsbury was surrounded by the enemy and in an 'ill condition' because two castles in Montgomeryshire had lately been 'basely and treacherously lost'. Earnley had also been required to investigate suggested foul play in the loss of Oswestry.[86] Another local commander, Sir Michael Woodhouse, warned Rupert that he feared treachery before Shrewsbury fell to a night attack, claiming the townsmen neglected to post sufficient guards.[87] Richard Symonds listed it as 'betrayed to the rebells in winter 1644', while *Mercurius Aulicus* soon claimed that Rupert had recaptured and hanged twelve of the turncoats that betrayed the town.[88] Yet parliamentarian sources anxiously denied they had utilized treachery. Thomas Malbon wrote that Mytton 'did very secretlie & cu'inglie enter into Shrowesbury, althoughe not att the Gates, nor by any knowledge of theim in the Towne'.[89] Mytton and Reinking's own

[81] Norman Tucker, *Denbighshire Officers in the Civil War* (Denbigh, 1964), 81; Newman, 1, 310; *Portland MS*, 153.

[82] BL, E30(1), *Mercurius Aulicus*, 774.

[83] BL, Add. MS 18981, fo. 237; *Portland MS*, 280; Andrew R. Warmington, *Civil War, Interregnum and Restoration in Gloucestershire, 1640–1672* (Woodbridge, 1997), 64; Newman, 219.

[84] Keith Lindley, 'Sir Richard Browne, first baronet (*c.*1602–1669), parliamentarian army officer and lord mayor of London', *ODNB*.

[85] Ludlow, *Memoirs*, i, 139; Beinecke Rare Book and Manuscript Library, Osborn Shelves, fb87, fo. 75r.

[86] BL, Add. MS 18981, fo. 299r–v.

[87] Ibid., fos. 27, 40.

[88] Richard Symonds, *Richard Symonds's Diary of the Marches of the Royal Army*, ed. Charles Edward Long and Ian Roy (Cambridge, 1997), 172; BL, E276(18), *Mercurius Aulicus*, 16–23 March (Oxford, 1645), 1516.

[89] James Hall (ed.), *Memorials of the Civil War in Cheshire and the Adjacent Counties by Thomas Malbon of Nantwich, Gent., and Providence Improved by Edward Burghall, Vicar of Acton, near Nantwich* (Lancashire and Cheshire Record Society, 19, 1889), 163–4.

explanations of their success were deliberately vague, saying it 'was in agitation severall waies', and that Shrewsbury fell through 'severall tools at several times secretly convayed thither' and by the aid of two individuals 'lately got forth of Salop'.[90] Malcolm Wanklyn has recently argued that Shrewsbury fell not by treachery, but because its garrison was depleted, although he acknowledges many of the town regiment were disaffected.[91] Sir Samuel Luke reported to Essex that the royalists had grown accustomed to losing places in this fashion, and that Prince Maurice's letters to the king 'had certified the taking of Shrewsbury by Parliament's old and ordinary way, which they term a golden bridge.'[92]

Emboldened by Sir Trevor Williams' defection in Monmouthshire, Colonel Thomas Morgan sent a force to seize Chepstow castle in October 1645, while in March 1646 Corfe castle fell to what Sprigge described as a 'stratagem' of Colonel Bingham, parliamentary governor of Poole.[93] In December 1645 the parliamentarians captured Hereford by another night attack.[94] The governor, Sir Barnabas Scudamore, stood accused of selling the city, but he blamed the treachery of two of his officers who had previously defected, and three more that remained in the city.[95] Parliamentarian sources argued that Hereford was taken by surprise, but did not mention treachery—just that the city was 'very Craftely taken.'[96] However, they generously rewarded two renegades, Major Epiphanius Howard and Captain Daniel Alderne, for betraying the town. Each was freed from sequestration, offered rewards of £100, and allowed to nominate two friends to be discharged from sequestration.[97] The downfall of so many garrisons in this fashion impacted upon the royalist psyche. This is reflected in how notions of treachery featured in royalist literature and verse. Alexander Brome's lament 'On the loss of a garrison, meditation' included the lines:

> Town after town, field after field,
> This turns, and that perfidiously doth yield:
> He's banded on the traitorous thought of those
> That, Janus like, look to him and his foes.
> In vain are bulwarks, and the strongest hold,
> If the besieger's bullets are of gold…

[90] BL, E284(10), *Colonel Mittons Reply to Lievtenant Colonell Reinkings relation of the taking of Shrewesburie* (1645), 1; BL, E282(15), *A More Exact and Particular Relation of the Taking of Shrewsbury* (1645), 2.

[91] Wanklyn, *Warrior Generals*, 151, 271n.

[92] H. G. Tibbut (ed.), *The Letter Books of Sir Samuel Luke, 1644–45* (Publications of the Bedfordshire Historical Record Society, 42, 1963), 165.

[93] *Portland MS*, 286–7; Wing/S5070, Sprigge, *Anglia Rediviva*, 207.

[94] Ronald Hutton, *The Royalist War Effort 1642–1646* (2nd edn., 1999), 193.

[95] Ian J. Atherton (ed.), *Sir Barnabas Scudamore's Defence Against the Imputations of Treachery and Negligence in the Loss of the City of Hereford in 1645* (Akron, Ohio, 1992), 10, 44–6; Folger Shakespeare Library, *Sir Barnabas Scudamore's Defence: Vindicating him from those grand inputations o[f] treachery and negligence, in the late surprisall of Hereford* (1646), 2–3, 9, 10.

[96] *Portland MS*, 328–9; Hall (ed.), *Memorials of the Civil War in Cheshire*, 192n.

[97] Atherton (ed.), *Sir Barnabas Scudamore's Defence*, 46n; *Portland MS*, 395.

> Trust not in friends, for friends will soon deceive thee,
> They are in nothing sure, but sure to leave thee.[98]

In contrast, Parliament was fortunate that their failed conspiracy-led strategies were swiftly overshadowed by battlefield victories. When Colonel Dodding was suspected of intending to defect in Lancashire in April 1644, the Committee of Both Kingdoms issued secret orders to march 1,000 of the county's 'best horse and foot' to Dodding's quarters at Lancaster, ostensibly to combat the Westmorland royalists, but in reality to deprive Dodding of the opportunity of declaring himself, 'for that once done he is lost to all further service.'[99] This left south Lancashire's forces depleted when Rupert arrived and sacked Bolton in May. Lancashire commanders were reluctant to send forces out of the county, because they doubted their recruits' loyalty and feared 'secret plots within ourselves striking at our chief garrisons.'[100] Although several Lancashire colonels were suspected of treachery, none were prosecuted, with the victory at Marston Moor distracting attention from their failures.[101]

Likewise, the Committee of Both Kingdoms committed Fairfax to besiege Oxford in May 1645 because of intelligence from the side-changing earl of Sussex that the governor, William Legge, would surrender it.[102] Partly owing to Sussex's intelligence, in April 1645 a subcommittee under Viscount Saye was established to secretly treat for the surrender of royalist garrisons and the arrest of royalist spies.[103] The policy backfired by allowing the king's army free rein to sack Leicester, yet once the mistake was realised and Fairfax released, Naseby quickly followed. This overshadowed the previous failed strategy, protecting Saye and the New Model from their political enemies among the earl of Essex's supporters.

IV

The experience of defeat frequently intensified factional conflict. Rather than accepting that the enemy had proved superior in numbers, training, or leadership, internal recriminations usually ensued. Allegations of treachery were useful here because they deflected responsibility. The earl of Stamford diverted attention from his ineptitude by claiming that his major-general, James Chudleigh, defected not after but during the battle of Stratton. Then he attempted to associate his political enemy, Anthony Nicholls MP, with Chudleigh's alleged treachery.[104] Lord Hopton blamed the defeat of his

---

[98] Henry Morley (ed.), *The King and the Commons. Cavalier and Puritan Song* (1868), 103–4.

[99] *CSPD 1644*, 99–100.

[100] Ibid., 164.

[101] John Rosworm, 'Good Service Hitherto Ill Rewarded', in G. Ormerod (ed.), *Tracts Relating to Military Proceedings in Lancashire during the Great Civil War* (Chetham Society, 2, 1844), 222, 226, 230; *CSPD 1644*, 173.

[102] Michael Mahony, 'The Savile Affair and the Politics of the Long Parliament', *Parliamentary History*, 7 (1988), 218; Patricia Crawford, 'The Savile Affair', *EHR*, 90 (1975), 73, 78–9.

[103] Mahony, 'The Savile Affair and the Politics of the Long Parliament', 218.

[104] BL, E67(27), *Articles of Agreement Betweene His Excellency Prince Maurice, and the Earle of Stamford, Upon the Delivery of the City of Excester, the fifth of September, 1643. Together with a Letter Relating*

forces at Alton on a treacherous officer in the earl of Crawford's horse regiment.[105] Waller claimed that his failure to take Basing House was due to traitors in the ranks 'that putt themselves upon this service only to overthrow itt'.[106] The duchess of Newcastle excused her husband's defeats as having occurred in his absence through 'Jugling, Treachery, and Falshood' amongst his subordinates.[107] According to the losing commanders, all three major battles in Yorkshire were determined by treachery. Sir Thomas Fairfax blamed his major-general, John Gifford, for treacherously delaying deployment at Adwalton Moor and not committing the reserves.[108] John, Lord Belasyse, excused his failure to hold Selby through the treachery of one Captain Wilson letting Fairfax's horse into the town.[109] Sir Hugh Cholmley and Sir Philip Monckton voiced rumours that the side-changer Sir John Urry betrayed Rupert's cavalry at Marston Moor.[110] Yet P. R. Newman considered that 'stories such as this should always be treated with the gravest suspicion as indicating less a reality than a frame of mind among the defeated.' In this case, they were consequent upon Urry's defection several weeks after the battle.[111]

Such recriminations clearly fuelled factional conflicts on both sides. Lord Willoughby was finished as a parliamentarian commander after allegations that his treachery was responsible for the disastrous siege of Newark in March 1644. One of Willoughby's officers, Lieutenant-Colonel Bury, published an account of it that questioned Willoughby's allegiance, and rumours soon circulated in London that Willoughby's treachery was due to his envy of the earl of Manchester, 'and desire to see his forces broken'. This intensified an ugly confrontation with the earl that led to violence at Westminster.[112]

Essex's army was beset with recriminations after their disaster in Cornwall. This was because on 8 August 1644 the king and the royalist high command wrote to Essex, urging him to negotiate to avoid bloodshed and join the king in imposing a fair peace on parliament.[113] A favourite relative of Essex, Lord Beauchamp, was selected to deliver the letter, but Essex's reply on 10 August indignantly refused to break his trust, claiming that parliament had not authorized him to conduct such negotiations.[114] After Lostwithiel this left at least six of Essex's senior officers vulnerable to charges of premature surrender and corresponding with the enemy.

---

the Earle of Stamfords Proceedings in the West. Sept. 20 (1643), 3–4; *House of Lords MS*, HMC, 5th Report, Part I, Report and Appendix (1876), 111, 114.

[105] Chadwyck Healey (ed.), *Bellum Civile*, 72.

[106] *Portland MS*, 155.

[107] Margaret Cavendish, duchess of Newcastle, *The Life of the Thrice Noble, High and Puissant Prince William Cavendishe, Duke, Marquess and Earl of Newcastle* (1667), 50, 118.

[108] Bodl., MS Fairfax 36, fo. 8r–v; TNA, SP 16/513/part i/107–8.

[109] Folger Shakespeare Library, V.a.216 Belasyse Memoirs, fo. 13v.

[110] Bodl., MS Clarendon 23, fo. 153v; BL, Lansdowne MS 988, fo. 328r; Wanklyn, *Warrior Generals*, 107.

[111] P. R. Newman, *The Battle of Marston Moor, 1644* (Chichester, 1981), 67.

[112] Clive Holmes, 'Colonel King and Lincolnshire Politics, 1642–1646', *HJ*, 16 (1973), 459; *CJ*, iii, 387–9: BL, Add. MS 31,116, fos. 112v, 114r; *Cowper MS*, HMC, 12th Report, Appendix, Part II (1888), ii, 342.

[113] BL, Add. MS 78205, fos. 61–2; DRO, 1392 M/L 1644/54.

[114] Wanklyn, *Warrior Generals*, 118, 121; DRO, 1392 M/L 1644/54; Beinecke Rare Book and Manuscript Library, Osborn Shelves, fb156, fo. 114.

Among these was Colonel John Butler, commander of Essex's own regiment, who was captured at Boconnoc on 4 August and released on parole. Butler stood accused of deserting his post and circulating a paper of instructions from the king's army. Butler showed the papers to Colonel Thomas Tyrrell, who acquainted Skippon and sent copies to Sir Philip Stapleton. Stapleton was dismissive of the allegations, but Skippon initially wanted Butler court-martialled, although he may have relented, supposedly telling Anthony Nicholl: 'It was not good for an officer to fall upon another. It would make a fraction in the Army.'[115] The London diarist Thomas Juxon considered Butler guilty of treachery, and suspected that Colonel Edward Aldrich, captured and paroled alongside him, was also culpable. He considered that the king had 'shamefully dismantled our army by the neglect and treachery of our great officers'.[116] Suspicions arose that Colonel John Dalbier was allowed to escape from Boconnoc in return for becoming a royalist agent.[117] Essex deflected blame from his own officers to the Devonian Colonel John Were, accusing him of 'playing the Judas' and changing sides.[118] The disaster in Cornwall and the failure at Newbury thereafter excited rumours that the parliamentarian command was full of traitors and time-servers; John Syms believed that Essex had cashiered forty of his officers, and that Manchester had hanged three of his colonels for treachery 'who confessed at their death, that they did not fight for the cause, but for honour & gain, & for to lengthen out the war'.[119]

Essex's resignation speech of 2 April 1645 vouched for his officers, pleading they be granted a speedy trial.[120] On 8 May he reminded both Houses that Colonels Butler, Tyrrell, Dalbier, and Commissary Copley had remained long in prison without charge.[121] This unresolved business fuelled political hostility to the New Model among Essex's clients; Sir Samuel Luke blasted Skippon for having 'dealt so unworthily' with Essex in Cornwall.[122] With hindsight, this infighting appears to have promoted the emergence of a more successful command; none of Essex's colonels suspected of treachery in the west were commissioned in the New Model, although many opposed it without success as reformadoes in 1647.[123]

Barbara Donagan has recently argued that conflict within the royalist command was even more damaging.[124] This situation was inflamed by suspicions of treachery reaching the highest levels. Sir Edward Nicholas considered that perfidy and ill-discipline were rife in Oxford in May 1643. Praying that 'we may be preserved from treachery', he warned Rupert that 'since I see treachery not punished...I am apt to believe the traitors will multiply'.[125] After the Scottish Covenanters invaded

[115] Beinecke Rare Book and Manuscript Library, Osborn Files, 10,923.
[116] Juxon, *The Journal of Thomas Juxon*, 58–60, 64.
[117] Mark Stoyle, *Soldiers and Strangers: An Ethnic History of the English Civil War* (New Haven, 2005), 107.
[118] *CSPD 1644*, 493–4; *CJ*, iii, 667.
[119] BL, Add. MS 35297, fo. 56v.
[120] Beinecke Rare Book and Manuscript Library, Osborn Shelves, fb156, fo. 124.
[121] BL, Add. MS 31116, fo. 209r.
[122] Tibbut (ed.), *Letter Books of Sir Samuel Luke*, 324.
[123] Beinecke Rare Book and Manuscript Library, Osborn Shelves, fb155, fos. 237–9.
[124] Donagan, *War in England*, 245.
[125] BL, Add. MS 18980, fos. 59–60.

in January 1644 there were suspicions at court over the loyalty of Lieutenant-General King, earl of Eythin, who was known to be discontented, friends with the earl of Leven, and hoping to return to Swedish service.[126] In addition, Henry, Lord Wilmot, Lieutenant-General of Horse, Henry, Lord Percy, General of Artillery, and Thomas Savile, earl of Sussex, were all arrested on suspicion of treachery between August 1644 and January 1645.[127] In November 1645 Fairfax supposedly sent Dr William Stane to interview General Goring about 'whether my Lord Savile had any grounds for his report' that Goring would defect with his cavalry in exchange for pardon and for the protection of his estates.[128] The king's uncertainty extended to his own family. By August 1645 he feared for Rupert's loyalty at Bristol and his clients at Oxford and Newark, William Legge and Sir Richard Willis. Rupert had already advised the king to make peace, and with his brother, the Elector Palatine, welcomed in London, the prospect of Rupert falling away looked increasingly likely.[129] Charles was already suspicious of the Elector, enquiring of him in September 1644 'upon what invitation you are come. Then the design of your coming'.[130] These doubts were behind the backlash against Rupert after he surrendered Bristol, when several of the Prince's favourites were arrested and imprisoned.[131]

By 1645 there was clearly awareness that premature surrender was a particular problem among royalists. During his imprisonment in the Tower in 1646, Monck noted: 'You ought to be careful you have no Officer in chief that is covetous, or given to pillaging. For such men are good to no body, but themselves and the Enemy; and are most commonly easily corrupted with mony. Such men ought by no means to be made Governours of Towns.'[132] Exemplary punishment was inflicted on Lieutenant-Colonel Francis Windebank, shot in April for surrendering Bletchingdon.[133] Rupert's call for a court martial to clear himself for surrendering Bristol was followed by similar demands from Viscount Ogle at Winchester and Sir Barnabas Scudamore at Hereford. Losing so many strongholds in this fashion promoted violent infighting. In December 1645 Sir Nicholas Throckmorton told Sir Thomas Lunsford that he lost Monmouth basely, and both were imprisoned to prevent a duel.[134] Distrust among royalists featured strongly in the second civil war, with royalists in London

---

[126] Ian Roy and Joyce Macadam, 'Why did Prince Rupert fight at Marston Moor?', *JSAHR*, 86 (2008), 239–40.

[127] Bodl., MS Clarendon 24, fos. 6, 22; Symonds, *Richard Symonds's Diary*, 49, 106–7; Ronald Hutton, 'The Structure of the Royalist Party' *HJ*, 24 (1981), 562–3; Stuart Reid, 'Henry Percy, Baron Percy of Alnwick (*c.*1604–1659), royalist army officer', *ODNB*.

[128] Bodl., MS Clarendon 26, fo. 51.

[129] Hutton, 'The Structure of the Royalist Party', 567.

[130] Beinecke Rare Book and Manuscript Library, Osborn Files, 17829.

[131] Ian Roy, 'William Legge (1607/8–1680), royalist army officer', *ODNB*.

[132] Wing/A864, George Monck, *Observations Upon Military & Political Affairs. Written by the Most Honourable George Duke of Albemarle, &c. Published by authority* (1671), 114–15.

[133] P. R. Newman, *The Old Service: Royalist Regimental Colonels and the Civil War 1642–46* (Manchester, 1993), 124–5.

[134] Symonds, *Richard Symonds's Diary*, 276.

denounced for turning informers and identifying their fellows to parliament for financial gain.[135] Royalist newsbooks gave the Scots defeated at Preston little sympathy, accusing 'false Brethren in the Scottish army' of betraying their comrades for monetary reward.[136] In Ireland too, royalists and confederates blamed Cromwell's capture of Drogheda and Wexford upon cowardice and treachery as their high command turned on one another. Micheál Ó Siochrú has recently stressed how the confederates' most effective printed propaganda was directed at their own comrades, and how they 'commonly ascribed every military setback to the actions of traitors.'[137]

V

These selected examples appear to have told a rather partial or hindsight-driven story of royalist failure and parliamentarian success in determining how treachery informed strategy. There were some royalist successes, such as the defection of Sir Richard Grenville in March 1644 with parliament's plans for their spring campaign. Yet parliament overcame and was better placed to deal with these setbacks. This was in part because, as John Ellis has detailed at length, parliament was developing superior structures for the gathering and dissemination of military intelligence.[138] Intelligence of Goring's continued absence, possibly delivered by a renegade or double agent, endowed Fairfax with great advantages at Naseby. Furthermore, by 1645 parliament was able to broadcast their superiority in military intelligence with publications showcasing the king's correspondence at Naseby and Lord Digby's at Sherburn-in-Elmet.[139] Parliament also proved more resilient because, as Ann Hughes has shown, its several committees, the Lords and Commons, and the regional associations, all offered alternative arenas in which the discredited could hope for redress.[140] Failed commanders such as Essex, Manchester, Stamford, and Willoughby continued participating in the cause even after their dismissal from command. Although close to panic, parliament's war effort evaded collapse in 1643. To galvanize support, propagandists such as William Prynne and John Vicars increasingly portrayed the war as an apocalyptic struggle for Godly religion against popery and tyranny, warning of the dire punishment that treacherous backsliders would suffer in this world along

---

[135] *Sutherland MS*, HMC, 5th Report, Appendix (1876), 151.

[136] Jason McElligott, *Royalism, Print and Censorship in Revolutionary England* (Woodbridge, 2007), 75.

[137] Micheál Ó Siochrú, 'Oliver Cromwell and the Massacre at Drogheda', in David Edwards, Pádraig Lenihan and Clodagh Tait (eds.), *Age of Atrocity: Violence and Political Conflict in Early Modern Ireland* (Dublin, 2007), 277, 282; Micheál Ó Siochrú, *God's Executioner: Oliver Cromwell and the Conquest of Ireland* (2008), 74, 116, 146.

[138] John Ellis, *'To Walk in the Dark': Military Intelligence during the English Civil War, 1642–1646* (Stroud, 2011), 53, 165, 197.

[139] Ibid., 193; Ian Gentles, *The New Model Army in England, Ireland and Scotland, 1645–1653* (Oxford, 1992), 460.

[140] Hughes, 'The King, the Parliament and the Localities', 241, 257–61.

with divine retribution in the next.[141] To press home the point, one tract printed a fictitious duologue between a cavalier and a recent convert to parliament's cause. The cavalier gloated: 'I hear you have converted, I thought you had been wiser than to turne in a time when all men are leaving them.' To this the convert replied nobly: 'It is no matter, my conscience is not led with outward probabilities.' Regardless of parliament's military losses, the convert held that people should change sides upon principle because the royalist cause was tainted with popish conspiracy.[142] Alongside such propaganda initiatives, conspirators and would-be defectors were uncovered and arrested, enabling opinion to be galvanized against them during the process of trial and execution. In the meantime, the Vow and Covenant, and then the Solemn League and Covenant, shored up support and won new allies.

In contrast, the royalist focus of loyalty to an individual proved less flexible and less equipped to galvanize support in the aftermath of military failure. In royalist disputes the king's word was final. Leading royalists felt inclined to forsake the struggle if they feared they were irredeemably out of royal favour. Even local disputes between royalists might lead to alienation and defections amongst those whom the king decided against.[143] While treachery did not ultimately cause the royalists to lose the war, by 1645 it clearly accelerated a loss of support in their heartlands. There was quarrelling and subversion within many garrisons in the Welsh marches and West Midlands which robbed the king of his capacity to rebuild after Naseby.[144] In apportioning blame for the royalist defeat in 1646, historians have often looked elsewhere, pointing to disastrous advice from the king's advisers—principally Lord Digby. Ronald Hutton has contrasted Rupert's contempt for Digby's inclination to clandestine treachery with his honest preference for storming enemy strongholds. Digby attempted to subvert officers at Gloucester, Aylesbury, and Abingdon.[145] Yet even Rupert was not above such behaviour, and was personally complicit in plots against Aylesbury and Bristol in 1643.[146] This reflects a more general double standard and uneasiness about how far it was honourable to capture places by such means. Among the seven ways George Monck listed to win castles and towns, 'by Treachery' was placed first; but he gave no advice on how to accomplish it. This was striking, because he gave plentiful advice on means that he considered less effective, as well as how to defend garrisons from treachery.[147] This embodies the contradictory impulses felt towards side-changing; subverting enemy

---

[141] BL, E33(18), John Vicars, *A Looking-Glasse for Malignants: or, Gods hand against God-haters... Together with a caveat for cowards and unworthy (either timorous or treacherous) newters* (1643); BL, E251(6), William Prynne, *The Doome of Cowardize and Treachery or A Looking-Glass for Cowardly or Corrupt Governours, and Souldiers who through Pusillanimity or Bribery betray their Trusts, to the publick Prejudice*, 23 October (1643).

[142] BL, E250(6), *The Reformed Malignants or a Discourse upon the Present State of our Affaires, Betwixt a Cavalier and a Convert*, 4 September (1643), 1, 3–4.

[143] Hughes, 'The King, the Parliament and the Localities', 241, 251, 257–61.

[144] Hutton, *The Royalist War Effort*, 189–93.

[145] Hutton, 'The Structure of the Royalist Party', 565.

[146] Patrick McGrath, 'Bristol and the Civil War', in R. C. Richardson (ed.), *The English Civil Wars: Local Aspects* (Stroud, 1997), 101–2.

[147] Monck, *Observations Upon Military & Political Affairs*, 118, 132–4.

commanders was practical and extremely worthwhile, but somehow remained unmanly and not something to boast about.

The war aims on both sides fluctuated and were ill-defined. By utilizing allegations of treachery as a weapon in factional politics, protagonists argued over the true nature and aims of their cause. In this way the label 'turncoat' became culturally constructed, and something which changed dramatically over time, particularly with the radicalization of the parliamentary cause from 1647. Therefore, although treachery came to shape strategy and political infighting, factional rivalries themselves came to define and determine those described as turncoats. During the second civil war, so much royalist activity revolved around defecting parliamentarians that it dominated their strategy more than ever. The Prince of Wales promised converts from parliament's forces a full pardon and their pay arrears, while Langdale changed his plans when the governor of Skipton castle would not defect.[148] There were mass defections from the fleet, as well as from Kent and Essex's trained bands. Tynemouth, Pontefract, Scarborough, Pembroke, and Tenby castles were taken as a result of side-changing, along with Berwick-upon-Tweed and the Munster towns in Ireland, while further plots were instigated against parliamentarian garrisons at Chester, Gloucester, Holy Island, King's Lynn, and Stafford, along with Beaumaris and Denbigh castles.[149] Such dispersed conspiracies were so difficult to coordinate that ultimate failure was likely; but nevertheless, they delivered a crushing blow to the confidence of parliamentarians that their comrades shared their priorities.

Parliamentarian strategy in 1648 revolved around extinguishing the military threat inflamed by these defections. Consequently, those who remained steadfast grew radicalized and vindictive. Severe punishment of those perceived as turncoats became more routinely employed. Trials and executions for 'breach of trust' brought about a wider definition of treason that eventually came to encompass the king himself. A powerful factor in prompting the king's trial and execution was the realization that if his life was spared, parliamentarian vulnerability to treachery and defection would continue, with victory in a third war far from guaranteed. Killing the king might narrow the parliamentarian coalition further, but at least those that remained could be trusted. In this way, fear of traitors and turncoats ultimately shaped the political strategy of regicide, and determined the course of the English Revolution.

---

[148] BL, E454(8), *The Declaration of His Highnesse the Prince of Wales, to Sir Marmaduke Langdale*, 25 July (No place, 1648), 4; Jack Binns, *Yorkshire in the Civil Wars: Origins, Impact and Outcome* (Pickering, 2004), 135.

[149] *Portland MS*, 463, 472, 505–8; Ashton, *Counter-Revolution*, 347–8, 375, 400, 402–6, 411–20, 465; Bodl., MS Carte 130, fos. 65–6.

7

The language of treachery in newsbooks and polemic

This chapter examines how the phenomenon of side-changing was described in print and what purposes these descriptions served. The printed propaganda of both sides sought to secure consent, instil political participation, and stimulate monetary contributions.[1] Printed accounts of the actions of side-changers potentially addressed all these objectives, and enabled the meaning of defections to be more publicly and widely contested. Print became a powerful medium through which to shape notions of turncoating and to contest what constituted treacherous conduct. Printed propaganda did not merely comment upon the conflict, it fuelled and shaped it. Jason Peacey has shown how the promulgation of news became more closely managed in the 1640s, and how print could be used to undermine rivals on one's own side.[2] Print rendered the internal operations of both sides' politics a matter of perception and discussion. Stories of the impact, presence, and tactics of factions were important because they shaped the ways contemporaries behaved, 'and because members of the political elite needed to engage with, and manipulate, public perceptions.'[3] This shift to a public discourse raises methodological problems as printed narratives adopted a variety of forms from character assassinations to self-defences. There are obvious problems with using printed tracts for factual information, especially anything relating to the fortunes of war; much false news was deliberately propagated to misinform, deflect attention from other matters, or stimulate fund-raising initiatives.[4] Newsbooks and printed declarations published accounts of defections in the hope that they would encourage more. Even before Edgehill, the king's declaration at Shrewsbury in October 1642 boasted that several enemy captains and many of their soldiers had recently joined them '& sayeth the greatest part of the enemy's men profess they will never fight if they see his Majesty's banner in the field'.[5] Some such claims were extremely damaging even when they proved untrue or grossly exaggerated. On 7 September 1644, *Mercurius Aulicus* claimed that Essex's cowardice in abandoning his army in

---

[1] Jason Peacey, *Politicians and Pamphleteers: Propaganda During the English Civil Wars and Interregnum* (Aldershot, 2004), 323.

[2] Ibid., 27, 36, 202, 237.

[3] Jason Peacey, 'Perceptions of Parliament: Factions and the "Public"', in John Adamson (ed.), *The English Civil War: Conflict and Contexts, 1640–1649* (Basingstoke, 2009), 104–5.

[4] Peacey, *Politicians and Pamphleteers*, 242.

[5] BL, Add. MS 78205, fo. 14.

Cornwall had instigated 'many thousands' of his infantry to defect in order to revenge themselves on him.[6] Some reported defections never actually occurred. In January 1643, Captain John Fenwick was reported to have retired from Newcastle's army out of disgust at the Catholic influence in command. Yet Fenwick remained loyal and was killed at Marston Moor.[7] Subsequent royalist defectors quickly emulated this appeal to anti-Catholic prejudice when currying favour with parliament.[8]

Educated contemporaries fashioned themselves as healthily sceptical of the printed news, despite their thirst for it. When Mr Porter relayed Oxford's news to the governor of Dartmouth, he commented: 'Sir, news here is as various as the rainbow for colours, I can ascertain you but little for true'.[9] John Hotham confided to the earl of Newcastle in March 1643: 'I am grown to believe nothing because I think our masters of both sides feed us with such meat as they think fittest for us.'[10] Newsbooks themselves pandered to these expectations by printing similar sentiments: 'I hope you will not be so severe to expect Truth in every circumstance; for all mercuries having the plant *Mercurie* predominant at their Nativities, cannot but retaine a twang of Lying'.[11] Similarly, in 1647 Samuel Sheppard's first issue of his new royalist serial *Mercurius Elencticus* acknowledged the political fluidity behind the production of serial newsbooks, before promising truthfulness and political constancy in its reporting:

> Roome for another *Mercury*, one Ile warrant you that was better bred then to tell Lyes, or to startle at the noyse of a squirting Ordnance. One that values not a *Forty shillings fine*, nor feares a *Forty dayes Captivity*. No Weathercock, nor Changeling, no tame Citizen, Committee or Excise man, no Rebell, nor Traytor, so assure your selves, no *Parliament man*, and then no matter what I be; my heart is honest, and my Intelligence true.[12]

I

The language used to describe side-changers in print consisted of a colourful vocabulary of insult appreciated at all social levels. There was clearly a large popular appetite for stories of turncoats and treachery. Thomas Juxon and John Syms both took great care to record instances of side-changing, however small-scale.[13] To ruin a defector's name, propagandists drew upon images of treachery from the Bible,

[6] BL, E10(20), *Mercurius Aulicus*, 36th week, 1–7 September (Oxford, 1644), 1154.

[7] BL, E86(40), *The Kingdomes Weekly Intelligencer*, no. 5, 24–31 January (1643), 38; Newman, 130.

[8] See the cases of Captain William Bushell and Captain Doughty who defected to parliament in December 1643 and May 1645: *CJ*, iii, 328; BL, Add. MS 11331, fo. 157r.

[9] DRO, 1392 M/L 1644/24.

[10] Bodl., MS Nalson III, no. 6.

[11] BL, E73(2), George Wither, *Mercurius Rusticus: Or, A Countrey Messenger* (1643), 1–2.

[12] BL, E412(30), *Mercurius Elencticus*, no. 1, 29 October–5 November (1647), 1.

[13] Thomas Juxon, *The Journal of Thomas Juxon, 1644–1647*, ed. Keith Lindley and David Scott (Camden Society, 5th series, 13, 1999), 41–2, 44, 48, 55, 58, 64, 69–73; BL, Add. MS 35297, fos. 7r, 15v–16v, 26r–27r, 34r–v, 38r, 47r, 56v, 61r–v, 64r, 67v, 71r, 78r–v, 81r, 95v, 119v.

literature, or the stage to generate enduringly derisive nicknames for side-changers. Behind this abuse lurked the thoughtfully crafted insult typical of seventeenth-century litigation over defamation.[14] Terms such as base, rogue, and knave were used to deny gentility, while fictitious material was propagated in vilifying side-changers in order to turn particular individuals into hate-figures for popular consumption. Baseness, lying, irreligion, and cowardice were the most frequent themes, while occasionally sexual incontinence was implied. Notorious side-changers could scarcely have their name printed without some cursing reminder of their defection: *The Scottish Dove* referred to 'perfidious Hurry'.[15] Another serial referred to Sir Hugh Cholmley as 'perfidious and backsliding'.[16] James Chudleigh was 'infamous and treacherous Chudleigh',[17] while Sir Alexander Carew was an 'apostate'.[18] Urry's name was scarcely printed without some reference to his side-changing, and was commonly given as 'turn-coat Urry'.[19] During 1648, Edward Wogan and Matthew Boynton were customarily referred to as 'renegado Wogan' and 'treacherous Boynton'.[20]

The most frequent aspersion was to strip side-changers of their gentility in order to eject them from the community of honour and render them incapable of further public trust. One serial maintained that Sir Hugh Cholmley 'deserves not the name of a Gentleman'.[21] Although the local enemies of Colonel John Poyer utilized many representations of subversion in their damning of him, a denial of his gentility was at the heart of their accusations: he was the father of bastards, an indiscriminate plunderer, the leader of a lawless rabble, 'a great Swearer and quarreler'—but above all, he was 'born to nothing, sprung up from a Turn-spit to a Glover'.[22] The most elaborate and fulsome denial of gentility was reserved for Sir Richard Grenville.[23] After his former professions of loyalty, parliament found his betrayal particularly galling. About a week after his defection in March 1644, two gibbets were erected at the Royal Exchange and at Palace-Yard, Westminster, where Sir Richard Grenville, dubbed the 'grand Apostate and Renegado of England', was declared a traitor with this written proclamation fixed to the gibbets:

[14] Richard P. Cust and Andrew J. Hopper (eds.), *Cases in the High Court of Chivalry, 1634–40* (Publications of the Harleian Society, new series, 18, 2006).

[15] BL, E6(19), *The Scottish Dove*, no. 44, 9–16 August (1644), 347.

[16] BL, E10(22), *The Kingdomes Weekly Intelligencer*, no. 74, 24 September–1 October (1644), 594.

[17] BL, E105(17), *Mercurius Civicus, Londons Intelligencer*, no. 5, 1–8 June (1643), 39.

[18] BL, E250(8), *A Perfect Diurnall of Some Passages in Parliament*, no. 8, 4–11 September (1643), 57.

[19] BL, E74(4), *A True and Punctuall Relation of the Severall Skirmishes Performed*, 28 October (1643), 2.

[20] BL, E640(14), *Mercurius Politicus Comprising the Summ of All Intelligence*, no. 63, 14–21 August (1651), 1008.

[21] BL, E95(2), *The Kingdomes Weekly Intelligencer*, no. 14, 28 March–4 April (1643), 110.

[22] Wing/S3579A, *A Short Comment upon the Grounds and Reasons of Poyers Taking up Armes in these Second Insurrections* (1649), 1, 5.

[23] The invective against Grenville was so bitter that one eighteenth-century antiquarian listed much of it for Dr Charles Burney's collection: BL, Stowe MS 768, fos. 1–36.

Whereas Richard Greenvile hath of late presented his service unto the Parliament and hath been entertained by the Parliament as Colonell of a Regement of Horse: And whereas the said Greenvile, contrary to his promise, ingagement, and honour of a Souldier, hath basely, unworthily, and faithlessly deserted the said service and feloniously carried away the money paid unto him in regard of the said service. These are to proclaime the said Richard Greenvile, Traitor, Rogue, Villaine, and Skelum, not onely uncapable of Military imployment, but of all acquaintance and conversation with men of honesty and honour. And this Proclamation in the meane time to be nailed on the Gallowes, whilst it shall please God to deliver the said Greenvile into the hands of Justice, that he himselfe may supply the roome of this Proclamation.[24]

This proclamation envisaged his death as a common felon and stripped Grenville of his gentility—a status with which the terms 'traitor, rogue, and villain' were incompatible. The term 'skellum', denoting particular contempt, signified a rascal, scamp, scoundrel, or villain.[25] London's press seem to have reserved it to Grenville, who was henceforth uniquely known as 'Skellum Grenville'. The strength of this denunciation was exceptional, and even startled some royalists.[26]

The parliamentarian press sought to shift blame for defecting onto side-changers themselves by representing them as cruel, rapacious, and transgressors of military law. James Chudleigh was damned by the earl of Stamford's friends, eager to deflect attention from Stamford's disastrous generalship. He was scorned as 'perfidious *Chudley*', and 'a double minded wretch', who maliciously wounded a captured parliamentarian officer with his rapier.[27] Newsbooks might depict side-changers as hated and illegitimate by those who had suffered under their misrule: after his arrest, Plymouth's women 'fell upon' Sir Alexander Carew, and 'would have beaten out his braines, if the Maior of the Towne had not rescued him'; whilst at Scarborough castle's surrender, local women 'could hardly be kept from stoning of Sir *Hugh Cholmley*'.[28] Stereotypical accounts of women moved to such violence became a staple of propaganda in developing villain figures.

Stories soon circulated of Grenville's inclination to summary justice and his penchant for hangings. He was accused of cruelty to pressed recruits, treating them as beasts 'as Drovers use to do Oxen'.[29] After having forced one parliamentarian

[24] BL, E252(24), *A Perfect Diurnall of Some Passages in Parliament*, no. 33, 11–18 March (1644), 263.

[25] J. A. Simpson and E. S. C. Weiner (eds.), *The Oxford English Dictionary*, 20 vols. (2nd edn., Oxford, 1989), xv, 590; Amos C. Miller, *Sir Richard Grenville of the Civil War* (1979), 67–70.

[26] BL, Add. MS 18980, fo. 31.

[27] BL, E70(13), *Strange, True, and Lamentable Newes from Exeter, and Other Parts of the Western Countreyes Shewing how Cruelly the Resolute Cavaliers have dealt with the Inhabitants since the Departure of that Right Noble Commander the Earl of Stamford*, 11 October (1643), sig. A2v.

[28] BL, E67(3), *Certaine Informations from Severall Parts of the Kingdome*, no. 34, 4–11 September (1643), 259–60; BL, E294(15), *An Exact Relation of the Surrender of Scarborough Castle*, 21 July (1645), 4. A Catholic siege engineer in Dartmouth was also supposedly almost 'torne in peeces by the Women of the town, for his cruelty in burning of houses, and other villainous acts': Wing/S5070, Joshua Sprigge, *Anglia Rediviva: Englands Recovery* (1647), 171.

[29] BL, E254(6), *Perfect Occurrences of Parliament*, no. 31, 19–26 July (1644), sig. A3v; BL, E258(32), *Perfect Occurrences of Parliament*, no. 10, 28 February–7 March (1645), sig. K2r; BL, E260(8), *Perfect Passages of each dayes Proceedings in Parliament*, no. 23, 26 March–2 April (1645), 180–1.

captive to hang another, he was depicted 'sitting on his horse beholding the spectacle'.[30] Another tract reported that he hanged a countryman who asked for his horse back from one of Grenville's captains. Allegedly this was an arbitrary judgement, delivered on the spot: 'this is growne a custome with Skellum, as wee are informed, without any triall.'[31] Feeding from one another, these stories multiplied and generated an image of Grenville as a consistent transgressor of military law. Such villainy narratives became highly marketable, and Mark Stoyle has suggested that they were not entirely unfounded.[32]

The language employed against Grenville dehumanized him with bestial metaphors. The Captain Grenville condemned in 1644 for attempting to betray Plymouth was derided as 'a spawne of Sir Richards', and 'a whelp of Skellum *Greenviles*', as if treachery had been infused into his very blood.[33] *Mercurius Britanicus* mocked him as 'the Cornish Elfe', reporting the failed efforts against Plymouth of 'Dicke Greeneville and his Choughs'.[34] Bestial metaphors were also used in Captain John Legard's account of Scarborough's betrayal, which derided his treacherous lieutenant as a 'Cerberus', while Lucy Hutchinson also used this term to describe a cheating lackey.[35] However, Grenville remains an extreme example in England at least. Such bestial metaphors, while often directed at Irish rebels or English Catholic royalists, were comparatively rarely applied to side-changers.[36]

Another means of tarnishing a side-changer's reputation was to depict their defection as motivated by spite or self-interest. One London serial highlighted depictions of Sir Edward Dering in the royalist press as having defected out of pique because the king had not bestowed offices such as the shrievalty of Kent or the deanery of Canterbury upon him. It countered that Dering had defected for the right reasons, being 'not ashamed to say, he hath offended, in adhering to the Cavaliers.'[37] This claim was mocked the following month, when *Mercurius Aulicus* retorted that Sir Richard Grenville 'did not petition the Members at Westminster to be a Deane, a Secretary, or a Sheriffe, and upon a denyall wheele off to the adversary', but broke with the parliament when they were showering favour upon him. By stressing Grenville's self-denial, the royalists argued his defection was the more

[30] BL, E47(1), *A Continuation of the True Narration of the Most Observable Passages in and about Plymouth, from January 26. 1643. till this present*, 10 May (1644), 6.

[31] BL, E258(38), *Perfect Passages of each dayes Proceedings in Parliament*, no. 21, 12–19 March (1645), 162.

[32] Mark Stoyle, *West Britons: Cornish Identities and the Early Modern British State* (Exeter, 2002), 93–5.

[33] BL, E10(30), *Mercurius Civicus*, no. 71, 26 September–3 October (1644), 665–6; BL, E10(22), *The Kingdomes Weekly Intelligencer*, 595.

[34] BL, TT E16(25), *Mercurius Britanicus*, no. 57, 4–11 November (1644), 453; BL, E24(16), *Mercurius Britanicus*, no. 65, 6–13 January (1645), 517.

[35] BL, E95(9), *A True and Exact Relation of all the Proceedings of Sir Hugh Cholmleys Revolt deserting the Parliament*, 7 April (1643), 7; Lucy Hutchinson, *Memoirs of the Life of Colonel Hutchinson*, ed. N.H. Keeble (1995), 306.

[36] Andrew Hopper, 'The Popish Army of the North: Anti-Catholicism and Parliamentarian Allegiance in Civil War Yorkshire, 1642–46', *Recusant History*, 25 (2000), 21–2; Kathleen M. Noonan, '"The Cruel Pressure of an Enraged, Barbarous People": Irish and English Identity in Seventeenth-Century Policy and Propaganda', *HJ*, 41 (1998), 154–6.

[37] BL, E31(21), *The Kingdomes Weekly Intelligencer*, no. 42, 30 January–7 February (1644), 328.

principled and their cause therefore the most righteous.[38] Base, mercenary motives could be ascribed to the enemy, suggesting that their loyalty was unconscionable and easily bought. Marchamont Nedham mocked those tasked with hunting down London's royalist underground press, jeering that by offering them 'a six penny Advantage in Salary', he would 'make them all of my Faction.'[39] Multiple side-changers could be depicted as giddy and inconstant; *Mercurius Aulicus* warned parliamentarians in January 1644: 'Do not boast of my Lord of Bedford and Holland, till you know how long they'll stay with you.'[40]

Attacks upon the military honour of side-changers were intended to unman them and destroy their public legitimacy. The simplest means was an allegation of cowardice. By 1645 Sir Hugh Cholmley was blasted as the 'Liver hearted *Cholmley*', and 'his cowardship'.[41] The word renegade was adapted to 'runagado' to impute cowardice. Used from the early seventeenth century, 'runagado' was applied to faithless rebels, cowardly runaways, and Christians converted to Islam.[42] Horatio Carey and Major Brookbank were both derided as a 'runnagado', the later for fleeing to the enemy at Edgehill.[43] When Sir Richard Grenville was called a runagado in one newsbook, John Syms copied the term into his personal journal.[44] *Mercurius Anti-Pragmaticus* later denounced Grenville as a 'snivelling Coward', and 'His Majestys Marchpaine Champion', who soiled himself at news that parliament's forces approached.[45]

Print also utilized xenophobic prejudices. In particular, parliamentarians were increasingly suspicious of their own foreign officers and soldiers after so many defected in 1643.[46] When one parliamentarian newsbook reported the defection of Sergeant-Major Griffith's troop in Lincolnshire, it claimed that the defectors were French and that the troop's Englishmen remained loyal.[47] *Mercurius Britanicus* condemned the Frenchman Major Francis Dowet as a 'perjur'd Renegado' and 'no English-man, and whether he hath any Christian-name I know not.'[48] *Mercurius Aulicus* employed the stereotype of the ungrateful, avaricious, and hypocritical Scot to ridicule Colonel James Wemyss, Waller's artillery commander captured at Cropredy Bridge. It declared that although the king had given Wemyss a generous salary as master gunner of England before the war, Wemyss treacherously repaid him by deliberately targeting Charles' person at Cropredy with his artillery, and by

---

[38] BL, E37(26), *Mercurius Aulicus*, 9th week, 25 February–2 March (Oxford, 1644), 857.

[39] BL, E464(12), *Mercurius Pragmaticus*, no. 25, 12–19 September (1648), sig. Jv.

[40] BL, E30(1), *Mercurius Aulicus*, 2nd week, 7–13 January (1644), 781.

[41] BL, E258(27), *A Perfect Diurnall of Some Passages in Parliament*, no. 82, 17–24 February (1645), 653–4.

[42] Simpson and Weiner (eds.), *Oxford English Dictionary*, xiv, 265.

[43] BL, E 252(27), *Perfect Diurnal of Some Passages in Parliament*, no. 36, 1–8 April (1644), 282; BL, E252(16), *Perfect Diurnal of Some Passages in Parliament*, no. 25, 8–15 January (1644), 199;

[44] BL, E47(1), *A Continuation of the True Narration of the Most Observable Passages in and about Plymouth*, 7–9; BL, Add. MS 35297, fo. 26r.

[45] BL, E416(7), *Mercurius Anti-Pragmaticus*, no. 5, 11–18 November (1647), 5.

[46] Mark Stoyle, *Soldiers and Strangers: An Ethnic History of the English Civil War* (New Haven, 2005), 104–6.

[47] BL, E94(14), *The Kingdomes Weekly Intelligencer*, no. 13, 21–28 March (1643), 104.

[48] BL, E298(24), *Mercurius Britanicus*, no. 95, 25 August–1 September (1645), 852.

selling to parliament the new leather guns he had invented at Lambeth 'in the same place where the Gun-powder-Traytors practiced'. *Aulicus* mocked Wemyss's protestations of loyalty when brought before the king after his capture, claiming he had said '*Gud feith his heart was always with His Majestie*'.[49]

Unable to exact revenge upon side-changers safely residing among the enemy, the frustration of some pamphleteers produced wishful thinking. The *Scottish Dove* represented Grenville as tormented by guilt: 'run away *Grinvile*, who flyes like guilty *Cain* from every shadow, frightened by his fancies, and tormented by a prickling, galled conscience for symptoms of misery; hell within and a halter at Westminster that makes the man as mad as a March hunted hare'.[50] *Mercurius Britanicus* depicted him as so haunted by fears of the gibbet 'that his dreaming conscience is terrified and startles every minute at Triangle Apparitions.' This serial tititlated readers with a series of revenge fantasies about Grenville, that 'dappered Dick with the plundred pearls in his ears, which would show very glorious in a Pillory'. It longed for the day that would 'bring that dapper Heathen into the compasse of a Penny-halter.'[51] The *Scottish Dove*, cheated of Cholmley's execution by Scarborough castle's surrender on terms,[52] consoled readers with hopes that in future Cholmley and Grenville 'may meet at an English tree, to cut a Caper', and be 'exalted on an *English* Oake'.[53] The *Parliaments Post* reflected more soberly that Grenville had hanged more men than all the king's commanders combined, and that the 'like measure which he hath given to others, may be now returned to himself.'[54]

Side-changers frequently attracted accusations of irreligion and apostasy. In 1644 Cholmley was branded a 'treacherous Apostate' who had burnt down Whitby and massacred its civilians.[55] The term 'apostate' was frequent, but satanic metaphors were rarely employed, although *The Scottish Dove* hailed Grenville as 'the worst of the worst of men', whose 'Serpentine policie' had 'gayned the Devils love and his best ayd'.[56] *Mercurius Britanicus* preferred a more general denunciation of Grenville's irreligion, calling him 'heathen', and 'little pagan Dicke, the shame of that family'.[57]

In a society where the Bible was omnipresent in everyday speech, both sides resorted to Biblical allegory to denounce inconstancy.[58] Parliament's fast sermons utilized the plethora of Old Testament kings who turned away from God.[59] One alleged side-changer

---

[49] BL, E2(6), *Mercurius Aulicus*, 26th week, 29 June (Oxford, 1644), 1056.

[50] BL, E3(3), *The Scottish Dove*, no. 43, 2–9 August (1644), 338.

[51] BL, TT E16(25), *Mercurius Britanicus*, no. 57, 4–11 November (1644), 453; BL, E24(16), *Mercurius Britanicus*, no. 65, 6–13 January (1645), 517.

[52] BL, E270(33), *The Scottish Dove*, no. 71, 21–28 February (1645), 556.

[53] BL, E294(20), *The Scottish Dove*, no. 93, 25 July–1 August (1645), 734.

[54] BL, E304(6), *The Parliaments Post Faithfully Communicating to the Kingdome the Proceedings of the Armies on Both Sides*, no. 21, 30 September–7 October (1645), 6.

[55] BL, E252(24), *A Perfect Diurnall of Some Passages in Parliament*, no. 33, 11–18 March (1644), 259.

[56] BL, E277(15), *The Scottish Dove*, no. 77, 4–11 April (1645), 606–7.

[57] BL, E18(12), *Mercurius Britanicus*, no. 59, 18–25 November (1644), 468.

[58] Christopher Hill, *The English Bible and the Seventeenth-Century Revolution* (1993), 32.

[59] Ibid., 79–108.

facing execution in Smithfield supposedly warned that 'there are many Achans still in the Camp.'[60] This inferred from Joshua 7:20–26 that, much like the Israelites at Ai, parliament would never prove victorious until it rooted out those among them who had offended God. Another tract compared Sir George Chudleigh's backsliding to that of Lot's wife in Genesis 19:26. It quipped that despite obtaining a royal pardon, Chudleigh stood 'in need of more pardons then one.'[61]

Predictably, the most common Biblical allusion was to Judas Iscariot. Judas was a commonplace insult, its use extending far down the social scale. Francis Brabant complained to the Court of Chivalry in 1637 that a neighbour had said 'that I had betrayed my master Sir Richard Greenvill and that I was Iscariot'.[62] By comparing treacherous backsliders to the betrayer of Christ, propagandists implied that the injured party was on God's side. The *Scottish Dove* dubbed Cholmley 'Judas Cholmley',[63] while Grenville was likened to Judas and Cain for guilt in betraying God's cause.[64] Grenville's defection was depicted as motivated by his covetousness of the money parliament had entrusted to him for recruiting his regiment, and that 'like *Judas* he carried the bag with him'.[65] Commonplace identifications of Judas in the press were replicated in complaints of disgruntled commanders, such as Essex's accusation that Colonel John Were 'hath played the Judas and is revolted.'[66] The pamphleteer Henry Walker was scorned as a Judas by royalists for his broken declarations of loyalty to the king.[67] In 1647 the royalists blasted the Scots for selling the king to the English parliament—one tract observing that 'Iscariot was but a puny Scot in avarice', and rhyming:

> *Judas* before a Traytor *Scot* shall weare
> A Saintly Rubrick in Times Calendar.[68]

Sir Archibald Johnston was heckled in church by a woman who accused him of killing Montrose, 'betraying the king like Judas and trying to make himself king instead.'[69] Royalists developed these condemnations further after the king's trial, commonly comparing the trial commissioners and regicides to Jews, Caiphas, and also to Judas, to emphasize their treachery.[70]

---

[60] BL, E13(8), *A More Exact and Perfect Relation of the Treachery, Apprehension, Conviction, Condemnation, Confession, and Execution, of Francis Pitt, aged 65. Who was executed in Smithfield on Saturday, October the 12. 1644, for endeavouring to betray the garrison of Rushall-Hall in the county of Stafford, to the enemy*, 18 October (1644), 6.

[61] BL, E37(20), *A Declaration Published in the County of Devon by that Grand Ambo-dexter, Sir George Chudleigh* (1644), 4, 7.

[62] College of Arms, Curia Militaris, Acta (5), fo. 45.

[63] BL, E270(33), *The Scottish Dove*, 556.

[64] BL, E3(3), *The Scottish Dove*, 338; BL, TT E16(25), *Mercurius Britanicus*, no. 57, 4–11 November (1644), 453.

[65] BL, E35(23), *The Weekly Account*, no. 36, 29 February–6 March (1644), last page.

[66] *CSPD 1644*, 493–4.

[67] Joad Raymond, 'Henry Walker (*fl.*1638–1660), journalist and preacher', *ODNB*.

[68] BL, TT 669.f.11(103), *Judas Justified by his Brother Scot*, 3 December (1647).

[69] John Coffey, 'Sir Archibald Johnston, Lord Wariston (*bap.* 1611–d. 1663), lawyer and politician', *ODNB*.

[70] Jason McElligott, *Royalism, Print and Censorship in Revolutionary England* (Woodbridge, 2007), 59; Ann Hughes, 'A "Lunatic Revolter from Loyalty": The Death of Rowland Wilson and the English Revolution', *History Workshop Journal*, 61 (2006), 200.

The Levellers too portrayed their defeat as wrought by the betrayal of a Judas figure. After the army mutiny was quelled at Burford, one of the ringleaders, Cornet Henry Denne, was spared execution after displaying penitence before the generals, who were eager to vindicate their own conduct by controlling the last words of the condemned.[71] Thereafter, Denne was persuaded to write a tract acknowledging his errors and praising Fairfax and Cromwell's mercy, in order to convert others 'out of that dangerous and destructive Faction.'[72] The Levellers' version of events was very different. Rather like the earl of Stamford's earlier treatment of James Chudleigh, they depicted Denne as treacherously in league with the enemy generals all along. One Leveller pamphlet dubbed him 'that wretched *Judas Den*', appointed by the generals 'to be most zealous and forward of any man for us, the better to compasse our ruine and lead us like poor sheep to the slaughter'. According to the Levellers, Denne was then pardoned that he might 'vindicate and justify all those wicked and abominable proceedings of the Generall, Lievtenant Generall, and their officers against us, howling and weeping like a Crocodile', while Denne's pamphlet made him a *'perfect Rogue and villain upon everlasting Record'*.[73]

II

The providential arguments deployed against side-changers in print appealed to all social strata, drawing heavily from stories of God's punishing of dreadful sinners which had long circulated in written and oral culture. Alexandra Walsham has argued that prior to the civil wars, contemporaries' readiness to interpret signs of divine providence 'represented an area of relative cultural consensus', so it follows that both sides were eager to demonstrate instances of it that favoured their cause.[74] It became an overused device in printed polemic as both sides circulated narratives of providential judgements, particularly those referring to the fate of side-changers. There was concern that defectors should not be seen by their former comrades to prosper in their new allegiance. Such stories were designed to play upon the fears of prospective defectors that they would not be well received by the other side. In August 1642, one tract fancifully claimed that the royalist council of war had condemned Goring despite his important defection in their favour: 'they sweare as soon as they come to *Portsmouth*, they will have Goring out by head and shoulders; for that he that betrayed the King before, and the trust of the Parliament now, will be true to neither King nor Parliament, but turne like a Weather-cocke.'[75] Another newsbook maintained that when Cholmley defected, as soon as he 'had kissed the

---

[71] BL, E556(1), *A Declaration of the Proceedings of His Excellency the Lord General Fairfax in the Reducing of the Revolted Troops*, 23 May (1649), 11.

[72] BL, E556(11), *The Levellers Designe Discovered: Or the Anatomie of the Late Unhappie Mutinie: Presented unto the Souldiery of the Army under the command of His Excellency the Lord Fairfax; for prevention of the like in others. Written by Henry Denne, an actor in this Tragaedy* (1649), 3.

[73] BL, E571(11), *The Levellers (falsly so called) Vindicated, or The Case of the Twelve Troops (which by Treachery in a Treaty) was Lately Surprised, and Defeated at Burford truly stated* (1649), 6–8.

[74] Alexandra Walsham, *Providence in Early Modern England* (Oxford, 1999), 115, 280, 333.

[75] BL, E109(29), *An Extract of a Letter from Yorke*, 5 August (1642), 5.

Queenes hand, shee turned her backside upon him before he could rise, as if she had taken his perfidiousnesse in scorne'. It then falsely claimed that the royalists would endanger him in the forlorn hope in all their military engagements, 'for they take him to be such an unfaithfull wretch, as is not fit to be tursted [*sic*] either by King, Queene, or Parliament.'[76] If the honour of a side-changer was slighted by their newly chosen side, then the object of changing sides was futile.

An impulse to gloat at the come-uppance of side-changers led several newsbooks to publish rumours of their untimely deaths. In December 1643 both *Mercurius Civicus* and the *Perfect Diurnal* wrongly claimed that 'Renegado Urry is for certain lately dead.'[77] The *Perfect Diurnal* reported in April 1644 that 'Runnagado *Cary*' was among those slain or taken at Cheriton fight.[78] This serial was also premature in reporting Grenville's death after he was shot in the belly at Wellington.[79] Such deaths were interpreted as manifestations of divine retribution and indicators of God's will. Clodagh Tait has recently stressed that reports of strange and miraculous deaths were very important because 'remarkable news might travel very quickly and have a direct effect on public opinion and actions'.[80] When Grenville was wounded, the London press were eager to raise providential arguments. One serial rejoiced that he had received 'a brace of Bullets in his groin' as a 'just judgement of God', because Grenville was 'a notable Whoremaster', and 'a notable prophaner of the Lords day'. Furthermore, it was particularly providential because he 'received this wound on the Lords day, and in the West Country, where he hath hanged and murthered so many men.'[81] Joshua Sprigge noted the fate of Major Sadler, as 'a righteous hand upon a false man'. Originally a parliamentarian, Sadler defected to the royalists but was recaptured at Tiverton's surrender. Condemned to death by the New Model's council of war, he escaped to Exeter, where the royalists executed him for treacherously deserting his post at Tiverton.[82]

Providential arguments not only celebrated the death of renegades; they also sought to deter prospective side-changers. In response to parliament's collapsing support in 1643, John Vicars produced a tract blasting side-changers and 'timorous or treacherous newters' as 'God haters', detailing their grisly fates as a providential warning. He claimed that one London apprentice, Charles Rose, marched out as a parliamentarian soldier but secretly planned to desert and 'make halters to hang the Round-heads'. Near Aylesbury, he was struck mad and found naked on the highway. Rejected by his own father, he returned to London, where he died,

---

[76] BL, E95(2), *The Kingdomes Weekly Intelligencer*, 110.

[77] BL, TT E252(12), *A Perfect Diurnall of Some Passages in Parliament*, no. 22, 18–25 December (1643), 175; BL, TT E79(18), *Mercurius Civicus: London's Intelligencer*, no. 31, 21–28 December (1643), 346.

[78] BL, E252(27), *A Perfect Diurnall of Some Passages in Parliament*, no. 36, 1–8 April (1644), 282.

[79] BL, E260(18), *A Perfect Diurnall of Some Passages in Parliament*, no. 90, 14–21 April (1645), 718.

[80] Clodagh Tait, ' "The Just Vengeance of God": Reporting the Violent Deaths of Persecutors in Early Modern Ireland", in David Edwards, Pádraig Lenihan and Clodagh Tait (eds.), *Age of Atrocity: Violence and Political Conflict in Early Modern Ireland* (Dublin, 2007), 148.

[81] BL, E260(22), *Perfect Occurrences of Parliament*, no. 17, 18–25 April (1645), sig. R4v.

[82] Wing/S5070, Sprigge, *Anglia Rediviva*, 144–5.

declaring: 'He was a dogge, he was a damned wretch'. Vicars related how another deserter at Cambridge, forced to dice for his life after his court martial, unwittingly revealed his cavalier sympathies as he threw them, exclaiming: 'Now for God and the King'. A captured Lincolnshire clergyman submitted in Newark to take what Vicars called the 'Oxonian Protestation or Covenant against the Parliament', only to be struck mad 'and utterly distracted in his senses' afterwards. A 'Mr Standidge' of Lancashire was repaid for his 'unhappy backsliding' from parliament's cause by a fatal bullet that glanced off a wall during the siege of Manchester. Vicars used the case of a London merchant, one Joseph Latch, to caution those whose material interests compromised their allegiance. Despite being pious and well-affected, Latch supposedly went to Oxford to negotiate safe passage of his goods overland from Bristol to Manchester. Imprisoned by the royalists, he was released only upon promising never to aid parliament again. After his return he grew sick and tormented by guilt, crying out: 'I am in hell, I sinke lower and lower; O was there ever such an hypocrite as I am, and therefore I must be damned, and I alone must have my portion with *Judas*'. These cautionary tales were intended to establish that because the parliamentary cause was owned by God, traitors and turncoats had nowhere to hide, but 'God can and will find them out at last'.[83] Those considering defecting might be discouraged by detailing the terrifying judgement which God meted out upon those who had already done so.

Another tract warning against the dangers of backsliding was William Prynne's *The Doome of Cowardize and Treachery* (see Fig. 7.1), written in October 1643 to orchestrate support for the forthcoming prosecution of Nathaniel Fiennes. This was a cheap and mass-produced tract hoping to reach a mass audience of soldiers. In it, Prynne blended the adjectives 'cowardly', 'mercenary', and 'treacherous' together, writing that this was 'an Age of Timidity and Treachery'. He concluded that exemplary capital justice was required for those who betrayed their trusts for the purpose of deterrence and to make parliament's officers and soldiers more diligent and incorruptible.[84]

However, newsbooks might also applaud incoming defectors to magnify the value of their conversion and the consequent damage done to the enemy. In this way, *Mercurius Aulicus* declared that Lord Mordaunt's defection in April 1643 was a harbinger of doom for the rebels: 'It seems the Winter of the cause is now drawing on, the fairest leaves would not else fall away so fast'. Quick to contrast this blow to parliament with supposed royalist solidity, *Aulicus* interpreted it as a judgement upon the relative value of each side's cause: 'in all this time, not one of all His Majesties soldiers have fallen away unto the Rebels, except they have bin guilty of

---

[83] BL, E33(18), John Vicars, *A Looking-Glasse for Malignants: or, Gods hand against God-haters. Containing a most Terrible yet True Relation of the many most Fearefull Personall Examples (in these present times, since the yeere, 1640.) of Gods most Evident and Immediate Wrath against our Malevolent Malignants. Together with a Caveat for Cowards and Unworthy (either Timorous or Treacherous) Newters* (1643), 10–11, 16, 23–5, 28–30.

[84] BL, E251(6), *The Doome of Cowardize and Treachery or a Looking-glass for Cowardly or Corrupt Governours, and Souldiers who through Pusillanimity or Bribery Betray their Trusts, to the Publick Prejudice*, 23 October (1643), 1, 20.

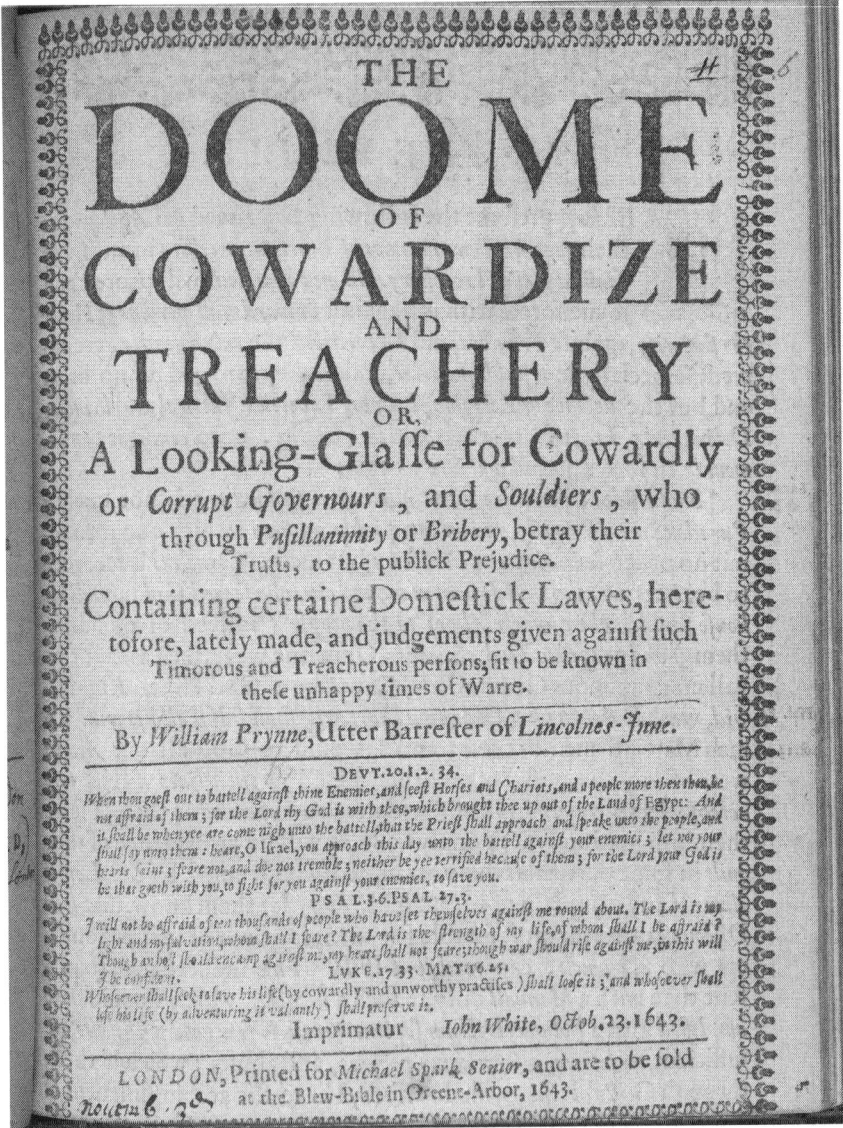

Fig. 7.1. William Prynne, *The Doome of Cowardize and Treachery or, A Looking-Glasse for Cowardly or Corrupt Governours, and Souldiers, who through Pusillanimity or Bribery, betray their Trusts, to the publick Prejudice*. London, 23 October 1643. (© The British Library Board: BL, TT E251(6).)

murder, felonie, or some other such crime of like capitall nature, for which they were to suffer death had they tarried longer.'[85]

III

Beneath the printed treatment of side-changing often lurked specific political objectives. Printed news aspired to influence future allegiance and provoke individual defections: royalist newsbook writers, well aware of Viscount Inchiquin's growing disaffection, were praising him for six months before he defected from parliament in April 1648.[86] Propaganda against side-changers tended to increase and accentuate the divisions between royalists and parliamentarians by printing uncompromising condemnations of the enemy. Bitterness against former colleagues—frequently a potent factor in individual defections—found its way into print, deepening antipathy and distrust. Therefore, it would seem logical that the most heavily committed activists on both sides were those most inclined to sponsor propaganda that vilified side-changers.

How defectors ought to be denounced and how repentant renegades should be received became contested matters within the printed news and factional politics generated by both sides. *The True Informer* was initially sceptical of Dering's conversion, raking up how his 'learning' and 'excellent parts' had inflicted great injury on the Commonwealth. It even claimed that Dering pretended that his defection was 'of his own accord'.[87] In 1644 the *Parliament Scout* advocated that while repentant side-changers might be pardoned they should not be invested with trust, because such would 'run as fortune favours', and were no better than neutrals, putting their own interests before the cause: 'if opportunity offer, they will turne again, and if the wind blow strong, whirle about.' It also argued that reformed royalists should not be allowed to compound for their estates until after the war, as early compositions risked 'a secret supply to the enemy' and were unfair because they placed a higher financial burden upon parliament's loyal supporters.[88]

Establishing the factional alignment of key parliamentarian serials is complicated, as it was often a matter of perception. Although once thought a middle group newsbook, the *Parliament Scout* was believed by one Scots Covenanter to be a mouthpiece for the Independents, and by February 1645 it was considered that its editor, John Dillingham, opposed the Uxbridge peace negotiations.[89] Jason Peacey has shown how *Mercurius Britanicus* frequently shifted its position between 1643 and 1646, owing to changing political circumstances and the turnover of

---

[85] BL, E99(22), *Mercurius Aulicus*, 15th week, 9–16 April (Oxford, 1643), 187.

[86] McElligott, *Royalism, Print and Censorship in Revolutionary England*, 66.

[87] BL, E31(10), *The True Informer*, 27 January–3 February (1644), 151.

[88] BL, E32(11), *The Parliament Scout Communicating his Intelligence to the Kingdome*, no. 33, 2–9 February (1644), 283–4.

[89] Valerie Pearl, 'Oliver St. John and the "Middle Group" in the Long Parliament: August 1643–May 1644', *EHR*, 81 (1966), 506; Joyce Macadam, 'Soldiers, Statesmen and Scribblers: London Newsbook Reporting of the Marston Moor Campaign, 1644', *Historical Research*, 82 (2009), 106; Peacey, *Politicians and Pamphleteers*, 260, 297.

personnel in the key roles of patron, licenser, and editor. His article challenges earlier views that *Britanicus* was established to praise Essex and thereby stave off his feared defection. Instead, Peacey argues that from August 1643 it was initially concerned with rebutting *Mercurius Aulicus*, and attacking those peers and MPs who had already defected or were suspected of plotting to do so. It accused religious moderates in the Westminster Assembly of Divines of treachery, and defended Nathaniel Fiennes during his court martial, leading Peacey to suggest that it represented the Saye–Pym group.[90] However, by 4 March 1644 the earl of Essex was licensing *Britanicus*, with John Rushworth, the licenser of news, challenging him for control from April.[91] Another of its purposes was to intensify internal discord among the royalists, courting Lord Wilmot with sympathetic coverage after his arrest by the king in August 1644.[92] When Marchamont Nedham took over as chief editor from September 1644, it grew increasingly critical of the king, voicing fears that the Uxbridge negotiations were a cover for royalist treachery. By January 1645 it was seeking to discredit Essex, prompting another takeover from the earl that February.[93] By April Nedham was praising Essex's constancy and fidelity, but by May Captain Thomas Audley took over the licensing, winning back the serial for the Independents. It was soon lauding Fairfax and denouncing the king with uncompromising vitriol after the publication of the *King's Cabinet Opened*. In October 1645 Nedham made the tantalizing promise that Lord Digby's recently captured correspondence would unmask traitors within parliamentarian ranks.[94]

Yet London's serial press did not just settle scores within the parliamentarian coalition. It also sought to provoke disunity in royalist ranks. For instance, *The Kingdomes Weekly Intelligencer* attempted to undermine Newcastle's army in January 1643 by suggesting that Lord Savile, Sir William Savile, and Sir Thomas Gower had been placed under armed guard because, displeased by the Catholic influence in command, they were suspected of plotting to desert to Fairfax.[95] In this way the press might attempt to render enemy commanders incapable of further service. George Monck lamented that commanders were so vulnerable to slander: 'if he fail, or prove unfortunate, he is calumniated, scandalised', and that just 'one hour causeth the loss of that reputation, which hath been thirty years acquiring.'[96] Joyce Macadam has stressed the broader objectives of printed news, and how it became 'a key instrument of psychological warfare for bolstering morale at home, and fomenting doubt and discord among the enemy.'[97] On the royalist side, *Mercurius Aulicus* developed similar objectives, and has recently been characterized as 'a

[90] Jason Peacey, 'The Struggle for *Mercurius Britanicus*: Factional Politics and the Parliamentarian Press, 1643–6', *Huntington Library Quarterly*, 68 (2005), 518–22.

[91] Ibid., 524–5.

[92] Macadam, 'Soldiers, Statesmen and Scribblers', 110.

[93] Peacey, 'The Struggle for *Mercurius Britanicus*', 529–30.   [94] Ibid., 533–4, 538.

[95] BL, E86(40), *The Kingdomes Weekly Intelligencer*, 38.

[96] Wing/A864, *Observations upon Military & Political Affairs. Written by the most honourable George Duke of Albemarle, &c. Published by Authority* (1671), 3, 15–16.

[97] Macadam, 'Soldiers, Statesmen and Scribblers', 113.

vehicle for the Laudian faction at court, which ignored the views of moderate royalists.'[98]

In Ireland, retrospective accusations of treachery surrounding the death of Sir Charles Coote were advanced within the protestant coalition to discredit the marquis of Ormond. Coote's savagery against the native Catholic population earned him notoriety in the confederate play *A Tragedy of Cola's Furie*, published at Kilkenny in 1646. When Coote was accidentally shot dead by one of his own men at Trim in May 1642, it was later suggested that his death was no accident but an assassination to weaken the protestant forces and make way for Ormond's realignment of the government forces through the Cessation.[99]

Jason McElligott has recently highlighted that side-changing was particularly prominent among the pamphleteers and propagandists themselves—in particular, four writers who went over to the king from parliamentarian or neutral standpoints in 1647: John Crouch, John Hackluyt, Samuel Sheppard, and Marchamont Nedham.[100] These writers did not restrict themselves to a royalist audience but during 1648 increasingly sought to persuade parliamentarians and neutrals to convert as they had done. Their presence in London unsettled parliament's shaky grip on the capital during much of the New Model's absence in summer 1648.[101] They produced royalist propaganda, often at considerable personal risk, until they were captured and imprisoned. All eventually recanted their royalism in the 1650s while Nedham, Crouch, and Hackluyt went on to write for interregnum regimes whose propaganda became considerably reliant on former royalists. Blair Worden has questioned how these working relationships functioned with the memory of past enmity.[102] Their tergiversations invited hostility, and royalist contemporaries found Nedham's post-Restoration attempts to refashion himself as a royalist unconvincing. Anthony Wood called Nedham a 'weather-cock', valuing 'money and sordid Interest rather than Conscience'. Samuel Butler called him 'a Mercury with a winged conscience, the Skip-Jack of all fortunes, that like a Shittle-cock drive him which way you will, falls still with the cork end forwards.'[103] Even Worden has depicted Nedham as an 'agile reverser of his allegiances', who enjoyed his 'shifts of adherence', adding that his stated reasons for abandoning royalism in 1650 were almost identical to his justification of writing for the restored monarchy eleven years subsequently.[104] Yet these writers' abandonments of royalism were, like the printer William Dugard's, in order to avoid life-threatening hardship and imprisonment. Their 'pragmatism and reluctant accommodation' was comparable to that

---

[98] Peacey, *Politicians and Pamphleteers*, 189.

[99] Kevin Forkan, 'Inventing a Protestant Icon: The Strange Death of Sir Charles Coote', in Edwards, Lenihan and Tait (eds.), *Age of Atrocity*, 209, 212–15; Patricia Coughlan, 'Enter Revenge: Henry Burkhead and Cola's Furie', *Theatre Research International*, 15 (1990), 1–17.

[100] McElligott, *Royalism, Print and Censorship in Revolutionary England*, 94.

[101] Ibid., 39–40.

[102] Ibid., 107–10, 124, 168, 181; Blair Worden, *Literature and Politics in Cromwellian England: John Milton, Andrew Marvell, Marchamont Nedham* (Oxford, 2009), 10.

[103] McElligott, *Royalism, Print and Censorship in Revolutionary England*, 118.

[104] Worden, *Literature and Politics in Cromwellian England*, 10, 14–15.

of Thomas Hobbes—Dugard later claiming that his recantation was under threat of execution.[105] Recently, historians have been increasingly uncomfortable with depicting propagandists who changed sides as completely unprincipled. They were seeking to make a living in difficult circumstances rather than amass great fortunes, while their shifting positions often correlated with fundamental changes in the nature of the parliamentarian and royalist causes.[106] Blair Worden and Joad Raymond have pointed to elements of political constancy in Nedham, such as his enmity to Presbyterians, while McElligott has stressed Nedham's consistent opposition to religious persecution and intolerance, even comparing his conversion to royalism with Edward Hyde's in 1642.[107]

[105] McElligott, *Royalism, Print and Censorship in Revolutionary England*, 137–8, 167.
[106] Peacey, *Politicians and Pamphleteers*, 288, 301–2.
[107] McElligott, *Royalism, Print and Censorship in Revolutionary England*, 112, 119, 125; Worden, *Literature and Politics in Cromwellian England*, 27–30.

8

Honour, reputation, and the self-fashioning of elite side-changers

This chapter will investigate side-changing from the perspectives of those who engaged in it, as they sought to forge a respectable self-image for contemporaries or posterity. Many explained away their former allegiance by depicting themselves as having arrived on the wrong side by accident, stratagem, or necessity. Examining how gentry defectors fashioned their defections takes us to the heart of elite notions of loyalty, honour, and political identity. The interface between these has been a key concern of post-revisionist historiography, which aims to understand how codes of honour interacted with individuals' religious and political preferences.[1] It also builds upon the growing interdisciplinary engagement with the self-fashioning of early modern elites. Literary scholars have pointed to an increased self-consciousness in contemporaries' letters and essays, while the urge toward autobiographical writing was often triggered by the traumatic experience of changing sides.[2] Such self-reflection 'certainly served some individuals as a means of easing tensions in their lives', and for some became a balm for injured honour.[3]

Older, traditional conceptions of honour stressed ancient lineage, blood, pedigree, outward display, and hunting. These ideas persisted alongside a more recent tradition that stressed virtue, education, sobriety, restraint, magistracy, godliness, and public service.[4] Yet these traditions were not mutually exclusive and were often blended or appropriated for different purposes and audiences. Richard Cust has recently contended that by the 1620s, Renaissance humanism, classical republicanism, and English Calvinism had blended to generate an image of the virtuous, incorruptible 'public man'. Drawing upon the writings of the Stoics, such as Plutarch, Seneca, and Cicero, this political culture stressed virtue and constancy as

---

[1] John Adamson, 'Introduction: High Roads and Blind Alleys—The English Civil War and Its Historiography', in John Adamson (ed.), *The English Civil War: Conflict and Contexts, 1640–1649* (Basingstoke, 2009), 27.

[2] Ronald Bedford, Lloyd Davis, and Philippa Kelly (eds.), *Early Modern Autobiography: Theories, Genres, Practices* (Ann Arbor, 2006), 4–6; Muriel C. McClendon, Joseph P. Ward, and Michael MacDonald (eds.), *Protestant Identities: Religion, Society and Self-fashioning in Post-Reformation England* (Stanford, 1999), 12.

[3] Brigitte Glaser, *The Creation of the Self in Autobiographical Forms of Writing in Seventeenth-Century England: Subjectivity and Self-fashioning in Memoirs, Diaries, and Letters* (Heidelberg, 1999), 14, 273.

[4] Richard Cust, 'Honour and Politics in Early Stuart England: The Case of Beaumont v. Hastings', *P&P*, 149 (1995), 60; Mervyn James, *English Politics and the Concept of Honour, 1485–1642, P&P*, supplement, no. 3 (1978), 92.

paramount determinants of nobility. In theory, the gentry were supposed to refrain from private interests to prioritize their duty to serve the public.[5] Such notions of service were reflected in the kind of literature that filled the gentry's commonplace books:

> Mark those that meanly truckle to your power
> They all deserted and changed sides before,
> And would tomorrow Mahomet adore.
> On higher springs true men of honour move
> Free is their service, and unbought their love.
> When danger calls and honour leads ye way
> With joy they follow, and with pride obey.[6]

Brought up under such expectations, it was clearly problematic for gentlemen to change sides without impugning their honour. Clarendon elucidated this by arguing that few side-changers prospered in their new allegiance: 'We scarce find, in any story, a deserter of a trust or party he once adhered to, to be prosperous, or in any eminent estimation with those to whom he resorts...neither hath it been in the power or prerogative of any authority to preserve such men from the reproach and jealousy and scandal that naturally attend upon any defection'.[7] Penetrating how side-changers sought to circumvent such difficulties might advance the historiography on rhetoric, self-fashioning, and honour among the notoriously status-obsessed English gentry.[8]

Archival sources for studying the self-representation of gentry side-changers are scattered but plentiful. Many wrote letters to justify themselves to friends and contemporaries, or corresponded with enemy officers in attempts to coordinate defections. Extensive legal notes survive from trials of recaptured side-changers such as Sir John Hotham and Colonel John Morris, providing insights into how they defended their actions.[9] The Hotham papers contain plentiful material relating to their trials.[10] Particularly rich sources are the memoirs of side-changers such as Sir Hugh Cholmley.[11] Seeking to defend reputations for posterity, memoirists were prone to selective memory in constructing how they wished to be remembered by family and friends. There are also several thousand cases dealt with by the

---

[5] Richard Cust, 'The "Public Man" in Late Tudor and Early Stuart England', in Peter Lake and Steve Pincus (eds.), *The Politics of the Public Sphere in Early Modern England* (Manchester, 2007), 119, 126, 129.

[6] Beinecke Rare Book and Manuscript Library, Osborn Shelves, b115, fo. 12: poem 'The Man of Honour', in an anonymous seventeenth-century commonplace book.

[7] Edward Hyde, earl of Clarendon, *History of the Rebellion and Civil Wars in England Begun in the Year 1641*, ed. William Dunn Macray, 6 vols. (Oxford, 1888), iii, 248–9.

[8] Richard Cust, 'Catholicism, Antiquarianism and Gentry Honour: The Writings of Sir Thomas Shirley', *Midland History*, 23 (1998), 40–70; Cust, 'Honour and Politics in Early Stuart England'; Barbara Donagan, 'The Web of Honour: Soldiers, Christians, and Gentlemen in the English Civil War', *HJ*, 44 (2001), 365–89.

[9] HHC, Hotham MS, U DDHO/1/35; BL, Egerton MS 1048, fos. 101–4.

[10] Andrew Hopper (ed.), *The Papers of the Hothams, Governors of Hull during the Civil War* (Camden Society, 5th series, 39, 2011), 118–58.

[11] Sir Hugh Cholmley, *The Memoirs and Memorials of Sir Hugh Cholmley of Whitby 1600–1657*, ed. Jack Binns (YASRS, 153, 2000).

Committee for Compounding.[12] This committee set fines for royalists to pay to free their estates from sequestration. Cases before this committee included parliamentarians ordered to pay fines for their former royalism. Their petitions provide a further source, once allowance is made for their shaping by legal counsel and committee procedure. They naturally minimized the royalism of their earlier careers. For example, Thomas Simpson of Bishop Auckland petitioned that he had spent more than £400 in raising his troop for parliament in 1644, but played down his earlier royalism as short-lived and forced upon him. His conversion narrative recounted his escape from hanging by the royalists, and was endorsed by his parish minister and the parliamentarians Ferdinando, Lord Fairfax, and Colonel Francis Wren. Yet despite this impressive effort he was still fined £50 to discharge his estates.[13]

Gentry side-changers may have acted to protect themselves, family, and estates, and to profit by victory, but most denied self-interested motives. They frequently faced suspicions that they sought to side with the strongest. Consequently, many sought to 'spin' their past actions to support a self-image of constancy, reliability, and untarnished honour. This chapter explores how they approached this, in response to contemporary notions of side-changing and what it entailed. It focuses upon the self-representation of several professional officers who deserted parliament for the king early in war, along with the power of self-representation in print culture, before unpicking the self-fashioning of Sir Hugh Cholmley, the two Hothams, and Murrough O'Brien, Viscount Inchiquin.

The early Stuart gentry self-consciously fashioned their public reputations, particularly through the manipulation of ritual, rhetoric, and print. They compared political activity to 'ascending the stage' and worried about humiliation in the eyes of a 'news-hungry public'.[14] Civil war amplified such concerns. Provincial officers were notoriously sensitive about how their reputations stood in Oxford or London, and where they were placed in factional conflicts.[15] Facilitated by cheap print, a cult of personality among rival commanders emerged, and officers became subjects of life narratives.[16] Side-changers might deflect the abuse, discussed in the previous chapter, by claiming political constancy. When the earl of Holland defected in August 1643 he refused to apologize for his previous parliamentarianism or admit any offence whatsoever. This proved a major obstacle to his integration into royalism, despite his armed attendance at Newbury.[17] In November 1643 he returned to parliament and published a self-justificatory tract in which he compared himself to rivers and streams: 'naturally are they inclined to revert, and to looke backe to their Channells, and long-kept course againe.'[18]

---

[12] *CCCD*.

[13] TNA, SP 23/181/361–77.

[14] Richard P. Cust, 'Wentworth's "Change of Sides" in the 1620s', in Julia F. Merritt (ed.), *The Political World of Thomas Wentworth, Earl of Strafford, 1621–1641* (Cambridge, 1996), 64.

[15] Barbara Donagan, *War in England, 1642–1649* (Oxford, 2008), 108–9.

[16] Kevin Sharpe and Steven N. Zwicker (eds.), *Writing Lives: Biography and Textuality, Identity and Representation in Early Modern England* (Oxford, 2008), 19–20.

[17] Hyde, *History of the Rebellion*, iii, 195.

[18] BL, E32(14), *A Declaration Made to the Kingdome by Henry, Earle of Holland*, 10 February (1644), 6.

When he was executed in 1649 for a second bout of armed royalism, he argued that he had always been faithful to parliament—a remarkable claim for a man who had deserted them twice. Yet for Holland this was essential for his self-regard and posterity. He argued that the cause, not he, had changed. He claimed, quite sincerely, that 'I have never gone off from those Principles that ever I have professed.'[19] Indeed, by 1649 he could claim greater constancy to parliament's war aims of 1642 than the regicides, who most parliamentarians considered had perverted their cause. Holland provides an extreme example of how changed circumstances left individuals vulnerable to the slur of being turncoats. As the parliamentarian coalition fractured in 1648, there were many left like him, disenfranchised and unrepresented.

I

Most professional officers who defected to the king during 1642–3 claimed that they never intended to participate in rebellion. Although this seems suggestive of royalist propaganda, it remains persuasive, because until September 1642 it was doubtful whether civil war was possible, owing to the king's failure to recruit an army. Officers who enlisted in parliament's army for Ireland found themselves channelled into Essex's army, with their terms of service changed without consultation. This prompted several high-profile incidents of turncoating, beginning with the spectacular defection of Sir Faithful Fortescue's troop during the battle of Edgehill. Raised in summer 1642, this troop was intended for Ireland, and Fortescue could reasonably argue that it was never his intention to oppose the king in England. He remained a committed royalist thereafter, fighting at Worcester in 1651.[20] Another defector from the army for Ireland became the civil wars' most notorious side-changer. Sir John Urry, a Scotsman with continental military experience, was often depicted as exemplary of the professional whose own interests outweighed service to either side. His cornet adopted the motto of Francesco Sforza, Duke of Milan: 'Nemo me impune lacessit' ('No one attacks me with impunity').[21] This motto suggests an aggressive attachment to his martial honour. Nevertheless, when Urry defected in June 1643, probably through concern that his low rank slighted his reputation, he carefully 'professed repentance for having been in rebellion'. Consequently, he was 'magnified and extolled' at Oxford, commissioned, and knighted. Importantly, Urry sought to protect himself from charges of betraying trust by resigning his parliamentarian commission a month before he defected. *Mercurius Aulicus* reported on 21 April 1643 that he was retiring to Scotland, while Urry himself later claimed to have refused an

---

[19] Barbara Donagan, 'A Courtier's Progress: Greed and Consistency in the Life of the Earl of Holland', *HJ*, 19 (1976), 348, 352.

[20] Basil Morgan, 'Sir Faithful Fortescue (*b.* in or before 1581, *d.*1666), royalist army officer', *ODNB*; P. R. Newman, *The Old Service: Royalist Regimental Colonels and the Civil War 1642–46* (Manchester, 1993), 57–8; Newman, 142; Hyde, *History of the Rebellion*, ii, 360, 363.

[21] Ian Gentles, 'The Iconography of Revolution: England 1642–1649', in Ian Gentles, John Morrill and Blair Worden (eds.), *Soldiers, Writers and Statesmen of the English Revolution* (Cambridge, 1998), 100.

oath not to enter royalist service.[22] Although Urry's successful negotiation of his defection owed something to professional codes of conduct, it was more firmly grounded in his potential usefulness to the royalist cause.[23] Despite his precautions, many speculated on whether he would defect again—which he did, so often that he was commonly described as 'of turncoat memory.'[24]

Another defector who returned from Ireland was James Chudleigh of Ashton, Devon. Clarendon recalled that Chudleigh originally offered himself to the king in December 1642, but was rebuffed because of his parliamentarian family and his part in revealing the Army Plot in 1641.[25] London propagandists praised Chudleigh's 'immortal Fame', for 'his discreet and valient carriage' against the Cornish, and he was appointed Sergeant-Major-General to the earl of Stamford's parliamentarian western army.[26] After several engagements, Chudleigh was captured at the battle of Stratton on 16 May 1643. Royalists maintained that he changed sides several days later, but parliamentarians claimed that Chudleigh defected during the battle itself. This enabled Stamford to divert attention from his own ignominious flight to reproach Chudleigh's treachery for the defeat. Chudleigh's self-regard did not take kindly to such treatment; his military reputation had hitherto been promoted in print by boastfully exaggerating his successes while blaming others for reverses.[27] Hoping to utilize Chudleigh's example to provoke further defections, the royalist press at Oxford printed his self-defence. The tract blended Chudleigh's fiery indignation with personal attacks on Devon parliamentarians to fashion his defection as motivated by conviction. Chudleigh maintained that his captors treated him honourably and persuaded him that the royalist cause was just. He argued that his new friends were more inclined to peace than 'the factious Tumult of the Citty of Exeter' who maintained their cause through abusing religion. He urged his former comrades to negotiate a treaty. Clearing himself of treachery, he maintained that he had led Devon's parliamentarians in good faith, declaring: 'Twas not without excessive continued paines, that I had put that Tumultuous body into a serviceable posture in the field.' He claimed that while he lay wounded at Stratton, other parliamentarian commanders, 'that I am never likely to meet with in the field', fled to Exeter 'to passe the time in making Aldermen, and women believe them valiant, whiles all the world knows the contrary.'[28] Diverting attention from his own inconstancy, he contrasted himself with former colleagues whom he depicted as corrupted by urban and feminine

[22] BL, E100(18), *Mercurius Aulicus*, 16th week, 16–22 April (Oxford, 1643), 205; Hyde, *History of the Rebellion*, iii, 55, 58.

[23] Edward M. Furgol, 'Sir John Urry (*d.* 1650), army officer', *ODNB*; Ian Gentles, *The English Revolution and the Wars in the Three Kingdoms, 1638–1652* (Harlow, 2007), 241.

[24] Bodl., MS Clarendon 23, fo. 153v; Beinecke Rare Book and Manuscript Library, Osborn Shelves, b169, fo. 152; Cholmley, *Memoirs and Memorials*, 137; Donagan, *War in England*, 49.

[25] Hyde, *History of the Rebellion*, iii, 73–4.

[26] BL, E100(6), *A Most Miraculous and Happy Victory Obtained by James Chudleigh Serjeant Major Generall of the Forces under the E. of Stamford*, 29 April (1643), 3.

[27] Chudleigh claimed that he overawed the royalists 'by beating in his six Scouts with three of ours and our shadows, we are left the onelie defence of this Countie': BL, E100(17), *Speciall Passages and Certain Informations from Severall Places*, no. 38, 25 April–2 May (1643), 310–12.

[28] Wing/C3983, James Chudleigh, *Serjeant Major James Chudleigh his Declaration to his Country-men* (Oxford, 1643), 1–5.

influences and therefore incapable of masculine, military honour. Stamford also charged Chudleigh's father, Sir George, with cowardice and treachery, dealing an insufferable blow to Sir George's long-established reputation as a leading 'patriot' and 'father of his country' in Devon.[29] By September 1643 Sir George Chudleigh had resigned as lieutenant-general, withdrawn from parliamentarian allegiance, and claimed royal pardon. By November he had penned a self-defence 'to satisfy his friends' that was quoted approvingly by *Mercurius Aulicus*.[30] In March 1644 the London press responded by blasting his claim to constancy in a popular pamphlet referring, in its title, to 'that Grand Ambo-dexter' (see Fig. 8.1).[31]

Officers returning from Ireland to desert parliament for the king stressed their military skill and personal worth, often expressing an aggrieved sense of betrayal or injured honour. Sir Richard Grenville remains their most notorious exemplar. He returned in 1643 and became lieutenant-general to Sir William Waller, but joined the king at Oxford on 7 March 1644. His treachery was particularly flagrant because he had taken the Solemn League and Covenant, and reportedly pledged in the Commons that 'he would never take up Arms against, but for the Parliament, and die in the defence of them with his last drop of blood.'[32] Writing to Speaker Lenthall on 8 March, Grenville justified himself in a mocking and self-congratulatory tone. He declared that parliament had slighted him by deliberately frustrating his legal affairs, accusing them of 'a design to have a hold and engagement on me in a service I was so ill-satisfied in.' Then he argued that parliament's imposition of unlawful oaths, overstepping precedents, and confiscation of delinquents' estates had driven him to the king. If, as Clarendon maintained, Grenville later hinted that he planned this defection before he left Ireland, Grenville's claim that his parliamentarianism was a ruse to deceive the enemy was well calculated to mitigate his guilt and ingratiate himself with his new friends.[33] On arriving in Devon, his letter urging Plymouth to surrender explained his defection further. It insisted he had wanted to keep out of the war, initially refusing parliament's 'great tokens of favour' to serve them. Arguing that he was provoked into turning on parliament, he fell into customary royalist arguments that parliamentarians used religion as 'the cloak of rebellion', and that they were directed by 'sectaries of infinite kinds which would not hear of a peace.' Grenville reflected on having broken the Covenant by enclosing a tract entitled 'the Iniquitye of the Covenant', but Plymouth's governor ordered it burned by the common hangman in the market-place.[34]

[29] Mary Wolffe, *Gentry Leaders in Peace and War: The Gentry Governors of Devon in the Early Seventeenth Century* (Exeter, 1997), 158–64.
[30] BL, E75(37), *Mercurius Aulicus*, 44th week, 29 October–4 November (Oxford, 1643), 625.
[31] 'Ambi-dexter' was a term applied, from the early seventeenth century, to double-dealers supporting both sides during a conflict: BL, E37(20), *A Declaration Published in the County of Devon by that Grand Ambo-dexter, Sir George Chudleigh baronet* (1644), 3–7.
[32] Thomas Juxon, *The Journal of Thomas Juxon, 1644–1647*, ed. Keith Lindley and David Scott (Camden Society, 5th series, 13, 1999), 44; BL, E250(16), *A Perfect Diurnall of Some Passages in Parliament*, no. 11, 25 September–2 October (1643), 88.
[33] Amos C. Miller, *Sir Richard Grenville of the Civil War* (1979), 67–70.
[34] The tract Grenville enclosed was almost certainly: BL, E36(10), *The Iniquity of the Late Solemne League or Covenant, Discovered by Way of a Letter to a Gentleman Desiring Information upon the Poynt*, 9 March (1644); BL, Add. MS 35297, fos. 31r–32v; BL, E47(1), *A Continuation of the True Narration of the Most Observable Passages in and about Plymouth*, 10 May (1644), 9–12.

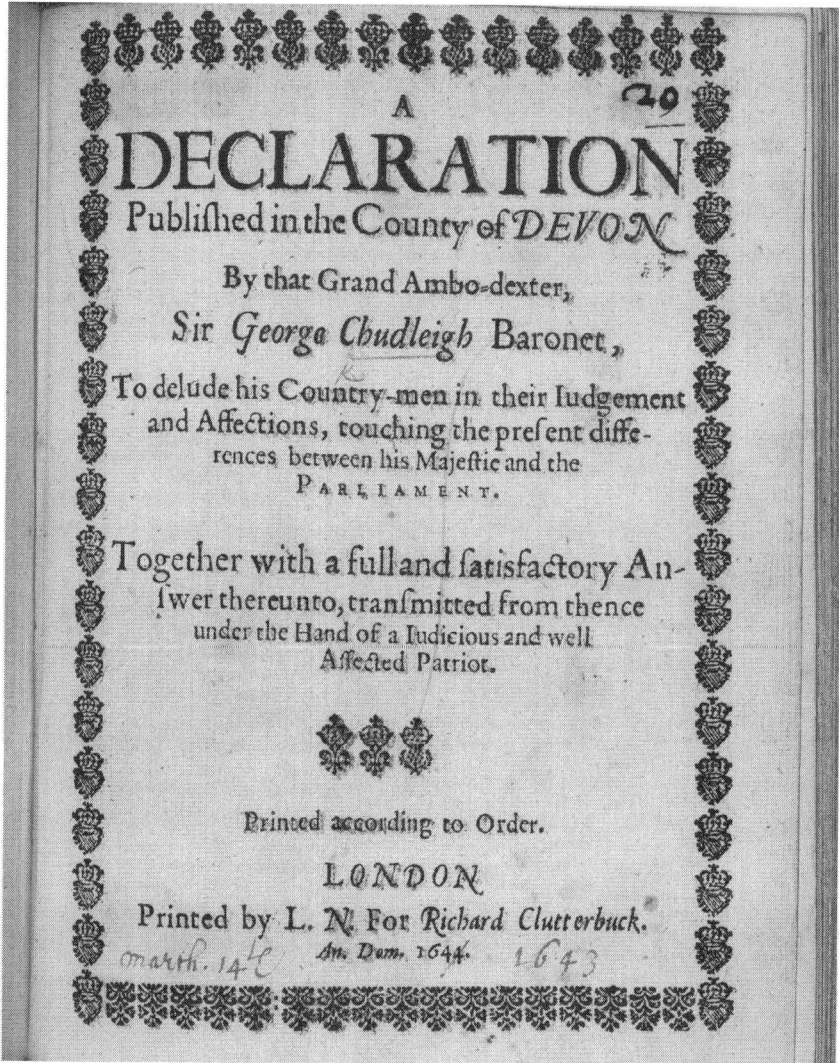

Fig. 8.1. Parliamentarian propaganda against turncoats. *A Declaration Published in the County of Devon By that Grand Ambo-dexter, Sir George Chudleigh Baronet, To delude his Country-men in their Iudgement and Affections, touching the present differences between his Majestie and the Parliament. Together with a full and satisfactory Answer thereunto, transmitted from thence under the Hand of a Iudicious and well Affected Patriot.* London 1644. (© The British Library Board: BL, E37(20).)

Thereafter, Grenville proved an energetic commander, albeit one who tended to inflame conflict within the royalist command. On 20 January 1646 he was arrested for refusing a commission from the Prince of Wales, and within the year penned an immodest defence that exaggerated his successes while blaming others for royalist setbacks.[35] Despite his previous parliamentarianism he boldly declared his 'services and intention was ever found faithful to his majesty and to the contrary can no man take him in any kind.'[36] He even complained to the Prince of Wales' council that Lord Goring's men would rather 'take to the enemies party, than to be subject to my course of discipline.'[37] He presented himself as the victim of conspiratorial lords on the prince's council and a sufferer for unsullied loyalty. This was an image very different from his previous posturing as the champion of Cornish particularism in attempting to promote a separate negotiated peace between Cornwall and parliament.[38]

In January 1654 Grenville penned another manuscript self-justification which again avoided mentioning his former parliamentarianism. By then he had accused Clarendon of plotting with Cromwell, for which the exiled Charles II forbade Grenville from his presence. This affront robbed Grenville of the spiritual comforts of other exiled royalists who consoled themselves with reputations for constancy and integrity. Grenville remonstrated that his loyalty was 'sufficiently tried' and that he was one of the crown's 'faithfullest servants', adding 'I pray God it be not made a crime to be loyal.' He declared: 'all that know me rightly, have known experience of my impartiality in service of His Majesty.'[39] In further protest, Grenville drafted an embittered autobiography that placed military service and loyalty at the heart of his concept of honour. It made the remarkable claim: 'My former time spent hath been as a soldier, (as were all my ancestors, since the Conquest of England, anno 1066) ever constantly for services of the crown of England.'[40] Espousing older, traditional notions of honour, he held that his pedigree, blood, and martial valour were guarantors of loyalty. He recounted his success against the Irish rebels in 1642, and claimed to have been invited by letters to return to serve the king in England. He passed over his service under Waller, and again failed to explain how he joined the royalist cause. His final response was to adopt the tone of stoic forbearance and retirement that was customary for English gentry to employ during moments of political failure.[41] He wrote that he would 'make my peace with God and man: and to find a quiet dying place in my native land: and never again touch with any kind of worldly affairs.' Yet his bitterness overwhelmed

---

[35] Bodl., MS Clarendon 27, fos. 77–80.

[36] Ibid., fo. 79.	[37] Ibid., fo. 3.

[38] Mark Stoyle, *West Britons: Cornish Identities and the Early Modern British State* (Exeter, 2002), 110.

[39] Bedford, Davis, and Kelly (eds.), *Early Modern Autobiography*, 9; Bodl., MS Clarendon 47, fo. 242.

[40] 'Sir Richard Grenville's single defence against all aspersions (in the power or aim) of malignant persons: and to satisfy the contrary': Bodl., MS Clarendon 47, fo. 312r.

[41] Ann Hughes, 'Men, the "Public" and the "Private" in the English Revolution', in Lake and Pincus (eds.), *The Politics of the Public Sphere*, 201–2.

his attempted forbearance. Intimating that it was now too late for him to continue in royalist service, he echoed the earl of Strafford's reported disillusion with the Stuarts, quoting Psalm 146: 'O put not your trust in Princes, nor in any child of man, for there is no help in him.'[42] Grenville's attachment to his lineage and martial honour left him ill-equipped to engage in a service suffering from contested command structures, imploding factional politics, and a collapsing war effort. His language of loyalty and service scarcely suppressed his vitriol, providing a thin veil for his inconstancy and the conditional nature of his allegiance.

II

Newsbooks' coverage of side-changers influenced the self-fashioning employed by defectors and their expectations of future treatment. Many side-changers turned to the powerful medium of print to communicate their motives. Some self-justifications were intended to be read by their fellow gentry, but others were cheaper pamphlets for a popular audience. On occasions, the side-changer's new masters sought to dictate what form these took or to edit the text for polemical purposes, making it difficult to trace how far a defector's self-narrative was actually composed by others. Publishing a self-justificatory declaration was established practice by summer 1643. These texts ranged from a passage in serial newsbooks to fully dedicated pamphlets, and were often published quickly after the defection.[43] Through them, propagandists sought to maximize the damage which defections inflicted upon the enemy. Declarations of parliamentarians who became royalists stressed how low-born social subversives, anarchy, and religious confusion dominated the parliamentary ranks, while their opposite counterparts trumpeted disgust at the Cessation in Ireland and the strength of popery at court.

Sergeant-Major Robert Kirle and Sir Edward Dering constitute telling examples of each. Kirle's eight-page pamphlet claimed to publish a letter he had written to a friend at Windsor in February or March 1643, soon after his defection to Oxford. His avowed purpose in writing for a supposed parliamentarian audience was to 'free myself from the imputation of dishonour, and undeceive others.' He excused himself by claiming that having recently returned from soldiering abroad, his ignorance of events led him unwittingly into parliament's army. He argued that his defection was free of necessity, ambition, and malice, but was rather 'a perfect discovery of those false lights, that have hitherto misled me, and a deep apprehension of the horrour which attends the persevering in such errors.' Then he linked religious plurality and social subversion, a cornerstone of royalist propaganda:

...certaine I am, that all the Officers of no one Company were of the same Opinion what religion they fought for...Some liked the Chaplain of the Regiment, another thought his Corporall preached better...and one would thinke, that every Company

---

[42] Bodl., MS Clarendon 47, fo. 316r–v; Ronald G. Asch, 'Thomas Wentworth, first earl of Strafford (1593–1641), lord lieutenant of Ireland', *ODNB*.

[43] BL, E244(30), *Mercurius Aulicus*, 1st week, 1–7 January (Oxford, 1643), 6.

had been raised out of the severall Congregations of Amsterdam...if they cannot prove any of quality to be a Papist, yet as he is a Gentleman, he shall want grace; and that is title enough to possesse the estates of all that are more richer then themselves.[44]

How, if at all, Kirle explained this pamphlet when he returned to parliament in September 1644 remains unknown, but his case illustrates how effectively self-defences were turned to partisan propaganda.[45]

This process grew more sophisticated as the war lengthened. Jason Peacey's extensive research on Sir Edward Dering has recently highlighted that when Dering deserted Oxford for London in February 1644, parliament forced him into a dec-laration to explain himself. An ailing Dering wished to accept parliament's offer of pardon to return home to settle his affairs before he died.[46] He was granted liberty upon submitting an apologetic petition, but its contents were humiliatingly made public, and the Kent county committee insisted he publicly repudiate royalism in 'no volume, but an epitome...a little pamphlet, which will better sink into the common people's brain than any long volume.' An unenthusiastic Dering eventu-ally promised 'the pamphlet you command shall go out sudden and unpolished', and that it would 'be a piece of a penny, fit...for the vulgar.'[47] It was published on 1 April, and pleased parliament by trumpeting key claims of parliamentarian prop-aganda to a mass audience. Dering expressed disgust at Catholic officers dominat-ing the king, and abhorrence of the Cessation in Ireland. His condemnation of the Oxford Parliament as 'an anti-Parliament' was conveniently timely, while his tirade against Laudian-popish ceremonies and the '*Dionysian* Orgy' of organ music at Oxford was calculated to appeal to the Godly: 'One single groan in the Spirit, is worth the *Diapason* of all the Church-Musick in the world.'[48]

Despite attempts at a constancy narrative, Dering admitted to a genuine conver-sion, comparing himself with Saint Paul, 'from a Persecuter, I was made a Con-vert.' He joined the king in summer 1642 as 'the most unwilling man that ever went', even claiming that he had advised Charles to return to Westminster with just forty servants. Dering stressed that he chose to return, professing himself 'very sorry for bearing Arms against the Parliament.'[49] This was a godsend for parliamen-tary propaganda, as Dering had been a particularly vocal MP, renowned for court-ing popularity by circulating his speeches. It was widely anticipated that reports of

---

[44] BL, E246(35), *A Copy of a Letter Writ from Serjeant Major Kirle, to a Friend in Windsor* (1643), 2–3.

[45] Newman, 219; J. and T. W. Webb (eds.), *Memorials of the Civil War between Charles I and the Parliament of England as it affected Herefordshire and the Adjacent Counties*, 2 vols. (1879), ii, 98, 238, 350–3; BL, E339(9), *The Gallant Siege of the Parliament's forces Before Ragland Castle*, 30 May (1646).

[46] Jacqueline Eales, *Community and Disunity: Kent and the English Civil Wars, 1640–1649* (Faver-sham, 2001), 15.

[47] Jason Peacey, 'Sir Edward Dering, Popularity and the Public, 1640–1644', *HJ*, 54 (2011), 981.

[48] BL, E40(5), *A Declaration by Sir Edward Dering Knight and Baronet*, 1 April (1644), 8–11.

[49] Ibid., 2–3, 6, 7–8.

his defection would lead other royalists to defect or withdraw their allegiance.[50] Indeed, Sir Anthony Ashley Cooper was among several who changed sides soon after, surrendering himself at Hurst castle on 24 February 1644. Like Dering, he emphasized political principles before his personal interests, remarking that the Catholics at court and the Cessation in Ireland were 'destructive to religion and state'. Ashley Cooper resigned his royalist commissions well before changing sides, and maintained that therefore he had not acted dishonourably nor been unfaithful. Parliament evidently considered his principled conversion genuine; by August 1644 he was commissioned as field marshal-general in Dorset, remaining a loyal and energetic commander thereafter.[51]

Print was also seized upon as a means to counteract rumour and defend reputations. When Colonel John Were found himself the scapegoat for the earl of Essex's disaster in Cornwall, he turned to the popular eight-page pamphlet to clear his name and 'to vindicate my reputation, more pretious, then my life'. He stood accused of quitting his posts, prematurely surrendering, and voluntarily defecting to the enemy. He denied these charges, attributing them to 'the meere guilt of rumour, or by some aspersion cast upon me by the subtile enemy, whose interest is the discord of friends.'[52] However, he admitted that after the surrender, when he was wet, sick, and in fear for his life, he accepted the offer of a former officer of his who had already defected to spend the night in royalist quarters, with the promise of being returned to his men the next day. Were claimed that the royalists broke this promise, and by placing him under duress, forced him to pledge himself to serve the king: 'I promised to serve the King, but with a secret reservation to my selfe, no further then he complyed with his Parliament, holding it no sinne to deceive them that had been twice perfidious to me.' He eventually escaped and made his way to Taunton, where he raised men for parliament and would have remained in military service there were it not for London's pamphleteers publishing 'the scandall of my revolt'.[53] In response he made his way to Southampton to clear his name, but was arrested by Essex's orders and sent as a prisoner to London's Compter on 7 November 1644.[54] Embittered by his treatment, he admitted to having spoken words tending to Essex's dishonour 'in some passion which might have been well left unsaid'. Nevertheless, he demanded a trial 'above all things', for 'my present sufferance not so much grieving me as the present scandall I lye under,

---

[50] Edmund Ludlow, *The Memoirs of Edmund Ludlow, Lieutenant-General of the Horse in the Army of the Commonwealth of England, 1625–1672*, ed. C. H. Firth, 2 vols. (Oxford, 1894), i, 86; Francis Bickley (ed.), *Report on the Manuscripts of the late Reginald Rawdon Hastings, esq.*, HMC, 78, 4 vols. (1930), ii, 122; BL, E32(1), *A Continuation of Certain Speciall and Remarkable Passages Informed to the Parliament*, no. 6, 1–8 February (1644), 7; BL, E32(11), *The Parliament Scout Communicating his Intelligence to the Kingdome*, no. 33, 2–9 February (1644), 278–80.

[51] Tim Harris, 'Anthony Ashley Cooper, first earl of Shaftesbury (1621–1683), politician', *ODNB*; Patrick Little, 'Four Dorset Turncoats', unpublished paper delivered at a civil war conference at the Dorset Record Office, Dorchester, 2002.

[52] I am most grateful to Tim Wales for his notes on Colonel John Were. BL, E21(34), *The Apologie of Colonell John Were in Vindication of his Proceedings since the Beginning of this Present Parliament* (1644), 1.

[53] Ibid., 4–6. Thomas Juxon had been misinformed that Were was a Cornishman who had betrayed his regiment to the king: Juxon, *The Journal of Thomas Juxon*, 59.

[54] *CJ*, iii, 667, 678, 689.

and the frequent scoffings of the disaffected'.[55] Having mobilized support from Essex's political enemies, including Waller and Hesilrige, Were refused to play the part Essex had assigned him, instead trumpeting his constancy 'though the Parliament was then at its lowest ebbe', and maintaining that he was the first and last gentleman to raise a regiment in Devon for parliament. To present himself as the unjustly persecuted man of martial honour, he claimed that he was more anxious to clear his name among parliament's soldiery than their politicians, although of course his release from imprisonment depended more upon the latter.[56] He was not bailed until 4 November 1645.[57] His case is one among many that indicate both how allegations of treachery fuelled factional politics, and how treachery could be read back into events retrospectively, because of a state of mind among the defeated, and the need to divert responsibility in the explanation of military disasters.

III

This section examines the self-fashioning of Sir Hugh Cholmley and the Hothams, governors of Scarborough and Hull. Cholmley's memoirs and memorials set about justifying his defection in a much different way from the pamphlets and newsbooks discussed above. He penned his memoirs in the changed circumstances of 1656, and the passage of time allowed greater opportunity for refashioning and self-deception.[58] Kevin Sharpe and Steven Zwicker have discussed how such memoirists were concerned to produce exemplary accounts, 'written for use', and designed as a counsel and guide for others.[59] Cholmley addressed them to his sons for the defence of his good name. They made several false claims, including that when he defected in March 1643 Scarborough's whole garrison 'was immediately settled for the King without the least mutiny or disturbance.'[60] Anxious that posterity would regard him as inconstant, he maintained that he did not break his trust with parliament. Instead, they broke their trust with him, by altering the grounds of the war, failing to supply him, and allowing his name to be slandered in London. He claimed that his motives were not 'for any perticuler ends of my owne, but merely to performe the duty and alleagance I owed to my Soveraigne, and which I did in such away as was with out any deminution of my honour either as a gentleman or souldier.'[61]

During 1648 Cholmley had written an earlier retrospective justification for Clarendon, entitled 'Memorialls tuching Scarbrough', in which he explained his

---

[55] BL, E21(34), *The Apologie of Colonell John Were*, 7–8. For his words against Essex see *LJ*, vii, 258.

[56] Ibid., 1–2.

[57] *CJ*, iv, 334.

[58] Glaser, *Creation of the Self*, 5.

[59] Sharpe and Zwicker (eds.), *Writing Lives*, vi, 4, 13, 19.

[60] Cholmley, *Memoirs and Memorials*, 144.

[61] Ibid., 105.

parliamentarianism as arising from an 'apprehension that persons ill affected to the peace of the kingdome did intrude themselves into imployment.' He contended that by undertaking Scarborough's governorship, he kept out more dangerous alternatives, while his more impartial disposition enabled him to promote peace from a position of armed strength. He claimed that his Protestation and allegiance oaths required him to defend the king, and that he twice urged Speaker Lenthall to negotiate a peace treaty, lamenting that the 'kings faire and reasonable propositions' went unheeded.[62] Cholmley had indeed complained to Lenthall, and when the Commons responded by ordering him to quit Scarborough, he refused.[63] Instead, on 20 March 1643 he travelled in disguise to York to secretly negotiate his defection with the queen. One of his initial conditions, later overtaken by events, was that he be granted three weeks to return his commission to Essex, so that when he turned royalist he might not be charged with betraying his trust.[64]

Like Chudleigh and Grenville, Cholmley magnified the injuries his honour received from parliament. In December 1642 he was chastised in parliament for disobeying Lord Fairfax's orders, and by January 1643 he bitterly complained of his treatment in the press, warning Lenthall that 'my former actions did never deserve those representations of them which were in print, nor any belief of them.'[65] In March, he lamented that parliament slighted him by not sending sufficient supplies.[66] His sensitivity was partly due to his upbringing, himself admitting that his father was of a 'haughty sperret and chollericke', swore too much, and was prone to duels and rude behaviour towards his servants and the country people. His father struck a gentleman in Star Chamber, and Sir Hugh himself struck down a trained bandsman for insolence in 1639.[67] Close attention to lineage, reputation, and local standing shaped Cholmley's notion of honour. His pew in Whitby parish church, which 'completely straddles the chancel arch', has been described as an 'incredibly vulgar' display of status.[68]

Cholmley's representation to his sons of selfless cavalier loyalty is less than convincing. His defection was dictated by the local military situation, for he sought to prevent Scarborough being besieged.[69] If the northern royalist army was not so large and threatening to his estates, Cholmley's royalism may have been less forthcoming. Furthermore, his honour was soon questioned by the comrades he had deserted. Fearing to come abroad, his terms with the queen insisted that he remain Scarborough's governor. He surrounded himself with servants armed with pistols, and almost came to blows with his officers, at least six of whom deserted him with

[62] Ibid., 140, 143.

[63] For Cholmley's complaint to Lenthall, see *Portland MS*, 90; BL, E85(17), *Newes from Yorke. Being a True Relation of the Proceedings of Sir Hugh Cholmley since his comming to Scarborough* (1643), sig. A2r.

[64] Cholmley, *Memoirs and Memorials*, 142–3.

[65] *CJ*, ii, 893; *Portland MS*, 90; BL, Harleian MS 164, fo. 298r.

[66] BL, E95(9), *A True and Exact Relation of all the Proceedings of Sir Hugh Cholmley's Revolt*, 7 April (1643), 4.

[67] Cholmley, *Memoirs and Memorials*, 70–1, 99.

[68] Felicity Heal and Clive Holmes, *The Gentry in England and Wales, 1500–1700* (1994), 338.

[69] Jack Binns, *'A Place of Great Importance': Scarborough in the Civil Wars* (Preston, 1996), 96.

about 100 troopers.[70] Endeavouring to dissuade him from changing sides, one captain claimed to have warned him 'what a dishonour it would be to himselfe, and what a stain to his posterity.'[71] Cholmley was ordered to be impeached for high treason in the Commons on 2 April 1643. In October 1645 his exemption from pardon was proposed.[72] The press, whose invective against him was vicious, amplified the condemnation. Compelled by this savaging, Cholmley crafted a self-image of personal constancy and injured honour, beset by the inconstancy of his former cause and comrades. This portrayal was recurrent among sympathetic representations of side-changing. His protestations persuaded Clarendon, who clearly admired him, and even Gardiner, who compared him favorably with the Hothams, saying he appeared 'to have had the nobler nature, and to have been actuated by the purer motives.'[73]

The correspondence of disaffected officers with enemy commanders was a perennial fear of leaders on both sides. Numerous such letters survive between the earl of Newcastle and Sir John Hotham and his eldest son, John Hotham. The Hothams' conspicuous parliamentarianism cooled as, like Cholmley, their estates became threatened by Newcastle's army. The younger Hotham entered into a frequent, friendly correspondence with Newcastle from December 1642, eventually pledging that he would defect at an opportune moment and bring with him his father, Hull, Beverley, and Lincoln, along with disaffected parliamentarians in Lincolnshire and the East Riding.[74]

Hotham presented himself to Newcastle as trustworthy, honest, constant, and an effective commander whose defection might be procured should parliament err. He maintained his change of sides would be conditional upon this point, otherwise 'I should have been the scorn and by word of every boy in the street.'[75] Although he posed as disdainful of heeding gossip among the common sort, he remained especially sensitive about his public standing. On 3 April 1643 he warned Newcastle that Cholmley's defection had 'drawn such a jealousy upon me and our people talk at large.'[76] He indicated his desire to change sides, but in such a way 'as not to bring upon me the odious name of knavery.' He held out the hope that parliament's mistreatment of him would permit his defection without staining his honour, which he remarked was 'like a woman's honesty, not to be repaired if once touched.' Meanwhile, he ingratiated himself by warning Newcastle that he was mocked at court by Lady Cornwallis, who said 'that you were a sweet General, lay in bed until eleven o'clock and combed till 12, then came to the Queen, and so the work was done, and that General King did all the business.' He warned Newcastle: 'You can expect nothing at court, truly the women rule all.'[77] By pointing to the

---

[70] TNA, SP 28/138/3, SP 28/129/6, fo. 9

[71] BL, E95(9), *A True and Exact Relation*, 5–7.

[72] BL, Add. MS 31116, fo. 40r; BL, Harleian MS 164, fo. 351r; BL, Harleian MS 166, fo. 271r.

[73] Samuel R. Gardiner, *History of the Great Civil War, 1642–1649*, 4 vols. (1987), i, 105.

[74] HHC, Hotham MS, U DDHO/1/14, 18, 20, 28–9; Bodl., MS Tanner 62, fos. 71, 83, 90; BL, Add. MS 32096, fos. 248–51; *Portland MS*, 80–84, 89, 99, 109, 699–707.

[75] HHC, Hotham MS, U DDHO/1/27.

[76] Ibid., DDHO/1/12, 29.

[77] Ibid., DDHO/1/12; *Portland MS*, 109, 701.

inversion of gender roles at court, he shrewdly appealed to Newcastle's frustration with gossips jealous of his success in raising a large army. Here the concept of women's unnatural engagement in high politics blended with notions of secrecy, intrigue, and deception as feminine attributes.[78] The younger Hotham contrasted this with the virtues of the open, masculine friendship, personal loyalty, and constancy that he offered the earl. His repeated self-justificatory references to his honour strung Newcastle along and were intended to protect the Hotham estates from royalist soldiers, until, prepared with strong arguments against having broken their trust, his family were ready to defect.

By June 1643 the younger Hotham was at Nottingham, where, clashing with parliament's other local commanders, he was arrested on suspicion of treachery.[79] On 22 June Hotham was dragged from his bed and incarcerated in Nottingham castle. There he wrote to the queen, inviting her to arrange his rescue. En route under guard to Leicester, Hotham escaped, allegedly justifying himself to Captain Rossiter that 'we had better be subject to one than 300 tyrants', and 'you shall see in a short time that there will be never a Gentleman but will be gone to the King.' He rode to Lincoln, where he discoursed with Lord Willoughby, Captain Purefoy and others, allegedly boasting that 'now he had got out of the protection of the Parliament he would keep out'.[80] The queen informed Newcastle on 27 June of Hotham's escape, remarking 'I hope now, that he will be prudent: better late than never.' She informed the king that Hotham 'hath sent to me that he would cast himself into my arms, and that Hull and Lincoln shall be rendered.'[81] Once at Lincoln, Hotham wrote to his father of his escape, and prepared the ground for his defection by writing a letter of protest to Speaker Lenthall on 24 June. This was read in the House of Commons three days later. It complained that his arrest constituted an attack on his gentility that was doubly grievous because he had been the first man in arms for parliament. It declared that:

> Colonel Cromwell had employed an Anabaptist to accuse him, and that one Captain White had been employed against him who was lately but a yeoman. That so much injustice had not been exercised upon any gentleman, in any age or time when arbitrary power was at the height. That the valour of these men had only yet appeared in their defacing of churches.[82]

[78] S. H. Mendelson and Patricia Crawford, *Women in Early Modern England, 1550–1720* (Oxford, 1998), 403; Hughes, 'Men, the "Public" and the "Private" in the English Revolution', in Lake and Pincus (eds.), *Politics of the Public Sphere*, 196, 208n.

[79] Lucy Hutchinson, *Memoirs of the Life of Colonel Hutchinson*, ed. N. H. Keeble (1995), 108–9; *CJ*, iii, 138.

[80] Anna Maria Diana Wilhelmina Stirling, *The Hothams: Being the Chronicles of the Hothams of Scorborough and South Dalton from their hitherto unpublished family papers*, 2 vols. (1918), i, 79–80; Hutchinson, *Memoirs*, 109; BL, E21(16), *Mercurius Civicus: London's Intelligencer*, no. 81, 5–12 December (1644), 744–5, 749.

[81] Mary Anne Everett Green (ed.), *The Letters of Queen Henrietta Maria* (1857), 191, 220–1; BL, E292(27), *The Kings Cabinet Opened or, Certain Packets of Secret Letters & Papers, written with the Kings own hand, and taken in his Cabinet at Nasby-Field* (1645), 33.

[82] BL, Harleian MS 164, fo. 234r–v.

Once reunited with his father, on 28 June Hotham wrote to Newcastle that the preconditions for his defection had now been satisfied; he had been so maltreated by parliament that 'no man can think my honour or honesty is further engaged to serve them.'[83] The Hothams understood that owing to the damage they had done royalism, their defection needed to deliver a large force and territory into royalist control. The resultant procrastination led to widespread speculation about Hull's betrayal weeks before the Hothams' final arrest there on 29 June 1643.[84] They remained untried for seventeen months, but Sir John Hotham's defence in December 1644 provides another excellent source for a side-changer's self-fashioning.

Written to save his life, its dramatic language magnified Sir John's former services in securing Hull and emphasized the danger to his person. As with other contemporary prison writings, Sir John sought to validate his conduct and overturn the suspicions that led to his confinement.[85] Referring to April 1642, Sir John declared that he did not seek 'to have a part to play unprecedented by any', adding 'I sat down with joy under the name and hazard of a traitor.' He argued that his 'single endeavours' raised, paid, and maintained more than 3,000 men. He claimed that there was no evidence of his involvement in a plot to betray Hull, that he had been arrested and imprisoned without charge, and that his trial by martial law was illegal. He criticized the 'ill management', and 'backwardness' of the Fairfaxes for having brokered a treaty of neutrality in September 1642, and for failing to reinforce him to contest the queen's passage to York in February 1643.[86]

Despite this forceful defence, what doomed father and son was their shared tendency, common among defectors, to respond impulsively to perceived slights. When John Hotham returned to Hull after escaping from his first arrest at Nottingham, Sir John procured the signatures of his council of war to a strikingly peremptory letter to parliament, demanding that Cromwell and his 'Anabaptist rogues', 'be delivered to justice' for causing his son's wrongful imprisonment. The letter prepared the ground for their long-considered defection, stating explicitly that their sense of injury freed them from the obligations of their former allegiance:

> There is nothing in this world, next to their duty to God Almighty, dearer to men of honour than their reputations; neither is there any thing that falls out with more regret to them, than to have that violated by those whom they esteem their friends, and of whom, they conceive, they have had just right to expect other dealings. This letter is occasioned by the most unjust and perfidious wrong offered to one of our society here, which, as we conceive, was ever put on any man; and, we are further persuaded, that no age or history can produce the like example: and truly, it gives us all just cause to look to our own conditions, who are by the king esteemed traitors; and if we shall be subject to be abused by such mischievous instruments as these are, who

    [83] Stirling, *The Hothams*, i, 81.
    [84] John Tickell, *History of the Town and County of Kingston-upon-Hull* (Hull, 1798), 465–8.
    [85] Dosia Reichardt, 'The Constitution of Narrative Identity in Seventeenth-Century Prison Writing', in Bedford, Davis and Kelly (eds.), *Early Modern Autobiography*, 119–20.
    [86] HHC, Hotham MS, U DDHO/1/34, 35, 40; Basil N. Reckitt, *Charles the First and Hull, 1639–1645* (2nd edn, Howden, 1988), 119–28.

have been the cause of this gentleman's wrong, we certainly remain in a sad condition; and, we think, we shall be excused before God and man, to do the best we can for our own preservation.[87]

The Hothams stressed blood, pedigree, and lineage in their ideas about honour because their capacious kinship network, provided by eight ill-fated wives, related them to all the East Riding's leading parliamentarians.[88] Boasting an unbroken succession from father to son since the twelfth century, it was hardly surprising that their concept of honour stressed pedigree. Continuity of lineage was held to prove a family's virtue, as longer, purer pedigrees concentrated levels of noble blood.[89] Partly due to this, they had grown notoriously sensitive to perceived slights. On the scaffold Sir John admitted that for 'rash words, anger and such things, no man has been more guilty.'[90] Strafford considered that Sir John was 'extreme sensible of honour, and discourtesies perhaps a little overmuch.' In 1642 John Hampden sent placatory letters reassuring Hotham that his honesty remained unquestioned.[91] Their aggressive sense of honour left them ill-equipped to obey commands from Lord Fairfax or accept parliament's failure to send sufficient supplies. They probably considered their Yorkshire baronetcy equal or superior to Fairfax's Scottish barony. A letter among the Hotham papers concerning John Hotham and Lord Fairfax lamented of the 'unhappy difference twixt men so equally worth.'[92] Only a family particularly strident about its status would acclaim an esquire the equal of a baron, while Sir John warned the Fairfaxes to 'give not law to those from whom you ought to receive.'[93] The hostility towards the Fairfaxes in Sir John's defence also reflected how the trial became entwined with factional power struggles at Westminster over new-modelling parliament's armies.[94]

IV

Another example of a local commander who utilized written correspondence to justify his side-changing was Murrough O'Brien, Viscount Inchiquin and Lord

[87] Tickell, *History of the Town and County of Kingston-upon-Hull*, 458–60.

[88] Bulstrode Whitelock, *Memorials of English Affairs from the Beginning of the Reign of Charles the First to the Happy Restoration of King Charles the Second*, 4 vols. (Oxford, 1853), i, 206; Hyde, *History of the Rebellion*, iii, 526–9; Sir Henry Slingsby, *The Diary of Sir Henry Slingsby of Scriven, Bart.*, ed. Daniel Parsons (1836), 92; Sir William Dugdale, *The Visitation of the County of Yorke* (Surtees Society, 36, 1859), 386.

[89] Cust, 'Catholicism, Antiquarianism and Gentry Honour', 49; Stirling, *The Hothams*, i, 21.

[90] John Morrill, *The Nature of the English Revolution* (1993), 184; Heal and Holmes, *The Gentry in England and Wales*, 171; Stirling, *The Hothams*, i, 96–7.

[91] Philip Saltmarshe, *History and Chartulary of the Hothams of Scorborough in the East Riding of Yorkshire, 1100–1700* (York, 1914), 112; HHC, Hotham MS, U DDHO/1/8.

[92] HHC, Hotham MS, U DDHO/1/60.

[93] BL, E240(30), *Reasons Why Sir John Hotham, Trusted by the Parliament, Cannot in Honour agree to the Treaty of Pacification made by some Gentlemen of York-shire at Rothwell*, 29 September (1642), 2, 8.

[94] Andrew Hopper, *'Black Tom': Sir Thomas Fairfax and the English Revolution* (Manchester, 2007), 60–2.

President of Munster. Jane Ohlmeyer has argued that his rivalry with the Boyles and the military difficulties he faced in Munster do much to explain his changing sides in 1644 and 1648.[95] Much like Cholmley and the Hothams before him, he justified himself with the language of slighted honour. Having first served the king, accepted the Cessation and sent forces into royalist service in England, Inchiquin defected on 17 July 1644. This shift has often been attributed to Charles I denying Inchiquin Munster's Lord Presidency, but it was sparked by a conspiracy of native Irish to seize Cork and other Munster towns that July.[96] Inchiquin justified his defection to parliament by rejecting the Cessation, and by writing to his brother that the king 'hath put this kingdom and us into the power of the Irish'.[97] He received a commission from Westminster to be Lord President of Munster in January 1645.[98]

Inchiquin changed sides again, abandoning parliament on 3 April 1648. This second defection has been attributed to frustrated ambition, lack of recognition for his services, and the failure of pay and supplies from London.[99] His change of sides, well anticipated by royalists, had been pending for some time; Inchiquin had articulated his frustrations in parliament's service for over a year beforehand. A native Irishman, Inchiquin felt that he was unfairly censured for his actions before he converted to parliament's cause, whilst he was irritated that Westminster had failed to send a committee to aid the financing of his forces.[100] The situation was inflamed further when parliament's new Lord Lieutenant of Ireland, Philip Sidney, Lord Lisle, landed at Monkstown, near Cork, on 20 February 1647. Immediately thereafter, Inchiquin complained of his orders being countermanded, and that Lisle sought to render him 'incapable of all command'. In a long letter of complaint to Speaker Lenthall on 16 March 1647, Inchiquin fashioned himself as a patient sufferer, calmly restraining himself as his officers were affronted by Lisle's orders and purged from command: 'In a more strict and rigid manner they handle all that have any relation to me, or Major General Jephson, and no crime can be so penal as to have either a dependency on, or an affection to either of us, or command under us.' The 'scorn and insolency' of those newly landed with Lisle were such 'as must necessarily exasperate the most patient to very high resentment.' The campaign of Inchiquin's rivals, Lord Lisle and Lord Broghill, extended to slighting him in councils of war, and withholding pay from Inchiquin's own regiments, whilst settling those of others. An aggrieved Inchiquin added: 'That they seem to find much fault with the ordering and conduct of affairs here before they came and

---

[95] Jane Ohlmeyer, 'The Baronial Context of the Irish Civil Wars', in John Adamson (ed.), *The English Civil War: Conflict and Contexts, 1640–1649* (Basingstoke, 2009), 119.

[96] Gardiner, *History of the Great Civil War*, i, 333; Gentles, *The English Revolution*, 210, 223; Patrick Little, 'Murrough O'Brien, first earl of Inchiquin (*c*.1614–1674), nobleman and army officer', *ODNB*.

[97] BL, Add. MS 46928, fo. 40r.

[98] Beinecke Rare Book and Manuscript Library, Osborn Shelves, fb155, fos. 277–9; BL, Egerton MS 1048, fo. 29.

[99] Robert Ashton, *Counter-Revolution: The Second Civil War and its Origins, 1646–8* (New Haven, 1994), 400–2.

[100] BL, Add. MS 46931A, fos. 92, 141.

yet amend little themselves.' He wrote stoically to Lenthall that he had endured all these slights 'with all submission to His Excellency's pleasure, to avoid giving any impediment to the service'. If parliament accepted that he was 'a person so inacceptable as I am seemingly made to be', he offered his resignation.[101]

By April 1647 Inchiquin remarked that parliament's treatment of him degraded the historical position of the office of Lord President, but that despite the many affronts he endured 'I will punish no man for it, leaving that to the state'. Preparing the stage for his defection upon the grounds of slighted honour, he added: 'It were more to my satisfaction to be handsomely removed than to continue in the service on those terms'.[102] This suggested that to Inchiquin, the conditions of his service were as important as the cause, and that his show of civil gentility was a learned front. His self-fashioning of stoic restraint in his letters to parliament are challenged by the testimony of Sir Adam Loftus and Sir John Temple on 23 April, who reported him as threatening them with violence whilst angrily mustering 200 reformado officers and former cavaliers in his house.[103] Indeed, Inchiquin had won an unsavoury reputation among his native countrymen as 'Murrough of the Burnings', which appears at odds with his effected temperance and moderation.[104]

On 21 May 1647 Inchiquin renewed his complaint to Lenthall that he was slighted at Westminster for granting protections to the Irish living near his Munster garrisons. He explained that without supplies from elsewhere, he was constrained to do so because these Irish made contributions to the upkeep of his forces. Rather, these allegations were a political ploy by his enemies: 'That it is and hath been strongly laboured and designed not [only] to rob me of all esteem in the opinion of that honourable house, but deprive me of all employment...as they desire I should seem to bee unfaithful therein'.[105] Here, Inchiquin's rivals played upon xenophobic prejudice to craft an image of him as a treacherous native Irishman. Lisle's father, the earl of Leicester, considered that as Inchiquin was a native Irishman, whose 'kindred being almost all in rebellion', he was 'incapable by the laws of Ireland to be governor or commander in chief'.[106] Inchiquin complained that 'Sir Arthur Loftus did most unworthily traduce the President and with him the whole Irish nation', and that Broghill had taunted one of Inchiquin's harpers that he 'was as arrant a rebel as any was in Ireland'.[107]

When Fairfax's army's charges against the eleven members accused him of treason, Inchiquin responded to Fairfax and Lenthall to vindicate himself on 25 August 1647. He claimed that his enemies had misrepresented him, and that if he was guilty as charged he would have put himself 'out of the reach of justice'. He

[101] BL, Add. MS 46931A, fos. 97–9, 103–6. Furthermore, Inchiquin considered that his officers were systematically discredited by being put upon dishonourable employments and under the command of scornful inferior officers: BL, Add. MS 46931B, fo. 185.
[102] BL, Add. MS 46931A, fo. 190.
[103] *Portland MS*, 419.
[104] Micheál Ó Siochrú, *God's Executioner: Oliver Cromwell and the Conquest of Ireland* (2008), 12.
[105] Bodl., MS Tanner 58, fo. 109.
[106] G. Dyfnallt Owen (ed.), *Report on the Manuscripts of the Right Honourable Viscount De L'Isle, V.C.*, HMC 77, Volume VI, Sidney Papers, 1626–1698 (1966), 566.
[107] BL, Add. MS 46931B, fo. 184.

remarked that he had supported his officers' petition for their pay, not to prepare the grounds for their defection, but to induce them to remain loyal to Westminster.[108] Given the insulting manner in which Inchiquin conceived he had been treated, his loyalty to parliament for the remainder of 1647 is striking, and is only partially explained by Lord Lisle's return to London. Instead, Inchiquin's festering dissatisfaction became widely known, and played upon by royalist commanders and propagandists. Prior to his defection in April 1648, Inchiquin remonstrated with Lenthall on 31 January that his soldiers were every day dying from want, and that without supplies from England there was no means to preserve them from ruin.[109]

Although military necessities do much to explain Inchiquin's defection in April 1648, his anxieties at the Vote of No Addresses and the increasingly radical nature of the English Independents also contributed.[110] This was reflected in his self-justification to his former comrades, communicating these grounds of principle in a letter to Colonel Michael Jones on 15 July that his change of sides was 'to establish his Majesty in his just rights', and 'settle his authority over this kingdom, where probably we may suddenly restore the Protestant Religion to its former lustre and laws to their force', as well as to restore the king and parliament in England 'to their just rights, privileges, and genuine freedom'.[111] Whilst Inchiquin's shifting might seem 'fickle and duplicitous' in England, perhaps even reflective of a 'tribal ambition', they reflect the dilemmas faced by many other Munster Protestants, to whose cause Inchiquin fashioned himself as a constant champion.[112]

V

From the wavering of county magnates like Sir John Hotham to the business-like transactions of career soldiers such as Sir John Urry, gentlemen communicated their defections in widely differing ways to vindicate themselves and establish the 'truth' of their actions. It remains difficult to disentangle their self-interest from political loyalties and contemporaries may not always have envisioned such distinctions. Yet despite these differences, several collective similarities emerge. Few defections occurred among Godly parliamentarians, while the Hothams, Chudleigh, Cholmley, Grenville, and Urry were hardly noted for attachment to Puritans. Although side-changers had been brought up with civic humanist notions of serving the public, which some vocalized in their self-justificatory narratives, many defections appear grounded upon older concepts, enshrining lineage, pedigree, and martial values at the centre of their self-worth. This supports Richard Cust's

---

[108] Ibid., fos. 195, 197.
[109] *Portland MS*, 443.
[110] Michael Braddick, *God's Fury, England's Fire: A New History of the English Civil Wars* (2008), 530; Ó Siochrú, *God's Executioner*, 53.
[111] *Portland MS*, 486–7.
[112] Joseph Cope, *England and the 1641 Irish Rebellion* (Woodbridge, 2009), 156; Jane Ohlmeyer, 'The Marquis of Antrim: A Stuart Turn-Kilt?', *History Today*, 43 (1993), 17.

arguments that the early Stuart gentry were adept at employing a variety of concepts of honour in their self-representation to meet changing needs, occasions, and audiences. For example, the composition narratives tend to emphasize their faithfulness to the parliamentary cause from the outset, propaganda conversion narratives focused most on the alienating features of the enemy, and memoirs and autobiographies for posterity were most inclined to stress personal principle and constancy.

The status-obsessed nature of the English gentry inclined those most sensitive about perceived slights to be prone to side-changing. Those temperamental about rank and standing appear more conditional in their allegiance and less able to fully commit to serving a cause. It is revealing that so many side-changers conceived themselves slighted by comrades before they changed sides. Defections were rarely hasty decisions, but more usually the culmination of growing disillusionment. Although both sides developed mechanisms for redressing slighted honour and containing factional conflict, when these failed changing sides became the ultimate sanction for those snubbed or marginalized.[113] As Patrick Little has observed, it was often 'a reaction against the old masters, not a sudden burst of enthusiasm for the new ones.'[114] However, side-changers claimed to be following their consciences, and therefore acting with due principle and constancy. Sensitive about defending reputations for posterity, they fashioned narratives of constancy through selective memory and avoidance of compromising details. Some resigned their commands weeks before defecting to protect themselves from charges of betraying their trust. Many professed or experienced genuine political conversions, seeking to downplay or explain away their former allegiance. Others displaced the slur of inconstancy onto former comrades; it was not the 'turncoat' but those around them who had changed. Their experience confirms that by the 1640s the English gentry were remarkably adept at projecting a variety of self-representations for different purposes and audiences.

Many of these self-representations are comparable to the arguments used by French politicians after 1815 to justify their past support for Napoleon: for example, that they had not sworn loyalty to the Bourbons, that they remained constant to their personal principles regardless of the regimes they had served, and that the nation should not be deprived of their competence in conducting government. Louis XVIII accepted Benjamin Constant's excuse in his *Mémoire Apologétique* that he defected to Napoleon during the Hundred Days only to temper Bonaparte's excesses. Many of these French 'girouettes' also felt the urge to pen self-justificatory memoirs. The multi-volume tomes compiled by Etienne-Denis Pasquier to justify his past support for Bonaparte were scornfully considered to have produced 'a theory for every situation, a defence for every cause, and an apology for every

---

[113] Ann Hughes, 'The King, the Parliament and the Localities during the English Civil War', *JBS*, 24 (1985), 259–63; Ian Atherton, 'Royalist Finances in the English Civil War: The Case of Lichfield Garrison, 1643–5', *Midland History*, 33 (2008), 66–7.
[114] Little, 'Four Dorset Turncoats'.

inequity.'[115] Pasquier gave the same retrospective justification as Sir Hugh Cholmley did for his parliamentarianism: that if he had stood aside, more seditious and unscrupulous people would have taken his place.[116]

Although contemporary commentators such as Clarendon and recent historians such as Blair Worden agree that defectors were scorned, this reaction was not universal.[117] Instead, much depended on how the side-changer managed their defection, or how successfully it was managed for them. In July 1643 Sir John Berkeley recommended James Chudleigh to Rupert as having 'been of infinite consequence to this service both by his courage, skill and activity and he deserves to have a particular encouragement'.[118] Some defectors remained true despite unfavourable subsequent circumstances, so we should be wary of discountenancing all declarations of principle in self-justificatory statements. Neither should all defections be interpreted as cynical opportunism; many followed tortuously difficult questions of conflicting loyalties. That so many parliamentarians joining the king in 1643 remained steadfast thereafter is striking.[119] Some defectors became valued and trusted by their new comrades, and Barbara Donagan has argued that despite many being executed 'the record is dotted with turncoats who survived and prospered.'[120] Those able to persuade themselves and enough others that they changed sides from conscience might retain their own sense of honour and public reputation, despite bitter condemnations by those they deserted.[121]

---

[115] Alan B. Spitzer, 'Malicious Memories: Restoration Politics and a Prosopography of Turncoats', *French Historical Studies*, 24 (2001), 51–6.

[116] Ibid., 59; Cholmley, *Memoirs and Memorials*, 104.

[117] Blair Worden, *The English Civil Wars 1640–1660* (2009), 51.

[118] BL, Add. MS 18980, fo. 89. Even Hyde mourned 'gallant' Chudleigh's death at Dartmouth in October 1643: Hyde, *History of the Rebellion*, iii, 238.

[119] Newman, *The Old Service*, 40–1, 121.

[120] Prominent examples included in the *ODNB* are Sir Anthony Ashley Cooper, Bussy Mansell, Sir Edward Massey, Sir Trevor Williams, and Henry Mordaunt, second earl of Peterborough.

[121] Donagan, 'The Web of Honour', 382–3.

9

Trial and execution: defectors and military justice

This chapter will examine the trial and execution of recaptured defectors, before turning to the deportment of the side-changers themselves in the contested public arenas of court and scaffold as they sought to fashion an attractive self-image for posterity. It aims to insert the experience of the civil war side-changer into the wider historiography of the agency, rhetoric, and purpose surrounding early modern public executions. The behaviour of the condemned solicited differing political interpretations from contemporaries eager to read meaning into their deaths while their executions were justified or condemned in print. For example, whereas the royalist martyrologies of the 1660s stressed constancy, honour, and sacrifice, the earl of Leicester observed of those royalist insurgents in 1651 who petitioned for mercy: 'It seems that for all theyr great words and obstinacy in refusing to acknowledge this Parlement and government, they can change theur minde and be humble when theyr lives are in danger.'[1]

The execution of recaptured side-changers and those suspected of treachery was considered customary practice in continental Europe during the Thirty Years' War.[2] Professionals who had served on the continent were not slow to import the practice; the Irish general Thomas Preston justified his hanging of a royalist prisoner to Ormond in 1643 by claiming that the victim had previously defected from the Confederates. Maintaining that this was the 'custom of the country wherein I serve', he urged Ormond to follow his example.[3] Yet recaptured defectors in Britain and Ireland were not always despatched in this fashion, despite Mark Stoyle's point that the 'wide sanction given to such punishments reinforces the impression that changing sides was seen as mean and contemptible.'[4] When more pragmatic concerns prevailed, some side-changers were exchanged, pardoned, set to manual labour, or given lesser sentences. The manner in which they were treated reveals the particular concerns of the contending parties at specific moments.

Death sentences for recaptured side-changers were usually pronounced by councils of war, and were intended to serve several purposes. Firstly, they were envisaged

---

[1] G. Dyfnallt Owen (ed.), *Report on the Manuscripts of the Right Honourable Viscount De L'Isle, V.C.*, HMC 77, Volume VI, Sidney Papers, 1626–1698 (1966), 607.

[2] Geoffrey Parker, *Empire, War and Faith in Early Modern Europe* (2002), 169.

[3] *Calendar of the Manuscripts of the Marquess of Ormonde preserved at Kilkenny Castle*, new series, vol. 1, HMC (1902), 57. Micheál Ó Siochrú has argued that Preston referred to the Spanish Netherlands, where he had acquired his military education: Micheál Ó Siochrú, 'Atrocity, Codes of Conduct and the Irish in the British Civil Wars, 1641–1653', *P&P*, 195 (2007), 65n.

[4] Mark Stoyle, *Loyalty and Locality: Popular Allegiance in Devon during the English Civil War* (Exeter, 1994), 112.

as an exemplary deterrent to prevent future defections and overawe those wavering into compliance. Secondly, they demonstrated God's providence against backsliders. Thirdly, they underlined the legitimacy of the cause and the political institutions it represented. This chapter examines how parliamentarians and royalists framed their military laws regarding side-changers, how they applied them in practice, and how far Charles Carlton's claim that parliament grew harsher than the royalists is justified.[5] This bias in the evidence owes much to parliament's victories in 1646 and 1648, with the royalists rarely finding themselves in a position to inflict exemplary justice. With the coming of the second civil war, parliamentarians grew more severe in sentencing their former adherents to death. This reflected the changed conditions of 1648, and parliamentarians' increased usage of a language of employment and trust in contrast to royalist emphases upon love and personal loyalty.[6] This process had revolutionary results as trials and executions for 'breach of trust' brought about a wider definition of treason that came to encompass the king himself. Finally, the chapter discusses how side-changers' engagement in scaffold dramas, dying speeches, and posthumous martyrologies helped define, contest, and communicate the meaning of the conflict to a wide audience.

I

Both sides mass produced cheap, portable pamphlets that established military laws hoping to govern their forces' behaviour. Officers were required to have such pamphlets read to their companies weekly so that none could claim ignorance. Complete implementation was patchy; both king and parliament lamented in subsequent revisions of these laws that their commanders had forborne from full enforcement.[7] Barbara Donagan has already conducted an excellent discussion of these laws,[8] so this analysis will focus more narrowly on those laws which applied specifically to side-changers.

The laws for Essex's army were first published in September 1642, subsequently being revised and enlarged in May and November 1643.[9] A similar set was pub-

---

[5] Charles Carlton, *Going to the Wars: The Experience of the British Civil Wars, 1638–1651* (1994), 198.

[6] Barbara Donagan, 'The Web of Honour: Soldiers, Christians, and Gentlemen in the English Civil War', *HJ*, 44 (2001), 376.

[7] BL, E75(34), *Lawes and Ordinances of Warre, established for the better conduct of the army, by His Excellency the Earl of Essex, Lord Generall of the forces raised by the authority of the Parliament, for the defence of king and kingdom. Together with a declaration of the Lords and Commons in Parliament, concerning the regulating of great inconveniences in His Excellencies army* (1643), sig. C1v–C2r; Margaret Griffin, *Regulating Religion and Morality in the King's Armies, 1639–1646* (Leiden, 2004), 132–4.

[8] Barbara Donagan, *War in England, 1642–1649* (Oxford, 2008), 144–56.

[9] BL, E116(34), *Lawes and Ordinances of Warre, established for the better conduct of the army by His Excellency the Earle of Essex Lord Generall of the forces raised by the authority of the Parliament, for the defence of the king and kingdom*, 12 September (1642); Wing (2nd ed.)/E3314A, *Laws and Ordinances of Warre, established for the better conduct of the army, by His Excellency the Earl of Essex… Together with a declaration of the Lords and Commons in Parliament, concerning the regulating of great inconveniences in His Excellencies army*, 13 May (1643); BL, E77(25), *Laws and Ordinances of Warre, established for the better conduct of the army, by His Excellency the Earl of Essex… And now inlarged by command of His Excellency; and printed by his authority*, 25 November (1643); BL, E75(34), *Lawes and Ordinances of Warre*.

lished for the earl of Warwick's projected army in November 1642, while Essex's revised laws of 1643 were reissued to the New Model in 1645.[10] Side-changing was not specifically mentioned, but defectors fell under the general article for desertion: 'No man that is inrolled shall depart from the Army or Garrison, or from his Colours without licence, upon paine of death.'[11] Essex established that those corresponding with the enemy without his direction could 'be punished as Traitors and Rebells', while those surrendering a garrison prematurely could expect execution. Seditious and mutinous speeches were punishable by death, as was passing a mile or more out of camp without orders. Providing intelligence to and fraternizing with the enemy were hindered by an article that restricted communication with enemy messengers, drummers, or trumpeters to senior officers. Anxieties over spies were reflected in the article prescribing death for those who presented themselves to a muster with a false name, surname, or place of birth.[12] The revised orders of 1643 specified death for all who failed to enrol in a company within their first three days.[13] From November 1643 anyone who came into parliament's army's headquarters or garrisons without a drum, trumpet, or pass risked being hanged as a spy.[14] Martial law was also imposed upon civilians by an ordinance of parliament on 16 August 1644 that condensed Essex's *Laws and Ordinances of Warre* into seven articles, adding that whoever took up arms against parliament, having first taken the National Covenant, would 'die without mercy'.[15]

The king's first military articles, published at York in 1642, had a similar relevance for side-changers as those first issued by Essex. There were comparable provisions against departing the camp, mutinous, and seditious speeches, while a specific article pronounced death for those employed as spies and guides who proved treacherous.[16] However, separate orders published for the royalist northern army under the earl of Newcastle had more specific provisions dealing with treachery. They contained capital articles against providing intelligence to the enemy and surrendering defensible towns. Those who corresponded with the enemy without authority from Newcastle faced death, while a unique article pronounced death upon any regiment that 'shall treat with the Enemy, or enter into any League with him without our leave or our Generals'.[17] This reflected royalist anxieties over those Yorkshire colonels' loyalties who had only recently engaged in a short-lived

---

[10] BL, E127(31), *Lawes and Ordinances of Warre, established for the better conduct of the army by His Excellency the Earle of Warwick Lord Generall of the forces raised by the authority of the Parliament, for the defence of the Citie of London and the counties adjacent*, 19 November (1642); Donagan, *War in England*, 148.

[11] BL, E116(34), *Lawes and Ordinances of Warre*, sig. C1v.

[12] Ibid., sig. A3v, B1v, B4v, C1r, D2r.

[13] Wing (2nd ed.)/E3314A, *Laws and Ordinances of Warre*, sig. B1r.

[14] BL, E77(25), *Laws and Ordinances of Warre*, sig. B1v.

[15] C. H. Firth and R. S. Rait (eds.), *Acts and Ordinances of the Interregnum, 1642–1660*, 3 vols. (1911), i, 486–8.

[16] Wing/C2493B, *Military Orders and Articles established by His Majestie, for the better ordering and government of His Majesties army* (York, 1642), 4, 6, 13.

[17] BL, E127(23), *Orders and Institutions of War, made and ordained by his majesty, and by him delivered to his Generall His Excellence the Earle of Newcastle. With the said Earles speech to the army at the delivery and publishing the said orders prefix* (1642), 5–6.

neutrality treaty with Lord Fairfax.[18] The king's revised orders of 1644 threatened death for unwarranted communication with the enemy 'in any place of strength', and stipulated that no soldier could be received into pay without taking a royalist oath and his name being formally listed.[19]

While neither side printed a law that provided exclusive criteria for dealing with side-changers, both upheld many articles under which they could be executed. The laws became more detailed, numerous, and refined in response to how the war was conducted—a process in itself shaped by the experience of side-changing. We now turn to how these articles were applied in practice during the first civil war.

II

A full reconstruction of the application of martial law against side-changers remains impossible owing to the lack of surviving court martial records, with only Sir William Waller's for 1644, John Lambert's for 1647–8, and those for the republican army in Scotland in 1651 known to be extant.[20] Yet a general view can be acquired from newsbook sources, correspondence, and parliamentary and private journals. One of the earliest executions appears to have been in Worcester market on 7 October 1642, noted by Nehemiah Wharton as intended 'for the villain that betrayed our troops into the hands of Prince Rupert'.[21] The first large-scale hangings were imposed upon recaptured defectors by Essex's council of war after Reading's surrender in April 1643 (as noted in Chapter 4).

Later in 1643, martial law was employed against civilian royalist conspirators in London and Bristol, who were not turncoats at all, but royalist sympathizers residing in parliamentarian garrisons. Colonel Nathaniel Fiennes employed martial law against Alderman Robert Yeamans and George Bourchier for plotting to betray Bristol in March 1643. The royalist high command warned of retaliation if they were executed yet on 30 May Yeamans and Bourchier were hanged, drawn, and quartered—Yeamans outside his own house.[22] In London in the aftermath of Waller's plot, a court martial sentenced the civilians Nathaniel Tompkins and Richard Chaloner to be hanged for conspiracy under the provisions of Essex's *Laws*

[18] Austin Woolrych, 'Yorkshire's Treaty of Neutrality', *History Today*, 6 (1956), 696–704.
[19] Wing/C2497A, *Military Orders and Articles Established by His Majesty, for the better ordering and government of His Majesties army. Also two proclamations, one against plundring and robbing. The other against selling or buying of armes and horse, printed by His Majesties command at Oxford by Leonarch* [sic] *Lichfield* (Oxford, 1644), 18, 20.
[20] Waller's court at Farnham sentenced John Boreham and Richard Kiddle to hang for desertion and suspected turncoating in spring 1644: John Adair, 'The Court Martial Papers of Sir William Waller's Army, 1644', *Journal of the Society for Army Historical Research*, 44 (1966), 206–11; Carlton, *Going to the Wars*, 384n; WYAS, Wakefield, C469/1: Minutes of the parliamentarian council of war at Ripon, Knaresborough, York, and Pontefract, 1647–8.
[21] *CSPD 1641–3*, 398–400.
[22] Bodl., MS Clarendon 22, fo. 31; John Lynch, *For King & Parliament: Bristol in the Civil Wars* (Stroud, 1999), 54–5.

and Ordinances of War. Chaloner was hanged outside his own house in Cornhill on 5 July.[23] Clarendon maintained that these executions were to overawe citizens inclined to peace.[24] On 27 November 1643 Daniel Kniveton was hanged in Cornhill for bringing the king's declaration forbidding the taking of the Covenant. Arriving from Oxford without a pass from parliament or Essex was considered 'contrary to the Law of Armes, London being now a Garrison Towne.'[25] By 1645 civilian commissioners in Kent employed martial law against civilians conspiring to betray Dover castle. A gentleman and a yeoman were executed, alongside a former sergeant or lieutenant in the trained band.[26] Resort to martial law, even against civilians, became increasingly prevalent.

In December 1643 Nathaniel Fiennes was tried by Essex's council of war at St Albans for prematurely surrendering Bristol in July 1643. Sir Simonds D'Ewes considered that Fiennes had acted with cowardice if not treachery, but William Prynne argued that such cowardice and surrender prior to the 'uttermost extremity' was deemed treasonous by the recently revised *Laws and Ordinances of War* under which Fiennes was tried.[27] Although found guilty, Fiennes' political connections and his importance as son of Viscount Saye and Sele secured a pardon from Essex—a luxury that was rarely afforded officers of lesser rank elsewhere. *The Perfect Diurnal* reported that the recaptured side-changer, Major Brookbank, was shot on the orders of Essex's council of war in January 1644 for having defected at Edgehill.[28] Captain Thomas Steele was shot at Nantwich on 29 January 1644 for surrendering Beeston castle without a fight. Having dined with the enemy commander, Steele was suspected of treachery and in danger of being lynched by Nantwich's garrison before the council of war passed sentence.[29] On 9 July 1644 the recaptured defector Captain Arnold Howard was hanged at Barnstaple's High Cross, and Essex was enraged when the royalist governor of Exeter retaliated by

[23] Stephen Wright, 'Richard Chaloner (*d.* 1643), conspirator', *ODNB*; BL, E251(6), *The Doome of Cowardize and Treachery or a Looking-Glass for Cowardly or Corrupt Governours, and Souldiers who through Pusillanimity or Bribery betray their Trusts, to the Publick Prejudice*, 23 October (1643), 18.
[24] Edward Hyde, earl of Clarendon, *The History of the Rebellion and Civil Wars in England Begun in the Year 1641*, ed. William Dunn Macray, 6 vols. (Oxford, 1888), iii, 37, 49.
[25] BL, Add. MS 31116, fo. 96r; David Martin Jones, *Conscience and Allegiance in Seventeenth-Century England: The Political Significance of Oaths and Engagements* (New York, 1999), 129; BL, E77(27), *Certain Informations from Severall Parts of the Kingdome*, no. 46, 27 November–4 December (1643), 358.
[26] BL, E294(20), *The Scottish Dove*, no. 93, 25 July–1 August (1645), 732.
[27] BL, Harleian MS 165, fo. 245v; *A Complete Collection of State-Trials and Proceedings Upon High Treason, and Other Crimes and Misdemeanours from the Reign of King Richard II to the end of the Reign of King George I*, 8 vols. (1730), i, 745–802; Adele Hast, 'State Treason Trials during the Puritan Revolution, 1640–1660', *HJ*, 15 (1972), 46; BL, E77(25), *Laws and Ordinances of Warre*, see Thomason's note on the frontispiece stating that these were different from the former, and that Fiennes was tried under them.
[28] BL, E252(16), *Perfect Diurnall of Some Passages in Parliament*, no. 25, 8–15 January (1644), 199; John Rushworth, *Historical Collections of Private Passages of State*, 8 vols. (1721), v, 297.
[29] James Hall (ed.), *Memorials of the Civil War in Cheshire and the Adjacent Counties by Thomas Malbon of Nantwich, Gent., and Providence Improved by Edward Burghall, Vicar of Acton, near Nantwich* (Lancashire and Cheshire Record Society, 19, 1889), 91–2.

hanging a parliamentarian sea captain, thinking the royalists 'bloudy minded to execute a man in cold blood'.[30]

The ceremonial hanging in effigy of Sir Richard Grenville on a Westminster gibbet for his defection in March 1644 indicated parliament's frustration at having trusted him, but also his likely fate should he fall into parliamentarian hands.[31] After his arrest by the Prince of Wales' council in January 1646, Grenville requested to be tried or discharged with increasing urgency as the New Model closed in.[32] After the defection of Grenville, their lieutenant-general, the court martial papers of Waller's army unsurprisingly include measures pertinent to side-changing, such as the order of 25 April 1644 for all absentee officers to return upon pain of death, and the trials of Captain Thomas Ducton and Edward Palmer for spying for the enemy.[33]

Sir Alexander Carew and the two Hothams were the most prominent parliamentarians executed by court martial prior to 1649. Sentenced at London's Guildhall in October and December 1644, they were tried, not under Essex's *Laws and Ordinances of War*, but rather by parliament's recent ordinance for martial law of 16 August 1644. This established in London a functioning commission that could deliver capital sentences with just twelve of its fifty-six commissioners sitting. The charges against Carew and the Hothams fell under the second and seventh articles of endeavouring to betray a town and deserting their trust to adhere to the enemy.[34] Carew pleaded that these articles 'did not looke backward, but forward, and therefore that he ought not to be tried by them.'[35] Likewise, Sir John Hotham pleaded that his prosecution under this ordinance was illegal, as it post-dated his alleged crimes by fourteen months. He maintained that martial law was not in force in Yorkshire during 1643, claiming that parliament always refused his requests for martial law while he was governor of Hull.[36] These defences were overruled as 'insufficient' and unduly reflecting 'upon the wisdome and justice of the Parliament'.[37] Although Carew and Hotham were well connected, the surrender of maritime towns critical to parliament was a weighty matter, with the faction in favour of new modelling the army ranged against them. Their trials and executions furthered the process whereby parliament broadened its definition of treason to punish backsliders and breakers of trust.

---

[30] Carlton, *Going to the Wars*, 198; Richard W. Cotton, *Barnstaple and the Northern Part of Devon in the Great Civil War* (1889), 273–7.

[31] BL, Stowe MS 768, fo. 6; BL, TT E254(6), *Perfect Occurrences of Parliament*, no. 31, 19–26 July (1644), sig. A3v; *Calendar of State Papers Venetian, 1643–1647*, ed. A. B. Hinds, vol. 27 (1926), 86; Amos C. Miller, *Sir Richard Grenville of the Civil War* (1979), 69–70.

[32] Bodl., MS Clarendon 47, fo. 80.

[33] Adair, 'Court Martial Papers', 209–10, 219; BL, 669 f.10(6), *Concilium apud Fernham*, 13 May (1644).

[34] The fifty-six commissioners included thirteen peers, seven knights and baronets, twenty-one colonels, five lieutenant-colonels, and three majors: Firth and Rait (eds.), *Acts and Ordinances of the Interregnum*, i, 486–8.

[35] BL, E18(5), *Mercurius Civicus: London's Intelligencer*, no. 78, 14–21 November (1644), 723–5.

[36] Bodl., MS Nalson 22, no. 137.

[37] BL, E18(5), *Mercurius Civicus*, 725.

III

Numerous minutes of the royalist council of war survive, suggesting that it was even busier in trying and sentencing commanders for premature surrendering or corresponding with the enemy.[38] Between 1643 and 1645 it tried under these charges Colonel Richard Feilding, Sir Richard Cave, Charles, Lord Paulet, Lieutenant-Colonel Francis Windebanke, William, Viscount Ogle, Sir Barnabas Scudamore, and Prince Rupert himself. Unsurprisingly therefore, Ian Roy has stressed its role in investigating and disciplining royalist officers. It was presided over by Charles himself, or his lord general, and consisted of high-ranking army officers and privy councillors. It sat in Christ Church, Oxford, or accompanied the king on campaign. Increasingly, royalist garrison commanders actually requested trial by it to clear their names after questionable surrenders.[39]

On 29 April 1643 Colonel Richard Feilding was charged with 'severall foule suspicious passages' in surrendering Reading to Essex. Although he was tried before the council of war, evidence against him was compiled by Secretary Nicholas, Lord Chief Justice Heath, and Dr Thomas Rives, the King's Advocate. According to John Belasyse, who was also in Reading, Feilding had 'pretended to command as eldest Col[onel]' once the governor, Sir Arthur Aston, was incapacitated. Feilding claimed that the king approved his terms for a truce—terms which he could not then break once the king arrived to relieve Reading. Sir Edward Dering noted that many in Oxford clamoured for justice against Feilding for betraying the town. Two full days of hearing followed, with Feilding defending his employment of a female spy in Essex's camp; but on 4 May the council sentenced Feilding to be beheaded. Within a week the king granted Feilding a pardon, but not before he had been twice reprieved upon the scaffold.[40] The stigma of treachery dogged him for life, along with persistent rumours that he was bribed by Essex or his kinsman the earl of Denbigh.[41]

Royalists were divided over how to treat Feilding. Clarendon later considered him innocent both of cowardice and 'base compliance with the enemy'. He dated the emergence of factions at Oxford to divisions that the trial engendered, betraying his retrospectively roseate view of royalist politics in the war's early days.[42] However, on 11 May Secretary Nicholas warned Rupert: 'since I see treachery... not punished, I am apt to believe the traitors will multiply'.[43] The Prince of Wales pleaded for mercy for Feilding, while one of Sir Samuel Luke's spies picked up on controversy over the intended method of execution, along with fanciful

---

[38] BL, Harleian MS 6802, 6804, 6851, 6852.

[39] Ian Roy, 'The Royalist Council of War, 1642–6', *Bulletin of the Institute of Historical Research*, 35 (1962), 152, 158, 167.

[40] Folger Shakespeare Library, V.a.216, Belasyse Memoirs, fos. 10v–11r; BL, Stowe MS 184, fos. 53v–54r; BL, E102(1), *Mercurius Aulicus*, 18th week, 30 April–6 May (Oxford, 1643), 130; I. G. Philip (ed.), *The Journal of Sir Samuel Luke* (The Oxfordshire Record Society, 29, 1947), i, 65.

[41] Samuel R. Gardiner, *History of the Great Civil War, 1642–1649*, 4 vols. (1987), i, 130; Donagan, *War in England*, 104.

[42] Hyde, *History of the Rebellion*, iii, 30.

[43] BL, Add. MS 18980, fos. 59–60.

rumours that if Feilding was not shot, Rupert would retire abroad in protest.[44] One parliamentarian newsbook sought to inflame such perceived divisions by praising Feilding for his strict observance of the terms, though it proved unfavourable to the royalists, claiming he hath 'gained such a badge of honour, that not any Cavalier in the Kings Army hath hitherto deserved the like.'[45]

Nicholas was equally sure of Sir Richard Cave's guilt for surrendering Hereford to Waller.[46] Cave was acquitted in June 1643, notwithstanding Colonel Herbert Price's testimony that Cave had sought to surrender to save Hereford from plunder, and that he deliberately dismissed the royalist cavalry before Waller approached. His defence that the city was untenable and the garrison too small was apparently accepted. A broadsheet was published to repair his reputation, although he may still have been considered culpable and was removed from command.[47] In May 1644 Lord Charles Paulet, brother to the marquis of Winchester, was tried by a council of war, presided over by the earl of Forth, for conspiring to betray Basing House. Evidences were prepared against him, and Secretary Nicholas sent Forth the recent reprint of the book of military orders to remind him of his duty. Forth advised the king on an appropriate sentence through the Advocate General, and again the king decided on pardon.[48]

By 1645, more streetwise royalist garrison commanders prepared strong defences before surrendering. When Viscount Ogle was besieged in Winchester castle he invited his officers to set their hands in private to their opinions whether or not to surrender, one by one. When Ogle was examined at Oxford he demanded a full court martial, and was able to document that only two majors had wanted to continue the fight. On 12 November 1645 the court martial concluded 'that no stain of conduct or courage could be fastened upon him; and no more could have been done by any governor than was done by the Lord Viscount Ogle'. Still unsatisfied that his honour was beyond reproach, and mindful of the examples of Cave and Feilding, Ogle then requested the king change the date of his viscountcy to after the court martial.[49] After the fall of Hereford in December 1645, its governor, Sir Barnabas Scudamore, was accused of accepting money to betray the city. He rode to Worcester to face the charges, and was imprisoned without trial for seven months. He composed a pamphlet which blamed his subaltern officers, but the king considered him guilty. One newsbook erroneously reported his execution,

[44] Malcolm Wanklyn, *The Warrior Generals: Winning the British Civil Wars* (New Haven, 2010), 245n; Philip (ed.), *Journal of Sir Samuel Luke*, i, 69.

[45] BL, E249(3), *A Perfect Diurnall of the Passages in Parliament*, no. 48, 1–8 May (1643), unpag., 3 May.

[46] Francis Bickley (ed.), *Report on the Manuscripts of the Late Reginald Rawdon Hastings, esq.*, HMC, 78, 4 vols. (1930), ii, 100.

[47] Folger Shakespeare Library, V.b.2 Scudamore Collection, 1618–1657 (4 and 5); BL, 669 f.7(26), *The Iudgement of the Court of Warre upon the charge laid against Sir Richard Cave, for the Delivery up of Hereford* (Oxford, 1643); Ian J. Atherton (ed.), *Sir Barnabas Scudamore's Defence Against the Imputations of Treachery and Negligence in the Loss of the City of Hereford in 1645* (Akron, Ohio, 1992), 36; BL, Stowe MS 184, fo. 54r.

[48] I. G. Philip (ed.), *The Journal of Sir Samuel Luke* (The Oxfordshire Record Society, 33, 1952–3), iii, 267–8; *CSPD 1644*, 143, 147, 151.

[49] BL, Add. MS 27402, fos. 98–101.

and although Scudamore was released when Worcester surrendered, his loyalty remained besmirched thereafter.[50]

The most prominent royalist defendant was Rupert himself, charged with prematurely surrendering Bristol, in a court martial at Newark on 18 and 21 October 1645. Rupert demanded the trial, having drafted his defence and a copy of the surrender articles. Although Charles cleared his nephew of 'the least want of courage or fidelity', Rupert considered the discharge of his friend Sir Richard Willis from Newark's governorship as an affront from Digby. Charles Gerard seconded him and declared Digby a traitor. This provoked an armed confrontation in Newark market, with the king ordering the new governor, John Belasyse, to draw up the royal guards to confront Rupert's men 'with swords & pistols ready'. Although bloodshed was averted, an offended king issued passes to Rupert and Maurice to travel overseas. Willis subsequently challenged Belasyse to a duel, and the new governor was placed under guard to prevent his responding. The whole affair illustrates just how divisive trials under martial law for treachery could become, as the royalist cause imploded into infighting and personal vendettas.[51]

The royalist council of war rarely imposed capital sentences for treachery upon officers of field rank, and their implementation was still more infrequent. Little appears to have been instigated to examine the suspicions directed at the colonels Sir Thomas Gower, Thomas Blague, and Henry Hunks, although the latter was exonerated by a court of inquiry. In explaining Lieutenant-Colonel Francis Windebanke's execution for surrendering Blethingdon House in April 1645, P. R. Newman considered the sentence 'unusually severe'.[52] While the council of war often imparted mercy to high-status defendants, it was less forgiving to those without field rank. One of the first executions was that of one Blake, an informant to Essex, hanged soon after Edgehill.[53] In October 1643 Nicholas informed Henry Hastings that the king approved of the sentence upon a conspirator to betray Belvoir castle, and required Hastings's council of war to likewise judge the captain who surrendered Eccleshall castle.'[54] In December 1643 a Captain Hurst was shot in Oxford for having mortally wounded Sir Thomas Byron.[55] In April 1644 a Captain Wilson was condemned to death for 'treachery or cowardice' in allowing Fairfax to break into Selby.[56] Civilian officials might also suffer; the bailiff of Bewdley was suspected of complicity in 'Tinker' Fox's raid in May 1644, for which he appears to have been hanged by Rupert the following March.[57]

[50] Atherton (ed.), *Sir Barnabas Scudamore's Defence*, 24–38.

[51] BL, Harleian MS 6852, fos. 317r–19v; Folger Shakespeare Library, V.a.216, Belasyse Memoirs, fos. 19v–21r.

[52] Newman, 418; P. R. Newman, *The Old Service: Royalist Regimental Colonels and the Civil War 1642–46* (Manchester, 1993), 124–5.

[53] Wanklyn, *Warrior Generals*, 22, 238n.

[54] Bickley (ed.), *Report on the Manuscripts of the late Reginald Rawdon Hastings*, ii, 105.

[55] Philip (ed.), *Journal of Sir Samuel Luke*, iii, 222; Newman, 56.

[56] Folger Shakespeare Library, V.a.216, Belasyse Memoirs, fo. 13v.

[57] C. D. Gilbert, 'A Dramatic Incident in Royalist Worcestershire: "Tinker" Fox's Raid on Bewdley of May 1644', *Midland History*, 35 (2010), 132, 134.

Respect for due process of military law was upheld by royalist exiles in dealing with traitors. In December 1655 the double agent Henry Manning was discovered to be a government spy. After a lengthy trial before an improvised court headed by the marquis of Ormond and Sir Edward Nicholas, which revealed considerable malice in Manning's letters to Thurloe, he was taken to a wood near Cologne and privately 'pistolled' by Sir James Hamilton and William Armorer.[58]

I V

Parliamentarians sharpened their retribution against recaptured side-changers during the second civil war. Until 1646 both royalists and, to a lesser extent, parliamentarians had occasionally proved merciful towards those of high rank suspected of treachery. The second civil war transformed this. Executions of recaptured side-changers became more frequent, jeopardizing previously observed codes of conduct. Parliament interpreted royalist uprisings in England and Wales as acts of treason against a settled state. Even before the renewal of armed hostilities, in January 1648 parliament redefined the laws of treason to hang, draw, and quarter Captain Burley for attempting to rescue Charles from the Isle of Wight.[59] Once the fighting resumed, defections of parliamentarian officers and men in Kent, Essex, South Wales, and the north became treasonous crimes demanding exemplary justice.[60] On 8 June the Commons authorized Fairfax's council of war to try defectors among Kent's and Essex's insurgents. On 21 July this was broadened into authorizing Fairfax to grant commissions to try by martial law all former parliamentarians among those captured.[61] *The Moderate* reported on 22 August 1648 that anyone who had taken the Negative Oath or Covenant and thereafter borne arms against parliament could be executed without mercy.[62] This encompassed royalist parole-breakers, and brought the total into thousands—far too many for parliament to realistically execute. Therefore, enforcement was restricted to those considered especially troublesome and corrupting. At Yarmouth, two defectors were sentenced but one was pardoned, and the punishment of defectors in Scarborough castle was left to the discretion of local colonels Hugh Bethell and Francis Lascelles.[63] Resorting to severity reflected how shaken the parliamentarians were by the fracturing of their coalition and the scale of defections. They articulated this anxiety through a language of breach of trust that had been 'ubiquitous in contemporary political

---

[58] Geoffrey Smith, *Royalist Agents, Conspirators and Spies: Their Role in the British Civil Wars, 1640–1660* (Farnham, 2010), 199–200, 204.

[59] *CSPD 1648–9*, 13–14; BL, E520(36), *Perfect Occurrences*, no. 58, 4–11 February (1648), 403–4.

[60] Barbara Donagan, 'Atrocity, War Crime, and Treason in the English Civil War', *American Historical Review*, 99 (1994), 1139, 1156, 1161–2.

[61] Rushworth, *Historical Collections*, vii, 1145, 1198; *CJ*, v, 589, 642.

[62] BL, E461(16), *The Moderate Impartially Communicating Martial Affaires to the Kingdome of England*, no. 7, 22–29 August (1648), sig.G2r–v.

[63] Donagan, 'Atrocity, War Crime, and Treason', 1156; Rushworth, *Historical Collections*, vii, 1272.

discourse', but was now especially invoked by vengeful parliamentarians, first towards defectors and parole-breakers, but eventually against the king himself.[64]

This backlash was first evidenced by Fairfax and Cromwell's attitudes in South Wales. Among Colonel Horton's captives in May 1648, former parliamentarian officers under Laugharne were quickly court-martialled and executed.[65] Although their rank and file were granted quarter, Cromwell considered the officers who surrendered to mercy at Pembroke castle twice as culpable as the royalists 'because they have sinned against so much light, and against so many evidences of Divine Providence going along with and prospering a just Cause, in the management of which they themselves had a share.'[66] Cromwell was angry because they had defied God's judgement in having granted parliament victory in 1646. He was outraged when the treble side-changer Colonel Humphrey Mathews was admitted into composition after Pembroke's surrender. He stressed that Mathews had apostatized, was 'the desperatest promoter of the Welsh Rebellion amongst them all', and that parliament's soldiers had 'not had a more dangerous enemy'. Cromwell threatened that his officers were astonished to witness God's providence so flouted and 'to see their blood made so cheap'.[67] In August 1648, when the Prince of Wales warned Fairfax that his royal honour was 'highly concerned' in the preservation of those captured at Pembroke, and threatening retaliatory severity upon parliamentarian prisoners, Fairfax responded in terms of breach of trust, declaring that it was 'not so much that they were in hostility against them (I suppose) as that they have betrayed the trust they reposed in them to the sad engaging this kingdom again in war & blood'.[68]

Although parliament ordered the court martial of Major-General Rowland Laugharne, and Colonels Rice Powell and John Poyer in June 1648, they were imprisoned without trial in Windsor castle until April 1649. A court martial at Whitehall from 4 to 12 April condemned all three to death. Laugharne's wife petitioned that her husband's one foolish act 'might not cause all his former evident services to be forgotten', and the Council of State relented by ordering that one death would suffice. This was selected by a child drawing lots, and when Poyer proved unlucky his fate was considered providential, as he had been the first in rebellion.[69] Another officer who defected with Laugharne, Lieutenant-Colonel John Butler, was selected for trial in the High Court of Justice on 29 October

---

[64] Howard Nenner, 'Loyalty and the Law: The Meaning of Trust and the Right of Resistance in Seventeenth-Century England', *JBS*, 48 (2009), 859, 868.

[65] Rushworth, *Historical Collections*, vii, 1131–2.

[66] Arthur Leonard Leach, *The History of the Civil War (1642–1649) in Pembrokeshire and on its Borders* (1937), 205–6; Thomas Carlyle (ed.), *Oliver Cromwell's Letters and Speeches: with Elucidations*, 3 vols. (1857), i, 278.

[67] BL, Sloane MS 1519, fo. 186. Matthews had served as a captain under Sir John Hotham in Hull before recruiting royalist infantry in Wales in 1643. In arms for parliament again by October 1645, he defected with Laugharne in 1648: Newman, 249; Ron Slack, *Man at War: John Gell in his Troubled Time* (Nottingham, 1997), 73; TNA, SP 28/138/; TNA, E121/5/7, no. 12.

[68] BL, Add. MS 19399, fos. 58, 60; BL, Egerton MS 2618, fo. 27.

[69] Leach, *History of the Civil War in Pembrokeshire*, 189, 212–13; Robert Ashton, *Counter-Revolution: The Second Civil war and its Origins 1646–8* (New Haven, 1994), 421; BL, E527(35), *Perfect Occurrences*, no. 115, 9–16 March (1649), 901.

1651. His eventual fate remains unclear, although his widow petitioned Charles II in 1662 and was granted relief on the basis that Butler was 'slain by Cromwell'.[70]

In June 1648 a plot to betray Chester to the insurgents was uncovered, and two of the conspirators were shot after a trial organised by Colonel Duckenfield.[71] In other places, parliamentarian officers were unsure of the local legal arrangements. In July 1648 Colonel Mytton complained to Speaker Lenthall that the parliamentarian sentinels engaged by royalist officers to betray Denbigh castle could not be tried because no officer present 'hath power to proceed against them by Martial Law'.[72] Parliament's county committees also lacked the resources to house the large numbers of prisoners taken. Sir Arthur Hesilrige, governor of Newcastle-upon-Tyne, complained in July 1648 that if he did not receive orders concerning the recaptured side-changers in his custody 'they will be suddenly knit up'. Unable to maintain his prisoners, he recommended their transport to foreign plantations.[73] When Colonel Philip Monckton's contingent of Pontefract royalists was defeated at Willoughby Field on 5 July 1648, the Nottinghamshire county committee requested permission to try several at the Assizes and banish others overseas. Parliament responded that county committees should nominate captured insurgents for trial at the Assizes and prepare evidence against them.[74]

Some side-changers never made it to trial. John Dalbier, formerly quartermaster-general to the earl of Essex, was slain by troopers under Colonel Adrian Scroop at St Neots on 10 July. Although Scroop merely reported that Dalbier was mortally wounded, Ludlow later claimed that the troopers 'to express their detestation of Dalbeir's [*sic*] treachery, hewed him in pieces'.[75] The following month, Lieutenant-Colonel Henry Lilburne was slain at Tynemouth castle. Local parliamentarians were concerned to make his fate an exemplary warning: one tract exhorted perfidious governors elsewhere to repent, and his head was placed on a spike over the castle gate.[76]

The shooting of Lucas and Lisle at Colchester for breaking their paroles has long obscured the fate of those side-changing officers specifically exempted from Fairfax's terms of surrender on 26 August.[77] Among them were Colonel James Till, Colonel Sawyer (or Sayers), Lieutenant-Colonel Henry Farr, and Major Stephen

---

[70] Newman, 51–2; *CSPD 1651*, 502; *CSPD 1661–2*, 335, 354, *CCAM*, 711, TNA, SP 29/53/35.

[71] Hall (ed.), *Memorials of the Civil War*, 214–16.

[72] *Portland MS*, 475.

[73] P. R. Hill and J. M. Watkinson (eds.), *Major Sanderson's War: Diary of a Parliamentarian Cavalry Officer* (Stroud, 2008), 58; *Portland MS*, 476–7. In this context 'knit up' denotes 'to string up, to hang': J. A. Simpson and E. S. C. Weiner (eds.), *Oxford English Dictionary*, 20 vols. (2nd edn., Oxford, 1989), viii, 497.

[74] Portland MS, 477; *CJ*, v, 629.

[75] *Portland MS*, 478; Edmund Ludlow, *The Memoirs of Edmund Ludlow, Lieutenant General of the Horse in the Army of the Commonwealth of England, 1625–1672*, ed. C. H. Firth, 2 vols. (Oxford, 1894), i, 198.

[76] Horatio A. Anderson, 'Tynemouth Castle: The Eve of the Commonwealth', *Archaeologia Aeliana*, 2nd series, 15 (1892), 223–4; BL, E459(4), *A Terrible and Bloudy Fight at Tinmouth Castle*, 16 August (1648), 3. Lilburne's widow petitioned in 1660 that his head was 'cut off and set upon the castle': TNA, SP 29/13/121.

[77] Donagan, *War in England*, 354, 356.

Smith.[78] Captain Robert Vesey of the Essex militia had already been captured during the siege, and parliament had ordered his court martial for inciting his men to change sides.[79] Farr commanded the earl of Warwick's regiment, and led the largest contingent of 1,000 defectors, allegedly summoning them to muster without disclosing his plan to defect. Although later recaptured, he escaped his death sentence by slipping into hiding. More were to be court-martialled and exemplary justice was threatened, but retribution was not immediate and their fates remain unclear, as no further executions had followed by 2 September.[80]

The hardening of parliamentarian attitudes towards side-changers in 1648 is best illustrated by the lengthy and rancorous siege of Pontefract. On 2 June 1648 this robust castle was betrayed to the insurgents by Colonel John Morris, a disbanded parliamentarian officer who had also suborned Major Ashby, Ensign Smith, and Sergeant Floyd of the garrison to join him.[81] Morris had served against the Irish during 1642–3, and returned to serve the king in England, claiming to have distinguished himself at Nantwich.[82] He changed sides after parliament captured Liverpool in November 1644, and some royalists suspected him of betraying the town.[83] Quickly commissioned colonel by Lord Fairfax, he participated in besieging Pontefract castle from April 1645.[84] A year after parliament took the castle, Sydenham Poyntz warned Lenthall that Morris was heading a plot to betray it.[85] Morris was subsequently imprisoned at York, but owing to his personal charisma and friendship with Colonel Robert Overton, the castle's governor, he was discharged home, from where he masterminded the castle's betrayal. With promise of rewards he persuaded eight garrison soldiers, including the sergeant of the watch, to defect and to aid him in admitting his confederates while the garrison slept (see Fig. 9.1).[86]

Understanding his probable fate should he be recaptured, Morris consciously fashioned himself as beyond reproach in self-absolving letters to the besieging commanders. On 20 September 1648 he surmised to Colonel Charles Fairfax: 'I should be much ashamed that there should be just occasion of any complaint of me, of any

---

[78] Brian Lyndon, 'Essex and the King's Cause in 1648', *HJ*, 29 (1986), 25, 27, 29–30, 34; *Beaufort MS*, HMC, 12th Report, Appendix, Part IX (1891), 22; *CSPD, 1644*, 533–4; Donagan, *War in England*, 317, 319, 363, 381; Newman, 372; *LJ*, x, 478.

[79] BL, E449(30), *The Earl of Norwich, Lord Capel, & Sir Charles Lucas, their peremptory answer, in refusing to surrender Colchester, upon the Lord Generalls conditions* (1648), 7; Rushworth, *Historical Collections*, vii, 1161; *CJ*, v, 611.

[80] BL, E461(24), *A True and Exact Relation of the Taking of Colchester* (1648), 3; Rushworth, *Historical Collections*, vii, 1250.

[81] Jack Binns, *Yorkshire in the Civil Wars: Origins, Impact and Outcome* (Pickering, 2004), 142.

[82] For details of Morris's service in Ireland see: WYAS, Sheepscar, WYL, 119/3, fos. 146–7.

[83] A mutiny of troops from Ireland had prompted the garrison's surrender: *CCCD*, 2409; TNA, SP 23/101/671–83; BL, Add. MS 18981, fos. 287–8, Robert Ashton, 'John Morris (c.1615–1649), army officer', *ODNB*; H. G. Tibbut (ed.), *The Letter Books of Sir Samuel Luke, 1644–45* (Publications of the Bedfordshire Historical Record Society, 42, 1963), 377.

[84] BL, Add. MS 11331, fo. 70r.

[85] Henry Cary (ed.), *Memorials of the Great Civil War in England from 1646 to 1652*, 2 vols. (1842), i, 174.

[86] WYAS, Sheepscar, WYL 119/3, fo. 148–53; Hyde, *History of the Rebellion*, iv, 396–400.

COL.ᵗ JOHN MORRIS.

Son & Heir of Matthias Morris of North-   Elmsall, in the County of York, Esq.ʳ bred
to the Military Profession in Ireland, under   Thomas Wentworth, the great Earl of
Strafford, and distinguished there for his   eminent bravery. He was prevailed on,
while very young, to enter into the Rebel   Army, but repented of his error; retired to
his estate, and on the 3.ᵈ of June, 1646, re-   deemed his reputation for loyalty; by the
almost romantic surprisal of the strong Castle   of Pontefract, aided only by eight persons.*
He held that Fortress against the usurpers till   after the Murder of the King; was promised
his life at the surrender, in respect to his gallantry   in its defence; but was afterwards seized, tryed,
and condemned at York; and having been put to death there, in August, 1649, was buried, at his own request, at Wentworth, near the grave of the noble Patron and instructor of his youth. Colonel Morris
married Margery, eldest daughter of Dʳ Robert Dawson, Bishop of Clonfert & Kilmacduagh, in Ireland,
by whom he had two sons, Robert, who died without issue, and Castilion, who left a numerous pro-
geny, many of whom settled in, or about Leeds, but the family is believed to be now extinct.

* One of whom, Capt. Thomas Paulden, published, in 1702, a narrative of that Enterprize, which was
reprinted in 1719, for the benefit of Col. Morris's widow.

Engraved from an Original Picture, in the Possession of Sir Mark Masterman
Sykes, of Sledmire in the County of York, Barᵗ

London, Published by Robert Wilkinson, N.º 58, Cornhill.

Fig. 9.1. Colonel John Morris. (Special Collections of the University of Leicester, University of Leicester Library, Fairclough Collection of Portrait Prints, EP36A.)

breach of my word which hitherto I could never be taxed with'.[87] On 6 October Morris complained that Fairfax had imprisoned his father: 'I know so much what belongs to martial discipline, that you have in this point overshot yourself, neither have I done anything which I durst not appeal to any soldier whatsoever'.[88] Fairfax replied that Morris was incapable of trust, and that it was the misery of Pontefract castle 'that a gentleman commands them not nor indeed a man sensible of common honesty.' Fairfax despised having to write to Morris, adding: 'Your aspersions upon my family are easily wiped off, they trouble me no more then the barking of a cur'. He warned Morris that if threats to execute parliamentarian prisoners were implemented, this would 'but proclaim you the scum of this country and must be retaliated'.[89] Yet in November it was Fairfax who hanged a former parliamentarian soldier recaptured from the garrison, prompting Morris to complain: 'I desire to know by what article you hanged him, for some of yours here shall taste of the same sauce.' Fairfax's reply demonstrated to Morris what he could expect when the siege was concluded: 'The crimes objected (as I have it by relation) he learnt of his chief. He was an intelligencer and the betrayer of a trust.'[90] Morris persisted that Fairfax had not identified which article of war had been invoked, and that the man hanged had never been a parliamentarian: 'It is impossible for him to betray a trust that never had any reposed in him.' Morris threatened to retaliate, and stop writing to Fairfax, declaring that he desired 'to deal with men of understanding and with them that are capable of reason'.[91] Yet the besiegers' severity persisted, inflamed by Colonel Rainsborough's murder by a party from the castle. Mr Beaumont, vicar of South Kirkby, was hanged on Baghill, in full view of the garrison, for passing intelligence to the garrison and for complicity in betraying the castle.[92]

The eventual terms of surrender proposed by Morris were wildly unrealistic. He proposed that he should be exempted from sequestration, granted an armed convoy homeward, and that none in the garrison should be sued at common law, civil law, or martial law for any acts committed since 1641.[93] Instead, Morris and five others, 'faithless to their former trust or guilty of other notorious & bloody crimes', were exempted from terms imposed by Major-General John Lambert on 19 March 1649.[94] Of those exempted, Major Ashby, Sergeant Floyd, and Henry Austwick hid in a vault under the round tower, but Morris, along with Cornet Blackburn and Ensign Smith, succeeded in breaking out of the castle before it was handed over. Smith was shot in the escape, but Morris, disguised as a beggar, evaded capture for ten days before he was betrayed and eventually delivered to York castle.[95]

[87] BL, Add. MS 36996, fo. 104.
[88] Ibid., fo. 109.
[89] Ibid., fos. 110–11.
[90] Ibid., fo. 137.
[91] Ibid., fos. 138–9.
[92] WYAS, Sheepscar, WYL 119/7, fo. 74; Ralph Josselin, *The Diary of Ralph Josselin, 1616–1683*, ed. Alan Macfarlane (Records of Social and Economic History, new series, 3, Oxford, 1976), 158.
[93] WYAS, Sheepscar, WYL 119/3, fos. 87–9.
[94] Ibid., fos. 81–2.
[95] BL, Add. MS 36996, fos. 181, 184; WYAS, Sheepscar, WYL 119/7, fos. 74, 241–2; Ashton, 'John Morris', *ODNB*.

Denied trial by council of war, Morris was indicted by a Yorkshire jury on 16 August and sentenced to be hanged, drawn, and quartered at the York Assizes. The sentence's grisly nature reflected that the siege lasted nine months and had proved particularly bitter—Yorkshire's committee for sequestrations later remarking that it 'cost much blood and treasure.'[96] The unsoldierly trial and traitor's death imposed upon Morris had a political purpose 'to assert publicly and visibly the new sovereign powers of the state.'[97]

The earl of Holland was captured after his failed insurrection in July 1648. Unlike most executed side-changers, he was not tried by council of war or the Assizes. Rather, on 6 March 1649 he was condemned by a high court of justice established by act of parliament.[98] Despite a letter urging clemency from General Fairfax, alongside petitions from his countess, and his brother, the earl of Warwick, the Rump voted on 8 March by 31 votes to 30 not to postpone his execution.[99] The following day Holland stood for two hours upon the scaffold at New Palace Yard, Westminster, before he was beheaded, 'expecting pardon as it was thought' (see Fig. 9.2).[100]

During and after the second civil war, contemporary notions of turncoating were embittered by the persistence of Stuart support in Scotland and Ireland. Captain Edward Wogan defected with his troop in March 1648, riding from Worcester to Edinburgh on a forged pass. Joining the Engagers, Wogan escaped to Ireland after the defeat at Preston. He was recaptured near Waterford in December 1649, prompting his colleagues to threaten the execution of Captain Caulfield, a parliamentarian prisoner, if he was harmed. This provoked an incensed response from Cromwell on 4 January 1650:

> And withal to let you know, That if any shall put such conditions on me that I may not execute a Person so obnoxious as Wogan, who did not only betray his trust in England, but counterfeited the General's hand, thereby to carry his men (whom he had seduced) into a Foreign Nation, to invade England, under whom he had taken pay, and from whose service he was not discharged; and with the said Nation did invade England; and hath since, contrary to the said trust, taken up arms here...I am resolved to deal with Colonel Wogan as I shall see cause.[101]

Cromwell's understanding of treason now embraced royalist attempts to mobilize Scots and Irish forces to invade England, but remaining at its heart was that Wogan had betrayed his trust and was therefore automatically at his mercy. When Cromwell recaptured Kentish officers who had defected in 1648 at Gowran in Ireland, he ordered them shot.[102]

[96] TNA, SP 23/101/671.
[97] Donagan, *War in England*, 397.
[98] Beinecke Rare Book and Manuscript Library, Osborn Shelves, fb 155, fos. 306–9.
[99] *CJ*, vi, 159.
[100] Dyfnallt Owen (ed.), *Report on the Manuscripts of the Right Honourable Viscount De L'Isle*, 587.
[101] Carlyle, *Oliver Cromwell's Letters and Speeches*, iii, 414–15.
[102] John Morrill, 'The Drogheda massacre in Cromwellian context', in David Edwards, Pádraig Lenihan and Clodagh Tait (eds.), *Age of Atrocity: Violence and Political Conflict in Early Modern Ireland* (Dublin, 2007), 246.

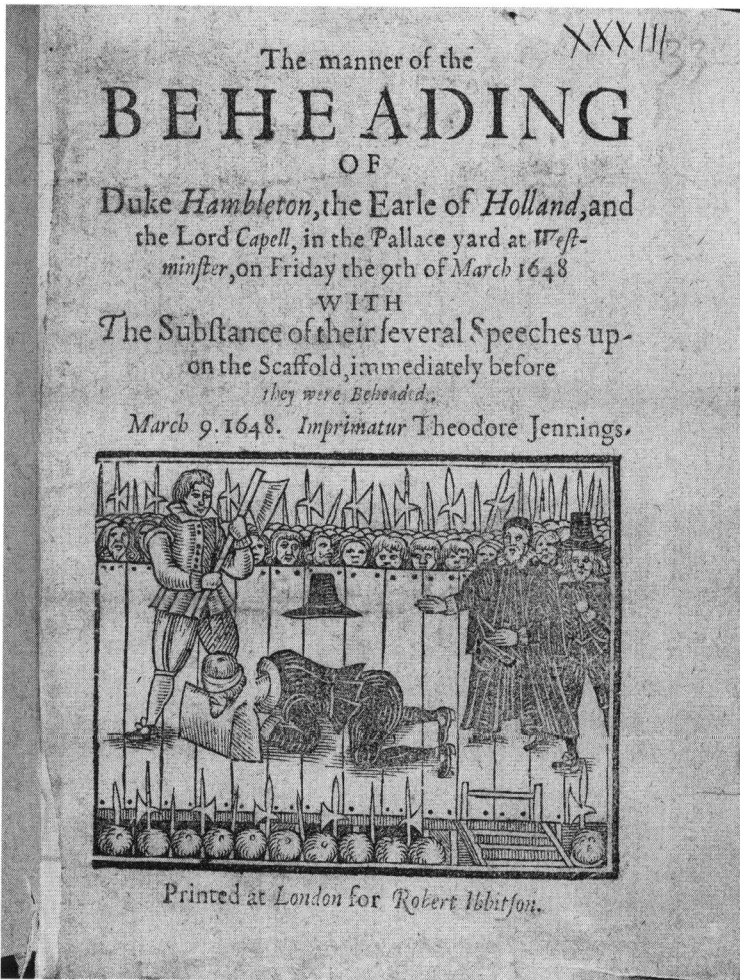

Fig. 9.2. Execution pamphlet for Henry Rich, Earl of Holland. James Sibbald, *The Manner of the Beheading of Duke Hambleton, the Earle of Holland, and the Lord Capell, in the Pallace Yard at Westminster, on Friday the 9th of March 1648 with The Substance of their several Speeches upon the Scaffold, immediately before they were Beheaded*. London 1649 (1648 O.S.). (© The Bodleian Library, University of Oxford, Wing (2nd edn.)/S3719.)

The Long Parliament moved away from its initial understanding of treason as levying war against the king or adhering to the king's enemies, albeit as they themselves defined.[103] It turned the concept of breach of trust against side-changers, and eventually against the king himself. Sir John Strangeways remarked in 1647 'that the king is king by an inherent birth-right; they say his kingly office is an office

---

[103] Hast, 'State Treason Trials', 37.

upon trust.' This concept was eventually used as the basis of the charges against Charles I.[104] Following the regicide, the Rump further broadened its definition of treason to punish its enemies. By May 1649 it had embraced the Levellers by including incitement to mutiny or any criticism of the new regime.[105] Two years later, captured royalists could be executed merely for communicating with Charles Stuart in contravention of the act of parliament of 12 August 1651. When the former parliamentarian Captain John Benbow was shot in Shrewsbury on 15 October, he was executed under the provisions of this act rather than for having changed sides.[106] Among his judges was Lieutenant-Colonel Simon Finch, a former royalist.[107]

V

This final section examines how the behaviour of side-changers during their trial and execution was reported—in particular, their dying speeches. This not only demonstrates defendants' self-justificatory strategies, but also how execution pamphlets communicated their claims or those of the tribunals executing them. The meanings of scaffold speeches outside a civil-war context have been explored by James Sharpe, Peter Lake, and Michael Questier. While Sharpe examined the dying speeches of felons, Lake and Questier concentrated on executions of Roman Catholics. Sharpe argued that public execution was an 'elaborate ceremony and ritual' intended to reinforce the government's legitimacy. The condemned 'were the willing central participants in a theatre of punishment', during which it was customary for them to make a last speech acknowledging the justice of the sentence and warning others against their bad end. Clergymen on the scaffold would guide the condemned about how to behave and ensure that they died repentant to aid their reconciliation with God. Sharpe argued that this demonstrated an 'internalization of obedience' among the condemned.[108] Even before the civil wars, such executions spawned a pamphlet literature reaching a wider audience than the crowds who witnessed them. They purported to include the dying speech, and were sometimes penned by the clergymen present, with a 'didactic and normative' purpose to communicate the government's expectations of its subjects. Although suspiciously stereotyped to deliver what the authorities wished people to hear, with acts of defiance rarely reported, for Sharpe these tracts provided useful evidence illuminating 'the nature of ideological control' in a state with only a limited capacity to enforce

---

[104] Nenner, 'Loyalty and the Law', 866, 868.

[105] Hast, 'State Treason Trials', 39, 53.

[106] Hall (ed.), *Memorials of the Civil War in Cheshire*, 223; BL, E282(15), *A More Exact and Particular Relation of the Taking of Shrewsbury* (1645), 4; Norman Tucker, *Royalist Officers of North Wales 1642–1660: A Biographical List* (Denbigh, 1961), 17; BL, E643(15), *The Perfect Tryall and Confession of the Earl of Derby, at a Court-Marshall holden at Chester the first day of October, in the year of our Lord God, 1651* (1651), 2, 5.

[107] Donagan, *War in England*, 235.

[108] J. A. Sharpe, '"Last Dying Speeches": Religion, Ideology and Public Execution in Seventeenth-Century England', *P&P*, 107 (1985), 144–7, 156, 159.

public order.[109] Sharpe suggested that the scaffold behaviour of seventeenth-century felons bore important similarities to that of most Tudor traitors such as Robert Devereux, earl of Essex, who died compliant, acknowledging their sins and accepting their sentences as just.[110]

During the civil wars, parliament overcame its anxieties about tumultuous assemblies to permit large crowds to witness the executions it ordered. It implicitly recognized that these were occasions where it might bid for popular support. Yet such communication was not one way; audiences considering themselves informed about due procedure might participate in these rituals. On both sides, the tribunal passing sentence could not always control scaffold events, and if they were ill-managed, such occasions might glorify the condemned.[111] The scaffold experience of condemned side-changers supports Sharpe's suspicion that during political executions, victims were more likely than felons to be defiant and unrepentant.[112] Through conspicuous displays of courage, some showed signs of turning the occasion to favour their cause, convincing onlookers that God was with them. Their last speeches enabled them to set agendas, as words delivered in the face of death were considered especially weighty. In this way both sides competed to utilize the scaffold drama to rally support and win converts, just as Catholic victims and Protestant authorities had done under Elizabeth and James I. Competing interpretations of scaffold events were played out in the pamphlet literature that increasingly accompanied executions for treason.[113]

The pamphlet describing Francis Pitt's execution for attempting to betray Rushall Hall to the Staffordshire royalists illustrates many of Sharpe's arguments, but it also carried a particular agenda for the competing factions at Westminster. Pitt was a Wolverhampton yeoman and previous Godly supporter of parliament. Supposedly seduced by his royalist landlord, Colonel Thomas Leveson, he changed sides and was condemned to be hanged by the court martial at London's Guildhall in October 1644. The two ministers penning the narrative stressed that Pitt accepted his sentence, even making a penitential speech on the ladder to warn others against the royalists' popery and to avoid his fate as a 'dissembling Hypocrite'. Then, Pitt urged parliament to not just 'use their power as a Net to catch the small Fishes, and let the great ones escape: I desire that great offenders may be brought to condign punishment as well as lesser ... for there are many Achans still in the Camp.'[114] This pamphlet, published immediately prior to the trial of Sir Alexander Carew and the Hothams, channelled the power of Pitt's dying words to influence public opinion

---

[109] Ibid., 147–8, 155, 158.

[110] Ibid., 157–8; Lacey Baldwin Smith, 'English Treason Trials and Confessions in the Sixteenth Century', *Journal of the History of Ideas*, 15 (1954), 476–7, 480–3, 491, 494.

[111] P. Lake and M. Questier, 'Agency, Appropriation and Rhetoric under the Gallows: Puritans, Romanists and the State in Early Modern England', *P&P*, 153 (1996), 64, 73, 97, 100.

[112] Sharpe, '"Last Dying Speeches"', 155n.

[113] Lake and Questier, 'Agency, Appropriation and Rhetoric', 74–5, 106.

[114] BL, E13(8), *A More Exact and Perfect Relation of the Treachery, Apprehension, Conviction, Condemnation, Confession, and Execution, of Francis Pitt, aged 65. Who was executed in Smithfield on Saturday, October the 12. 1644, for endeavouring to betray the garrison of Rushall-Hall in the county of Stafford, to the enemy*, 18 October (1644), 3, 5–6, 8–9.

against them, its postscript conventionally declaring: 'the words of a dying man are wont to take a deep impression'.[115]

Condemned side-changers appear to have feared that God would punish them if they died completely unrepentant. Therefore, many combined denial of the charges with emulating the customary acknowledgement of felons that they deserved death for more general sins.[116] For instance, Captain Thomas Steele, shot for surrendering Beeston castle prematurely, made a 'longe confession and repentance of his Synnes', including fornication, but nevertheless, at his death, 'disclaimed all treachery'.[117] Ralph Bennet, a parliamentarian messenger hanged in Chester in 1645, 'died with much courage, and told them he was hanged for his other sins and not for his relation to this cause'.[118] Likewise, Sir Alexander Carew accepted responsibility for his death and confessed his sins, 'especially my Pride, and my stout hearted-nesse'. Yet he refused to acknowledge the sentence as just, claiming he was condemned for an intention, not an act, and that as 'whatsoever I say is not to be believed' he would therefore 'have leave to hold my peace.' Turning to his companions on the scaffold, and the troublesome issue of his family's future reputation, he orated: 'These are my kindred, my ancestors were counted honest men.' Speaking of his forefathers' deaths, immediately before he was beheaded he repeated his mother's last words.[119] His stance of repenting his sins but denying particular guilt impressed Thomas Juxon, who considered Carew's death resolute.[120] The following week, the scaffold behaviour of John Hotham was similar. He confessed his sins, but *Mercurius Civicus* disapproved of his refusal to acknowledge his particular offences, his behaving in a 'peremptory' manner, and his deeply provocative listing of the services he had performed for parliament.[121] Although the final demeanour of Sir John Hotham 'was more humble and penitent than his sonnes', he also maintained his innocence, despite newsbooks' claims that his guilt was clearly established.[122]

A hierarchy of execution was observed in sentences for treachery pronounced by differing tribunals on both sides. Beheading was usually prescribed for noblemen and those thought deserving of dignity. After that, shooting was permitted those worthy of a soldier's death. Hanging—the fate suffered by plebeian felons—was reserved for spies, betrayers of garrisons, and those considered particularly culpable. Hanging gentlemen was considered particularly vindictive, as to 'hang a gentleman was to dishonour and declass him.'[123] Worst of all was to be

---

[115] Ibid., 10, 16.

[116] Sharpe, ' "Last Dying Speeches" ', 150, 155.

[117] Hall (ed.), *Memorials of the Civil War in Cheshire*, 117–18; Henry Newcome, *The Autobiography of Henry Newcome M.A.*, ed. Richard Parkinson, 2 vols. (Chetham Society, 26, 1852), i, 95.

[118] BL, Add. MS 11331, fo. 146r.

[119] BL, E22(6), *The Speech or Confession of Sir Alexander Carew Baronet: Who was Beheaded on Tower-Hill on Munday Decemb. 23. 1644. Published by Authority* (1644), 5–7.

[120] Thomas Juxon, *The Journal of Thomas Juxon, 1644–1647*, ed. Keith Lindley and David Scott (Camden Society, 5th series, 13, 1999), 71.

[121] BL, E23(9), *Mercurius Civicus: London's Intelligencer*, no. 84, 26 December–2 January (1645), 773.

[122] BL, E24(9), *Mercurius Civicus: London's Intelligencer*, no. 85, 2–9 January (1645), 776.

[123] Donagan, *War in England*, 182.

hanged, drawn, and quartered as a traitor to the state—a fate inflicted upon enemies of the republic from 1649, and enemies of the Restoration from 1660. Parliamentarians seemed readier to degrade renegade officers by hanging them. John Syms recorded that Captain Howard, hanged at Barnstable in July 1644, desired 'that he might be shot to death: but the Lord Roberts tells him that that was too honourable a death for him'.[124] In such cases, victims were unlikely to play along as penitent traitors. Captain Bartholomew Ellicott, hanged in Farnham market-place in December 1643, died condemning the council of war 'in a miserable condition, justifying himself' in his new allegiance.[125] When Captain Joseph Grenville was court-martialled for attempting to betray Plymouth in September 1644, he was hanged on a gallows below Mount Gould. He died 'confessing nothing nor seeming to be sorry for his fault.'[126] Syms recorded that three more turncoat officers were hanged at Mount Gould on 21 February 1645, and that each 'gave no tokens of remorse for their sin nor any signs of repentance for what they had done but died very senselessly as being obdurated and hardened in mischief'. Rather than being troubled at their failure to behave as penitent traitors, for Syms their brazen defiance doubly warranted their execution; it was a great relief that such obdurate and dangerous villains had been unmasked and despatched. The insult to these officers was deepened when one Benjamin Cloak was afforded a more honourable shooting at the foot of their gallows for having given a password to the enemy. Although Cloak claimed innocence, he obliged his tormentors by acknowledging his sins of Sabbath-breaking and drunkenness 'which when a man is given unto he will soon fall into all other sins, and of lying and swearing.'[127]

In March 1649 the earl of Holland's scaffold demeanour emulated the defiance shown by earlier side-changers. Anticipating this, the Rump denied him an effective platform. Arriving on the scaffold, he perceived that his voice would not reach the people beyond the soldiers surrounding it, and said: 'It is to no purpose (I think) to speak anything here.'[128] Yet his dying speech could not be denied, and he fashioned himself as constantly faithful to parliament and the public:

> I have never gone off from those principles that ever I have professed... There may be alterations and changes that may carry them further then I thought reasonable, and truly there I left them, but there hath been nothing that I have said, or done, or professed, either by Covenant, or Declaration, which hath not been very constant, and very clear upon the principles that I ever hath gone upon.[129]

---

[124] BL, Add. MS 35297, fo. 38r.

[125] Carlton, *Going to the Wars*, 198; G. N. Godwin, *The Civil War in Hampshire, 1642–1645* (1904), 130.

[126] BL, Add. MS 35297, fo. 47r: *CJ*, iii, 667.

[127] BL, Add. MS 35297, fo. 61r.

[128] BL, E546(21), *The Several Speeches of Duke Hamilton Earl of Cambridge, Henry Earl of Holland, and Arthur Lord Capel, upon the Scaffold immediately before their Execution, on Friday the 9. of March. Also the Several Exhortations, and Conferences with them, upon the Scaffold, by Dr Sibbald, Mr Bolton, & Mr Hodges. Published by special authority* (1649), 17.

[129] Ibid., 18–19.

Although he forgave his judges and acknowledged his death as God's judgement for his sins, he did not play the part required by the court. Rather, he called for a Stuart Restoration, pointing to the injustice of the sentence and illegality of his trial.[130] Fashioning himself a tragic, wronged victim, who had surrendered to the offer of quarter, he called to the solider who captured him: 'You little thought I should have been brought to this, when I delivered myself to you upon conditions'. This was intended to embarrass the court, which contended that if a promise of quarter had been made, it could only protect Holland 'from the military, not the civil sword'.[131] He then doffed his hat to Captain Watson among the mounted guards, exclaiming: 'God be with you sir, God reward you sir.'[132] Gallows gestures were highly significant, and Holland appears to have copied the king's action of stretching out his hand as a signal for the executioner to strike.[133]

Considering the trouble he had caused them, parliament granted John Poyer a dignified death; driven in a coach from Whitehall to Covent Garden, he was shot by a file of six firelocks on 25 April 1649. Poyer pleaded to Colonel Charles Fleetwood that he had served parliament 'in their lowest ebb of affairs', had withstood bribes from Charles Gerard, and that his defection had not been intentional but forced upon him by desperation, despair, and his 'bloody enemies' conspiring against him.[134] His dying speech stressed his constancy and loyalty: 'my affections to the Parliament did not alter...I was always honest with them until an unhappy disaster which hath brought this misery to me.'[135] He declared that he 'ever acted for the liberty and freedom of the subject', but expressed penitence at his revolt and freely forgave all, desiring in vain that his death might bring an end to the armed conflict. His generous deportment granted the fledgling Commonwealth a measure of much-craved legitimacy.[136]

No such clemency was afforded Colonel John Morris, tried at York by the Assize judges John Puleston and Baron Thorpe on 16 August 1649. He complained that the court had no jurisdiction nor precedent to try him, as the new treason law post-dated his alleged crime. Instead he claimed he was tried for 'soldierly acts' deserving of a court martial. Being forced to enter a plea, he pleaded not guilty. He objected that the prosecution's witnesses along with sixteen of the jury, including the foreman Mr Brooke, were his personal enemies. He requested legal counsel and a copy of his indictment, but both were denied.

---

[130] Ibid., 20, 23, 25–6.

[131] Ludlow, *Memoirs of Edmund Ludlow*, i, 221.

[132] BL, E546(21), *The Several Speeches of Duke Hamilton Earl of Cambridg*, [sic] *Henry Earl of Holland, and Arthur Lord Capel*, 32.

[133] Ibid., 36; Lake and Questier, 'Agency, Appropriation and Rhetoric', 75.

[134] *Report on the Manuscripts of F.W. Leybourne-Popham, esq., of Littlecote, co. Wilts*, HMC 51 (Norwich, 1899), 14–15.

[135] Leach, *History of the Civil War in Pembrokeshire*, 214.

[136] BL, E552(3), *The Declaration and Speech of Colonell John Poyer immediatly before his Execution in Covent-Garden neer Westminster, on Wednesday, being the 25. of this instant April, 1649. With the Manner of his Deportment, and his Proposals to the People of England*, 26 April (1649), 2–3.

He claimed he had a valid commission issued by the Prince of Wales, but Judge Puleston refused to have it read, remarking: 'Sir it will do you no good you may as well show a commission from the pope as this one'.[137] Morris warned the court that his death would not quell royalist resistance, and that if he was executed, Ormond would order reprisals in Ireland. He denied having 'acted anything contrary to my allegiance'. Morris's accomplice, Cornet Blackburn, refused to speak, 'being he that has spoken so much cannot be heard.'[138] When the sheriff insisted upon manacling them, Morris vowed not to attempt to escape, and appealed that such an act disgraced all soldiers, protesting that the consequent 'shame and dishonour doth more trouble me than loss of [my] life'. Manacling was reserved for plebeian felons, and therefore denied both Morris's gentility and his martial honour in the very public arena provided by his trial.[139] Morris concluded by defying the court, blessing the king, and thanking God that he would die in a just cause.[140] On 23 August, after another failed escape attempt three days earlier, Morris and Blackburn were led out to York's Tyburn to die with thirty others—mostly convicted felons.[141] This practice, like the manacling, was intended to degrade them by association, and had previously been inflicted upon condemned Catholic priests.[142] They were to be hanged, drawn, and quartered as traitors. En route to the gallows, Morris declared his innocence of betraying the royalist garrison at Liverpool, and made the conventional declaration of constancy that if he had a thousand lives he would 'willingly lay them down for the cause'. He maintained that he died in the Protestant faith, which 'I have been bred in, without the least wavering'. Perceiving no contradiction between befriending the parliamentarian colonels Forbes, Overton, and Fairfax, and seeking to do the king future service, he proclaimed: 'I have been alwayes faithfull to my Trust'.[143] Yet not all were convinced by such counterfactual declarations. The earl of Leicester considered that the severity against Morris was not due to his involvement in Rainsborough's death, which was 'not layd to his charge at his tryall', but was rather because he had betrayed parliament's trust, 'having ridden in theyr troupes'.[144] Even the royalist William Blundell considered Morris an

[137] BL, Egerton MS 1048, fos. 101–2.

[138] Ibid., fos. 102–3; BL, E572(27), *An Exact Relation of the Tryall & Examination of John Morris, Governour of Pontefract-Castle, at the Assizes held at York: Together with his Speeches, Prayers, and other passages immediately before his death, the 23. of August 1649. Whereunto is added, the Speech of Cornet Blackburne, executed at the same time*, 7 September (1649), 1–5; Dyfnallt Owen (ed.), *Report on the Manuscripts of the Right Honourable Viscount De L'Isle*, 592–3; Donagan, 'Atrocity, War Crime, and Treason', 1161, 1164n.

[139] When Morris's gaolers came to put irons on him in prison before the trial, he assaulted them and attempted to escape: WYAS, Sheepscar, WYL 119/7, fo. 242.

[140] BL, Egerton MS 1048, fo. 104.

[141] BL, Add. MS 21417, fo. 314; BL, Egerton MS 1048, fo. 104. Blackburn was sentenced specifically for having murdered Rainsborough at Doncaster, not for having betrayed his trust: WYAS, Sheepscar, WYL 119/7, fo. 246.

[142] Lake and Questier, 'Agency, Appropriation and Rhetoric', 86.

[143] BL, E572(27), *An Exact Relation of the Tryall & Examination of John Morris*, 1–2; *A Complete Collection of State-Trials*, vii, 323.

[144] Dyfnallt Owen (ed.), *Report on the Manuscripts of the Right Honourable Viscount De L'Isle*, 593.

unsavoury character, recounting that in Ireland he had hanged a gentlewoman 'only because she looked (as he was pleased to phrase it) like an Irish lady'.[145]

The scaffold behaviour of Sir John Urry, beheaded at Edinburgh in May 1650, is less clear. He blamed others for his death, claiming to have been led astray, although he supposedly died bravely and 'behaved himself somewhat like a Souldier'. David Stevenson argued that he died penitent, but Edward Furgol stressed his 'brave and constant demeanour at the end of a vacillating career.' His execution pamphlet utilized his notorious reputation for side-changing to warn 'how suddenly they that make not conscience of their wayes, may fall and leave nothing behind them, but ignominy and reproach.'[146]

Through a courageous scaffold performance, condemned side-changers could turn the crowd in their favour and bid for martyrdom. In this way the demises of both the renegade pirate, Captain Browne Bushell, and the Presbyterian minister, Christopher Love, were politically effective. Bushell was condemned for betraying Scarborough castle to Sir Hugh Cholmley.[147] He was tried before the High Court of Justice in Westminster Hall on 25 March 1651. Witnesses journeyed from Yorkshire to testify, and Luke Robinson, Scarborough's MP, led the prosecution. In his defence, Bushell denied that Scarborough was defensible for parliament in 1643. He was sentenced to beheading on Tower Hill on 29 March. He endeavoured to die a royalist martyr, arguing on the scaffold that his conscience convinced him that his initial parliamentarianism had been unlawful.[148] Declaring that he did not fear death, he expressed himself 'sorry that I ever drew my Sword for such ___ Masters', and avowed himself a loyal subject and member of the Church of England. He fashioned himself as following in the king's footsteps, asking if he faced the same axe and block that had despatched the king. Bushell's deportment was so impressive that the writer of his execution pamphlet feared the effect it had upon onlookers: 'The manner of this Gentleman at his departing, will cause many (especially those of his own fraternity) to eternize his Name; but it is disputable, whether conscience or courage, arm'd him with this Resolution'. The tract suggested that Bushell was not moved by love to the Stuarts, but rather by envy and hostility towards the republic (see Fig. 9.3).[149] In a similar vein, parliamentarians circumvented

[145] Kenneth Nicholls, 'The Other Massacre: English Killings of Irish, 1641–2', in Edwards, Lenihan, and Tait (eds.), *Age of Atrocity*, 181; William Blundell, *Crosby Records: A Cavalier's Notebook Being Notes, Anecdotes & Observations of William Blundell of Crosby, Lancashire, Esquire*, ed. T. Ellison Gibson (1880), 231.

[146] BL, E603(8), *Several Passages Concerning the Declared King of Scots, both by sea and land, communicated by letters, to persons of credit. Also, the confessions and speeches of the Laird Darsey, Major General Hurry, and Collonel Spotswood; made upon the scaffold at Edenburgh before their* Execution, 17 June (1650), 3, 6; David Stevenson, *Revolution and Counter Revolution in Scotland, 1644–1651* (2nd edn., Edinburgh, 2003), 137; Edward M. Furgol, 'Sir John Urry (d. 1650), army officer', *ODNB*.

[147] *CSPD 1650*, 220, 400.

[148] Ibid., 248, 332, 455; Jack Binns, 'Captain Browne Bushell: North Sea Adventurer and Pirate', *Northern History*, 27 (1991), 96, 102, 104.

[149] BL, E626(14), *The Speech and Confession of Capt. Brown-Bushel, at the Place of Execution on Saturday last, under the Scaffold on Tower-Hill: with the Manner of his Deportment, and his coming from the Tower in a scarlet cloak; as also his prayer, and desires to the people. Together with the manner of his tryall; and the articles and charge exhibited* [sic] *against him. Written by G.H. an eye-witnesse*, 31 March (1651), 3–6.

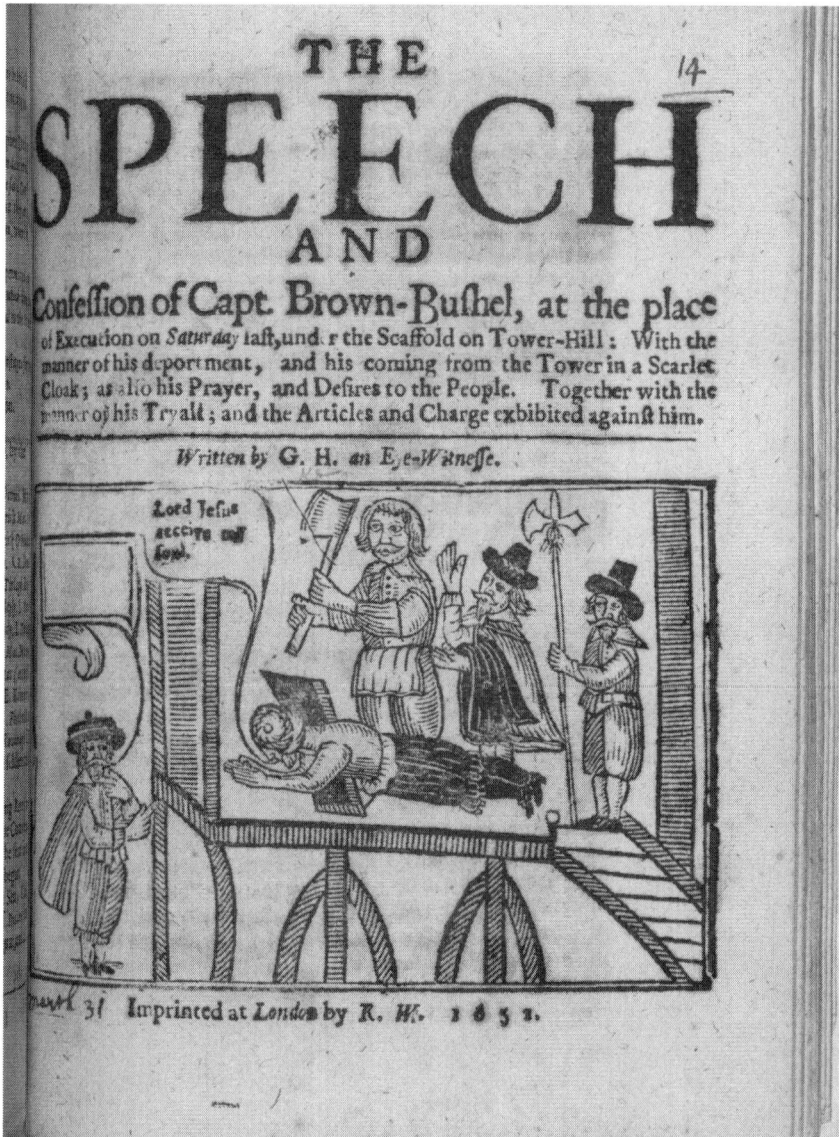

Fig. 9.3. Execution pamphlet for Browne Bushell. *The Speech and Confession of Capt. Brown-Bushel, at the place of Execution on Saturday last, under the Scaffold on Tower-Hill: With the manner of his deportment, and his coming from the Tower in a Scarlet Cloak; as also his Prayer, and Desires to the People. Together with the manner of his Tryall; and the Articles and Charge exhibited* [sic] *against him. Written by G.H. an Eye-Witnesse.* 31 March 1651. (© The British Library Board: BL, E626(14).)

the courage that Lucas and Lisle displayed at their executions by claiming that the pair were so intent on leaving an earthly legacy that they neglected their souls by dying unrepentant.[150]

Love followed Bushell to the block on 22 August 1651, after confessing that he had given money to Edward Massey. Defending his posthumous reputation, he claimed political constancy: 'I am also accus'd to be an Apostate, to be a Turncoat; but Bless my God, a High-Court, a long Sword, a bloody Scaffold, have not made me in the least to alter my Principles, or to wrong my Conscience'.[151] There was an inundation of printed works in favour of Love during and after his trial.[152] Love protested his innocence in print a fortnight before his execution, claiming that the evidence against him was insufficient.[153] On the scaffold he made a lengthy speech, warning: 'my blood it will be bad food for this Infant Commonwealth…Mine is not Malignant blood'. Although he acknowledged that he had sinned and deserved Hell, he proclaimed 'without vanity' that God had chosen him as a martyr, and that a heavenly 'crown of righteousness' awaited him.[154] The earl of Leicester noted that *Mercurius Politicus* interpreted Love's performance as 'barking against the Government.'[155] As with Bushell, this demanded a response from the Rump, who commissioned John Hall's *A Gagg to Love's Advocate* which refuted Love's arguments for mercy, defaming him as a 'blackmouth'd Rabshakeh'.[156] In addition, a final fourth section was inserted into the execution pamphlet itself. Following Love's printed speech, it revived the practice of Elizabethan Protestant writers of alleging that mental confusion among condemned Catholics disproved their claims to martyrdom.[157] These 'animadversions' warned onlookers against being 'made confident in evil by Mr Love's confidence at his death'. Rather, Love's confidence was 'in the face only', or if it was really in the heart, it 'lacked sufficient ground for the raising of it'. It argued that when traitors died unrepentant and 'full of confidence in God, whether real or pretended, it is a sore temptation upon men, not to be so tender or fearful of such practices, as the hatred and high displeasure of God against them, admonisheth them to be.'[158] (See Fig. 9.4.)

---

[150] Sharpe, '"Last Dying Speeches"', 154; Andrea Brady, '"Dying with Honour": Literary Propaganda and the Second English Civil War', *Journal of Military History*, 70 (2006), 20.

[151] *Weekly Journal or British Gazetteer*, 12 October (1717), 856.

[152] Jason Peacey, *Politicians and Pamphleteers: Propaganda During the English Civil Wars and Interregnum* (Aldershot, 2004), 263.

[153] BL, E790(5), Christopher Love, *A Cleare and Necessary Vindication of the Principles and Practices of me Christopher Love since my Tryall before, and Condemnation by, the High Court of Justice* (1651).

[154] BL, E641(10), *Mr Love's Case: Wherein is Published, First, his several petitions to the Parliament. Secondly, a full narrative of the late dangerous design against the state, written with Mr Loves own hand, and by him sent to the Parliament… Thirdly, Mr Loves speech and prayer on the scaffold on Towerhil, August 22. 1651. Printed by an exact copy, taken in short-hand by John Hinde. Fourthly, animadversions on the said speech and prayer* (1651), 25–7.

[155] Dyfnallt Owen (ed.), *Report on the Manuscripts of the Right Honourable Viscount De L'Isle*, 605; BL, E640(23), *Mercurius Politicus*, no. 64, 21–28 August (1651), 1019.

[156] BL, E640(28), *A Gagg to Love's Advocate: Or, An Assertion of the Justice of the Parliament in the Execution of Mr Love. By J.H. Esq.*, 25 August (1651), 22.

[157] Lake and Questier, 'Agency, Appropriation and Rhetoric', 76.

[158] BL, E641(10), *Mr Love's Case*, 32–3.

Fig. 9.4. Christopher Love. (Special Collections of the University of Leicester, University of Leicester Library, Fairclough Collection of Portrait Prints, EP58B, Box 2.)

VI

To conclude, it was not the purpose of scaffold speeches to divulge details about why individuals changed sides. While readily admitting a sinful life, most denied the charges, fashioning themselves as constant martyrs to die a 'good death' and secure their place in posterity. Yet after the Restoration, printed martyrologies reflected continuing unease over the meaning of the executions of side-changers, especially when contrasted to accounts describing more straightforward martyrs such as Lord Capel. One listed forty-one martyrs, of which at least six were side-changers—Morris, Benbow, Poyer, Holland, Bushell, and Love—yet the former parliamentarianism of Benbow and Morris went unmentioned, Bushell's was unclear, and Love was held to have 'dyed upon the Presbyterian Account'. Holland was afforded grudging praise, while the Hothams, Carew, and Urry were not even granted entries.[159] Poyer and Benbow were omitted from an earlier list of royal

[159] Wing/W3066, William Winstanley, *The Loyall Martyrology, Or, Brief Catalogues and Characters of the Most Eminent Persons who Suffered for their Conscience during the late times of Rebellion* (1665), 24, 27–8, 32, 34.

martyrs.[160] When *England's Black Tribunal* was reissued in 1680 as a manifestation of Tory loyalism during the Exclusion Crisis, Carew and the Hothams had been removed, with Morris and Holland the only side-changers remaining.[161] In this way the sacrifices of royalist defectors were downplayed and eventually massaged out of memory.

The theatre of execution became an arena for participation in political conflict in a new way during the civil wars. Changing notions of what constituted treason were 'asserted and resisted' on the scaffold before large crowds. Executions of side-changers were central to this process, because so many of them proclaimed their own political constancy at their death. Public debate about the condemned's behaviour and the meaning of their last speeches encompassed whether it was more honourable to remain constant to a transformed cause, or to follow the concerns of conscience in response to changing circumstances.[162] Competing interpretations of scaffold events became harder to control as execution pamphlets proliferated. After the regicide, the Rump was naïve to expect that royalist hard men such as Bushell and Morris would die the sort of obliging death suffered by Francis Pitt and John Poyer. Rather they would use the platform granted by their public executions to defy the regime, prolong the conflict, and rekindle royalist sympathies.

---

[160] Wing/R2135, *The Royal Martyrs, or, A List of the Lords, Knights, Officers, and Gentlemen, that were Slain (by the Rebels) in the Late Wars, in Defence of their King and Country as also of those Executed by their High Courts of (In)-Justice, or Law-Martial* (1663), 13.

[161] BL, E1805(1), *England's Black Tribunall. Set forth in the Triall of K. Charles, I. at the Pretended Court of Justice at Westminster Hall, January 22. Together with his Majesties speech, immediately before he was murdred on a scaffold erected at Whitehall-Gate, Tuesday, January 30. 1648. Also the severall dying speeches of the nobility and gentry, as were inhumanely put to death for their loyalty to their sovereign lord the King from 1642. to 1658* (1660), 97–103; Wing/E2949, *England's Black Tribunal set forth in the Tryal of King Charles I by the Pretended High Court of Justice in Westminster-Hall, January 20, 1648: together with His Majesties speech on the scaffold erected at White-Hall gate, Tuesday January 30, 1648: Also a perfect relation of the sufferings and death of divers of the nobility and gentry who were inhumanly murthered for their constant loyalty to their Soveraign Lord the King: together with their several dying speeches from the year 1642 to 1658* (1680), 87, 104.

[162] Michael J. Braddick, 'The English Revolution and its Legacies', in Nicholas Tyacke (ed.), *The English Revolution c.1590–1720: Politics, Religion and Communities* (Manchester, 2007), 32; Michael Braddick, *God's Fury, England's Fire: A New History of the English Civil Wars* (2008), 449.

Conclusion

Although the full extent of side-changing during the English Civil Wars and wider mid-century British and Irish conflicts can never be ascertained, it is hoped that this book has gone some way towards indicating the phenomenon's impact. From the grandest aristocrats to the humble common soldier, the evidence reveals that a bewildering number of contemporaries can be identified for whom side-changing became an important issue. English peers developed flexible views on loyalty, with up to a third having served both sides at some point, and more changing sides during the 1640s than those who remained loyal to parliament throughout. In the House of Commons, side-changing influenced factional definitions of what constituted 'the cause', fuelling infighting and the emergence of a more adversarial style of politics. Discrediting comrades as turncoats allowed individuals and parties to redefine the nature and purpose of their 'cause', often underlining their own legitimacy with claims to unswerving constancy and service, especially at the time of their cause's lowest ebb or greatest distress. Army officers might change sides for professional as well as political considerations, whilst their soldiers developed their own notions of loyalty and conditions of service, and were not always driven into side-changing by deferential or necessitous motives. The pattern of side-changing broadly reflected the fortunes of war, but was complicated by changing political circumstances as well as being subject to distinctive regional and local variations.

Military officers learned the practicalities of how to go about changing sides with success. Resigning a commission in advance might help protect one from charges of breach of trust. While some changed sides first and worried about vindicating themselves later, others agonized over their self-justifications for months beforehand. Cultivating friendly contacts among the enemy prior to defecting was advisable, as was bringing demonstrable benefit to one's new masters in terms of money, men, intelligence, supplies, or the control of towns, castles, or garrisons. Such action would enhance a defection's value and consequently the defector's political prospects. For instance, one embittered royalist considered that Marchamont Nedham's ability to realign himself successfully owed something to his possession of cyphers from both sides.[1] Although Barbara Donagan has persuasively argued that side-changing had a benign effect in making civil-war divisions less absolute, there is also a sense that on some occasions the reverse could prove true

---

[1] Blair Worden, *Literature and Politics in Cromwellian England: John Milton, Andrew Marvell, Marchamont Nedham* (Oxford, 2009), 25.

with particular defectors provoking extreme reactions.[2] Reputations were savaged in print with embittered, vituperative language, while capital sentences were increasingly imposed in cases of breach of trust. Therefore, ensuring that subordinates could be trusted before announcing oneself was another sensible precaution. Henry Lilburne sent those he was unsure of out of Tynemouth on errands before he delivered the castle to the royalist cause, thereafter murdering a corporal and supposedly threatening to pistol any further dissenters.[3] By the later seventeenth century the management of military defections became slick operations. In November 1688 the defection of cavalry under Lord Cornbury was meticulously plotted in advance so that former comrades were deceived and misdirected, while some troopers found themselves tricked into defecting.[4]

The importance of side-changing in shaping allegiance and determining the course of the wars ought now to be properly recognized. Side-changing was not marginal to the war's outcome. Both sides became obsessed with it, as fears or expectations of treachery frequently determined military strategies. When successive royalist garrisons in their heartlands of Wales and the West Midlands were betrayed from within during 1644 and 1645, this did much to undermine the morale and functional capacity of the royalist war-effort. A genuine change of heart was unnecessary for defections to prove militarily decisive, and the realization of defeat no doubt prompted much side-changing as damage limitation. For example, in the correct belief that parliament would prove victorious, the marquis of Antrim and Owen Roe O'Neill fatally undermined Ireland's royalist–confederate alliance in 1649 by negotiating with English parliamentarians in order to attempt to secure concessions.[5]

In 1648 the parliamentarian cause suffered an identity crisis and came close to destroying itself through the self-doubt unleashed by mass defections. Those who rode out the storm grew increasingly radicalized, embittered, and more anxious than ever about their men's allegiance.[6] Usual gauges of loyalty such as length of service became unreliable as parliament laid off much of its soldiery over the winter of 1647–48. On 10 July 1648 Colonel George Twisleton complained that despite his having discharged sixty soldiers who had formerly been royalists, 'Noe providence nor care can fence against treachery.' He bemoaned that the traitors in his ranks were men 'seduced who had served in these partes above four years, and never was of the enemyes party.'[7] Owing to such fears, from 1648 the harsh punishment of defectors became more routinely employed. Alongside this, the realization grew that if the king's life were spared, parliamentarians would continue to face

[2] Barbara Donagan, *War in England 1642–1649* (Oxford, 2008), 278.
[3] BL, TT E459(4), *A Terrible and Bloudy Fight at Tinmouth Castle*, 16 August (1648), 2; BL, TT E458(26), *Sir Arthur Hesilrige's Letter to the Honorable Committee of Lords & Commons at Derby-House, Concerning the Revolt and Recovery of Tinmouth-Castle*, 15 August (1648), 3–4.
[4] H. J. Yallop, 'Col. Ambrose Norton's Account of the Defection of Lord Cornbury –1688', *JSAHR*, 70 (1992), 231–8.
[5] Micheál Ó Siochrú, *God's Executioner: Oliver Cromwell and the Conquest of Ireland* (2008), 204.
[6] Donagan, *War in England*, 319n.
[7] *Portland MS*, 478–80.

treachery and backsliding from their comrades. In this way, fear of treachery and side-changing helped determine the course of the English Revolution; if so many could be executed for betraying their trust and turning against God's judgements, then why not the king?

Anxious about maintaining themselves in power, parliamentarians enlarged and redefined traditional concepts of treason throughout the 1640s.[8] Even from 1642, parliament had argued that the king was guilty of a breach of trust, through violating his coronation oath. The king's judges used this language of treachery against him during his trial, claiming that he had 'traitorously and maliciously declared war' on his subjects.[9] Arguments of breach of trust became central to justifying the regicide.[10]

Although both sides benefitted from side-changers' actions, the moral imperative to condemn the practice continued unabated. The downfall of renegades inspired self-satisfied gloating from contemporaries of all political persuasions. Sir Edward Nicholas remarked that when the earl of Holland abandoned Oxford in November 1643, 'Holland is returned to his vomit, and yet so far from being trusted at London as he is committed to the Black Rod.'[11] Sir John Hotham himself played upon such notions during his trial, putting it to his defence witnesses: had he not 'professed so publicly against the breach of trust, what a hateful crime it was, and how it rendered all a man's business unsuccessful?'[12] Sir Simonds D'Ewes reflected that Sir Alexander Carew had been so hotly engaged in promoting the war, and so violent against parliament's enemies that he provoked the judgement of God, and was thereby driven, like the Hothams, into ruining himself by treachery.[13] In October 1648 Walter Strickland wrote that parliament's former general, Sydenham-Poyntz, had defected but was 'now as little esteemed by them as by us; which I am glad to hear, that those whose consciences make their swords cut both ways, may know their wages in the scorn of both. I hope that time will discover all that walk one way and look another.'[14] Voicing such sentiments enhanced the commentator's own sense of worth and constancy, as well as deterring defections by linking side-changing with retribution.

Clarendon was most eager of all to demonstrate that side-changers never prospered, fabricating a cautionary tale about the execution of Colonel John Morris, maintaining that 'by a wonderful act of Providence' Morris 'was put to death in the same place where he had committed a fault against the King, and where he first performed a great service to the Parliament.'[15] Clarendon comforted himself that

[8] Adele Hast, 'State Treason Trials during the Puritan Revolution, 1640–1660', *HJ*, 15 (1972), 53.
[9] Blair Worden, *The English Civil Wars 1640–1660* (2009), 41, 101.
[10] Michael J. Braddick, 'The English Revolution and its Legacies', in Nicholas Tyacke (ed.), *The English Revolution c.1590–1720: Politics, Religion and Communities* (Manchester, 2007), 32.
[11] Francis Bickley (ed.), *Report on the Manuscripts of the late Reginald Rawdon Hastings, esq.*, HMC, 78, 4 vols. (1928–47), ii, 108.
[12] HHC, Hotham MS, U DDHO/1/41.
[13] BL, Harleian MS 165, fo. 165r–v.
[14] J. R. Powell and E. K. Timings (eds.), *Documents Relating to the Civil War, 1642–1648* (Navy Records Society, 105, 1963), 391.
[15] Edward Hyde, earl of Clarendon, *History of the Rebellion and Civil Wars in England Begun in the Year 1641*, ed. William Dunn Macray, 6 vols. (Oxford, 1888), iv, 406–7.

side-changers were rarely trusted, widely reproached, and scarcely ever prosperous. Yet he regretted that more was not done to win over Holland and Bedford in order to encourage more conversions.[16] This is indicative of the partisan double-standard at the heart of the phenomenon, where notions of constancy, honour, and service clashed with pragmaticism and political advantage. Particular instances of side-changing were not always considered reprehensible, especially by those who sought advantage from it. Gardiner observed this in action when parliament's council of war concurred with Lord Charles Paulet's plan to betray Basing House in spring 1644, 'which, if it had been conceived by Charles, they would have stigmatized as treachery, but which, as coming from themselves, they doubtless regarded as a mere stratagem of war.'[17] At the same time, they blasted Sir Richard Grenville for successfully defecting where Paulet had failed. While Cromwell vituperated Edward Wogan for betraying his trust with one hand, he sought to entice Viscount Inchiquin to do likewise with his other.[18]

Side-changing was even more pronounced in war-torn Scotland and Ireland, where it was a sensible survival strategy to adopt in negotiating the highly fluid and rapidly changing alliances of the 1640s. Jane Ohlmeyer has argued that if most political figures were 'obliged' to change sides in some way during the mid-century crisis this was especially true in the case of Ireland.[19] Here, allegiance was so tortuously complex that it can no longer be depicted as Protestant invaders warring against native Catholics. Micheál Ó Siochrú has recently pointed out that there is much evidence in Irish primary sources that many native Irish surrendered and entered into English service, including the New Model Army—some converting to Protestantism as they did so.[20] To explain the sudden side-changing that was so prevalent in 1640s Munster, Vincent Gookin claimed that his fellow Protestants had one consistent principle: that of 'profound reverence and submission to the power for the time being ruling over them.'[21] By the later 1640s resources became so scarce and internal divisions within English and Irish forces so pronounced that negotiating with enemy commanders became a necessary commonplace. Commanders as diverse as the marquis of Ormond, Viscount Inchiquin, Sir Charles Coote, Michael Jones, George Monck, and Owen Roe O'Neill wrote to one another seeking to inspire defections, win back old comrades, and build new coalitions.[22] When Jones declined Ormond's invitation to change his allegiance in response to the king's murder, he argued that this would be a breach of parliament's

---

[16] Ibid., iii, 146–51, 248–9

[17] Samuel R. Gardiner, *History of the Great Civil War, 1642–1649*, 4 vols. (1987), i, 319.

[18] Frederick Maurice, *The Adventures of Edward Wogan* (1945), 124.

[19] Jane Ohlmeyer, 'The Marquis of Antrim: A Stuart Turn-Kilt?' *History Today*, 43 (1993), 18.

[20] Ó Siochrú, *God's Executioner*, 204–10.

[21] T. C. Barnard, 'Crises of Identity among Irish Protestants, 1641–1685', *P&P*, 127 (1990), 71.

[22] Bodl., MS Carte 23, fo. 480r; Bodl., MS Carte 24, fos. 103v, 142; BL, Add. MS 46928, fo. 125r; *Portland MS*, 485–7, 513; BL, TT E562(1), *Generall Ovven Oneales Letter to Collonell Monck with the propositions of Owen Oneale, the Lords, gentry, and commons of the Confederate Catholiques of Ulster: to the most honourable, and potent, the Parliament of England. Together with Coll. Monck his answer. And Collonell Moncks Propositions to Owen Oneale, and the Rest of the Confederate Catholiques of Ulster* (1649).

trust.[23] This provoked Ormond to demonstrate that the parliamentarians did not have a monopoly on the concept of breach of trust. He accused Jones that by countenancing Pride's Purge and the regicide, he was guilty of the 'foulest breach of trust imaginable'.[24] The speed of changing political circumstances ensured that notions of treachery were highly partisan, subjective, and contested. Ohlmeyer has pointed to nobles with 'abysmal' reputations for 'disloyalty and treachery', such as Randal MacDonnell, marquis of Antrim, having some consistency to their aims. Even Antrim was far from unusual when compared to others such as Inchiquin and Broghill, who were 'obliged' by events to change sides. She has argued that notions of 'treachery' and 'patriotism' meant little in Gaelic territories, and that even a nobleman's loyalty to his sovereign was subordinated to concerns for his kinsmen and religion.[25]

The king's general in Scotland, the marquis of Montrose, was himself considered a turncoat by his enemies because he had formerly served the Covenanters, alongside several of his officers such as Colonels John Cochrane and John Middleton, and Lord George Gordon. The Scottish peerage also bred multiple side-changers such as the earl of Seaforth, dubbed a 'fence-sitter' by Ian Gentles, who may have only joined Montrose to protect his estates, before defecting to the Covenanters prior to the battle of Auldearn. John Stewart, Lord Traquair, was suspected of betraying Montrose in 1645, withdrawing his son from the royalist encampment, and passing intelligence to the Covenanters before the battle at Philiphaugh. William Cunningham, earl of Glencairn, had been a Covenanter in the first civil war but became a royalist thereafter.[26] As Scottish political developments were so fluid between 1646 and 1653 it is difficult to label the forces under the duke of Hamilton and David Leslie as side-changers merely because they were now fighting their former English allies. Many in these armies considered their political activities entirely consistent with the Solemn League and Covenant, and that their foes in the New Model Army were the real turncoats. Nevertheless, officers who might more confidently be considered as side-changers can still be identified among the Covenanter army in England during the first civil war. Lieutenant-Colonel William Henderson was dubbed a 'Reformeir' for having briefly served under Montrose before returning to the Covenanters, to be slain in the siege of Newcastle in October 1644.[27] Captain Thomas Rutherford was court-martialled and condemned to death in June 1644 for having 'treacherously surrendered' to Montrose the Covenanter garrison at South Shields fort.[28] Thereafter, the Covenanter forces

---

[23] Bodl., MS Carte 24, fo. 129r–v.

[24] Ibid., fo. 291r.

[25] Ohlmeyer, 'The Marquis of Antrim: A Stuart Turn-Kilt?', 13, 17–18.

[26] Ian Gentles, *The English Revolution and the Wars in the Three Kingdoms, 1638–1652* (Harlow, 2007), 257; J. R. M. Sizer, 'Stewart, John, first earl of Traquair (c.1599–1659), politician', *ODNB*; Geoffrey Smith, *Royalist Agents, Conspirators and Spies: Their Role in the British Civil Wars, 1640–1660* (Farnham, 2010), 32, 146, 174.

[27] C. S. Terry, 'The Siege of Newcastle-upon-Tyne by the Scots in 1644', *Archaeologia Aeliana*, 2nd series, 21 (1899), 217, 224.

[28] C. S. Terry, 'The Scottish Campaign in Northumberland and Durham between January and June, 1644', *Archaeologia Aeliana*, 2nd series, 21 (1899), 177.

in Yorkshire received a late influx of English royalists as the king's cause collapsed in April 1646.[29]

Charles II's murky double dealings with the marquis of Montrose and the Scottish parliament in April and May 1650 involved the prince negotiating for Covenanter support at the same time as he had authorized Montrose's expedition in the field against them. On 3 May he publicly ordered Montrose to disband and leave Scotland, but the following week, not knowing of his defeat, he privately requested him to remain in arms. Having publicly disowned Montrose's expedition, he appears to have made no attempt to negotiate for the life of his captured servant.[30] To deflect attention from this betrayal, the royalist serial *Mercurius Elencticus* circulated the falsehood that Montrose himself had been a turncoat, treacherously colluding with the English regicides to destroy all royalist forces.[31] Allegations of turncoating, however implausible, could prove highly effective political tools.

After 1649, successive interregnum regimes demanded the allegiance of former royalists. How converts were received depended much on the manner of their coming, the individual reputation of the convert, and perceptions of the nature of side-changing that had emerged from the 1640s. The considerable success of the Rump and Protectorate in winning over former royalists has long been recognized, while the work of Jason McElligott has highlighted the Rump's success in persuading royalist pamphleteers into collaborating with the republic's propaganda efforts.[32] When the male adult population were required to subscribe to the Engagement to be True and Faithful to the Commonwealth in January 1650, there was no requirement to approve the regicide, as the phrase 'as is now established' suggested no need to approve of past events.[33] The Engagement's repeal in January 1654 allowed even more former royalists to accommodate themselves with the Protectorate.[34] Some of John Thurloe's best intelligence agents were former royalists, and passing on information to Thurloe came to be seen by some exiles as a 'usual means of securing tolerant approval' in Protectorate England.[35] Parliamentary propaganda sought to encourage this process of rehabilitation, and in 1652 several tracts encouraged royalists to take advantage of the Rump's Act of Oblivion. One of these depicted two fictional cavaliers—'Sir Timothy Turn-coat' and 'Sir Rowland Resolute'—sensibly deciding to make their peace with parliament to avoid penury and hardship. The two agreed that most royalists fought and plotted only out of malice

[29] *LJ*, viii, 348–9, 366; *Portland MS*, 357.

[30] Austin Woolrych, *Britain in Revolution, 1625–1660* (Oxford, 2002), 480–1.

[31] BL, E602(10), *Mercurius Elencticus (For King Charls II.)*, no. 6, 20–27 May (1650), sig. F3r; BL, E602(21), *Mercurius Elencticus (For King Charls II.)*, no. 7, 27 May–3 June (1650), sig. G3v.

[32] Jason McElligott, *Royalism, Print and Censorship in Revolutionary England* (Woodbridge, 2007), 107–11, 137, 168, 178, 181.

[33] Edward Vallance, 'Protestation, Vow, Covenant and Engagement: Swearing Allegiance in the English Civil War', *Historical Research*, 75 (2002), 422.

[34] G. E. Aylmer, 'Collective Mentalities in Mid-Seventeenth-Century England: 4 Cross Currents: Neutrals, Trimmers and Others', *TRHS*, 5th series, 39 (1989), 7.

[35] Newman, 247, 415. Royalists who became informants to Thurloe include Joseph Bampfield, Francis Corker, Sir John Marley, Sir Richard Willis: Smith, *Royalist Agents, Conspirators and Spies*, 39, 84, 166, 205.

and hopes for revenge, alongside a desire to recover their fortunes: 'for a Gentleman without means, is like a Bag-pudding without suet'. At Sir Timothy's observation that leading cavaliers had all met with disgrace and ruin, save those pardoned by parliament, they resolved to lay down arms.[36]

As the 1650s advanced, abandoning royalism began to lose its stigma as former royalists, despairing of a Stuart Restoration, increasingly accepted the Protectorate. The Instrument of Government disabled in theory all who had fought against parliament since 1 January 1642 from sitting in the First Protectorate Parliament. Yet even here the door was left open. Converts were admitted if they had 'been since in the service of Parliament, and given signal testimony of their good affection thereunto.' One example was Robert Shapcote, elected MP for Tiverton in 1654 despite his opponents' claims that he was a royalist field officer who only defected to Essex in 1644. The Humble Petition and Advice also allowed former royalists to participate in government if they swore an oath abjuring Charles Stuart and were restored by Act of Parliament. It also allowed those Irish Protestants who had defected from Ormond and Inchiquin prior to 1650 back into public office. William Lockhart and Lord Cochrane constitute examples of Scots who had served Charles I and then become close to Cromwell.[37] Henry Oxinden reflected that even 'the most constant men must be content to change their resolutions according to the alterations of time.'[38] The presence of former royalists, now redefined as the 'well-affected' within interregnum government, led to unease among parliamentarians that they might derail indemnity proceedings and seek legal revenge upon their former enemies.[39] The parliamentarian coalition fractured further during the 1650s as radicals reinterpreted 'the cause', with many turning against Cromwell's elevation to Lord Protector. Responding to Cromwell's speech to the First Protectorate Parliament in September 1654, the Fifth Monarchist, John Spittlehouse, was arrested for denouncing Cromwell as a turncoat and a betrayer of the cause.[40] That year, Anna Trapnel crafted a similar narrative of betrayal, accusing Cromwell of backsliding and becoming the fourth horn on the beast in Daniel chapter 7.[41]

Unsurprisingly, in these circumstances allegations of turn-coating could be raised as a political weapon against rivals for office. In 1653 the bitter conflict at Hull between the Fifth Monarchist army chaplain, John Canne, and the lecturer at Holy Trinity, John Shaw, included a pamphlet controversy in which Canne defamed

---

[36] BL, E655(25), *The Cavaliers Jubilee: Or, Long Look'd for Come at Last: Viz. The Generall Pardon. In a Pleasant Dialogue between Sir Timothy Turn-coat, and Sir Rowland Resolute, Two Cavaliers that met accidentally, and were lately come over from beyond sea, upon the noise of the Generall Pardon, and their resolution to leave the service of the young Charles Stuart, and imbrace the Parliaments Protection in their Gracious Act of Oblivion* (1652), 4.

[37] Patrick Little and David Smith, *Parliaments and Politics during the Cromwellian Protectorate* (Cambridge, 2000), 36–7, 55.

[38] Worden, *Literature and Politics in Cromwellian England*, 16.

[39] Rachel Weil, 'Thinking about Allegiance in the English Civil War', *History Workshop Journal*, 61 (2006), 190.

[40] Bernard Capp, 'Spittlehouse, John (*bap.* 1612, *d.* in or after 1657), Fifth Monarchist', *ODNB*; BL, E813(19), John Spittlehouse, *An Answer to One Part of the Lord Protector's Speech* (1654).

[41] Ann Hughes, *Gender and the English Revolution* (2011), 79.

Shaw as 'a notable Turn-coate and Timeserver'. Canne complained that Shaw's 'scandalous actions' had been permitted because he was protected by his friends in the Rump, adding that 'Of late, Turn-coats, Time-servers, Apostates, and such like, have been most favoured, soonest heard and prefer'd'.[42] Shaw's enemies in Hull, who included the governor and many of his officers, petitioned Cromwell against him, claiming that Shaw had defended 'innocent Ceremonies' during the 1630s, and raking up Shaw's letter to the Archbishop of York of 22 August 1642 in which he denied that he opposed 'the Kings Majestie or Episcopacie'. This was going back a long way for evidence, but Shaw's enemies explained that he was only constant to parliament thereafter because he was 'always a complyer to the ruling times, and to great men'. They denounced Shaw as 'the greatest Turncoat in Yorkshire, insomuch as it is become a Proverb, John Shaw the Turn-coat'.[43] The argument became about defining the parliamentary cause, but it was really rooted in disagreements between the garrison and corporation, and the religious differences between the sectarian Canne and the more mainstream Godly Shaw. The conflict had famously witnessed the chancel and nave in Holy Trinity being divided by a wall, allowing them to preach simultaneously on either side of it. Considering that Shaw had strong parliamentarian credentials throughout the 1640s, the denouncements by his enemies suggest that even an elastic application of the term 'turncoat' could constitute worthwhile political leverage in the battle to position oneself as the true upholder of God's cause.[44] The episode also indicates that a thorough assessment of side-changing among the clergy is also overdue. There is no space to conduct this here, but such a study might commence with an investigation into passive conformity, assessing Gerald Aylmer's contention that to continue in their careers, all clergy had to be 'either partisans or conformists'.[45]

Blair Worden chose to end his recent overview of the civil wars with a quote from John Dryden, looking back from the vantage point of 1700: 'Thy wars brought nothing about.'[46] This reflects some cavalier insight into the ultimate political futility of the republican cause, but to suggest that the civil wars changed nothing is fanciful. Rather, ideas about loyalty and the nature of political participation changed dramatically because of the civil wars. As John Walter has argued, 'The Revolution opened up a new space for popular politics.'[47] New political identities along with a novel vocabulary to describe them emerged.[48] Prolonged conflict

---

[42] BL, E669(16), John Canne, *A Voice from the Temple to the High Powers* (1653), 33–4.

[43] *Witnesses produced against Mr John Shaw of Hull, attesting the Publike Charge against him, and much more* (1653), 2–3.

[44] Shaw had been a favourite of Lord Fairfax and had preached to his army at Selby in February 1643: Roger Hayden, 'John Canne (*d.*1667), Independent minister and printer', *ODNB*; Charles Jackson (ed.), 'The Life of Master John Shaw', in *Yorkshire Diaries and Autobiographies in the Seventeenth and Eighteenth Centuries* (Surtees Society, 65, 1875), 136, 140, 143–4.

[45] Aylmer, 'Collective Mentalities in Mid-Seventeenth-Century England: 4 Cross Currents', 3, 15.

[46] Momus to Mars in John Dryden's *A Secular Masque* (1700), cited in Blair Worden, *The English Civil Wars 1640–1660* (London, 2009), 165.

[47] John Walter, 'The English People and the English Revolution Revisited', *History Workshop Journal*, 61 (2006), 176.

[48] Weil, 'Thinking about Allegiance in the English Civil War', 184.

brought the question of personal allegiance into the public arena in new ways and to an unprecedented level. As all sides invited individuals to lend their support or cooperation, allegiance became something to be negotiated and constructed as well as commanded. Individuals participated in shaping the nature of the cause for which they stood, and those who felt marginalized, either by their comrades or by changing political circumstances, might choose to realign themselves. Alternatively, they might experience a change of sides forced upon them by events. These switches could have a major impact on future political developments as the rival coalitions unravelled. Although defections often sparked angry denunciations, it came to be recognized that in some contexts, side-changing could become an honourable as well as a necessitous course of action.

Epilogue

Treason doth never prosper; what's the reason:
Why, if it prosper, none dare call it treason.[1]

The prevalence and nature of civil-war side-changing had important consequences for the post-Restoration world. After 1660, most side-changers were protected by the Act of Indemnity. Only the most isolated and vulnerable were picked off by vengeful cavaliers such as the eighth earl of Derby, whose execution of William Christian for treason against the Lords of Man on 2 January 1663 reflected the peculiarly unique political circumstances on the Isle of Man.[2] Meanwhile, those who faced no such retribution, those whose loyalties had navigated the troubled 1640s with success, understandably incurred the resentment of those less flexible, adept, or fortunate. Three such Pembrokeshire gentlemen were ridiculed after 1660: 'Roger Lort: of any principle or religion to acquire wealth. Sampson Lort: he can pray as long as there is profit. James Lewis: forced from a Royalist to act as a Colonel for King and Parliament...loved more for doing no wrong than for doing any good.'[3] George Downing successfully redefined himself as a royalist in the 1660s, despite having been an army chaplain before becoming a diplomat in the interregnum. By doing so he forged a reputation as an 'able, mean, avaricious and treacherous man'. His trickery in capturing his former colonel, John Okey, earned him notoriety, as 'A Judas came to be known as an "arrant George Downing"'.[4] In Yorkshire, Joshua Greathead of Gildersome, a former major under Fairfax, betrayed his fellow northern plotters in 1663 and was remembered as 'a cunning knaveish man, it was a very dangerous thing to be in his company, he was hated by all good men, yea of his neighbours who all stood in awe of him'. Such notoriety inspired

[1] STC (2nd ed.)/12776, Sir John Harington, *The Most Elegant and Witty Epigrams of Sir Iohn Harington, Knight digested into Foure Bookes: three vvhereof neuer before published* (1618), sig. K4v.

[2] John Callow, 'The Limits of Indemnity: The Earl of Derby, Sovereignty and Retribution at the Trial of William Christian, 1660–63', *The Seventeenth Century*, 15 (2000), 204, 208.

[3] Arthur Leonard Leach, *The History of the Civil War (1642–1649) in Pembrokeshire and on its Borders* (1937), 220–1.

[4] Ruth Spalding (ed.), *Contemporaries of Bulstrode Whitelocke, 1605–1675* (Records of Social and Economic History, new series, 14, Oxford, 1990), 78; Ralph Josselin, *The Diary of Ralph Josselin, 1616–1683*, ed. Alan Macfarlane (Records of Social and Economic History, new series, 3, Oxford, 1976), 488.

allegations of his ghost haunting Gildersome.[5] During the 1660s it certainly made practical politics to disassociate oneself from those who were notorious for side-changing in the 1640s. For instance, it is unsurprising that not one of the more than 5,000 indigent royalist officers requesting relief in the 1663 list claimed to have served in Sir John Urry's regiment.[6]

John Lacy's play *The Old Troop* provides an example of the invective against turncoats on the Restoration stage. Having served as a royalist lieutenant during the civil wars, Lacy penned and performed this play that satirized 'Tell-troth', a turncoat character who engineered the betrayal of the parliamentarian garrison of 'Thieves den'. When 'Tell-troth' was interrogated on joining the troop, he said that he had left the parliamentarians because he 'lik'd 'em not' and that his captain was a hypocrite. He came not only out of love for the king, but for his own ends: 'I'l fight bravely for a Battel or two, then beg an old house to make a Garrison of, grow rich, consequently a coward, and then let the Dog bite the Bear, or the Bear the Dog, I'l make my own peace, I warrant you, and, in short, this is my business hither.'[7] Such satire reflected the disillusion shared by Clarendon that the royalist military folded too quickly in 1645–6, as lacking in devotion, many activists surrendered prematurely or changed sides to secure the best personal terms. Plays and literature of this nature offered solace to royalists who comforted or flattered themselves that their own activism had been unswerving.

At the same time, angry royalist censure of turncoats in public office during the 1660s assuaged their own consciences at having compromised themselves to live under the interregnum regimes. One broadsheet mocked the heralds for their side-changing during the interregnum, quipping: 'How comes it there was three Kings of Arms when there was no King in England?' It questioned: 'Whether they ought to come so neer his Majestie as to touch his Coat, seeing they have turned it so often?'[8] Adrian Ailes has shown how Edward Bysshe, parliament's Garter King of Arms, was allowed to remain in the College of Arms after 1660, although most of his fellow heralds and kings of arms appointed by parliament were demoted or ejected, several having served Charles I, the Rump, Cromwell, and Charles II consecutively.[9]

Considering the changed circumstances of 1660, it is highly problematic to see the many former parliamentarians who supported the Restoration as side-changers. The manner in which parliamentarians realigned themselves both during the Restoration and thereafter merits a separate study. However, the memory of those

[5] Michael Sheard (ed.), *Records of the Parish of Batley in the County of York* (Worksop, 1894), 14; D. H. Atkinson, *Ralph Thoresby, the Topographer: his Town and Times*, 2 vols. (Leeds, 1885), i, 54.
[6] Stephen Ede-Borrett, 'The Royalist Army at the Second Battle of Newbury, 27 October 1644', *JSAHR*, 77 (1999), 245; Wing/L2479, *A List of Officers Claiming to the Sixty Thousand Pounds, &c. Granted by His Sacred Majesty for the Relief of His Truly-Loyal and Indigent Party* (1663).
[7] John Lacy, *The Old Troop, or, Monsieur Raggou as it was acted at the Theatre-Royal* (1672), 7–8, 54–5; Julie Sanders, 'John Lacy (c.1615–1681), playwright and actor', *ODNB*.
[8] I am grateful to Adrian Ailes for this reference: Broadsheet entitled *Upon Sight of the Heralds Coat*, 8 May (1660), in Bodl. MS Ashmole 840, fo. 753r.
[9] I am grateful to Adrian Ailes for allowing me to read his unpublished paper 'A Pair of Garters: Heralds and Heraldry at the Restoration'.

who conspicuously profited from the Stuarts' return, despite having changed sides during the 1640s, such as George Monck, Anthony Ashley Cooper, Charles Howard, and Lord Broghill, were naturally stigmatized by disaffected republicans as turncoats and betrayers.[10] Lucy Hutchinson recalled that her husband so abhorred Ashley Cooper that he could not bear 'the mention of his name, and held him for a more execrable traitor than Monck himself.'[11] Monck's retrospective explanation that he had been working towards a royal restoration since before 1660 was trumpeted by his admirers, deepening the wounds of his former republican colleagues. John Toland considered that Monck intended a restoration before he left Scotland, and that consequently his 'Dissimulation, Treachery, and Perjury, are like to remain unparallel'd in history'.[12] One of Monck's relatives later felt it necessary to publish a vindication of him.[13]

Once the 'Restoration settlement' was completed, former parliamentarians and royalists had plentiful experience of tactical realignment for political and personal survival. As Ethan Shagan has suggested for their sixteenth-century forbears, some might even have ' "forged" new consciences', partially in response to new cultural pressures, to endure the sharp political fluctuations of the day.[14] By the 1660s the number and necessity of these shifts was increasingly more widely met with cynicism than with outrage. Geoffrey Parker has pointed to a similar process in Europe reeling from the Thirty Years' War, where doubt and 'a sense of resignation often replaced the dynamic providentialism that had led men to fight to the death with a clear conscience.'[15] When parliamentarians who had served successive interregnum regimes sought political prominence after the Restoration, broadside ballads, verse, and songs such as 'The Second Part of Saint George for England' complacently mocked naked opportunism, amoral time-serving, and irreligious hypocrisy as the true source of civil-war side-changing:

> But yet I am told,
> That the Rumpers do hold,
> That Saints may swim with the tyde:
> Nor can it be Treason,
> But Scripture and Reason,
> Still to close with the stronger side.[16]

The broadside ballad *A Turncoat of the Times* was published in 1665 by stationers John Wright and Thomas Vere, who had worked for parliament during the

---

[10] G. E. Aylmer, 'Collective Mentalities in Mid-Seventeenth-Century England: 4 Cross Currents: Neutrals, Trimmers and Others', *TRHS*, 5th series, 39 (1989), 6–7.

[11] Lucy Hutchinson, *Memoirs of the Life of Colonel Hutchinson*, ed. N. H. Keeble (1995), 273–4.

[12] John Toland, *The Art of Restoring. Or, The Piety and Probity of General Monk in Bringing about the Last Restoration, Evidenc'd from his own Authentic Letters* (1714), 38.

[13] George Granville, *A Letter to the Author of Reflexions Historical and Political, Occasioned by a Treatise in Vindication of General Monk, and Sir Richard Granville* (1732), 15, 17.

[14] Ethan Shagan, *Popular Politics and the English Reformation* (Cambridge, 2003), 309.

[15] Geoffrey Parker, *Empire, War and Faith in Early Modern Europe* (2002), 162.

[16] See also the invective against Ashley Cooper: Wing/B4851, Alexander Brome, *Rump: Or an Exact Collection of the Choicest Poems and Songs relating to the Late Times. By the Most Eminent Wits, from Anno 1639 to Anno 1661*, 2 vols. (1662), ii, 17–18, 161.

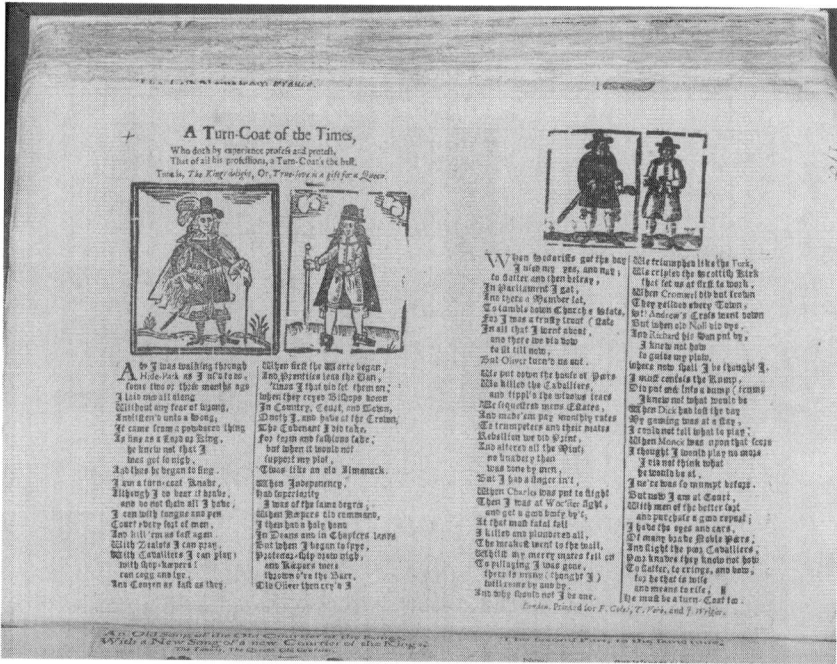

Fig. E.1. The memory of civil-war side-changing in a popular ballad. *A Turn-Coat of the Times, Who doth by experience profess and protest, That of all his professions, a Turn-coat's the best. Tune is, The Kings Delight, Or, True-love is a gift for a Queen.* 1665. In W. G. Day (ed.), *The Pepys Ballads*, 5 vols. (Cambridge, 1987), ii, 210. (© The Pepys Library, Magdalene College, Cambridge.)

1640s.[17] While this ballad derived sardonic amusement from the careerist shifting of English statesmen, it concluded that such skilful turncoating was almost an essential prerequisite for political success (see Fig. E.1):

> But now I am at Court,
> With men of the better sort
>   and purchase a good report;
> I have the eyes and ears,
> Of many brave Noble Peers,
> And slight the poor Cavalliers,
> Poor knaves they know not how
> To flatter, to cringe, and bow,
>   for he that is wise

---

[17] Jason Peacey, *Politicians and Pamphleteers: Propaganda during the English Civil Wars and Interregnum* (Aldershot, 2004), 44, 121–3; Stuart Handley, 'Thomas Vere (*d*.1682), jury foreman', *ODNB*.

and means to rise

He must be a turn-Coat too.[18]

Turncoats and treachery were consistently blamed for military defeats—not just in their immediate aftermath, but years or even decades later. Despite his royal pardon, Richard Feilding was long blamed for betraying Reading by recollections that he 'had been seen going surreptitiously into Essex's tents.'[19] Sir Philip Warwick considered that the earl of Norwich had acted in good faith during the Kent campaign in 1648, but that his 'ill success could not keep it from being vulgarly questioned.'[20] Sir Thomas Fairfax besmirched his major-general, John Gifford, as treacherous when explaining his greatest defeat in his memoirs twenty years after the event, despite Gifford having been exonerated and entrusted with the command of Cromwell's lifeguard in Ireland.[21] His story successfully deflected blame and was readily accepted by later memoirists and antiquarians.[22] The Victorian editor of the Fairfax correspondence reflected that of all the disadvantages suffered by the Fairfaxes in their northern campaigns, that 'there were traitors amongst their foremost men' was 'the greatest calamity of all.'[23]

Local customs, songs, and anniversary sermons emerged that celebrated the deliverances of besieged towns such as at Nantwich and Taunton.[24] In particular, the foiling of conspiracies generated thanksgiving days that celebrated the downfall of particular traitors and turncoats. In 1645 John Syms noted that 26 August was 'the day we kept as a day of thanksgiving for the delivery of the fort & island from Carew's treachery'.[25] The parish clerk of St Mary's, Beverley, noted the execution of the Hothams in the register alongside Naseby and other 'deliverances which God hath given to England against the wicked company of cavaliers'.[26] The Rump Parliament preserved the memory of their deliverances by making an example of individual side-changers, deliberately delaying Browne Bushell's execution to coincide with the eighth anniversary of his betrayal of Scarborough castle.[27]

---

[18] Wing/2123.2:362–3, *A Turn-coat of the Times. Who doth by Experience Profess and Protect, that of all Professions, a Turn-coat's the Best. To a Pleasant Tune much in Request* (1665); W. G. Day (ed.), *The Pepys Ballads*, 5 vols. (Cambridge, 1987), ii, 210. This popular broadside ballad spawned three further editions until 1690.

[19] Barbara Donagan, *War in England, 1642–1649* (Oxford, 2008), 104.

[20] Beinecke Rare Book and Manuscript Library, Osborn Shelves, fb87, fo. 91v.

[21] *CJ*, iii, 285, 341, 355, 518, 704; TNA, SP 16/513/part i/107–8; BL, E121/4/8, no.13; C. H. Firth and Godfrey Davies, *The Regimental History of Cromwell's Army*, 2 vols. (Oxford, 1940), ii, 639–41; *CSPD, 1653–4*, 66; Bodl., MS Fairfax 36, fo. 8r–v.

[22] Joseph Lister, *The Autobiography of Joseph Lister of Bradford in Yorkshire*, ed. Thomas Wright (1842), 19; William Grainge, *The Battles and Battlefields of Yorkshire* (York, 1854), 161; Lockwood Huntley, *The Fairfaxes of Denton and Nun Appleton* (York, 1906), 23; Norrison Scatcherd, *The History of Morley, in the Parish of Batley, and West-Riding of Yorkshire* (Leeds, 1830), 273.

[23] Robert Bell (ed.), *The Fairfax Correspondence: Memorials of the Civil War*, 2 vols. (1849), i, 34.

[24] John Lowe, 'The Campaign of the Irish Royalist Army in Cheshire, November 1643–January 1644', *Transactions of the Historical Society of Lancashire and Cheshire*, 111 (1959), 72; Joshua Toulmin, *The History of Taunton in the County of Somerset* (Taunton, 1822), 415, 423.

[25] BL, Add. MS 35297, fo. 81r.

[26] East Riding Record Office, PE 1/2, p. 152.

[27] Jack Binns, *Yorkshire in the Civil Wars: Origins, Impact and Outcome* (Pickering, 2004), 159.

The sheer extent of side-changing during the 1640s and 1650s redefined the shape of politics thereafter. Shifting allegiance was no longer the act of a handful of isolated, aberrant renegades; by the 1650s, sustained civil conflict had rendered it a practical necessity for large swathes of the political nation. The role of side-changers became more indispensable as sovereign powers increasingly recognized that they had to bid for the widest possible support; Cromwell strove for 'healing and settling', while Charles II promised indemnity to nearly all his father's enemies. The question became not whether one had changed sides, but when, where, why, how, and with whom one had gone about it. There were degrees of turncoating, and many contemporaries appear to have been acutely sensitive to its context. Rachel Weil has persuasively argued that the reception, fashioning, and refashioning of such conversions remain 'crucial aspects of the seventeenth century's revolutionary legacy'.[28]

Prominent politicians after the Restoration acquired nicknames that revelled in their inconstancy. Anthony Ashley Cooper was dubbed, by Marchamont Nedham, 'the Dorsetshire eel' for his shifting loyalties.[29] John Erskine, the Jacobite duke of Mar, was later nicknamed 'Bobbing John' for his political double-dealing.[30] Melinda Zook has recently stressed that even Robert Ferguson's striking political conversion from a 1680s' Whig to a 1690s' Jacobite was 'hardly unique', given that 'shifting with the wind was more or less a national pastime in Restoration England.'[31] Figures as diverse as Henry Care, Nathaniel Hooke, Sir James Montgomery, Charlwood Lawton, and Sir John Trenchard shifted their positions to 'remain politically viable in a fast-changing environment', while the non-juror William Sherlock was mocked by the song 'The weasel uncased' for his submission to William III.[32] Other clergymen were subsequently mocked for changing their denominational alignments in satirical prints,[33] as well as in popular songs such as *The Vicar of Bray*.[34] The chorus of one ballad of 1693, entitled *The Religious Turncoat*, is suggestive of the continuing stigma suffered by such clergymen for serving different religious regimes:

> A Turncoat is a cunning Man,
> That Cants to Admiration;
> And prays for any King, to gain
> The Peoples Approbation.[35]

---

[28] Rachel Weil, 'Thinking about Allegiance in the English Civil War', *History Workshop Journal*, 61 (2006), 183.

[29] Alan Marshall, 'Mechanic Tyrannie: Anthony Ashley Cooper and the English Republic', in John Spurr (ed.), *Anthony Ashley Cooper, First Earl of Shaftesbury 1621–1683* (Farnham, 2011), 31.

[30] Christoph v. Ehrenstein, 'John Erskine, styled twenty-second or sixth earl of Mar and Jacobite duke of Mar (*bap.* 1675, *d.* 1732), Jacobite army officer, politician, and architect', *ODNB*.

[31] Melinda S. Zook, 'Turncoats and Double Agents in Restoration and Revolutionary England: The Case of Robert Ferguson, the Plotter', *Eighteenth-Century Studies*, 42:3 (2009), 364, 366.

[32] Ibid., 366–70.

[33] William Pennock, *The Turncoats* (1709–10).

[34] D. M. Palliser, 'Popular Reactions to the Reformation during the Years of Uncertainty', in Christopher Haigh (ed.), *The English Reformation Revised* (Cambridge, 1987), 94; *Calliope: Or the Musical Miscellany: A Select Collection of the Most Approved English, Scots, and Irish Songs* (1788), 284–6.

[35] Wing/R912, *The Religious Turncoat: Or a Late Jacobite Divine turn'd Williamite* (1693).

Shifting and realignment soon became necessary tools of survival for many Scots and Irish as they navigated their way through the Jacobite Risings.

During the civil wars that engulfed the English-speaking peoples across the Atlantic, side-changing continued to remain prevalent. During the American Revolution, large numbers of colonists moved between loyalist and patriot camps. The most notorious of them, Benedict Arnold, is now a byword for treachery in United States history. The circumstances of Arnold's defection share many similarities with his seventeenth-century counterparts. He too proved highly temperamental about slights to his honour, and was partly motivated by his sense of grievances that he had suffered in the revolutionary cause. He had corresponded with the British General Clinton for more then a year beforehand, and after defecting published a self-justificatory narrative that trumpeted his political constancy.[36] Substantial side-changing also occurred during and after the American Civil War, in which about 3,000 Union prisoners swore loyalty to the Confederacy, while about 10,000 Confederates were recruited into the Union forces. Some southerners were nicknamed 'Galvanized Yankees' for accepting service against Native Americans in the west. Hoping that leniency would aid post-war reunification, President Lincoln appealed for the allegiance of southerners by offering pardons in return for an oath of loyalty to the Union.[37] Confederate prisoners were interviewed to determine their culpability and fitness for clemency. Rather like the cases of royalists brought before parliament's Committee for Compounding, successful Confederates did not articulate their political standpoints, but depicted their activism as imposed upon them either by force or youthful impetuousness.[38]

Side-changing during military conflicts remains important today. At times of rapid political change there is no shortage of media commentators endeavouring to predict the future course of events. To this end, the predominant direction and purpose of side-changing is repeatedly used as a prime indicator. In recent years political strategies have continually been adopted and incentives brokered in attempts to stimulate the practice among enemy forces in Libya, Iraq, and Afghanistan. In modern British politics the occasions when MPs change their political party still attract excited speculation as pundits attempt to unpick the wider significance of these episodes, particularly when they play out close to general elections.[39] The claims of civil-war side-changers have been reiterated in the justificatory narratives of modern British MPs. Emma Nicholson, Conservative MP for Torridge and West Devon, defected to the Liberal Democrats in 1995. After having long felt snubbed by her party, she maintained that 'it is the Conservative Party that has shifted, not my own views.'[40] When Shaun Woodward, Conservative MP

---

[36] John Shy, 'Benedict Arnold (1741–1801), army officer', *ODNB*.

[37] Peter Karsten, 'The American Democratic Citizen Soldier: Triumph or Disaster?', *Military Affairs*, 30 (1966), 37; Harold M. Hyman, 'Civil War Turncoats: A Commentary on a Military View of Lincoln's War Prisoner Utilization Program', *Military Affairs*, 22 (1958), 134–8.

[38] Hyman, 'Civil War Turncoats', 138; Weil, 'Thinking about Allegiance in the English Civil War', 186.

[39] Robert Leach, *Turncoats: Changing Party Allegiance by British Politicians* (Aldershot, 1995).

[40] http://www.independent.co.uk/opinion/profile-emma-nicholson-not-her-sort-of-party-1527965.html (accessed 20 September 2011).

for Witney, joined Labour in 1999 he echoed Nicholson's claims that his own party had left him, not the other way around. This left his former colleague Michael Ancram accusing him of self-interest and careerism, remarking: 'what he lacks is candour and honour'. Labour's plans to reward Woodward with a safe seat to contest the 2001 election unsettled many party activists.[41] The defection to Labour of the Conservative MP for Grantham and Stamford, Quentin Davies, sparked arguments that MPs had no right to defect, but instead ought to resign if they could no longer support the party for which they were elected. This argument harks back to the similar hard questions of public duty and private conscience that was faced by many civil-war side-changers. 'Turncoat' continues to be used in a derogatory fashion by the tabloids; the *Daily Mail* denounced the MP John Bercow as one in 2009, despite Bercow having never left the Conservative Party.[42]

The mid-seventeenth-century conflicts familiarized a majority of the British and Irish peoples with the practice of side-changing and many of its conventions. For perhaps the first time, the dichotomy between public duty and private conscience was felt by many thousands. It was not just statesmen and conspirators who learned how to change sides. During the Second Dutch War of 1665–7 an estimated 3,000 English sailors defected to the Dutch.[43] Jonathan Scott has argued that the Whigs of the Exclusion Crisis and the Tories of the subsequent loyalist reaction were, with the exception of some hardliners, essentially the same people. In time, many simply changed sides.[44] This was political behaviour learned in the 1640s. In this way, Charles de Rémusat's observation of post-Waterloo France might be applied equally to post-Restoration England: 'the public that scoffs at the people who have served strikingly different governments forgets that it has done the same itself'.[45]

[41] *The Independent*, 25 March 2011; http://news.bbc.co.uk/1/hi/uk_politics/571883.stm (accessed 20 September 2011).

[42] http://www.dailymail.co.uk/news/article-1186975/Browns-candidate-Speaker-Right-wing-turncoat-hated-Tory-MPs.html (accessed 20 September 2011).

[43] Peter Linebaugh and Marcus Rediker, *The Many Headed Hydra: The Hidden History of the Revolutionary Atlantic* (2000), 146.

[44] Tim Harris, '"Venerating the Honesty of a Tinker": The King's Friends and the Battle for the Allegiance of the Common People in Restoration England', in Tim Harris (ed.), *The Politics of the Excluded, c.1500–1850* (Basingstoke, 2001), 217; Jonathan Scott, *Algernon Sidney and the Restoration Crisis, 1677–1683* (Cambridge, 1991), 47–8.

[45] Alan B. Spitzer, 'Malicious Memories: Restoration Politics and a Prosopography of Turncoats', *French Historical Studies*, 24 (2001), 59.

APPENDIX 1

Defectors from the House of Commons at Westminster.

Name of member	Constituency	Month of exclusion
Sir George Goring	Portsmouth	August 1642
Sir Hugh Cholmley	Scarborough	April 1643
Sir William Ogle	Winchester	June 1643
Edmund Waller	St Ives	July 1643
Sir Henry Anderson	Newcastle-upon-Tyne	September 1643
Sir Alexander Carew	Cornwall	September 1643
William Constantine	Poole	September 1643
Sir John Harrison	Lancaster	September 1643
Sir John Hotham	Beverley	September 1643
John Hotham	Scarborough	September 1643
Sir Guy Palmes	Rutland	September 1643
John Dutton	Gloucestershire	January 1644
Edward Bagshaw	Southwark	January 1644
Sir Alexander Denton	Buckingham	January 1644
John Fettiplace	Berkshire	January 1644
William Glanvile	Camelford	January 1644
Sir Gerard Napper	Melcombe Regis	January 1644
Sir George Stonehouse	Abingdon	January 1644
Michael Wharton	Beverley	January 1644
William Bassett	Bath	February 1644
Henry Brett	Gloucester	February 1644
Sir Thomas Eversfield	Hastings	February 1644
Sir Thomas Peyton	Sandwich	February 1644
Sir Edward Littleton	Staffordshire	March 1644
Sir Henry Bellingham	Westmorland	October 1645
Sir John Price	Montgomeryshire	October 1645
John George	Cirencester	November 1646

APPENDIX 2

MP defectors from the king.

Name of member	Constituency	Month of defection
Sir Edward Dering	Kent	February 1644
Sir Anthony Ashley Cooper	Downton	February 1644
Sir Gerard Napper	Melcombe Regis	March 1644
Sir John Price	Montgomeryshire	October 1644
Sir John Fenwick	Northumberland	c. December 1644
Piers Edgecumbe	Camelford	March 1646
Richard Edgecumbe	Newport	March 1646
William Coryton	Launceston	March 1646
William Scawen	St Germans	March 1646
Sir Hugh Owen	Pembroke	Unclear

APPENDIX 3

Officer defectors from the army of the earl of Essex, 1642–45.[1]

Officer	Rank[*2]	Date of defection
Sir Faithful Fortescue	Lt-Colonel in earl of Peterborough's foot and captain of 74th troop of horse*	October 1642[3]
John van der Gerish	Lieutenant in Fortescue's horse*	October 1642[4]
John Balston	Lieutenant in earl of Peterborough's foot	October 1642[5]
Humphrey Brookbank	Lieutenant in Lord Willoughby's troop of horse	October 1642[6]
William St Leger	Captain of horse*	c.1642–3[7]
Bartholomew Elliot	Lieutenant in Charles Essex's foot	c.1642–3[8]
Joseph Wagstaffe	Lt-Colonel in John Hampden's foot	January 1643[9]
Robert Kirle	Captain of 68th troop of horse	February 1643[10]
Sir Hugh Cholmley	Colonel of foot	March 1643[11]
Lancelot Alured	Lt-Colonel in Sir Henry Cholmley's foot	March 1643[12]
Henry, Lord Mordaunt	Captain of horse	April 1643[13]
John Urry	Sergeant-major of horse to Sir William Balfour*	June 1643[14]
Horatio Carey	Sergeant-major of horse to Sir William Waller*	June 1643[15]
John Hotham	Lieutenant-General and captain of 30th troop of horse	June 1643[16]
William Pretty	Captain of 17th troop of horse	July 1643[17]
William, Earl of Bedford	General of horse, resigned Feb 1643	August 1643[18]
William Lower	Sergeant-Major in Thomas Ballard's foot*	October 1643[19]
Owen Parry	Sergeant-Major in Lord Wharton's foot*	1643[20]
Carlo Fantom	Lieutenant then captain in Arthur Goodwin's horse	1643[21]
Humphrey Mathews	Lt-Colonel of foot*	1643[22]
Arnold Haward	Lieutenant in Alexander Pym's horse	c.1643–4[23]
Sir Richard Grenville	Lt-General of horse to Sir William Waller*	March 1644[24]
Francis Dowett	Captain of 19th troop of horse*	April 1645[25]

1 BL, E117(3), *The List of the Army Raised under the Command of his Excellency, Robert Earle of Essex and Ewe, Viscount Hereford, Lord Ferrers of Chartley, Bourcheir and Lovaine: appointed Captaine Generall of the Army* (1642).

2 Entries marked with an asterisk denote those known to have served in Ireland, or to have enlisted in Lord Wharton's projected expedition of June 1642: BL, 669.f.6[31], *A List of the Field Officers chosen and appointed for the Irish Expedition, by the Committee at Guild-hall, London, for the Regiments of 5000 foot and 500 horse*, 11 June (1642).

3 Basil Morgan, 'Sir Faithful Fortescue (b. in or before 1581, d. 1666), royalist army officer', *ODNB*.

4 Peter Young, *Edgehill, 1642: The Campaign and the Battle* (Moreton-in-Marsh, 1998), 106, 273.

5 Young, *Edgehill, 152, 238;* Newman, 15.

6 BL, E252(16), *Perfect Diurnall of Some Passages in Parliament*, no. 25, 8–15 January (1644), 199; John Rushworth, *Historical Collections of Private Passages of State*, 8 vols. (1721), v, 297.

7 Bodl., MS Clarendon 21, fo. 120; Newman, 324.

8 Charles Carlton, *Going to the Wars: The Experience of the British Civil Wars, 1638–1651* (1992), 198; G. N. Godwin, *The Civil War in Hampshire, 1642–1645* (1904), 130.

9 *Portland MS*, 85; BL, E244(30), *Mercurius Aulicus*, 1st week, 1–7 January (Oxford, 1643), 6; Newman, 394; C. H. Firth, rev. Sean Kelsey, 'Sir Joseph Wagstaffe (bap. 1611?, d. 1666/7), royalist army officer', *ODNB*.

10 Newman, 219; BL, E246(35), *A Copy of a Letter Writ from Serjeant Major Kirle, to a Friend in Windsor* (1643).

11 Cholmley held his commission directly from Essex: Sir Hugh Cholmley, *The Memoirs and Memorials of Sir Hugh Cholmley of Whitby 1600–1657*, ed. Jack Binns (*YASRS*, 153, 2000), 140.

12 *Bouverie MS*, HMC, 10th Report, Appendix VI (1887), 90; BL, TT E95(9), *A True and Exact Relation of all the Proceedings of Sir Hugh Cholmleys Revolt*, 7 April (1643), 1.

13 BL, E99(22), *Mercurius Aulicus*, 15th week, 9–16 April (Oxford, 1643), 187; Newman, 262; Victor Stater, 'Henry Mordaunt, 2nd earl of Peterborough (bap. 1623, d. 1697), nobleman', *ODNB*.

14 Edward M. Furgol, 'Sir John Urry (d. 1650), army officer', *ODNB*.

15 Newman, 64.

16 Hotham held his captain's commission directly from Essex: David Scott, 'John Hotham (1610–1645), parliamentarian army officer', *ODNB*.

17 Young, *Edgehill*, 152; Newman, 305.

18 Victor Stater, 'William Russell, first duke of Bedford (1616–1700), politician', *ODNB*.

19 Newman, 238; David Kathman, 'Sir William Lower (c.1610–1662), playwright and translator', *ODNB*.

20 Young, *Edgehill*, 240; Newman, 287.

21 John Aubrey, *Aubrey's Brief Lives*, ed. Oliver Lawson Dick (Harmondsworth, 1949), 193–4; TNA, SP 28/10/137–9; John Wilson (ed.), *Buckinghamshire Contributions for Ireland 1642 and Richard Grenville's Military Accounts 1642–1645* (Buckinghamshire Record Society, 21, 1983), 115–20, 129.

22 Ron Slack, *Man at War: John Gell in his Troubled Time* (Nottingham, 1997), 73; Norman Tucker, *Royalist Officers of North Wales 1642–1660: A Biographical List* (Denbigh, 1961), 43.

23 Carlton, *Going to the Wars*, 198; Richard W. Cotton, *Barnstaple and the Northern Part of Devon in the Great Civil War* (1889), 273–7.

24 Ian Roy, 'Sir Richard Grenville, baronet (bap. 1600, d. 1659), royalist army officer', *ODNB*.

25 *CSPD 1644–5*, 362, 394.

Bibliography

The place of publication of printed works is London unless otherwise noted.

MANUSCRIPTS

Beinecke Rare Book and Manuscript Library, Yale University
Osborn files 10467: Declaration of the marquis of Montrose
Osborn shelves b101: The commonplace book of Ralph Assheton of Kirkby Grange
Osborn shelves b168: Short memorials of Thomas, 3rd baron Fairfax
Osborn shelves b169: Henry Guthrie, bishop of Dunkeld's history of the Scottish civil war
Osborn shelves fb87: Memoirs of Sir Philip Warwick
Osborn shelves fb94: The Pym correspondence
Osborn shelves fb155: The commonplace book of John Browne
Osborn shelves fb159: Miscellaneous parliamentary speeches and debates

Bodleian Library
MS Ashmole 840
MS Aubrey 8
MS Carte 6, 130, 224
MS Clarendon 21–27, 34, 46–47
MS Fairfax 30–37
MS Nalson 2, 3, 11, 13, 22
MS Tanner 56–64

British Library
Additional MS 10114: Parliamentary diary of John Harrington, 1646–1653
Additional MS 11692: Manuscripts presented by the Hon. P.P. Bouverie
Additional MS 15856: Copies of official documents during the reigns of Charles I and II, 1634–1658
Additional MS 15858: Original letters and correspondence of Sir Richard Browne and John Evelyn
Additional MS 18738: Autograph letters, 1433–1817
Additional MS 18979: Fairfax correspondence, 1625–1688
Additional MS 18980–1: Original letters, relating to the civil wars; addressed principally to Prince Rupert, 1642–1658
Additional MS 19399: Original letters, bills of privy seal, orders of Privy Council, and other documents, bearing the autograph signatures of royal and noble persons, principally of England
Additional MS 21417: Baynes correspondence
Additional MS 21506: Original letters and autographs of eminent persons, 1587–1835
Additional MS 28082: Army establishments, seventeenth and eighteenth centuries
Additional MS 28721: Miscellaneous papers
Additional MS 29747: Autograph letters
Additional MS 31116: Parliamentary journal of Lawrence Whitacre, 1642–1647
Additional MS 32096: State papers, historical documents, and official and private letters, 1086–1760, vol. 6.
Additional MS 34195: Collection of original letters, warrants and papers, 1576–1763
Additional MS 34274: Miscellaneous autograph letters

Additional MS 35297: John Syms's journal of the civil war, 1642–1649
Additional MS 36996: Fairfax papers, transcripts, 1645–1648
Additional MS 40883: Diary of Nehemiah Wallington, 1641–1643
Additional MS 44848: Copies of state papers, sixteenth and seventeenth centuries
Additional MS 46928–31: Egmont papers
Additional MS 62084: Pythouse papers, vol. IV
Additional MS 78205, Evelyn papers, vol. XXXVIII
Additional MS 78221, Evelyn papers, vol. LIV
Egerton MS 1048: Collection of historical and parliamentary papers, 1620–1660
Egerton MS 2146: Manuscripts and poems by Brian Fairfax
Egerton MS 2534: Official and private correspondence, 1560–1726, vol. II, 1650–1654
Egerton MS 2542: Nicholas papers
Egerton MS 2551: Royal warrants for creations of peers and baronets, appointments to offices, and grants of various kinds, 1654–1662
Egerton MS 2618: Historical letters and papers, 1556–1753
Egerton MS 2644–7: Correspondence of Sir Thomas Barrington
Egerton MS 2884: Sir Hugh Chomley's memoirs concerning the Hothams
Harleian MS 164–6: Parliamentary journal of Sir Simonds D'Ewes
Harleian MS 386: Collection of original letters concerning the D'Ewes family
Harleian MS 6851–2: Papers relating to the civil war, etc
Lansdowne MS 988: Bishop Kennet's collections, vol. LV
Sloane MS 1519: Original letters, 1574–1667
Stowe MS 184: Miscellaneous historical papers 1628–1653
Stowe MS 768: Extracts from newspapers 1643–1657

College of Arms, London
Curia Militaris: Records of the High Court of Chivalry, 1634–41

Devonshire Record Office, Exeter
Book 73/15, James White's chronicle
DD 36995, Order of city commissioners for the defence of Exeter, 1643
ECA, Book 64, Exeter city quarter sessions, 1642–1660
1392M/L: Seymour of Berry Pomeroy MS
1579A-0/17/36, Account of the loyalty of Totnes during the civil wars, 1664–1665

Durham University Library Archive
Mickleton–Spearman MS

East Riding of Yorkshire Record Office, Beverley
DDRI 43/8: Documents of the Bethell family of Rise Park

Folger Shakespeare Library, Washington D. C.
Bennet MS, X.d.483 (32)
V.a.216, 'A Brief Relation of the Life and Memoirs of John Lord Belasyse written and collected by his Secretary Joshua Moone'
V.b.2, Scudamore Collection, 1618–1657 (2), (6), (27)

Hull History Centre
C BRS/7: Papers relating to the Hothams and the civil wars
U DDCY: Cholmley MS
U DDHO: Hotham MS

U DDWB: Wickham-Boynton MS

Leicester, Leicestershire, and Rutland Record Office
DG21/275: Hazlerigg of Noseley MS

The National Archives, Kew
ASSI 45: Clerks of the assizes records, northern circuit
E121: Certificates for the same of crown lands
SP 16: State papers of the reign of Charles I
SP 19: Papers of the committee for advance of money
SP 22: Papers of the committee for plundered ministers
SP 23: Papers of the committee for compounding
SP 24: Papers of the committee for indemnity
SP 25: Council of State: books and accounts
SP 28: Commonwealth exchequer papers
SP 29: State papers of the reign of Charles II

Northumberland Collections Service, Woodhorn
(A) ZSW 6 and 7: Swinburne of Capheaton MS
SANT/ADM/4/1/2, Thorneton MS
SANT/BEQ/22/1/6: Transcript of Sir Thomas Glemham's letter of 2 February 1644

West Yorkshire Archive Service, Sheepscar
WYL 119/3, 5, 7: Bacon Frank of Campsall MS

West Yorkshire Archive Service, Wakefield
C469/1: Minutes of the parliamentarian council of war at Ripon, Knaresborough, York and
    Pontefract, 1647–1648.

PRINTED SOURCES

Newsletters
The contemporary tracts and newsbooks cited in the endnotes are too numerous
to be listed again here, but they were principally drawn from among the Burney
Collection, the Thomason Tracts, Early English Books Online, and the Civil War
Tracts at York Minster Library.

General
Adair, John, 'The Court Martial Papers of Sir William Waller's Army, 1644', *JSAHR* 44
    (1966), 205–26.
Aubrey, John, *Aubrey's Brief Lives*, ed. Oliver Lawson Dick (Harmondsworth, 1949).
Aubrey, John, *Brief Lives*, ed. Richard Barber (Woodbridge, 2004).
Bell, Robert (ed.), *The Fairfax Correspondence: Memorials of the Civil Wars*, 2 vols. (1849).
Bickley, Francis (ed.), *Report on the Manuscripts of the Late Reginald Rawdon Hastings*,
    HMC, 78, 4 vols. (1928–47).
Birch, T. (ed.), *A Collection of the State Papers of John Thurloe, esq.*, 7 vols. (1742).
Blundell, William, *Crosby Records: A Cavalier's Notebook Being Notes, Anecdotes & Observa-
    tions of William Blundell of Crosby, Lancashire, Esquire*, ed. T. Ellison Gibson (1880).
Bouverie MS, HMC, 10th Report, Appendix VI (1887).

Boyle, J. R. (ed.), *Memoirs of Master John Shawe, Sometime Vicar of Rotherham, Minister of St Mary's, Lecturer at Holy Trinity Church, and Master of the Charterhouse, at Kingston-upon-Hull. Written by himself in the year 1663–4* (Hull, 1882).

Braye MSS, 10th Report, Appendix VI (1887).

Bulstrode, Richard, *Memoirs and Reflections upon the Reign and Government of King Charles the Ist and K. Charles the II^d* (1721).

Burnet, Gilbert, *Bishop Burnet's History of his Own Time*, ed. Martin Joseph Routh, 6 vols. (2nd edn., Oxford, 1833).

Burton, Thomas, *The Diary of Thomas Burton, esq., Member in the Parliaments of Oliver and Richard Cromwell, from 1656 to 1659*, ed. John Towill Rutt, 4 vols. (1828).

Calendar of State Papers Domestic, 1641–1662.

Calendar of the Proceedings of the Committee for Advance of Money, 1642–1656, ed. Mary Anne Everett Green, 3 vols. (1888).

Calendar of the Proceedings of the Committee for Compounding (Domestic), 1643–1660, ed. Mary Anne Everett Green, 5 vols. (1889–92).

Carlyle, Thomas (ed.), *Oliver Cromwell's Letters and Speeches: With Elucidations*, 3 vols. (1857).

Carr, Ivor, and Atherton, Ian (eds.), *The Civil War in Staffordshire in the Spring of 1646: Sir William Brereton's Letter Book, April–May 1646* (Collections for a History of Staffordshire, 4th series, 21, 2007).

Carte, Thomas (ed.), *A Collection of Original Letters and Papers Concerning the Affairs of England from the Year 1641 to 1660. Found among the Duke of Ormonde's Papers*, 2 vols. (1739).

Cartwright, J. J. (ed.), 'Papers Relating to the Delinquency of Lord Savile, 1642–1646', *The Camden Miscellany, vol. 8* (Camden Society, 2nd series, 31, 1883).

Cary, Henry (ed.), *Memorials of the Great Civil War in England from 1646 to 1652*, 2 vols. (1842).

Cavendish, Margaret, duchess of Newcastle, *The Life of the Thrice Noble, High and Puissant Prince William Cavendishe, Duke, Marquess and Earl of Newcastle* (1667).

Cavendish, Margaret, duchess of Newcastle, *The Life of William Cavendish, Duke of Newcastle to which is added the true relation of my birth breeding and life by Margaret, Duchess of Newcastle* ed. C. H. Firth (1906).

Chadwyck Healey, Charles E. H. (ed.), *Bellum Civile: Hopton's Narrative of his Campaign in the West (1642–1644) and other papers* (Somerset Record Society, 18, 1902).

Cholmley, Sir Hugh, *The Memoirs and Memorials of Sir Hugh Cholmley of Whitby, 1600–1657*, ed. Jack Binns (YASRS, 153, 2000).

Clay, J. W. (ed.), *Abstracts of Yorkshire Wills* (YASRS, 9, 1890).

Cowper MS, HMC, 12th Report, Appendix, Part II (1888), vol. 2.

Cust, Richard P. and Hopper, Andrew J. (eds.), *Cases in the High Court of Chivalry, 1634–40* (Publications of the Harleian Society, new series, 18, 2006).

Day, W. G. (ed.), *The Pepys Ballads*, 5 vols. (Cambridge, 1987).

Denbigh MS, HMC, 4th Report, Part I, Report and Appendix (1874).

Dugdale, Sir William, *The Visitation of the County of Yorke* (Surtees Society, 36, 1859).

Dyfnallt Owen, G. (ed.), *Report on the Manuscripts of the Right Honourable Viscount De L'Isle, V.C.*, HMC 77, Volume VI, Sidney Papers, 1626–1698 (1966).

Earl de la Warr MS, HMC, 4th Report, Part I, Report and Appendix (1874).

Firth, C. H. (ed.), *The Clarke Papers*, 4 vols. (Camden Society, new series, 49, 54, 61, 62, 1891–1901).

Firth, C. H. and Rait, R. S. (eds.), *Acts and Ordinances of the Interregnum, 1642–1660*, 3 vols. (1911).

Green, Mary Anne Everett (ed.), *The Letters of Queen Henrietta Maria* (1857).

Hackett, John, *Scrinia Reserata: A Memorial Offered to the Great Deservings of John Williams, D.D.* (1692).

Hall, James, (ed.), *Memorials of the Civil War in Cheshire and the Adjacent Counties by Thomas Malbon of Nantwich, gent., and Providence Improved by Edward Burghall, Vicar of Acton, near Nantwich* (Lancashire and Cheshire Record Society, 19, 1889).

Hamper, William (ed.), *The Life, Diary and Correspondence of Sir William Dugdale* (1827).

Heath, James, *A Chronicle of the Late Intestine War in the Three Kingdoms* (2nd edn., 1676).

Hill, P. R. and Watkinson, J. M. (eds.), *Major Sanderson's War: Diary of a Parliamentarian Cavalry Officer* (Stroud, 2008).

Hinds, A. B. (ed.), *Calendar of State Papers Venetian, 1642–1652*, 3 vols. (1925–7).

Hodgson, John, *The Autobiography of Captain John Hodgson of Coley Hall, near Halifax*, ed. John Horsfall Turner (Brighouse, 1882).

Holmes, Clive, *The Eastern Association in the English Civil War* (Cambridge, 1974).

Holmes, Clive, *Seventeenth-Century Lincolnshire* (Lincoln, 1980).

Hope, E. (ed.), *A Puritan Parish Clerk: A Commentary on Current Events made in the Registers of S. Mary's Church, Beverley, by Nicholas Pearson, parish clerk 1636–1653* (Beverley, n.d.).

Hopper, Andrew (ed.), *The Papers of the Hothams, Governors of Hull during the Civil War* (Camden Society, 5th series, 39, 2011).

House of Lords MS, HMC, 4th Report, Part 1, Report and Appendix (1874).

House of Lords MS, HMC, 5th Report, Appendix (1876).

Hutchinson, Lucy, *Memoirs of the Life of Colonel Hutchinson*, ed. N. H. Keeble (1995).

Hyde, Edward, earl of Clarendon, *The History of the Rebellion and Civil Wars in England*, 3 vols. (Oxford, 1717).

Hyde, Edward, earl of Clarendon, *State Papers collected by Edward, Earl of Clarendon*, 2 vols. (Oxford, 1767–73).

Hyde, Edward, earl of Clarendon, *The History of the Rebellion and Civil Wars in England Begun in the Year 1641*, ed. William Dunn Macray, 6 vols. (Oxford, 1888).

Johnson, George William (ed.), *The Fairfax Correspondence: Memoirs of the Reign of Charles I* (1848).

Josselin, Ralph, *The Diary of Ralph Josselin, 1616–1683*, ed. Alan Macfarlane (Records of Social and Economic History, new series, 3, Oxford, 1976).

Journals of the House of Commons.

Journals of the House of Lords.

Juxon, Thomas, *The Journal of Thomas Juxon 1644–1647*, ed. Keith Lindley and David Scott (Camden Society, 5th series, 13, 1999).

Larkin, J. F. (ed.), *Stuart Royal Proclamations. Volume II. Royal Proclamations of King Charles I, 1625–1646* (Oxford, 1983).

Lister, Joseph, *The Autobiography of Joseph Lister of Bradford in Yorkshire*, ed. Thomas Wright (1842).

Lomas, S. C. (ed.), *Leyborne-Popham MS*, HMC 51 (1899).

Ludlow, Edmund, *The Memoirs of Edmund Ludlow, Lieutenant-General of the Horse in the Army of the Commonwealth of England, 1625–1672*, ed. C. H. Firth, 2 vols. (Oxford, 1894).

Manchester MS, HMC, 8th Report, Appendix, Part II (1881).

May, Thomas, *The History of the Parliament of England which began Nov. 3 M.DC.XL* (1812).

Morley, Henry (ed.), *The King and the Commons. Cavalier and Puritan Song* (1868).

Newcome, Henry, *The Autobiography of Henry Newcome M.A.*, ed. Richard Parkinson, 2 vols. (Chetham Society, 26 and 27, 1852).

The Parliamentary or Constitutional History of England, Being a faithful account of all the most remarkable transactions in Parliament from the earliest times to the Restoration of King Charles II, by several hands, 24 vols. (1751–1761).

Portland MS, HMC, 29, 13th Report, Appendix, Part 1 (1891), vol. 1.

Philip, I. G. (ed.), *The Journal of Sir Samuel Luke*, 3 vols. (Oxfordshire Record Society, 29–33, 1947–1953).

Powell, J. R. and Timings, E. K. (eds.), *Documents Relating to the Civil War, 1642–1648* (Navy Records Society, 105, 1963).

Poyntz, Sydnam, *The Relation of Sydnam Poyntz, 1624–1636*, ed. A. T. S. Goodrick (Camden Society, 3rd series, 14, 1908).

Raine, James (ed.), *Depositions from the Castle of York Relating to Offences Committed in the Northern Counties in the Seventeenth Century* (Surtees Society, 40, 1861).

Round MS, HMC 14th Report, Appendix, Part IX (1895).

Rous, John, *The Diary of John Rous, Incumbent of Santon Downham, Suffolk, from 1625 to 1642*, ed. Mary Anne Everett Green (Camden Society, 66, 1856).

Rushworth, John, *Historical Collections of Private Passages of State*, 8 vols. (1721).

Shaw, John, 'The Life of Master John Shaw', in *Yorkshire Diaries and Autobiographies in the Seventeenth and Eighteenth Centuries*, ed. Charles Jackson (Surtees Society, 65, 1877).

Slingsby, Sir Henry, *The Original Memoirs Written during the Great Civil War being the Life of Sir Henry Slingsby and Memoirs of Captain Hodgson, with notes*, ed. Sir Walter Scott (Edinburgh, 1806).

Slingsby, Sir Henry, *The Diary of Sir Henry Slingsby of Scriven, Bart.*, ed. Daniel Parsons (1836).

Spalding, Ruth (ed.), *Contemporaries of Bulstrode Whitelocke, 1605–1675* (Records of Social and Economic History, new series, 14, Oxford, 1990).

Sutherland MS, HMC, 5th Report, Appendix (1876).

Symonds, Richard, *Richard Symonds's Diary of the Marches of the Royal Army*, ed. Charles Edward Long and Ian Roy (Cambridge, 1997).

Thomas, P. W. (ed.), *The English Revolution III. Newsbooks I. Oxford Royalist*, 4 vols. (1971).

Tibbut, H. G. (ed.), *The Letter Books of Sir Samuel Luke, 1644–1645* (Publications of the Bedfordshire Historical Records Society, 42, 1963).

Trevelyan, Sir W. C., and Trevelyan, Sir C. E. (eds.), *Trevelyan Papers, Part III* (Camden Society, 1st series, 105, 1872).

Vicars, John, *Jehovah-Jireh: God in the Mount or England's Parliamentarie-Chronicle* (1644).

Walker, Sir Edward, *Historical Discourses Upon Several Occasions* (1705).

Warwick, Sir Philip, *Memoires of the Reign of King Charles I with a Continuation to the Happy Restauration of King Charles II* (1701).

Webb, J. and T. W., *Memorials of the Civil War between Charles I and the Parliament of England as it affected Herefordshire and the Adjacent Counties*, 2 vols. (1879).

Whitelock, Bulstrode, *Memorials of English Affairs from the Beginning of the Reign of Charles I to the Happy Restoration of King Charles II*, 4 vols. (Oxford, 1853).

Whitelocke, Bulstrode, *The Diary of Bulstrode Whitelocke, 1605–1675*, ed. Ruth Spalding (Records of Social and Economic History, new series, 13, Oxford, 1990).

Wildridge, Thomas Tindal (ed.), *The Hull Letters: Documents from the Hull Records, 1625–1646* (Hull, 1886).

Wilson, John (ed.), *Buckinghamshire Contributions for Ireland 1642 and Richard Grenville's Military Accounts 1642–1645* (Buckinghamshire Record Society, 21, 1983).

PRINTED SECONDARY WORKS

Books and edited collections

Adair, John, *By the Sword Divided: Eyewitnesses of the English Civil War* (1983).

Adamson, John, *The Noble Revolt: The Overthrow of Charles I* (2007).

Adamson, John (ed.), *The English Civil War: Conflict and Contexts, 1640–1649* (Basingstoke, 2009).

Amussen, Susan, and Kishlansky, Mark (eds.), *Political Culture and Cultural Politics in Early Modern England: Essays presented to David Underdown* (Manchester, 1995).

Andriette, Eugene A., *Devon and Exeter in the Civil War* (Newton Abbot, 1971).

Appleby, David J., *Black Bartholomew's Day: Preaching, Polemic and Restoration Nonconformity* (Manchester, 2007).

Ashton, Robert, *The English Civil War: Conservatism and Revolution, 1603–1649* (2nd edn., 1989).

Ashton, Robert, *Counter-Revolution: The Second Civil War and its Origins, 1646–8* (1994).

Atkinson, D. H., *Ralph Thoresby, the Topographer: His Town and Times*, 2 vols. (Leeds, 1885).

Barratt, John, *Sieges of the English Civil Wars* (Barnsley, 2009).

Bayley, A. R., *The Great Civil War in Dorset, 1642–1660* (Taunton, 1910).

Beaver, Daniel C., *Hunting and the Politics of Violence before the English Civil War* (Cambridge, 2008).

Bedford, Ronald, Davis, Lloyd, and Kelly, Philippa (eds.), *Early Modern Autobiography: Theories, Genres, Practices* (Ann Arbor, 2006).

Bennett, Martyn, *The Civil Wars in Britain and Ireland, 1638–1651* (Oxford, 1997).

Binns, Jack, 'A Place of Great Importance': Scarborough in the Civil Wars* (Preston, 1996).

Binns, Jack, *Yorkshire in the Civil Wars: Origins, Impact and Outcome* (Pickering, 2004).

Braddick, Michael, *God's Fury, England's Fire: A New History of the English Civil Wars* (2008).

Brunton, Douglas, and Pennington, Donald H., *Members of the Long Parliament* (2nd edn., 1968).

Carlton, Charles, *Going to the Wars: The Experience of the British Civil Wars, 1638–1651* (1994).

Carpenter, Stanley D. M., *Military Leadership in the British Civil Wars, 1642–1651: 'The Genius of this Age'* (2005).

Carpenter, Stanley D. M. (ed.), *The English Civil War* (Aldershot, 2007).

Christie, William Dougal, *A Life of Anthony Ashley Cooper, First Earl of Shaftesbury, 1621–1683*, 2 vols. (1871).

Cliffe, J. T., *The Yorkshire Gentry from the Reformation to the Civil War* (1969).

Cliffe, J. T., *Puritans in Conflict: the Puritan Gentry during and after the Civil Wars* (1988).

Collinson, Patrick, *Elizabethan Essays* (1994).

Cope, Joseph, *England and the 1641 Irish Rebellion* (Woodbridge, 2009).

Cotton, Richard W., *Barnstaple and the Northern Part of Devonshire during the Great Civil War, 1642–1646* (1889).

Coward, Barry (ed.), *A Companion to Stuart Britain* (Oxford, 2003).

Cromartie, Alan, *The Constitutionalist Revolution: An Essay on the History of England, 1450–1642* (Cambridge, 2006).

Cust, Richard P., *Charles I: A Political Life* (2005).

Cust, Richard P., and Hughes, Ann (eds.), *Conflict in Early Stuart England: Studies in Religion and Politics 1603–1642* (1989).

Dalton, C., *History of the Wrays of Glentworth*, 2 vols. (1880).

Denton, Barry, *Only in Heaven: The Life and Campaigns of Sir Arthur Hesilrige, 1601–1661* (Sheffield, 1997).

Donagan, Barbara, *War in England, 1642–1649* (Oxford, 2008).

Dunn, Diana (ed.), *War and Society in Medieval and Early Modern Britain* (Liverpool, 2000).

Eales, Jacqueline, *Puritans and Roundheads: The Harleys of Brampton Bryan and the Outbreak of the English Civil War* (Cambridge, 1990).

Edwards, David, Lenihan, Pádraig, and Tait, Clodagh (eds.), *Age of Atrocity: Violence and Political Conflict in Early Modern Ireland* (Dublin, 2007).

Ellis, John, *'To Walk in the Dark': Military Intelligence during the English Civil War, 1642–1646* (Stroud, 2011).

English, Barbara, *The Great Landowners of East Yorkshire, 1530–1910* (Hemel Hempstead, 1990).

Everitt, Alan, *The Community of Kent and the Great Rebellion, 1640–1660* (Leicester, 1966).

Everitt, Alan, *The Local Community and the Great Rebellion* (Historical Association Pamphlet, 70, 1969).

Firth, Charles Harding, *The House of Lords during the Civil War* (1910).

Firth, Charles Harding, and Davies, Godfrey, *The Regimental History of Cromwell's Army*, 2 vols. (Oxford, 1940).

Fissel, Mark Charles, *The Bishops' Wars: Charles I's Campaigns against Scotland, 1638–1640* (Cambridge, 1994).

Fletcher, Anthony, *The Outbreak of the English Civil War* (1981).

Foard, Glenn, *Naseby: The Decisive Campaign* (2nd edn., Barnsley, 2004).

Gardiner, Samuel R., *A History of England from the Accession of James I to the Outbreak of the Civil War, 1603–1642*, 10 vols. (1904).

Gardiner, Samuel R., *History of the Great Civil War, 1642–1649*, 4 vols. (1987).

Gent, Thomas, *Gent's History of Hull, Reprinted in Fac-simile of the Original of 1735* (Hull, 1869).

Gentles, Ian, *The New Model Army in England, Ireland and Scotland, 1645–1653* (Oxford, 1992).

Gentles, Ian, *The English Revolution and the Wars in the Three Kingdoms, 1638–1652* (Harlow, 2007).

Gentles, Ian, Morrill, John, and Worden, Blair (eds.), *Soldiers, Writers and Statesmen of the English Revolution* (Cambridge, 1998).

Glaser, Brigitte, *The Creation of the Self in Autobiographical Forms of Writing in Seventeenth-Century England: Subjectivity and Self-fashioning in Memoirs, Diaries, and Letters* (Heidelberg, 1999).

Godwin, G. N., *The Civil War in Hampshire (1642–1645) and the Story of Basing House* (1904).

Godwin, William, *History of the Commonwealth of England. From its Commencement, to the Restoration of Charles the Second*, 4 vols. (1824–8).

Grainge, William, *The Battles and Battlefields of Yorkshire* (York, 1854).

Granville, Roger, *The King's General in the West: The Life of Sir Richard Granville, Bart., 1600–1659* (1908).

Gratton, J. M., *The Parliamentarian and Royalist War Effort in Lancashire 1642–1651* (Chetham Society, 3rd series, 48, 2010).

Griffin, Margaret, *Regulating Religion and Morality in the King's Armies, 1639–1646* (Leiden, 2004).

Haigh, Christopher (ed.), *The English Reformation Revised* (Cambridge, 1987).

Hardacre, Paul, N. *The Royalists during the Puritan Revolution* (The Hague, 1956).

Harris, Tim (ed.), *The Politics of the Excluded, c.1500–1850* (Basingstoke, 2001).

Hatfield, C. W., *Historical Notices of Doncaster*, 3rd series (Doncaster, 1870).

Heal, Felicity, and Holmes, Clive, *The Gentry in England and Wales, 1500–1700* (Basingstoke, 1994).

Heath-Agnew, E., *Roundhead to Royalist: A Biography of Colonel John Birch, 1615–1681* (Hereford, 1977).

Henning, Basil Duke (ed.), *The House of Commons 1660–1690*, 3 vols. (1983).

Hibbard, Caroline, *Charles I and the Popish Plot* (Chapel Hill, 1983).

Hill, Christopher, *Puritanism and Revolution: Studies in Interpretation of the English Revolution of the Seventeenth Century* (1958).

Hill, Christopher, *The English Bible and the Seventeenth-Century Revolution* (1993).

Hirst, Derek, and Strier, Richard (eds.), *Writing and Political Engagement in Seventeenth-Century England* (Cambridge, 1999).

Holmes, Clive, *The Eastern Association in the English Civil War* (Cambridge, 1974).

Holmes, Clive, *Seventeenth-Century Lincolnshire* (Lincoln, 1980).

Hopper, Andrew, *'Black Tom': Sir Thomas Fairfax and the English Revolution* (Manchester, 2007).

Howes, Audrey, and Foreman, Martin, *Town and Gun: The 17th-Century Defences of Hull* (Hull, 1999).

Hughes, Ann, *Politics, Society and Civil War in Warwickshire, 1620–1660* (Cambridge, 1987).

Hughes, Ann, *The Causes of the English Civil War* (2nd edn., Basingstoke, 1998).

Hughes, Ann, *Gangraena and the Struggle for the English Revolution* (Oxford, 2004).

Hughes, Ann, *Gender and the English Revolution* (2011).

Huntley, Lockwood, *The Fairfaxes of Denton and Nun Appleton* (York, 1906).

Hutton, Ronald, *The Royalist War Effort, 1642–6* (2nd edn., 1999).

James, Mervyn, *English Politics and the Concept of Honour, 1485–1642* (P&P, supplement, 3, 1978).

Jennings, Stuart B., *'These Uncertaine Tymes': Newark and the Civilian Experience of the Civil Wars 1640–1660* (Nottingham, 2009).

Johnson, David, *Adwalton Moor, 1643: The Battle that Changed a War* (Pickering, 2003).

Jones, Colin, Newitt, Malyn, and Roberts, Stephen (eds.), *Politics and People in Revolutionary England: Essays in Honour of Ivan Roots* (Oxford, 1986).

Jones, David Martin, *Conscience and Allegiance in Seventeenth-Century England: The Political Significance of Oaths and Engagements* (New York, 1999).

Jones, Phil, *The Siege of Colchester, 1648* (Stroud, 2003).

Kane, Brendan, *The Politics and Culture of Honour in Britain and Ireland, 1541–1641* (Cambridge, 2010).

Keeler, Mary Frear, *The Long Parliament, 1640–1641: A Biographical Study of its Members* (Philadelphia, 1954).

Kenyon, John and Ohlmeyer, Jane (eds.), *The Civil Wars: A Military History of England, Scotland and Ireland, 1638–1660* (Oxford, 2002).

Knight, Jeremy, *Civil War & Restoration in Monmouthshire* (Logaston, 2005).

Lake, Peter, and Pincus, Steve (eds.), *The Politics of the Public Sphere in Early Modern England* (Manchester, 2007).

Laurence, Anne, *Parliamentary Army Chaplains, 1642–1651* (Woodbridge, 1990).

Leach, Arthur Leonard, *The History of the Civil War (1642–1649) in Pembrokeshire and on its Borders* (1937).

Lindley, Keith, *Fenland Riots and the English Revolution* (1982).

Linebaugh, Peter and Rediker, Marcus, *The Many Headed Hydra: The Hidden History of the Revolutionary Atlantic* (2000).

Little, Patrick, and Smith, David L., *Parliaments and Politics during the Cromwellian Protectorate* (Cambridge, 2000).

Lynch, John, *For King & Parliament: Bristol in the Civil Wars* (Stroud, 1999).

Manning, Brian, *The English People and the English Revolution* (2nd edn., 1991).

Manning, Roger B., *Swordsmen: The Martial Ethos in the Three Kingdoms* (Oxford, 2003).

Maurice, Sir Frederick, *The Adventures of Edward Wogan* (1945).

McClendon, Muriel C., Ward, Joseph P., and MacDonald, Michael (eds.), *Protestant Identities: Religion, Society and Self-fashioning in Post-Reformation England* (Stanford, 1999).

McElligott, Jason, *Royalism, Print and Censorship in Revolutionary England* (Woodbridge, 2007).

McElligott, Jason, and Smith, David L. (eds.), *Royalists and Royalism during the English Civil Wars* (Cambridge, 2007).

McElligott, Jason, and Smith, David L. (eds.), *Royalists and Royalism during the Interregnum* (Manchester, 2010).

Memegalos, Florene S., *George Goring (1608–1657): Caroline Courtier and Royalist General* (Aldershot, 2007).

Mendelson, S. H. and Crawford, Patricia, *Women in Early Modern England, 1550–1720* (Oxford, 1998).

Merritt, Julia F. (ed.), *The Political World of Thomas Wentworth, Earl of Strafford, 1621–1641* (Cambridge, 1996).

Miller, Amos C., *Sir Richard Grenville of the Civil War* (1979).

Morrill, John (ed.), *Reactions to the English Civil War, 1642–1649* (Basingstoke, 1982).

Morrill, John, *The Nature of the English Revolution* (Harlow, 1993).

Morrill, John, *Revolt in the Provinces: The People of England and the Tragedies of War, 1630–1648* (2nd edn., Harlow, 1999).

Morrill, John, Slack, Paul, and Woolf, Daniel (eds.), *Public Duty and Private Conscience in Seventeenth-Century England* (Oxford, 1993).

Newman, P. R., *Royalist Officers in England and Wales: A Biographical Dictionary, 1642–1660* (New York, 1981).

Newman, P. R., *The Old Service: Royalist Regimental Colonels and the Civil War, 1642–46* (Manchester, 1993).

Ollard, Richard, *This War Without An Enemy: A History of the English Civil Wars* (1976).

Ó Siochrú, Micheàl, *God's Executioner: Oliver Cromwell and the Conquest of Ireland* (2008).

Parker, Geoffrey (ed.), *The Thirty Years War*, 2nd edn. (1997).

Parker, Geoffrey, *Empire, War and Faith in Early Modern Europe* (2002)

Peacey, Jason, *Politicians and Pamphleteers: Propaganda during the English Civil Wars and Interregnum* (Aldershot, 2004).

Powell, J. R., *The Navy in the English Civil War* (1962).

Prior, Charles W. A., and Burgess, Glenn (eds.), *England's Wars of Religion, Revisited* (Farnham, 2011).

Raymond, Joad, *The Invention of the Newspaper: English Newsbooks 1641–1649* (Oxford, 1996).

Raymond, Joad, *Pamphlets and Pamphleteering in Early Modern Britain* (Cambridge, 2003).

Reckitt, Basil N., *Charles the First and Hull, 1639–1645* (2nd edn., Howden, 1988).

Richardson, R. C. (ed.), *Town and Countryside in the English Revolution* (Manchester, 1992).

Richardson, R. C. (ed.), *The English Civil Wars: Local Aspects* (Stroud, 1997).

Roebuck, Peter, *Yorkshire Baronets 1640–1760: Families, Estates and Fortunes* (Oxford, 1980).

Roots, Ivan, *The Great Rebellion, 1642–1660* (1966).

Russell, Conrad (ed.), *The Origins of the English Civil War* (Basingstoke, 1973).

Russell, Conrad, *The Fall of the British Monarchies, 1637–1642* (Oxford, 1991).

Saltmarshe, Philip, *History and Chartulary of the Hothams of Scorborough in the East Riding of Yorkshire, 1100–1700* (York, 1914).

Scatcherd, Norrison, *The History of Morley, in the Parish of Batley, and West-Riding of Yorkshire* (Leeds, 1830).

Scott, Christopher L., Turton, Alan, and Gruber von Arni, Eric, *Edgehill: The Battle Reinterpreted* (Barnsley, 2004).

Scott, David, *Politics and War in the Three Stuart Kingdoms, 1637–49* (Basingstoke, 2004).

Scott, Jonathan, *Algernon Sidney and the Restoration Crisis, 1677–1683* (Cambridge, 1991).

Seaver, Paul S., *Wallington's World: A Puritan Artisan in Seventeenth-Century London* (Stanford, 1985).

Shagan, Ethan, *Popular Politics and the English Reformation* (Cambridge, 2003).

Sharpe, Kevin, and Lake, Peter (eds.), *Culture and Politics in Early Stuart England* (1994).

Sharpe, Kevin, and Zwicker, Steven N. (eds.), *Writing Lives: Biography and Textuality, Identity and Representation in Early Modern England* (Oxford, 2008).

Sheard, Michael (ed.), *Records of the Parish of Batley in the County of York* (Worksop, 1894).

Simpson, J. A. and Weiner, E. S. C. (eds.), *The Oxford English Dictionary*, 20 vols. (2nd edn., Oxford, 1989).

Slack, Ron, *Man at War: John Gell in his Troubled Time* (Nottingham, 1997).

Smith, David L., *Stuart Parliaments, 1603–1689* (1999).

Smith, Geoffrey, *The Cavaliers in Exile, 1640–1660* (Basingstoke, 2003).

Smith, Geoffrey, *Royalist Agents, Conspirators and Spies: Their Role in the British Civil Wars, 1640–1660* (Farnham, 2010).

Spurr, John (ed.), *Anthony Ashley Cooper, First Earl of Shaftesbury 1621–1683* (Farnham, 2011).

Stevenson, David, *Revolution and Counter Revolution in Scotland, 1644–1651* (2nd edn., Edinburgh, 2003).

Stirling, Anna Maria Diana Wilhelmina, *The Hothams: Being the Chronicles of the Hothams of Scorborough and South Dalton from their Hitherto Unpublished Family Papers*, 2 vols. (1918).

Stoyle, Mark, *Loyalty and Locality: Popular Allegiance in Devon during the English Civil War* (Exeter, 1994).

Stoyle, Mark, *From Deliverance to Destruction: Rebellion and Civil War in an English City* (Exeter, 1996).

Stoyle, Mark, *Plymouth in the Civil War* (Devon Archaeology, no. 7, 1998).

Stoyle, Mark, *West Britons: Cornish Identities and the Early Modern British State* (Exeter, 2002).

Stoyle, Mark, *Soldiers and Strangers: An Ethnic History of the English Civil Wars* (2005).

Sunderland, Frederick Harold, *Marmaduke, Lord Langdale of Holme-on-Spalding Moor, Yorkshire (Colonel-General) and some events of his time* (1926).

Thomas, Sir Keith, *The Ends of Life: Roads to Fulfilment in Early Modern England* (Oxford, 2009).

Thomas-Stanford, Charles, *Sussex in the Great Civil War and the Interregnum, 1642–1660* (1910).

Tickell, John, *History of the Town and County of Kingston-upon-Hull* (Hull, 1798).

Toulmin, Joshua, *The History of Taunton in the County of Somerset* (Taunton, 1822).

Tucker, Norman, *North Wales in the Civil War* (Denbigh, 1958).

Tucker, Norman, *Royalist Officers of North Wales 1642–1660: A Biographical List* (Denbigh, 1961).

Tucker, Norman, *Denbighshire Officers in the Civil War* (Denbigh, 1964).

Tyacke, Nicholas (ed.), *The English Revolution c.1590–1720: Politics, Religion and Communities* (Manchester, 2007).

Underdown, David, *Pride's Purge: Politics in the Puritan Revolution* (Oxford, 1971).

Underdown, David, *Somerset in the Civil War and Interregnum* (Newton Abbot, 1973).

Underdown, David, *Revel, Riot and Rebellion: Popular Politics and Culture in England, 1603–1660* (Oxford, 1985).

Underdown, David, *A Freeborn People: Politics and the Nation in Seventeenth-Century England* (Oxford, 1996).

Walsham, Alexandra, *Providence in Early Modern England* (Oxford, 1999).

Walter, John, *Understanding Popular Violence in the English Revolution: The Colchester Plunderers* (Cambridge, 1999).

Walter, John, *Crowds and Popular Politics in Early Modern England* (Manchester, 2006).

Wanklyn, Malcolm, *The Warrior Generals: Winning the British Civil Wars* (New Haven, 2010).

Warburton, Eliot, *Memoirs of Prince Rupert and the Cavaliers*, 3 vols. (1849).

Warmington, Andrew R., *Civil War, Interregnum and Restoration in Gloucestershire, 1640–1672* (Royal Historical Society, Studies in History, new series, 1997).

Wedgwood, C. V., *The King's War, 1641–1647* (1958).

Wenham, Peter, *The Siege of York, 1644* (2nd edn., York, 1994).

Whiting, J. R. S., *Gloucester Besieged: The Story of a Roundhead City* (2nd edn., Gloucester, 1984).

Wilson, Peter H., *Europe's Tragedy: A New History of the Thirty Years War* (2009).

Wolffe, Mary, *Gentry Leaders in Peace and War: The Gentry Governors of Devon in the Early Seventeenth Century* (Exeter, 1997).

Wood, Alfred C., *Nottinghamshire in the Civil War* (Oxford, 1937).

Woolrych, Austin, *Britain in Revolution, 1625–1660* (Oxford, 2002).

Worden, Blair, *Roundhead Reputations: The English Civil War and the Passions of Posterity* (2001).

Worden, Blair, *The English Civil Wars 1640–1660* (2009).

Worden, Blair, *Literature and Politics in Cromwellian England: John Milton, Andrew Marvell, Marchamont Nedham* (Oxford, 2009).

Wroughton, John, *An Unhappy Civil War: The Experiences of Ordinary People in Gloucestershire, Somerset and Wiltshire, 1642–1646* (Bath, 1999).

Young, Peter, *Edgehill, 1642: The Campaign and Battle* (2nd edn., Moreton-in-Marsh, 1995).

Young, Peter, and Emberton, Wilfrid, *Sieges of the Great Civil War, 1642–1646* (1978).

Articles in journals

Adamson, J. S. A., 'The Baronial Context of the English Civil War', *TRHS*, 5th series, 40 (1990), 93–120.

Armstrong, Robert, 'The Long Parliament Goes to War: The Irish Campaigns, 1641–3', *Historical Research*, 80 (2007), 73–99.

Aylmer, G. E., 'Collective Mentalities in Mid-Seventeenth-Century England: 1 The Puritan Outlook', *TRHS*, 5th series, 36 (1986), 1–25.

Aylmer, G. E., 'Collective Mentalities in Mid-Seventeenth-Century England: 2 Royalist Attitudes', *TRHS*, 5th series, 37 (1987), 1–30.

Aylmer, G. E., 'Collective Mentalities in Mid-Seventeenth-Century England: 3 Varieties of Radicalism', *TRHS*, 5th series, 38 (1988), 1–25.

Aylmer, G. E., 'Collective Mentalities in Mid-Seventeenth-Century England: 4 Cross Currents: Neutrals, Trimmers and Others', *TRHS*, 5th series, 39 (1989), 1–22.

Barnard, T. C., 'Crises of Identity among Irish Protestants, 1641–1685', *P&P*, 127 (1990), 39–83.

Binns, Jack, 'Scarborough and the Civil Wars, 1642–1651', *Northern History*, 22 (1986), 95–122.

Binns, Jack, 'Captain Browne Bushell: North Sea Adventurer and Pirate', *Northern History*, 27 (1991), 90–105.

Binns, Jack, 'Sir Hugh Cholmley: Whitby's Benefactor or Beneficiary?', *Northern History*, 30 (1994), 86–104.

Bowen, Lloyd, 'Representations of Wales and the Welsh during the Civil Wars and Interregnum', *Historical Research*, 77 (2004), 358–76.

Brady, Andrea, '"Dying with Honour": Literary Propaganda and the Second English Civil War', *Journal of Military History*, 70 (2006), 9–30.

Broxap, Ernest, 'The Sieges of Hull during the Great Civil War', *EHR*, 20 (1905), 457–73.

Callow, John, 'The Limits of Indemnity: The Earl of Derby, Sovereignty and Retribution at the Trial of William Christian, 1660–63', *The Seventeenth Century*, 15 (2000), 199–216.

Capern, Amanda L., 'The Hotham Family and its Papers', *Archives*, 23 (1998), 100–17.

Clifton, Robin, 'Popular Fear of Catholics during the English Revolution, 1640–1660', *P&P*, 52 (1971), 23–55.

Colman, Clark S., 'The Paralysis of the Cumberland and Westmorland Army in the First Civil War, c.1642–45', *Transactions of the Cumberland and Westmorland Antiquarian and Archaeological Society*, 3rd series, 1 (2001), 123–39.

Coughlan, Patricia, 'Enter Revenge: Henry Burkhead and Cola's Furie', *Theatre Research International*, 15 (1990), 1–17.

Crawford, Patricia, 'The Savile Affair', *EHR*, 90 (1975), 76–93.

Cressy, David, 'The Protestation Protested, 1641 and 1642', *HJ*, 45 (2002), 251–79.

Cust, Richard, 'News and Politics in Early Seventeenth-Century England', *P&P*, 112 (1986), 60–90.

Cust, Richard, 'Honour and Politics in Early Stuart England: The Case of Beaumont v. Hastings', *P&P*, 149 (1995), 57–94.

Cust, Richard, 'Catholicism, Antiquarianism and Gentry Honour: The Writings of Sir Thomas Shirley', *Midland History*, 23 (1998), 40–70.

Daly, James, 'The Implications of Royalist Politics, 1642–6', *HJ*, 27 (1984), 745–55.

Donagan, Barbara, 'A Courtier's Progress: Greed and Consistency in the Life of the Earl of Holland', *HJ*, 19 (1976), 317–53.

Donagan, Barbara, 'Codes and Conduct in the English Civil War', *P&P*, 118 (1988), 65–95.

Donagan, Barbara, 'Prisoners in the English Civil War', *History Today*, 43 (1991), 28–35.

Donagan, Barbara, 'Atrocity, War Crime, and Treason in the English Civil War', *American Historical Review*, 99 (1994), 1137–66.

Donagan, B., 'Did Ministers Matter? War and Religion in England, 1642–1649', *JBS*, 33 (1994), 119–56.

Donagan, Barbara, 'Halcyon Days and the Literature of War: England's Military Education before 1642', *P&P*, 147 (1995), 65–100.

Donagan, Barbara, 'The Web of Honour: Soldiers, Christians, and Gentlemen in the English Civil War', *HJ*, 44 (2001), 365–89.

English, Barbara, 'Sir John Hotham and the English Civil War', *Archives*, 20 (1992), 217–27.

Forster, G. C. F., 'Faction and County Government in Early Stuart Yorkshire', *Northern History*, 11 (1975–6), 70–86.

Gentles, Ian, 'The Struggle for London in the Second Civil War', *HJ*, 26 (1983), 277–305.

Gentles, Ian, 'Why Men Fought in the British Civil Wars', *The History Teacher*, 26 (1993), 407–18.

Graham, Aaron, 'Finance, Localism and Military Representation in the Army of the Earl of Essex (June–December 1642)', *HJ*, 52 (2009), 879–98.

Graham, Aaron, 'The Earl of Essex and Parliament's Army at the Battle of Edgehill: A Reassessment', *War in History*, 17 (2010), 276–93.

Hanson, T. W., 'Three Civil War Notes', *Transactions of the Halifax Antiquarian Society* (1916), 249–58.

Hast, Adele, 'State Treason Trials during the Puritan Revolution, 1640–1660', *HJ*, 15 (1972), 37–53.

Hindle, Steve, 'Dearth and the English Revolution: The Harvest Crisis of 1647–50', *Economic History Review*, 61 (2008), 64–98.

Hirst, Derek, 'The Defection of Sir Edward Dering', *HJ*, 15 (1972), 193–208.

Holmes, Clive, 'Colonel King and Lincolnshire Politics, 1642–1646', *HJ*, 16 (1973), 451–84.

Hopper, Andrew, 'The Popish Army of the North: Anti-Catholicism and Parliamentarian Allegiance in Civil War Yorkshire, 1642–46', *Recusant History*, 25 (2000), 12–28.

Hopper, Andrew, 'The Self-Fashioning of Gentry Turncoats during the English Civil Wars', *JBS*, 49 (2010), 236–57.

Hopper, Andrew James, '"Fitted for Desperation": Honour and Treachery in Parliament's Yorkshire Command, 1642–3', *History*, 86 (2001), 138–54.

Howell, Roger, 'Newcastle's Regicide: The Parliamentary Career of John Blakiston', *Archaeologia Aeliana*, 4th series, 42 (1964), 207–30.

Howells, Brian, 'The Kidnapping of Griffith Jones of Castellmarch', *Trivium*, 15 (1980), 37–46.

Hughes, Ann, 'The King, the Parliament and the Localities in the English Civil War', *JBS*, 24 (1985), 236–63.

Hughes, Ann, 'A "Lunatic Revolter from Loyalty": The Death of Rowland Wilson and the English Revolution', *History Workshop Journal*, 61 (2006), 192–204.

Hutton, Ronald, 'The Worcestershire Clubmen in the English Civil War', *Midland History*, 5 (1979), 39–49.

Hutton, Ronald, 'The Structure of the Royalist Party', *HJ*, 24 (1981), 553–69.

Hutton, Ronald, 'Clarendon's History of the Rebellion', *EHR*, 97 (1982), 70–88.

Hyman, Harold M., 'Civil War Turncoats: A Commentary on a Military View of Lincoln's War Prisoner Utilization Program', *Military Affairs*, 22 (1958), 134–8.

Johnson, A. M., 'Bussy Mansell (1623–1699): Political Survivalist', *Morgannwg: The Journal of Glamorgan History*, 20 (1976), 9–36.

Karsten, Peter, 'The American Democratic Citizen Soldier: Triumph or Disaster?', *Military Affairs*, 30 (1966), 34–40.

Kelsey, Sean, 'The Death of Charles I', *HJ*, 45 (2002), 727–54.

Knight, Jeremy K., 'Taking Sides: Royalist Commissioners of Array for Monmouthshire in the Civil War', *Proceedings of the Monmouthshire Antiquarian Association*, 22 (2006), 3–18.

Lake, Peter, and Questier, Michael, 'Agency, Appropriation and Rhetoric under the Gallows: Puritans, Romanists and the State in Early Modern England', *P&P*, 153 (1996), 64–107.

Lowe, John, 'The Campaign of the Irish Royalist Army in Cheshire, November 1643–January 1644', *Transactions of the Historical Society of Lancashire and Cheshire*, 111 (1959), 47–76.

Lyndon, Brian, 'Essex and the King's Cause in 1648', *HJ*, 29 (1986), 17–39.

Macadam, Joyce, 'Soldiers, Statesmen and Scribblers: London Newsbook Reporting of the Marston Moor Campaign, 1644', *Historical Research*, 82 (2009), 93–113.

Mahony, Michael, 'The Savile Affair and the Politics of the Long Parliament', *Parliamentary History*, 7 (1988), 212–27.

Marston, J. G., 'Gentry Honor and Royalism in Early Stuart England', *JBS*, 13 (1973), 21–43.

Matar, Nabil, 'The Barbary Corsairs, King Charles I and the Civil War', *The Seventeenth Century*, 16 (2001), 239–58.

Matar, N. I., 'The Renegade in English Seventeenth-Century Imagination', *Studies in English Literature, 1500–1900*, 33 (1993), 489–505.

Miller, Amos C., 'Joseph Jane's Account of Cornwall during the English Civil War', *EHR*, 90 (1975), 94–102

Morrill, J. S., 'Mutiny and Discontent in English Provincial Armies, 1645–1647', *P&P*, 56 (1972), 49–74.

Morrill, J. S., 'The Religious Context of the English Civil War', *TRHS*, 5th series, 34 (1984), 155–78.

Mulligan, Lotte, 'Peace Negotiations, Politics and the Committee of Both Kingdoms, 1644–1646', *HJ*, 12 (1969), 3–22.

Mulligan, Lotte, 'Property and Parliamentary Politics in the English Civil War, 1642–6', *Historical Studies*, 16 (1975), 341–61.

Nenner, Howard, 'Loyalty and the Law: The Meaning of Trust and the Right of Resistance in Seventeenth-Century England', *JBS*, 48 (2009), 859–70.

Newman, P. R., 'The Royalist North: A Rejoinder', *Northern History*, 17 (1981), 253–5.

Newman, P. R., 'The Royalist Officer Corps, 1642–1660: Army Command as a Reflexion of the Social Structure', *HJ*, 26 (1983), 945–58.

Noonan, Kathleen M., '"The Cruel Pressure of an Enraged, Barbarous People": Irish and English Identity in Seventeenth-Century Policy and Propaganda', *HJ*, 41 (1998), 151–77.

Ohlmeyer, Jane, 'The Marquis of Antrim: A Stuart Turn-Kilt?' *History Today*, 43 (1993), 13–18.

Ó Siochrú, Micheál, 'Atrocity, Codes of Conduct and the Irish in the British Civil Wars, 1641–1653', *P&P*, 195 (2007), 55–86.

Peacey, Jason, 'The Struggle for *Mercurius Britanicus*: Factional Politics and the Parliamentarian Press, 1643–6', *Huntington Library Quarterly*, 68 (2005), 517–44.

Peacey, Jason, 'Sir Edward Dering, Popularity and the Public, 1640–1644', *HJ*, 54 (2011), 955–83.

Pearl, Valerie, 'Oliver St John and the "Middle Group" in the Long Parliament: August 1643–May 1644', *EHR*, 81 (1966), 490–519.

Philips, C. B., 'County Committees and Local Government in Cumberland and Westmorland, 1642–1660', *Northern History*, 5 (1970), 35–66.

Pollock, Linda, 'Honour, Gender and Reconciliation in Elite Culture 1570–1700', *JBS*, 46 (2007), 3–29.

Roberts, Stephen K., 'Welsh Puritanism in the Interregnum', *History Today*, 41 (1991), 36–41.

Roberts, Stephen K., 'Office-holding and Allegiance in Glamorgan in the Civil War and After: The Case of John Byrd', *Morgannwg: The Journal of Glamorgan History*, 44 (2000), 11–31.

Roberts, Stephen K., '"Specially Trusted by the Parliament": Thomas Carne of Brocastle, a Lost Civil War Commander', *Morgannwg: The Journal of Glamorgan History*, 50 (2006), 61–76.

Roy, Ian, 'The Royalist Council of War, 1642–6', *Bulletin of the Institute of Historical Research*, 35 (1962), 150–68.

Roy, Ian, 'England Turned Germany? The Aftermath of the Civil War in its European Context', *TRHS*, 5th series, 28 (1978), 127–44.

Russell, Conrad, 'Why did People Choose Sides in the English Civil War?', *The Historian*, 63 (1999), 4–9.

Ryder, I. E., 'The Seizure of Hull and its Magazine, January, 1642', *YAJ*, 61 (1989), 139–48.

Scott, David, '"Hannibal at our Gates": Loyalists and Fifth-Columnists during the Bishops' Wars—The Case of Yorkshire', *Historical Research*, 70 (1997), 269–93.

Scott, David, 'The "Northern Gentlemen", the Parliamentary Independents and Anglo-Scottish Relations in the Long Parliament', *HJ*, 42 (1999), 347–75.

Scott, David, 'The Barwis Affair: Political Allegiance and the Scots during the British Civil Wars', *EHR*, 115 (2000), 843–63.

Seddon, Peter, 'Landlords and Tenants: The Impact of the Civil Wars on the Clare Estates in Nottinghamshire, 1642–1649', *Transactions of the Thoroton Society of Nottinghamshire*, 113 (2009), 81–91.

Sharpe, J. A., '"Last Dying Speeches": Religion, Ideology and Public Execution in Seventeenth-Century England', *P&P*, 107 (1985), 144–67.

Smith, Lacey Baldwin, 'English Treason Trials and Confessions in the Sixteenth Century', *Journal of the History of Ideas*, 15 (1954), 471–98

Spitzer, Alan B., 'Malicious Memories: Restoration Politics and a Prosopography of Turncoats', *French Historical Studies*, 24 (2001), 37–61.

Stoyle, Mark, 'Sir Richard Grenville's Creatures: The New Cornish Tertia 1644–46', *Cornish Studies*, 2nd series, 4 (1996), 26–44.

Stoyle, Mark, 'The Road to Farndon Field: Explaining the Massacre of the Royalist Women at Naseby', *EHR*, 123 (2008), 895–923.

Terry, C. S., 'The Scottish Campaign in Northumberland and Durham between January and June, 1644', *Archaeologia Aeliana*, 2nd series, 21 (1899), 146–80.

Terry, C. S., 'The Siege of Newcastle-upon-Tyne by the Scots in 1644', *Archaeologia Aeliana*, 2nd series, 21 (1899), 180–258.

Trim, David, 'Calvinist Internationalism and the English Officer Corps, 1562–1642', *History Compass*, 4 (2006), 1024–48.

Underdown, David, 'The Problem of Popular Allegiance in the English Civil War', *TRHS*, 5th series, 31 (1981), 69–94.

Vallance, Edward, 'Protestation, Vow, Covenant and Engagement: Swearing Allegiance in the English Civil War', *Historical Research*, 75 (2002), 408–24.

Vallance, Edward, 'The Captivity of James II: Gestures of Loyalty and Disloyalty in Seventeenth-Century England', *JBS*, 48 (2009), 848–58.

Walter, John, 'The English People and the English Revolution Revisited', *History Workshop Journal*, 61 (2006), 171–82.

Weil, Rachel, 'Thinking about Allegiance in the English Civil War', *History Workshop Journal*, 61 (2006), 183–91.

Wood, Andy, 'Beyond Post-Revisionism? The Civil War Allegiances of the Miners of the Derbyshire "Peak Country"', *HJ*, 40 (1997), 23–40.

Wood, Andy, '"A lyttull word ys tresson": Loyalty, Denunciation, and Popular Politics in Tudor England', *JBS*, 48 (2009), 837–47.

Woolrych, Austin, 'Yorkshire's Treaty of Neutrality', *History Today*, 6 (1956), 696–704.

Yallop, H. J., 'Col. Ambrose Norton's Account of the Defection of Lord Cornbury –1688', *JSAHR*, 70 (1992), 231–8.

Zook, Melinda S., 'Turncoats and Double Agents in Restoration and Revolutionary England: The Case of Robert Ferguson, the Plotter', *Eighteenth-Century Studies*, 42 (2009), 363–78.

Unpublished theses

Bates, David, 'The Honour Culture of Royalist Officers in the North during the First Civil War, 1642–1646' (M.Phil. thesis, University of Birmingham, 2002).

Jones, Jennifer, 'The War in the North: The Northern Parliamentary Army in the English Civil War, 1642–1645' (Ph.D. thesis, York University, Canada, 1991).

Newman, P. R., 'The Royalist Army in the North of England, 1642–5' (D.Phil. thesis University of York, 1978).

Index

Printed and bound by CPI Group (UK) Ltd, Croydon, CR0 4YY